D0854681

AMERICAN WOMEN
AND THE
U.S. ARMED FORCES

*A Guide to the Records of Military Agencies
in the National Archives
Relating to American Women*

COMPILED BY CHARLOTTE PALMER SEELEY
REVISED BY VIRGINIA C. PURDY and ROBERT GRUBER

National Archives and Records Administration
Washington, DC

Published for the
National Archives and Records Administration
By the National Archives Trust Fund Board
1992

Library of Congress Cataloging-in-Publication Data

Seeley, Charlotte Palmer.
    American women and the U.S. armed forces : a guide to the records
of military agencies in the National Archives / compiled by
Charlotte Palmer Seeley ; revised by Virginia C. Purdy and Robert
Gruber.
        p. cm.
    Includes index.
    ISBN 0-911333-90-8
    1. Women and the military—United States—History—Archival
resources. 2. United States—Armed Forces—Women—History—Archival
resources. 3. United States. National Archives and Records
Administration. I. Purdy, Virginia Cardwell. II. Gruber, Robert
III. United States. National Archives and Records Administration
IV. Title.
U21.75.S44   1992
355'.0082—dc20   91-40430
                                                              CIP

Cover: Bernice Sansbury adjusts the spark plugs on a training
plane in September 1943. She was one of thousands of
American women active in the U.S. Navy's WAVES program
during World War II. 80-G-471686.

Table of Contents

Part I—Federal Records

Part II—Related Materials in Presidential Libraries

Preface

The holdings of the National Archives include a significant number of records about women. This guide, *American Women and the U.S. Armed Forces*, describes an important subset of these records: that is, the records about women who interacted with and eventually formed a part of the Nation's military service organizations.

Guides such as this one have been prepared at the National Archives since 1940, when the first *Guide to the Material in the National Archives* was published. Over time, new editions of this general guide have been published, and supplementary guides have been issued that focus on specific portions of Archives holdings. In this latter category are the *Guide to Federal Records Relating to the Civil War* (1962), the *Guide to Records in the National Archives Relating to American Indians* (1981), *Black History: A Guide to Civilian Records in the National Archives* (1984), and most recently the *Guide to the Holdings of the Still Picture Branch* (1990). The several references to photographs in *American Women and the U.S. Armed Forces* supplement those included in *War & Conflict* (1989), a picture book composed of reproductions of more than 1,500 archival images of American wartime experiences from the American Revolution through the Vietnam War.

The records described in this guide discuss women as wives and mothers of soldiers, suppliers of military goods and services, and participants in and victims of war. It is our hope that the publication of this guide will encourage researchers to use these records to discover both the changing and the constant aspects of the military experience of American women. It is particularly appropriate for such research to be undertaken as we observe the anniversary of World War II.

DON W. WILSON
Archivist of the United States

Introduction

Scope

IN.1. This guide describes records of Federal military agencies in the National Archives and related materials in Presidential Libraries that relate to American women. It is not, however, a comprehensive listing of every pertinent document. By noting major bodies of records that contain information about women and by providing examples of specific documents, the guide gives the researcher a starting point in the study of the role of the U.S. Government in the lives of American women. A guide to the records of civilian agencies that relate to American women among the records of civilian agencies is in preparation.

Women and the Armed Forces

IN.2. During the 18th and 19th centuries women had relatively little contact with military agencies. Women sought and received pensions based upon the service of male relatives. They served the Armed Forces as cooks, hospital matrons, and laundresses. A few were contract nurses and physicians, but until the Spanish-American War, most military nurses were men. Seamstresses worked for the Quartermaster making uniforms, and women worked in arsenals. Welfare agencies were staffed with women both as employees and as volunteers. They sometimes wrote to high-ranking government and military officials to inquire about relatives or friends in one of the services. In rare cases women ventured into the intelligence area as informants or disguised themselves as men and served as soldiers.

IN.3. Beginning with the period of the Spanish-American War, contract nurses were often women who had been trained in the burgeoning professional nursing schools, and many joined the Army Nurse Corps when it was established in 1901. With the establishment of the Navy Nurse Corps in 1908, military nursing became virtually a feminine monopoly.

IN.4. During World War I the U.S. Navy, having searched its legislative authorities without finding a prohibition against enlisting women, established the personnel category of yeoman (F), and the U.S. Marine Corps created the Women's Reserve. At the same time, women contributed much to the war effort as dietitians, "reconstruction aids" (physical therapists), telephone operators, and workers with welfare organizations such as the American Red Cross and the YMCA and YWCA.

IN.5. The Women's Auxiliary Army Corps (WAAC), established in May 1942, became the Women's Army Corps (WAC) in July 1943, and the Navy began recruiting women into its Women Accepted for Voluntary Emergency Service (WAVES) in July 1942. The women's Coast Guard Reserve was called the SPAR, an acronym from loose translation of the

Coast Guard motto, "Semper Paratis, Always Ready," and women in the U.S. Marine Corps were referred to simply as Women Marines. Women pilots joined the Women's Auxiliary Ferrying Service (WAFS) and the Women Airforce Service Pilots (WASP). In some cases, the acronym for the women's service became a nickname for the women in the service. Women in the WAC became Wacs; those in the WAVES became Waves; and Coast Guard women were called Spars.

IN.6. By the end of World War II, dietitians, physical therapists, and occupational therapists were generally referred to as medical specialists, and in 1947 the Women's Medical Specialist Corps was created with officers' commissions authorized. With the Army-Navy Nurse Act of 1947 and the Women's Armed Services Integration Act of 1948, the women's services became a permanent, integral part of the Armed Forces of the Nation. In 1955 men were admitted as medical specialists and nurses, and by the end of the 1970's there were no separate all-woman components in any branch of the armed services.

IN.7. Civilian women were also closely associated with the military in the 20th century. The families of military personnel were a continuing responsibility for the services. Women's organizations sought to contribute to the welfare of service personnel and their families and sometimes to influence military personnel policies. In wartime, women stepped into industrial and other traditionally male jobs. Women entertainers performed overseas, sometimes in primitive surroundings to help raise troop morale. And always there were prostitutes.

The Records

IN.8. The basic organizational unit to which all records in the National Archives are assigned is called a record group (RG), and each record group is assigned a number. A record group most frequently consists of the records of a single agency, such as the Veterans Administration (RG 15). Records of a number of agencies are sometimes brought together into a collective record group on the basis of similar functions or other relationship. An example of such a collective record group is Records of Temporary Committees, Commissions, and Boards (RG 220).

IN.9. The National Archives endeavors to keep records in the order in which they were maintained by the creating agency, in the belief that this best preserves their integrity and interrelationships. Agency filing systems were designed for administrative purposes when the records were active and not for the benefit of future researchers. A major reason for the preparation of guides such as this is to help subject-oriented researchers to understand the complexities of recordkeeping systems and to locate materials of interest among the vast quantities of records. For information on the major records classification scheme used in Army agencies, see Appendix B.

IN.10. Within a record group, the basic archival unit of control of records is the series, which is a body of records arranged in some serial order or logically grouped together for some other reason. For many record groups, the National Archives has prepared preliminary inventories or inventories, which describe the records series by series. A typical series description in an inventory entry includes the series title and covered dates (such as GENERAL CORRESPONDENCE, 1886–1926), the quantity of records in linear feet, and their arrangement. Often there is some indication of the subject content. Relevant series are also described in this guide, but with emphasis on the subject matter, specific examples of relevant documents, and some practical guidance on using the records.

Format of This Guide

IN.11. This guide is arranged numerically by record group number. Each record group is described as nearly as possible in an order that reflects the organization of the agency.

IN.12. A record group description is headed by the name of the record group and its number:

Records of the Army Staff

Record Group 319

IN.13. Paragraphs are numbered in boldface and are composed of the record group number and a paragraph number separated by a period. If a paragraph is numbered **319.35,** the record group number is 319, and this is the 35th paragraph in the description of this record group. The index to the guide refers to these paragraph numbers rather than to page numbers.

IN.14. Series titles, including dates covered, appear in the narrative description in boldface, for example, **historical files of the Army Nurse Corps, 1900–47** (6 ft.).

National Archives Microfilm Publications

IN.15. Since the 1940's the National Archives has microfilmed many of the records in its holdings to preserve the records most frequently used and to make copies of the records available at a distance from the National Archives. Occasionally a large series will be microfilmed and the original records will be destroyed to save scarce records storage space.

IN.16. Microfilm publications have been assigned numbers preceded by an "M" or a "T." The T series was originally made up of copies of records that were expected to be used largely in a National Archives setting. M numbers were assigned to series that were also expected to be purchased by libraries and interested persons. The distinction has long disappeared, and all publications are now assigned M numbers. Many M-numbered publications are accompanied by descriptive pamphlets that provide the historical context or origin of the records and other information about the series. Publications are available for use at the National

Archives in Washington, DC, at 12 National Archives regional archives, and in many libraries. They are also for sale from the National Archives Trust Fund Board, Washington, DC 20408.

IN.17. When a series that has been microfilmed in its entirety is cited in this guide, the series title will be in bold as usual and will be followed by the publication number and the number of rolls of film. For example:

letters sent by the office of the Quartermaster General, 1818–70 (107 vols., 24 ft.), filmed as M745 (61 rolls)

If a microfilm publication includes only part of a series or combines the records in more than one series, the title of the publication is italicized. For example, *Revolutionary War Rolls* (M246, 138 rolls) includes two series. For a list of the microfilm publications that are cited in this guide, see Appendix C.

Restricted and Security Classified Records

IN.18. The use of some records in the National Archives, especially those of recent date, is subject to restrictions imposed by the Congress, the President, the Archivist of the United States, or the agency that created the records. In the case of personal papers donated either to Presidential Libraries or to the National Archives, restrictions imposed by the donor must be honored. To use security classified records, a researcher must sometimes obtain a security clearance in advance. On the other hand, some records described as security classified may have been declassified after the publication of this guide. Restrictions imposed to protect the privacy of individuals and corporations are usually inapplicable 75 years after the date of the records. In any event, it is wise for the researcher to get in touch with the National Archives in advance of a visit to be sure that pertinent records can be made available.

Acknowledgments

IN.19. In addition to the archivists whose names appear on the title page, many other staff members have contributed to this guide. Descriptions of audiovisual materials have been reviewed by Elizabeth Hill (still pictures), Leslie Waffen and William Murphy (sound recordings and motion pictures), and William Heynan (cartographic records). Descriptions of electronic records were reviewed by Margaret Adams. Among reviewers of descriptions of other records are Robin Cookson, Marion Johnson, Robert W. Krauskopf, Theresa Matchette, Lawrence H. McDonald, Timothy K. Nenninger, Geraldine N. Phillips, William Walsh, and Rita Wolfinger. Reviewing the description of materials in Presidential Libraries were Raymond Teichman, Tina Houston, Martin M. Teasley, David A. Horrocks, Dale C. Mayer, and William Johnson. The text was edited by Mary Anne O'Boyle and indexed by Jeanne Moody.

Part I
FEDERAL RECORDS

Records of the Veterans Administration

Record Group 15

15.1. The Veterans Administration was the result of policies and programs that date back to the American Revolution. The First Congress enacted legislation in 1789 to continue pensions provided in acts of the Continental Congress, and successive Congresses provided more and more liberal pensions based upon military service. In 1833 a Commissioner of Pensions was appointed to be under the joint direction of the Secretaries of War and the Navy. When the Department of the Interior was established in 1849, the Office of the Commissioner was transferred to it and became known as the Bureau of Pensions. In 1921 the Bureau of War Risk Insurance (created in 1914) and the Rehabilitation Division of the Federal Board for Vocational Education (created in 1918) were combined with the Bureau of Pensions and other services for veterans to form the Veterans Administration. Women were a concern of the agencies administering pensions, first as recipients of benefits related to the military service of deceased male relatives and later as claimants to benefits based on their own service as nurses and members of reserve and active military organizations.

Administrative Records

15.2. The Commissioner of Pensions was occasionally required to judge the worthiness of pension recipients, both men and women. Decisions to drop widows from pension rolls if they were found to have abandoned their children, engaged in adulterous cohabitation, or otherwise behaved in an unsuitable fashion are recorded in **excerpts from decisions of the Commissioner of Pensions, 1900–20** (4 vols., 7 in.), arranged alphabetically by subject. Many such decisions were appealed, as were denials of claims that were allegedly fraudulent. Administrative records relating to appeals include **digests of decisions and rulings of the Secretary of the Interior, the Commissioner of Pensions, and the Board of Review, 1871–96** (6 vols., 7 in.), arranged chronologically with indexes in four of the volumes; **records of decisions approved for publication, 1894–1920** (14 vols., 1 ft.), arranged alphabetically by surname of claimant; and **decisions of the Secretary of the Interior on appeals, 1849–96** (43 vols., 7 ft.), arranged alphabetically by surname of appellant and containing synopses of various types of cases. **Registers of appeals, 1867–70, 1880–84, 1887, and 1918–20** (4 vols., and an index), are arranged alphabetically by surname of claimant in the first volume, and thereafter by docket number. **"Departmental decisions, Appeal Section, Board of Review," 1904–7** (1 vol., 2 in.), unarranged, but indexed, are examples of similar decisions of the Secretary of the Interior.

15.3. That women were not above falsifying records to obtain pensions is evidenced in the cases summarized in **criminal and civil registers, 1875–1914** (22 vols., 4 ft.). The first 21 volumes are arranged chronologically with an alphabetical index in each by surname of defendant; the last volume is a name index of all of the defendants.

15.4. The importance of evaluating the legal marital status of applicants for pensions probably led to the compilation of **records relating to legal aspects of marital status ("marriage by States and general"), 1890–1917** (1 vol., 2 in.), arranged alphabetically by State, including miscellaneous material relating to marriage laws in various States and excerpts from decisions of the Commissioner of Pensions on the subject.

15.5. In 1890 a special enumeration of surviving veterans of the Civil War and their widows was taken. The resulting **special census schedules of surviving Union Civil War veterans or their widows, 1890** (190 bundles, 21 ft.), is arranged alphabetically by State or territory (Kentucky through Wyoming only) and was filmed as M123 (118 rolls). Although more information is supplied about the veterans than for the widows, an entry for a widow shows her name and post office address. **Tabulations pertaining to the special census schedules of Union Civil War veterans or their widows, n.d.** (6 vols., 6 in.), arranged alphabetically by State or territory except for Alaska, which was placed at the end, is also among the administratiive records of the Pension Bureau.

Pension Case Files

15.6. Three principal types of pensions were provided to servicemen and their dependents by the Federal Government. Disability or invalid pensions were awarded to servicemen for physical disabilities incurred in the line of duty; service pensions were awarded to veterans who served for specified periods of time; and widows' pensions were awarded to women and children whose husbands or fathers had been killed in action or had served specified periods. Of these, widows' case files are obviously those most likely to yield information about women, but occasionally an application for a veteran's invalid pension may have some information about his wife. Of the widows' applications, rejected applications usually contain more information than successful applications because rejected or contested applications were often submitted to special examiners who sought affidavits from relatives and neighbors to prove or disprove a claim.

15.7. Applications for pensions were made under several public and private acts of Congress. Public acts, under which the majority of pensions were awarded, encompassed large classes of veterans or their dependents who met common eligibility requirements. An applicant rejected under the terms of an early act often reapplied for benefits under later, more liberal laws.

15.8. Application procedures varied according to the act under which benefits were claimed. Generally the process required an applicant to appear before a court of record in the State of his or her residence to describe under oath the service for which a pension was claimed. A veteran's widow was required to provide, in addition, information concerning the date and place of her marriage. A widow who married for the second time lost her pension based upon her deceased husband's service. For those who applied for renewal of their pensions after their subsequent marriages had dissolved, there are **remarried widows' indexes** to their most recent names. An entry usually shows for each case the name of the claimant and the name, service, application number, and date of application of the soldier on whose service the original application was based.

15.9. In most of the series of case files noted below, the dates are the dates on which the applications were made, not those of the military service on which applications were based. The information about women in widows' applications usually tells more about their circumstances at the time of their application than about their experiences in the period of the war in which their husbands served. For example, a woman whose husband served in the War of 1812 might have waited to apply for a pension under the act of 1871, the first one to provide a pension for any surviving War of 1812 veteran or his widow whether or not the man was wounded or killed during the war.

15.10. There are a number of indexes and other finding aids to the case files. A **list of application and certificate numbers assigned to pension case files based on service between 1774 and 1865** (60 ft.), is arranged in numerical sequence. Cases appear in rough order by war and thereunder by type; for example, most successful widows' applications based on War of 1812 service are found together, separated from disapproved widows' applications or from any veterans' applications for the same war. Entries were made on cards divided into columns for "Army," "Navy," "1812," "Old Wars," "Indian Wars," and "Mexican War." ("Old Wars" designates service between 1783 and 1861 not associated with a particular war.) Each case file number is entered under the appropriate heading followed by the name of the applicant. A format in pension number sequence was used for *Numerical Index to Pension Claims, 1812–1930* (A1158, 359 rolls), which also includes both application numbers and certificate numbers but is not arranged by war. Alphabetical name indexes, filmed as T316, T317, T318, and T288, mix the names of men and women regardless of date of application or certificate.

15.11. Case files of pension and bounty-land warrant applications based on Revolutionary War Service, 1800–1900 (1,098 ft.), filmed as M804 (2,670 rolls), are arranged alphabetically by surname

5

of veteran and numbered with an alphabetical designation: "S" for "survivors" (veterans), "W" for widows, and sometimes "R" for rejected claims. A **name index,** filmed as M312 (15 rolls), consists of Max E. Hoyt's "Index of Revolutionary War Pension Applications, A–S," from the *National Genealogical Quarterly*, and the face sides of the Revolutionary War pension and bounty-land warrant application files, T–Z. The new married names of widows who remarried are cross-referenced. One woman who received a pension as a veteran and therefore has a file number beginning with "S" is Deborah Sampson Gannett. Her file, S32722 (M804, roll 1045), contains her sworn testimony that she served more than 2 years in a Massachusetts regiment disguised as a man named "Robert Shurtleff."

15.12. An 1832 law allowed the widow or orphans of a veteran who died while receiving a pension to claim the final payment due the veteran at the time of his death. In the same year the United States assumed Virginia's half-pay-for-life obligations to the State's veterans. **Case files of claims for half pay and pensions based on Revolutionary War service, 1800–59** (6 ft.), filmed as M910 (18 rolls), in large part concerns applications of heirs of deceased Virginia pensioners under these laws.

15.13. Early laws that provided for protection of the frontier and a regular peacetime military establishment also provided for pensions for the widows and children of men who died in such service. In addition, there are a few early widows' applications based on their later husbands' civilian service in **case files of pension applications based on death or disabiity incurred in service between 1783 and 1861, except in the War of 1812 and the Mexican War ("miscellaneous service, Old Wars"), 1800–1930** (111 ft.). The "Old Wars Index" (T316) applies to this series of case files.

15.14. Case files of pension and bounty-land warrant applications based on service in the War of 1812, 1812–1910 (1,279 ft.), are arranged alphabetically, usually under the name of the veteran but occasionally under the name of a widow. An alphabetical **name index** to these files has been microfilmed as M313 (102 rolls).

15.15. Military service after 1855 no longer entitled a veteran or his widow to bounty land. **Case files of bounty-land warrant applications based on service between 1812 and 1855** and **disapproved applications based on Revolutionary War service, 1800–1900** (2,580 ft.), arranged alphabetically by name of veteran, and **case files of bounty-land warrant applications of Indians based on service between 1812 and 1855, 1812–1900** (36 ft.), unarranged, are the last bounty-land warrant applications.

15.16. Beginning in 1892, a series of acts authorized pensions for surviving officers and enlisted men (or their widows or other dependents) who had served in the Army or Navy during Indian wars or disturbances between 1817 and 1898. Widows of Regular Army and Volunteer veterans and enrolled Indian scouts are represented in **case files of approved and disapproved pension applications of veterans of Indian Wars and of widows and other dependents of veterans of Indian Wars ("Indian widows' originals"), 1892–1926** (627 ft.), arranged alphabetically by surname of veteran.

15.17. The first pension law for widows and orphans of Mexican War soldiers who died in the war was approved by Congress, July 21, 1848, but it was not until 1887 that a pension based on a veteran's Mexican War service alone was available to his widow. There are two series of case files, both arranged alphabetically by surname of veteran: **case files of approved and disapproved pension applications of veterans of the Mexican War and of widows and other dependents of veterans of the Mexican War based on service alone, 1887–1926** (962 ft.), and **case files of approved and disapproved pension applications veterans of the Mexican War and of widows and other dependents of veterans of the Mexican War, based on death or disability, 1847–1930**.

15.18. **Case files of disapproved applications of widows and other dependents of Navy veterans ("Navy widows' originals"), 1861–1910** (105 ft.), arranged numerically by application or file number (NWO 9 to NWO 29,239), have been filmed on microfiche as M1274, and **case files of approved pension applications of widows and other dependents of Navy veterans (Navy widows' certificates"), 1861–1910** (591 ft.), arranged numerically by certificate or file number (NWC 623 to NWC 21,617), have been filmed on microfiche as M1279.

15.19. Beginning with the case files for pension applications based on Civil War service, some women who had served as nurses became eligible for pensions in their own right. Letters and affidavits of these women, of doctors who could attest to their service with the Medical Department of the Army during the war, and depositions of former patients, friends, relatives, and colleagues appear in such applications. Some women who could qualify either on their own service or as widows of male veterans applied for widows' pensions because the widows were given larger awards. Sarah A. Chadwick (WC 849,664) and Sarah A. Clapp (WC 601,330) applied as widows even though they themselves had served. Their records are in **case files of approved pension applications of widows and other dependents of veterans of the Army and Navy who served mainly in the Civil War and the War with Spain ("Civil War and later widows' certificates"), 1861–1934** (31,267 ft.), arranged numerically by certificate number (WC 2 to WC 1,651,647). Case files of rejected applications are in **case files of disapproved pension applications of widows and other dependents of veterans of the Army and Navy who served mainly in the Civil War and the War with Spain ("Civil War and later widows' originals"),**

1861–1934 (3,040 ft.), arranged numerically by application number (WO 2 to WO 1,644,996). Mary E. Merrill was pensioned as a nurse. Her file (SC 984,854) is in **case files of approved pension applications of veterans who served in the Army and the Navy mainly in the Civil War and the War with Spain ("Civil War and later survivors' certificates"), 1861–1934** (15,903 ft.), arranged numerically by certificate number (SC 9,487 to SC 999,999). Case file number SC 276,360 documents the pension allotted to Emma Alvira Smith Porch, who was a despatch bearer, guide, scout, and spy in the Department of the Missouri during the Civil War. Rejected applications of veterans are in a similar series of **"survivors' originals," 1861–1934** (2,267 ft.), arranged numerically by application number (SO 7 to SO 1,654,862). There is also a supplementary series of **case files of pension applications based on service in the years 1817–1917 and 1921–40 ("C" and "XC" series)** (10,385 ft.), arranged by number assigned regardless of prefix (C or XC 2,270,002 to 3,0223,602). These applications (except those based on service in the Revolutionary War, the War of 1812, or World War I) were made after 1934, and some case files withdrawn from previous series were assigned new file numbers. The **name indexes** to case file series for the Civil War and later (except the "C" and "XC" series), were filmed as T288 (544 rolls). The indexes contain a good deal of information about each entry and include the names of some well-known women such as Mary Ann Ball Bickerdyke, Cloe Annette Buckel, Isabella Fogg, Annie Wittenmyer, and Dr. Mary E. Walker.

15.20. In addition to nurses who applied for pensions based on their own service, a few other women claimed to have served as soldiers in the Union Army. For example, Kady Brownell, who claimed that she was wounded while serving with her husband's Rhode Island regiment, won a pension under a special act (file SC 279,843), but Eunice Godfrey's application, containing a description of her duties as cook and nurse (file WO 478,192), was rejected. Amanda Tyler Looney also failed to receive a pension as a veteran cook and nurse with the 16th Independent Battery of Ohio Light Artillery because she was not hired by the War Department. Emma Edmonds Seelye's sworn declaration stated that she enlisted in Detroit as Franklin Thompson, and she received a pension (SC 282,136) under a special act. Other such cases must be discovered by using the name indexes to the various application case files.

Financial Records and Pension Control Registers

15.21. Pension payment records are also useful to locate records of female pensioners. **Pension agency payment books, 1805–1909** (2,430 vols., 575 ft.), are arranged alphabetically by agency and thereunder by class of pensioner, thereunder chronologically, and thereunder alphabetically by pensioner's surname. An **index** (4 ft.) is similarly arranged. Microfilm copies of **pension payment cards, 1907–33**, ar-

If any of the women who composed this Civil War volunteer unit submitted pension claims, their applications would now be part of Record Group 15, as would the claims of Civil War nurses and widows. 64-M-306.

ranged alphabetically by pensioner's name, are available as M850 (2,539 rolls). Seven series of **pension payment rolls** covering various time periods are all arranged alphabetically by State.

15.22. Among control registers and lists are several that may be useful to the study of women. Some women's claims in the **list of pension claims suspended and disapproved from 1818 to 1853** (3 in.) give the reason for adverse action. Specific to women's studies are the names in a **register of pension applications of widows and other dependents of veterans of early wars, 1849–88** (3 vols., 3 in.), arranged chronologically and thereunder alphabetically by first letter of claimant's surname, and **registers of pension applications of widows and other dependents [of men] who served in the Army and the Navy after March 4, 1861, 1883–1912,** arranged in four chronological subseries and thereunder alphabetically by the first three letters of pensioner's surname. A **list of widows and other dependents of veterans of early wars pensioned from 1831 to 1873** (2 in.) is arranged numerically by certificate number. Each entry gives the woman's name; the veteran's name, rank, organization, and war; the pension agency; dates of issue and commencement of payments; and the amount of the payments. The **register of pension certificates issued to widows of veterans of the War of 1812, 1880–1909** (1 vol., 1 in.), lists certificates numbered 29,298–35,521 and is arranged chronologically by date certificate was issued. **Registers of pension certificates issued to widows and other**

dependents of Army and Navy veterans between 1862 and 1914, **1877–1914** (73 vols., 15 ft.), list certificates numbered 1–775,590 and is arranged chronologically. An **incomplete list of pensioned widows and other dependents of Army veterans of early wars, n.d.** (6 in.), arranged alphabetically by initial letter of veteran's name, covers Old Wars pensioners. Information about some of the earliest Navy widows can be found in a **list of widows and other dependents of Navy veterans pensioned from 1800–1883,** (1 vol., 2 in.), arranged alphabetically by the first two letters of the pensioner's surname. **Lists of veterans and widows and other dependents of veterans pensioned under various laws enacted from 1818 to 1853** (14 vols., 4 ft.), arranged by State, thereunder chronologically by date of pension act and thereunder alphabetically by initial letter of pensioner's surname, demonstrate the changes in eligibility for widows under each new law. A **register of Navy veterans and widows and other dependents of Navy veterans granted pensions, July–December 1869** (1 vol., 2 in.), is arranged in two subseries, one for veterans and another for dependents, thereunder alphabetically by State in which the pension agency was located, and thereunder chronologically by date of pension certificate.

Legal Records, 1862–1933

15.23. Under a pension act of 1862, the Secretary of the Interior was authorized to appoint a special agent to investigate and prosecute persons suspected of fraudulent activity relative to pensions. From this authorization the Law Division developed, and in its records are case files concerning the criminal behavior of both men and women.

15.24. Case files of attorneys, agents, and others relating to the prosecution of pension claims and the investigation of fraudulent practices, 1862–1933 (286 ft.), are arranged alphabetically by name (usually that of the person accused of fraud) in two subseries, A–E and A–W, followed by unarranged papers. Some photographs have been segregated from the case files and placed at the end of the series. One type of fraud was the failure of Civil War widows to inform the Bureau of Pensions when they remarried. There is also documentation of the claims of both men and women to be special agents through whom applications for pensions had to pass. Records filed under "Mashville" [sic] concern cases in middle Tennessee and include documents showing that at least one woman found guilty of forgery was sent to a penitentiary. Also included are several files showing disbarment proceedings against attorneys who exacted exhorbitant fees from mothers and widows to press their pension claims. **Case files of attorneys and agents in the Philippine Islands relating to the prosecution of pension claims and the investigation of fraudulent practices, 1925–38** (1 ft.), arranged alphabetically, are similar.

15.25. The **index and digest of *Decisions of the Department of the Interior in Appealed Pension and Retirement Claims*, 1904** (1 vol., 2 in.), arranged alphabetically by subject, serves as a finding aid to the published *Decisions* (14 vols., 1887–1904). Among the general subject terms in the index that relate to women are: "Adulterous cohabitation," "Dependent relatives," "Fraud and mistake," "Husband and wife," "Marriage and divorce," "Nurses," and "Widows."

15.26. **Letters sent pertaining to alleged violations of pension laws and memoranda pertaining to Indian scouts, 1925–30** (5 in.), arranged alphabetically by name of the subject person, include many details (including names and certificate numbers) concerning widows of scouts and of Civil War and Spanish-American War veterans accused of collecting pensions fraudulently. **Correspondence with special examiners, 1887–1930** (25 ft.), also deals with suspicious cases.

15.27. During the 1890's the Pension Bureau received many complaints that unprincipled persons in the Southern States were making misleading statements concerning pensions for ex-slaves, including women. Bills to provide pensions for ex-slaves were introduced in Congress in 1890 and later, but none was enacted into law. Each time such a bill was proposed, new organizations emerged purporting to be Government agencies that, for a fee, could get pensions for ex-slaves. **Correspondence and reports pertaining to the ex-slave pension movement, 1892–1916** (7 in.) are unarranged.

General Administrative Files of the Rehabilitation Division

15.28. The Vocational Rehabilitation Act of 1918 provided for vocational training and employment assistance for veterans disabled during military service. The **card index to the general administrative files, 1918–25** (33 ft.), serves several series, including **registration supervisors' reports, July 1922–April 1923** (7 in.). These chronologically arranged reports deal with the employment objectives pursued by the men and women in training in December 1922 and include a list of schools and colleges where they received training and the number of trainees at each institution. The names of many women appear in **contracts for instruction, 1919–21** (3 ft.), arranged alphabetically by surname of instructor or institution. Among the women instructors are teachers of subjects from agronomy and animal husbandry to lip reading and mathematics. **Trainee record cards, 1918–28** (1,790 ft.), arranged alphabetically by trainees' surnames, provide information about each participating veteran. **Sample regional office training case files, 1918–28** (30 ft.), arranged numerically by district number, document the types of training given to former sevicemen and servicewomen.

Insurance Records of the Bureau of War Risk Insurance

15.29. The Bureau of War Risk Insurance was established in 1914 to insure the lives of officers and enlisted men in the Army and Navy and of Army and Navy nurses, to compensate for death or disability in the armed services, and to assist the families of enlisted men while the men were in the service.

15.30. In the **general correspondence of the director, 1917–31** (55 ft.), arranged according to a decimal classification scheme, there is correspondence with American War Mothers and the American Legion Auxiliary concerning legislation and related efforts on behalf of women beneficiaries of war risk insurance and of servicemen and their dependents needing care. In file 9.1 there is a 1920 bibliography of publications concerning the probability of the remarriage of widows. Correspondence with the American Red Cross (file 023.8) concerns benefits for dependents of servicemen in wartime. There are also classifications for occupational and physical therapy aides, nurses, nursing schools, dietitians, librarians, schools for employees, and welfare of employees, many of which contain records about women.

15.31. A memorandum documenting the decision of the Bureau's Allotment and Allowance Division to award allotment and allowances to the children in the custody of a World War I yeoman (F) is in the the division's **administrative correspondence, 1918–34** (3 ft.), arranged alphabetically by subject. The series includes regulations and correspondence with the general counsel and others concerning fraud, eligibility, and other matters relating to allotments. **Sample case files relating to applicants for allowances and allotments ("A and S series"), 1918–21** (4 ft.), are arranged in two subseries, "A" by application number and "S" by Army serial number. They contain completed application forms and related records for allotments, allowances, and exemptions for good cause from compulsory allotment of pay to spouses; decisions of the Legal Division; Allotment and Allowance Division correspondence; investigative reports; and personal letters of each subject couple. The records give information about the current and former spouses, children, family residence, and often the social and marital history of the couple.

15.32. Numerous letters from wives and mothers of service personnel describing their plight and asking for help are in the **general correspondence of the Civil Relief Section, 1918–20** (4 ft. 6 in.).

Audiovisual Records

15.33. "Veterans Report, Issue No. 4," is one of several Veterans Administration films that explain the organization of the VA and illustrate the educational, financial, medical, and rehabilitation services it provided after World War II. In this particular film, two women attend a pilot training school, and another works as an aerial photographer.

15.34. Most of the women shown in **photographs, 1944–62** (15-MFS, 4,798 items), of medical and other facilities and services of the VA are hospital personnel or volunteers. In addition to numerous pictures of women as nurses, occupational and physical therapists, dietitians, and administrative and clerical employees, there is at least one print showing women patients (item 120A). The photographs are arranged alphabetically by subject, and a list of the subject headings is available.

Records of the Army Air Forces

Record Group 18

18.1. In July 1914 the Aviation Section was established in the Signal Corps. An Executive order of May 20, 1918, divided the Aviation Section into two separate agencies: the Division of Military Aeronautics and the Bureau of Aircraft Production. In 1919 the Director of Aircraft Production was appointed Second Assistant Secretary of War and Director of the Air Service, responsible for both the Bureau of Aircraft Production and the Division of Military Aeronautics.

18.2. The Army Reorganization Act of June 4, 1920, made the Air Service a combat arm of the Army, and the Air Corps Act of July 2, 1926, changed the name of the Air Service to the Air Corps. In March 1935 the General Headquarters Air Force was created; it was renamed the Air Force Combat Command in 1941. A general reorganization of the War Department in 1942 united the Air Corps and the Air Force Combat Command into the Army Air Forces (AAF). The National Defense Act of 1947 redesignated the AAF as the U.S. Air Force under the newly created Department of the Air Force, which in 1949 became a department of the Department of Defense.

18.3. Women's names appear in the early records of the Army Air Corps as civilian employees and Army nurses in the **general correspondence, 1917–38** (546 ft.), of the Office of the Chief of the Air Corps, arranged, like other general correspondence series in this record group, according to the War Department decimal classification scheme. The following files contain records about women: 080 "Societies and Associations," which includes correspondence of Mrs. Henry L. Stimson, a member of the Army Relief Society, about relief to families of servicemen; 123 "Funds—General (Welfare Fund)," which contains letters from both Mrs. Stimson and Mrs. Henry H. Arnold; 123 "Pioneer Fund—Guinea Pig," which concerns a sociological survey of commissioned officers' families and the offer of scholarships for children of Air Corp officers; 211 "Nurses" which deals with transportation of civilian and Army nurses, employment of visiting nurses, overseas assignments, and living and working conditions for nurses; 230.38 "Reports of Civilian Employees of the

13

Bureau of Aircraft Production," which contains general statistics of women and men; 230.38 "Women—Number of Married Women, 1923–37," which includes reports from the field listing names, positions, and salaries of those making more than $2,000 annually; 230.5 "Absences"; 230.6 "Privileges and Welfare, 1918–38," which contains activity reports and correspondence of Air Corps welfare workers Lillian Capron, Nancy W. Finley, and other personnel with such persons as War Department Welfare Service Representative Mary Oliver and War Department Welfare Coordinator Anita Phipps; 230.82 "Discharges and Dismissals, 1918–1938," which consists of lists of personnel from charwoman to draftswoman and "production expert" removed from service by reductions in force. File 230.83 "Reduction in Force, 1901–38," contains information about men whose wives worked for the Federal Government or the District of Columbia, because the Economy Act of 1933 mandated that working wives be dismissed before men or single women. Other files containing information about women include 231.22 "Instructors, 1916–38"; 231.4A "Custodians, 1915–38"; 247 "Beneficiary Money, Burial Expenses"; 248.8 "Bureau of Aircraft Production (Civilian Employees)"; 248.8 "Bonus, 1918–32"; 260 "Pensions"; and 512 "Dependents." File 291.1 was used as a general file about women and contains some information about women pilots. File 292 pertains to the veteran status of men and women.

18.4. Records about women are also found in some of the same War Department decimal file numbers (211 "Nurses," 291.1 "Women and Marriage," and 291.1 "Marriage") in **general correspondence, January 1939–September 1942** (428 ft.), of the Commanding General, Headquarters, AAF. In addition, file 292 "Quasi-military persons" relates to dependency, pay allotments, and deaths of servicemen and contains a draft issuance announcing the organization of the Dependents Placement Division to help families of AAF personnel find jobs and training.

18.5. The 1939–42 general correspondence documents the origin of women's service in the AAF, first in the temporary Women's Auxiliary Army Corps (WAAC), and later in the permanent Women's Army Corps (WAC), which succeeded the WAAC in 1943. Wacs were assigned to all branches of the Army, including the AAF, where they were generally called "Air Wacs." File 220.31 (6 in.) pertains to assignments of enlisted personnel of the WAAC. Civilian women who worked for the Aircraft Warning Service before the creation of the WAC are represented by a few documents in file 322.5 "Aircraft Warning Service." Letters advocating a women's auxiliary Army corps or seeking to enlist in the prospective WAAC are in 322.5 (2 in.); correspondence after the establishment of the WAAC in 324.5 (2 in.) records men's attitudes, regulations about marriage, and duty stations for Wacs. A "survey of commercialized prostitution" in one American town and a letter from an irate mother about the activities of nurses and servicemen are in file 250.1 "Morals and Conduct."

18.6. Records in this same series of general correspondence document the origin of utilization of women pilots. In the fall of 1942 Nancy Harkness Love organized the Women's Auxiliary Ferrying Squadron (WAFS), a group of experienced pilots to ferry military aircraft within the United States for the Ferrying Division of the Air Transport Command of the AAF. Shortly thereafter, a second group of civilian women formed the Women's Flying Training Detachment (WFTD) in the Flying Training Command of the AAF, with Jacqueline Cochran as director to recruit and train women pilots. In June 1943 under Cochran's leadership the WAFS and the WFTD merged into one organization, the Women Airforce Service Pilots (WASP). Cochran soon moved into the new Office of the Special Assistant for Women Pilots in the Office of the Assistant Chief of Air Staff for Operations Commitments and Requirements. Letters of inquiry from women and Cochran's responses constitute file 322.5 "Women Applicants for the W.A.F.S."

18.7. The **general correspondence, October 1942–May 1944** (784 ft.), of the Office of the Commanding General contains applications from women who wished to serve in the air evacuation activities of the AAF, administrative records pertaining to nurses as patients and to flight nurses, and correspondence concerning Army Nurse Corps personnel assigned to the AAF. Files 291.1 "Women and Marriage" and 292 "Quasi-military persons" relate to women, both civilian and military. Records about the Air WAC are found under file numbers 210.31, 211, 220.31, 221, 221.02, 324.5, 333 (bulky), and 333.1 (bulky). File 322 (bulky) contains records about women in the Aircraft Warning Service. A small amount of correspondence relating to the employment of women physicians as contract doctors in Air Service Command Control Depots is in file 321.23 "Medical." Policy and operational records relating to the WASP and its parts, the WAFS and the WFTD, are also in this series. In file 324.5 "WAFS and WASP, September 1942–May 1944" (ca. 10 in.), there is Cochran correspondence, an undated study titled "Analyses of Women Pilots Program and Suggestions for its Development" (7 pp.), special orders and regulations, and information about women's flying accidents. File 231.21 "Women Pilots, 1942–44" (7 in.), includes sketches of uniforms and a copy of Gen. Henry H. Arnold's letter to Rep. Margaret Chase Smith regarding a proposal to commission women pilots in the AAF. File 353 "Women Flying Training" (5 in.) consists of more applications, programs of instruction, and studies, including reports on improper use of WASP pilots and on target towing by women pilots. Rosters of Wasps by trainee class and duty assignment are in 330.32. Correspondence with Special Assistant Secretary of War Julius Amberg and members of Congress regarding Rep. Robert C. W. Ramspeck's committee investigation of the feasibility of using and training women in the WASP is in file 333.5. File 726.1, reserved for records about "genito-urinary, venereal, prostitution, and sex vices," contains occasional items about women.

18.8. A review copy of "A Study of Factors Determining Family Size in a Selected Professional Group" (111 pages) is in file 292 of the Commanding General's **formerly security classified correspondence, January 1939–September 1942** (300 ft.). The data, collected from U.S. Army Air Corps personnel, is the basis of the "guinea pig" file noted above in paragraph 18.3. This series also contains a 291.1 "WAC" file of administrative memorandums.

18.9. The continuation of this series in the Commanding General's **formerly security classified correspondence, October 1942–December 1944** (819 ft.), contains records of Army nurses in file 211 "Nurses." These include correspondence and cross-references relating to the rescue of air evacuation nurses and enlisted men in enemy-held Albania in November 1943, pregnancy among nurses, increased grade for flight nurses, and reports on nurses assigned to stations of the Air Transport Command in Africa. "Discharge of Nurses' Military Service" is the title of a 211 bulky file. Records of Army Nurse Corps personnel attached to medical units are in file 314.7 "Medical Histories." Substantive WAC materials, including correspondence, station surveys, and reports, are in file 324.5 (10 in.). Among the reports are copies of inspection activities, and special reports of Lt. Col. Betty Bandel. These cover the recruitment of black women, potentially subversive WAC personnel, WAC detachments assigned to the Central Pacific to replace civilian personnel, and training in cryptography and photographic interpretation. Other 324.5 files containing records about women are "Independent Organizations," "WASP," "Women Pilots," and "WAC." Among the records are operations reports of ferrying activities, "Comments of the Director of Women Pilots with Respect to the Historical Report of Ferrying Division of Air Transport Command Concerning WASP in Said Division" (65 pp.), and information about the considerable amount of legislative effort on behalf of the women pilots.

18.10. File 231.21 "Women Pilots" in the **general correspondence, 1939–42** (6 ft.), of the Air Adjutant General, Headquarters, AAF, contains letters, many from women, urging the War Department to create an organization of women pilots and suggesting that Jacqueline Cochran be appointed its leader. There are also letters from General Arnold to Cochran and other women who had expressed an interest in women ferry pilots and to other organized women pilots. Press releases, telegrams, letters, and memorandums in this file relate to Cochran's appointment as director of Women's Flying Training and Nancy Harkness Love's assignment as head of a Woman's Auxiliary Flying Squadron. Lists of women invited for interviews with the Ferrying Division, Air Transport Command are also in this file. In file 231.21 "Civilian Pilots" are lists dated October 1940 of student pilots and of men and women with pilots' certificates.

18.11. In the **general correspondence, June 1944–1948** (1,112 ft.), of the Office of the Air Adjutant General, Headquarters, AAF, file

220.3 "WAC" (4 in.) covers the assignment and transfer of enlisted Wacs and WAC groups such as hospital orderlies, those assigned to overseas service, and black detachments. Additional WAC records are filed under 320 "AAF Detachments, WAC." Colonel Bandel's later correspondence is in file 324.5 "WAC" (8 in.). Subjects of her correspondence include training, status, strength, and activities of the Air WAC, and demobilization. The file also includes memorandums and reports of the staff directions and commands to Bandel. In a 324.5 "WASP" bulky file (5 in.) are Cochran's "Final Report on the Women Pilot Program," August 9, 1945 (53 pp.); studies, including one entitled "Medical Considerations of WASP" (65 pp.); and Cochran's official correspondence for 1944. File 510 "Dependents, 1944–46" (5 in.), includes issuances and correspondence pertaining to accommodations, travel, and movement of household goods of families of AAF personnel.

18.12. The Air Adjutant General's **formerly classified and secret decimal correspondence, 1945–October 1948** (505 ft.), contains additional Air WAC records. A 324.5 "WAC" file (1 in.) includes numerous cross-reference sheets to bulky files. Among these is a report (2 in.) of the Air Inspector, AAF Headquarters, Air Technical Sevice Commands, about an investigation of morale and welfare of Wacs at Newark Army Air Base, NJ, and at Toledo and Wright Fields, OH. There are also records of investigations of WAC squadrons in the Caribbean and of a WAC detachment at Andrews AFB, MD. Other subjects in the file are assignments, statistics, discipline for men and women, image problems (particularly in the Southwest Pacific), a possible women's air raid defense system, women pilots for the U.S. Air Force, plans for postwar reduction, and postwar employment of Wacs in the AAF.

18.13. Record copies of the **Army Air Forces monthly service journal, January 1932–September 1948** (4 ft.), named successively as the *Air Corps News Letter*, *Air Forces News Letter*, *Air Force*, and *AAF Review*, were maintained by the Office of Information Services, Headquarters, AAF. For the years 1942–45 there is an index that provides citations for articles concerning the WAFS, the WFTD, and the WASP, as well as the WAC, flight nurses, and WAVES. A special February 1946 issue on AAF veterans includes an article on ex-servicewomen. Photographs of many entertainers appear in the November 1948 issue, which reported on Operation Wing Ding in Madison Square Garden, a salute to those who performed for the troops during the war.

18.14. There are three folders labeled "WAC," "WAF," and "WASP" in **manuscripts of histories, briefs, and stories, 1942–48** (10 ft.), in the records of the Personnel Narratives Division of the Director of Information, Office of Public Relations. They contain newspaper clippings and material issued for recruiting and public relations purposes, including scripts, advertising, and stories and pictures of women in the AAF.

18.15. Photographs of women serving in various capacities are scattered throughout the records of the ground photography section of

17

photographs made by the overseas technical unit of the Air Transport Command, April 1943–August 1945 (18-AG, 25,000 items). The photographs are under missions 4, 6, 8, and A4. A catalog of still picture captions (18-CS, 7 vols.) arranged by mission number, identifies negative numbers for the series.

18.16. Motion pictures of Air Force women are accessed by using the Army Depository copy of a film card catalog (111-ADC), which includes World War II outtakes collectively known as combat film subjects, December 1942–45 (ca. 3,000 reels). There is considerable footage of Army and Navy nurses. An entire reel is devoted to duties at an evacuation hospital and another to the work of a flight nurse who traveled with wounded soldiers from Italy to the United States. American Red Cross women volunteers appear in segments about Guam, and several reels document their activities in Germany in December 1945. A WAC unit in Foggia, Italy, 1944, in quarters and on duty in 12th Air Force Headquarters, and presentation ceremonies at 12th Air Force Headquarters in Florence, Italy, at which Col. Blanche E. Kerner was awarded the Legion of Merit medal on May 10, 1945, are shown. Paulette Goddard, Betty Hutton, Ruth Carroll, and Jinx Falkenburg appear in films of USO touring groups during World War II.

18.17. Aviatrix Katherine Stinson appears in at least three photographs (numbers 18-HE-453, 18-HE-694, and 18-HE-695) of aircraft activities and personnel at Rockwell Field, San Diego (Erickson Collection), 1914–18 (1,230 items, 18-HE). There are women in the group photographs numbered 18-HE-613, 18-HE-628, and 18-HE-699.

Records of the Bureau of Ships

Record Group 19

19.1. The Bureau of Ships had its origins in the Bureau of Construction, Equipment, and Repairs established in the Navy Department by an act of August 31, 1842. That bureau was succeeded by several others, most of which were abolished by 1920, when the Bureau of Ships inherited many of its predecessors' functions. The Bureau of Ships was responsible for the design, construction, conversion, procurement, maintenance, and repair of ships and other craft. On March 9, 1966, by order of the Department of Defense, the Bureau of Ships was abolished, and its functions were transferred to the Secretary of the Navy, who delegated most of them to the Naval Ship Systems Command under the Chief of Naval Operations. Women are represented in the records of the Bureau and its predecessors as civilian employees, as Waves, and as ship sponsors.

19.2. Names of many civilian women who were employed or applied for jobs in the Bureau of Construction, Equipment, and Repairs appear in the alphabetical **index, 1896–1925** (76 ft.), to the **correspondence ("A" documents), 1896–1925** (1,313 ft.), of the office of the chief of the Bureau, which is arranged numerically with the letter "A" affixed before each number to distinguish the letters from those of other correspondence bearing other alphabetical designators. A few index cards identify civilian employees and yeomen (F) by name; other subject headings relating to women are "Draftsman, female," and "Force-clerical and drafting." Index cards for the names of individuals usually refer to the numbers of specific files, some of which are extensive. Therefore, **history cards, 1896–1925** (75 ft.), arranged numerically and thereunder chronologically, which note the types of documents and abstract the contents of each file, are useful.

19.3. The **general correspondence, 1925–40** (2,062 ft.), is arranged according to the *Navy Filing Manual* (NFM),which provides general subject access. There is also an **alphabetical index** (51 ft.) and **history cards** (156 ft.) to this and other series that are arranged according to the NFM. Documents in this correspondence indicate that women were employed as clerical and drafting staff in the 1920's and 1930's and that women's organizations were concerned with some issues relating to the work of the Bureau of Ships.

19.4. Among the records of the Bureau of Engineering, a predecessor of the Bureau of Ships, the **general correspondence, 1911–22** (1,250 ft.), includes evidence that women were employed in clerical positions there. There is an **index** (77 ft.) arranged in five major subject categories and thereunder alphabetically by subjects such as "employees." The **general correspondence, 1923–40** (2,300 ft.), is arranged by the NFM in which the file designation "LL" is for "Employees," many of whom were women in clerical positions. **Indexes** (100 ft.) to this series are arranged alphabetically and thereunder according to the NFM.

19.5. During World War II, 1,100 enlisted Waves under 290 WAVES officers replaced all but 50 of the Navy men previously on duty at the Bureau of Ships. In file QR8 of the Bureau's **general correspondence, 1940–45** (7,260 ft.), arranged according to the NFM, are records concerning the placement, training, housing, etc., of Waves, as well as WAVES officers' inspection reports. These reports give evidence of positions held by women in Washington, DC, and at Bureau field offices, Navy yards, test facilities, and contract plants.

19.6. Women and girls appear in numerous **photographs of launchings and construction, 1902–65** (19-LC, 19-LCA, 19-LCM, ca. 321,200 items). The women are usually identified by name and by relation to some official.

19.7. Among **photographs of launchings and commissionings of post World War II ships and nuclear submarines, 1946–66** (19-NV, 500 items), are many pictures of women sponsors and the families of naval personnel. For example, Mrs. George C. Marshall was photographed at the commissioning of the nuclear submarine named for the late General Marshall on April 29, 1966.

Records of the Bureau of Naval Personnel

Record Group 24

24.1. The Bureau of Naval Personnel originated as the Bureau of Navigation, established by an act of July 5, 1862, to be responsible for certain personnel functions relating to officers. Shortly thereafter, the Bureau of Equipment and Recruiting was assigned, among other duties, the handling of enlistments. The Office of Detail was responsible for appointing and instructing volunteer officers. In 1889 the Bureau of Navigation absorbed the Office of Detail and assumed the personnel functions of the Bureau of Equipment and Recruiting. In 1942 the name of the Bureau of Navigation was changed to Bureau of Naval Personnel (BUPERS). The Bureau is responsible for the recruitment, assignment, and separation of naval personnel, including women in the Yeomen (F), the Navy Nurse Corps, and the WAVES, and the training and education of officers and enlisted personnel, including supervision of the U.S. Naval Academy and other schools.

24.2. A few citations of records relating to women in the Bureau of Navigation correspondence appear in the series, **subject registers of letters sent and received ("correspondence/subjects"), 1896–1902** (8 vols., 3 ft.), which serves as a finding aid for several series of early correspondence. Sample entries are, "Families, of officers: transportation, living on ship," and "Passengers."

24.3. The Bureau's **general correspondence, 1889–1913** (2,337 ft.), is arranged by year or time period and thereunder numerically, and **general correspondence, 1913–25** (1,092 ft.), is arranged numerically. **Record cards, 1903–25** (97 ft.), arranged by numbers assigned to subjects, contain chronologically arranged abstracts of documents in the general correspondence. **Subject cards, 1903–43** (89 ft.), arranged alphabetically by subject, provide further subject access to these and later series of correspondence. Correspondence between the Bureau and the Bureau of Medicine and Surgery about the establishment of a nurse corps in the Navy, including applicable regulations, pay, appointments, duty assignments, transfers, and resignations, is in the pre-1913 series of the correspondence. The 1913–25 series of correspondence contains, in file 3209, records about the Women's Section of the Navy League and its school, which gave classes in first aid, home care, diet cooking, telegraphy, and military calisthenics. File 5204 includes a few letters sent and received concerning the training, assignment, and transfer of the women in that service. File 7487 documents women volunteers in the American Red Cross in the United States and overseas. In file 8414 "Nurses" there are copies of orders assigning and transferring Navy nurses to stations in the continental United States, England, France, and elsewhere during that period. File 9875 contains Secretary of the Navy Josephus Daniels' March 14, 1917, memorandum to the Bureau stating that women were eligible to be enrolled in the Naval Coastal Defense Reserve (class 4), thus paving the way for the establishment of the Yeomen (F). File 55400 "Welfare Organizations" includes documents relating to women's work with the Young Women's Christian Association (YWCA), the American Red Cross, and the American Library Association for the benefit of Navy personnel. In file 55414 there is a report on prostitutes, bootleggers, and isolation hospitals prepared by the Navy's Assistant District Director of the Commission on Training Camp Activities (CTCA) in New Orleans. Entries on the subject cards for "Yeomen" and "Naval Reserve Force-Yeomen (F)" point to a few other documents.

24.4. The Bureau's **general correspondence, 1925–45** (2,555 ft.), arranged numerically by subject according to the *Navy Filing Manual* (NFM) and thereunder chronologically, documents the increasing number of BUPERS functions involving women. The documents in the series are also abstracted in the aforementioned subject cards.

24.5. Because BUPERS was responsible for the U.S. Naval Academy, the Bureau received letters from women worried about etiquette at Academy functions and seeking exceptions to the Academy prohibition of the marriage of midshipmen within 2 years of graduation. The letters are under classification P7, which also contains numerous letters from wives, servicemen, and their lawyers concerning support for dependents during marriage, separation, and divorce.

24.6. Routine assignments and separations of Navy nurses are documented in the 1925–40 part of file OG/P16-3 (1 in.), which is continued for 1941–45 under classification OG. Also under OG (1941–45) are reports prepared by Navy Nurse Corps Superintendent Sue Dauser, showing the number of regular reserve nurses on active duty and in nonactive status. In the same World War II part of OG are records about women dentists, physicians, communications officers, and photographic interpreters in the Navy.

24.7. The Office of the Director of the Women Appointed for Voluntary Emergency Service (WAVES) was administratively under the Bureau of Navigation, and the QR classification (4 ft.) in the 1925–45 general correspondence constitutes the main body of records in the National Archives about WAVES. Letters deal with enlistment, training, assignment, discipline, and discharge of Waves and document policy decisions from planning through the early postwar period. Included are personal letters of application, evaluations for promotion, and other records about individual women. Lt. Comdr. (later Capt.) Mildred McAfee, first director

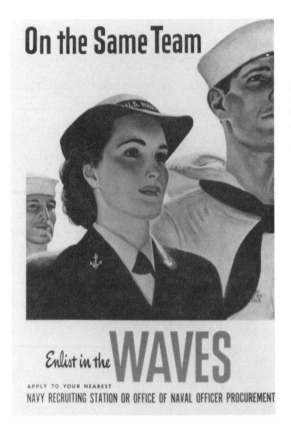

On the Same Team

Enlist in the WAVES

APPLY TO YOUR NEAREST
NAVY RECRUITING STATION OR OFFICE OF NAVAL OFFICER PROCUREMENT

The Bureau of Naval Personnel used this poster during World War II to recruit WAVES, or Women Appointed for Voluntary Emergency Service. 24-DP-6.

of the WAVES, and Virginia Gildersleeve, Chair of the Advisory Committee for Women in the Navy, signed many letters in the file.

24.8. Records of the training of both men and women at Link Trainer Instructor Schools are in file NC 153. File NC 157 contains correspondence with the commanding officer, Naval Reserve Midshipmen's School (WR) at Smith College, Northampton, MA, as well as issuances, mailgrams, revisions of curriculums, and lists of students. Personnel policy and actions for the Coast Guard Women's Reserve (SPARS) are also documented in this correspondence.

24.9. Other records that deal with women in this large correspondence series are filed under P3-2 "Medical Treatment, Pregnancy"; P7 "Domestic Relations, Marriages" (including those of nurses, Waves, civilian women employees, and wives of Navy men); P18-2 "Hours of Labor"; and P14-2 "Appointment and Employment." File NC 256 contains correspondence with the U.S. Naval Training School in the Bronx, NY (10 in.), which included the Hunter College Annex for enlisted women recruits. The series contains such diverse documents as an order for girdles and a ruling that separate statistics should be filed on availability reports for black enlisted women. Waves who received advanced training in communications attended Mount Holyoke College, South Hadley, MA, for which there is a folder of administrative correspondence with BUPERS (NC 162, ¼ in.).

24.10. The wide range of women's activities in welfare organizations is also documented in the 1925–45 correspondence series. Records about the American Red Cross include letters about garments knitted for sailors; the notification of families about casualties; and service as recreational aides in Iceland, as librarians in Alaska, and as nurses and hostesses in many parts of the world. Subject card entries indicate correspondence with or about the Navy Mothers' Club of America, the Navy Mothers League, the Navy Women's Overseas Service League, the Woman's Christian Temperance Union, and the YWCA.

24.11. Deck logs, July 1–19, 1937 (280 pages), of vessels engaged in the search for the lost plane of Amelia Earhart are among **logs of United States naval ships and stations, 1801–1946** (75,000 vols., 8,060 ft.). The logs containing Earhart material are available for the following participating vessels: U.S.S. *Colorado, Cushing, Dayton, Lamson, Lexington, Ontario,* and *Swan.*

24.12. Muster rolls of ships, January 1860–June 9, 1900 (366 vols., 36 ft.), are arranged in three chronological groups beginning with January 1, 1860–December 31, 1879, and thereunder alphabetically by name of vessel. In this first segment are several pages of muster rolls for the C.S.S. *Red Rover,* which was captured and coverted into the first Union hospital ship. On its rolls are the names of a nun, a black nurse, and a black laundress.

24.13. Muster rolls of ships and shore establishments, ca. January 1898–June 30, 1939 (3,539 vols., 681 ft.), are arranged in chronological periods and thereunder alphabetically by name or type of ship or shore unit. An **index to muster rolls of shore and aviation units** (2 ft.), arranged alphabetically by type or location of unit, is available. Among the earliest muster rolls containing names of women other than nurses are those that contain the names of World War I yeomen (F). Among locations where they served (usually in clerical positions) are B.F. Goodrich Co., Akron, OH; U.S. Naval Hospital, Guam; Naval Base Hospital No. 1, Brest, France; Allis-Chalmers Co., West Allis, WI; Naval Air Station, Cape May, NJ; Navy yards in many parts of the United States; and the Naval Reserve Enrolling Office, the Office of Naval Intelligence, the Office of the Naval Inspector of Ordnance, and the Office of Inspector of Machinery in Washington, DC. Information for each woman on the rolls usually includes name; rating; date, place, and terms of enlistment; date received on board; and dates and places of transfers. Volumes 1622 and 1445 of 1918–19 muster rolls, labeled "Navy Department Personnel," give the date of release from duty and the home address for each woman.

24.14. Microfilm copies of muster rolls of ships, stations, and other naval activities, September 1, 1939–January 1, 1949 (19,504 rolls), are arranged in subseries for ships, aviation units, and shore establishments, thereunder alphabetically by name of type of unit, and thereunder chronologically. They include the names of thousands of women who served the U.S. Navy and the U.S. Marine Corps in many ways. Marine Corps muster rolls include those for the Marine Corps Women's Reserve (MCWR) Battalion, Parris Island, SC, and for the MCWR Battalion, Marine Garrison Forces in Hawaii. Fifteen rolls of microfilm for MCWR units list the names of women who were trained at the U.S. Naval Training School for Enlisted Women at Hunter College, the Bronx, NY, 1943–45. For yeoman training schools in Stillwater, OK, and Cedar Falls, IA, there are two rolls each of women students. Roll S7744 contains muster rolls for the "Reserve Midshipmen's School (WR)," which are mainly lists of women Naval Reserve officer candidates training at Smith College. There are rolls for Storekeeper Schools in Naval Training Schools (WAVES) at Victoria Hotel, Boston (S7364), and in Milledgeville, GA (S7366). Names of enlisted Waves also appear on microfilm rolls for the Naval Dental School at the National Naval Medical Center, Bethesda, MD; for naval air stations such as the one at Pensacola, FL; and for auxiliaries of the Navy Relief Society in several cities. There are similar series of microfilmed muster rolls for January 1949–December 1956 (1,382 rolls) and **indexes to microfilm copies of muster rolls** (5 ft.) for 1941–46, 1946–48, and 1949–56.

24.15. The names of a few yeomen (F) appear in the subseries of reports for hospitals and naval stations in **reports of enlistments at receiving ships, training stations, hospitals, naval stations, and naval districts, January 1, 1913–June 30, 1926** (39 vols., 12 ft.), arranged randomly by type of activity reporting, and in **reports of enlistment in the Naval Reserve, January 1917–June 1919** (28 vols., 3 ft.), arranged by calendar or fiscal year, thereunder by place of enrollment, and thereunder by week or month.

24.16. Navy chaplains had considerable contact with the families of Navy personnel. The **general correspondence, 1916–40** (8 ft.), of the Chaplains Division is arranged alphabetically by subject and thereunder chronologically. Two subject headings that contain letters from or about women are "Funerals" and "Navy relief." Letters to the division from the Soldiers and Sailors Department of the National Woman's Christian Temperance Union are filed under "W.C.T.U." (1 in.).

24.17. The CTCA was established on July 26, 1917, to maintain morale, to provide recreation for men in training, and to handle problems of liquor and vice. After the war it became a permanent division of the Bureau of Navigation as the "Sixth Division," and, after 1921, as the Morale Division. Because the CTCA worked closely with welfare specialists from such organizations as the American Red Cross, the Young Men's Christian Association (YMCA), and the YWCA, the Commission's **general correspondence, 1918–20** (19 ft.), arranged according to a numerical classification scheme, contains documents relating to women who were on the staffs of those organizations. In addition, a few records relating to women appear in files bearing the following numbers and titles:

70   Clubs [one folder, "Mothers of Democracy"]

100 Employees [civilian and enlisted women]

213 Law enforcement [folders on individual women of CTCA's Section on Women and Girls, including documents about field work with women near training camps]

353 Correspondence with members of the Commission [some of whom were women]

388 [YWCA hostess houses for servicemen (1 in.)]

24.18. Motion pictures of Navy activities during and after World War I, 1917–27 (102 reels), arranged in a numerical system, were produced either by the Navy or by commercial firms for Navy recruiting purposes. Women appear in scenes as workers manufacturing gyroscopes for torpedoes at the Newport News, VA, Navy Yard (1918) and as American Red Cross nurses and Camp Fire Girls in a patriotic ceremony at the Statue of Liberty (1918). Mrs. Warren G. Harding is shown in one scene with the President aboard the Presidential yacht *Mayflower.*

24.19. The **"Administrative History of the Bureau of Personnel in World War II," n.d.** (15 vols., 1 ft.), consists of reports about each of the important activities of the Bureau. One volume (125 pp.) contains reports on the legislative and administrative history of the WAVES, including procurement standards, housing, discipline, and welfare of the women. Other volumes also include reports on Waves: "Physical Training for WAVES" in a volume on training, and "Live Entertainment," about Waves' activity in this field, in the volume on "The Welfare Activity." There is also a section on the Dependents' Welfare Division.

24.20. Waves were subject to regular Navy regulations and also to special regulations that applied only to women recorded in **"Regulations Governing Women Accepted for Voluntary Emergency Service, July 1942–November 1945"** (2 vols., 2 in.). One volume, labeled "NavPers-15085 (Restricted), 'Policies for the Administration of the Women's Reserve, USNR,' " contains printed regulations on procurement; military authority; pay and allowances; ranks, grades, rates, and classes; assignment to duty outside the continental United States; housing; uniforms; leave; discipline; marital status; and reenlistment, reappointment, recall, and separation. The second volume, "References in 'Policies for the Administration of the Women's Reserve, USNR,' " contains typewritten ad processed material. Both volumes are indexed.

24.21. The Special Services Division of the Welfare Activity managed welfare, recreation, and entertaiment of naval personnel. **General**

records of the Recreational Services Division, 1943–46 (30 ft.), arranged according to a subject-numeric classification scheme from "1— American Red Cross" to "65—Women's Reserve Division," is a basic source of information on the establishment and activities of units of the United Services Organization (USO) operating under naval jurisdiction. The series includes several files pertaining to Waves attached to the Welfare Activity, including those working with the USO and representing the Navy on the Joint Army-Navy Committee on Welfare and Recreation. Documents relating to Waves are in the "Personal Files of Personnel" section and in folders marked "35C NR, WV(S)" and "28C." Records about women entertainers are in annual reports (3 in.) of Camp Shows, Inc. In file 16 "Entertainment" scattered material about scheduling shows in which women appeared is followed by reports of performances and itineraries arranged by naval district. File 37 "Navy Mothers' Clubs" contains replies to offers of assistance and accounts of club activities. Women representing the YWCA, the YMCA, Traveler's Aid, and the separate YWCA for blacks participated in the USO work documented in file 61.

24.22. Over half of the **records of the Publicity and Advertising Section relating to the Navy recruiting program, 1940–45** (4 ft.), which are unarranged, deal with recruitment of Waves and Spars. The series includes enlistment posters, photographs of recruiting displays, and scrapbooks of clippings of articles, cartoons, and comic strips about service in the Navy.

24.23. There are a few portraits of wives included in the series **negatives of officers and enlisted men of the Navy and the Marine Corps and members of their families, 1917–36** (24-PD), and numerous posters relating to women in general and Waves in particular in **display posters, 1934–44** (24-DP), and **World War II recruitment posters, 1942–45** (24-PO).

Records of the Office of the Chief of Naval Operations

Record Group 38

38.1. The Office of the Chief of Naval Operations (CNO) was established in 1915 to coordinate naval operational activities. Under it were the Office of Naval Intelligence (ONI), the Board of Inspection and Survey, and the Naval Communications Service.

38.2. The CNO is the principal naval adviser to the President and the Secretary of the Navy on the conduct of war, the principal naval executive and adviser to the Secretary on the administration of the Department, and the naval member of the Joint Chiefs of Staff. He is responsible for the naval operating forces and associated bureaus and offices, manpower and logistical services, research and development plans and activities, naval strategic planning, the organization and training of naval forces, their preparation and readiness, and the maintenance of a high level of quality among personnel and components of the Navy.

38.3. The general correspondence of the Office from 1915 to June 30, 1942, is interfiled with that of the Office of the Secretary of the Navy (RG 80).

38.4. The later correspondence of the CNO, including the correspondence of the Deputy CNO (Air), is in CNO's **general correspondence, July 1, 1942–June 30, 1946** (436 ft.), arranged according to the *Navy Filing Manual* (NFM). The most frequently used file designations for records about women are QR-8, "Women's Reserve," and P-16-1, "Personnel Strength and Distribution." Yearly QR-8 files, 1942–46 (6 ft. total), cover training for women in ONI's Japanese language and crypt-analysis schools, names of enlisted Waves advanced in rating, names of women graduates of particular colleges who qualified for enlistment in officers' training, disciplinary action after complaints of residents near WAVES barracks, statistics on personnel requirements, WAVES officers in a peacetime Navy, and a conference on demobilization and postwar planning. File P4-2 contains documents about appointment of women to both WAVES and civilian jobs. File P7 includes cross-references to records relating to women's misconduct and disabilities and to illegitimate children of service personnel. The series is served by a **name and subject index** (2 ft.).

38.5. Beginning in 1941, the Commander-in-Chief, United States Fleet (COMINCH), was directly responsible to the President for creating war plans, executing operational commands, and making available for evaluation all pertinent information and intelligence. The district intelligence officer in the 13th Naval District included several items concerning women in his reports to COMINCH. Copies of the reports are in file A8-2 of a 1943 confidential subseries of **formerly security classified correspondence, 1942–45** (867 ft.), for the Headquarters, COMINCH. Both the correspondence and its **indexes** (107 ft.) are arranged by year, thereunder by type of security classification, and thereunder according to the NFM. Women's activities mentioned in intelligence reports included speaking on behalf of the American Civil Liberties Union to internees in a Japanese relocation center and participating in an allegedly suspect Flint, MI, organization called Loyal Mothers of America and in the Office Workers' Canteen, a union-sponsored Boston social hall. Some correspondence with the Bureau of Naval Personnel deals with housing and requests for additional women personnel.

38.6. In the **general correspondence, 1912–26** (305 ft.), of the Director of Naval Communications, arranged chronologically by year or period and thereunder by subject numbers, there is documentation of the many women employed in that division between the two world wars.

Records relating to yeomen (F) are scattered through file 38 for the years 1917–19. File 900 (2 in.) deals almost entirely with women clericals and telephone switchboard operators. File 901, concerning budget estimates, includes salaries for women communications personnel. File 904 records reductions in civilian personnel. There is a **subject index**.

38.7. The **general correspondence, 1942–45** (75 ft.), of the Postal Affairs Section of the Division of Naval Communications, arranged by year and thereunder by the NFM, contains material about Waves under file designations A(3-1) for organizational components and P(17-2WV) in which one folder is labeled, "Advancement in Rating, WAVES." There is also a **name index** (3 ft.).

38.8. Only a small amount of the **general correspondence ("cases"), 1899–1912** (80 vols., 31 ft.), of the ONI deals with women employees. However, in July 1899, shortly after ONI was established, Eva A. Marvin was hired away from the Department of the Interior because she was an "excellent typewritist" with proficiency in German. Her beginning salary was $1,000 per year, increased in 1907 to $1,300. A **general subject index** (12 ft.) includes a few entries for women translators.

38.9. Voluminous files on persons suspected of pro-German or anti-American sympathies, including some women, is in ONI **formerly confidential general correspondence, 1913–24** (45 ft.), for which there is a list of case numbers and names of persons who were subjects of the correspondence.

38.10. Material about the activities of Amelia Earhart and the search operations after her plane disappeared in the summer of 1937 is in ONI **formerly security classified general correspondence, 1929–42** (141 ft.), arranged according to the *Navy Filing Manual.* Filed under A4-3, the 170-page file includes letters from inquiring citizens and information about a January 7, 1939, report that Earhart was a Japanese prisoner in the Marshall Islands.

38.11. ONI received much of its information from naval attachés abroad. Most of the information transmitted was technical in nature, but one of the **formerly confidential reports of naval attachés, 1940–46** (413 ft.), is a brief report (B-7C17369/46), written in 1946, concerning 2,000 "brides and babies" of U.S. soldiers being transported from Europe to the United States by the U.S. Merchant Marine.

38.12. In ONI's records relating to investigations, 1917–30, the partial (A–H only) **list of persons suspected of being foreign agents, ca. 1917–20** (4 in.), contains the names of several women who either were in the Navy or were civilian employees. Activities of private citizens and organizations are also documented, including Mother Keebaugh's Army-Navy Club (file 20963-20). The ONI **formerly secret lists of agents, 1917–20** (½ in.), part of records relating to personnel, contain the names of several American women, including one purported to have been a prostitute in Japan. The **list of ONI personnel of naval districts, 1917–20** (1 ft.), includes both yeomen (F) and civilian employees.

38.13. Formulating policies for the training of aviation personnel was one of the functions of the Deputy CNO (Air) when that position was established in 1943. Lt. Joy Bright Hancock, later Director of the WAVES, worked in this office. In addition to training Waves to instruct male personnel, the office made recommendations to the Bureau of Naval Personnel for duty assignments of aviation personnel. File QR-8 "WAVES" (5 in.), in the **general correspondence, August 20–October 30, 1943** (30 ft.), covers the assignment of Waves to positions of aerologist, communication watch officer, aviation metalsmith, navigation instructor, and gunnery training device operator. Some letters complain about the audibility of the voices of women control tower operators. Much of the correspondence deals with requests for enlisted Waves as aviation radio personnel and evaluations of their performance in such positions.

38.14. The **general correspondence of the Naval Air Transport Service, 1941–43** (21 ft.), includes requests for enlisted women, letters about training Waves as instructors at the Link Instrument Trainer Instructor's School, and assigning them to duty as transport officers and pilots. The **index** (5 ft.) contains numerous entries under "WAVES." File A2-11/QR-8 includes records about uniforms, nonpreferential treatment, discipline, marriage, and resignations or discharges because of pregnancy.

38.15. Among **sound recordings** of the Office of the CNO are recordings of at least four radio broadcasts relating to women: messages from Seabees on Guam to mothers and sweethearts (38-35), a series of interviews with servicemen from Illinois about their families for broadcast in Peoria (38-19), a brief discussion of selecting a "Navy Mother of 1944" (38-4), and a plea from Adm. Chester Nimitz urging American women to take jobs in shipyards (38-5).

38.16. Photographs of World War I naval personnel from a series of miscellaneous photographs (HS, 335 items), arranged alphabetically by surname of sitter, contain pictures of two of women identified as agents.

Naval Records Collection of the Office of Naval Records and Library

Record Group 45

45.1. The Naval Records Collection was started in 1882 when the Librarian of the Navy Department began to collect naval documents relating to the Civil War for publication. The staff engaged in this task was called the Naval War Record Office and was known collectively with the library as the Office of Library and Naval War Records. During the early 1900's most of the bound records of the office of the Secretary of the Navy, all dated before 1886, were transferred to the Office of Library and Naval War Records, and the staff began collecting the older records of naval bureaus and records relating to naval personnel and operations during the American Revolution. In 1915 the office was named the Office of Naval Records and Library, and in 1919 it was merged with the Historical Section of the Office of Naval Intelligence. During the period between World War I and World War II, many documents were acquired from private and public sources. In August 1946 the Office of Naval Records and Library was combined with the Office of Naval History, which had been established in 1944 to prepare histories and narratives of naval activities during World War II.

45.2. Before 1830 there are few letters to women in the Secretary of the Navy's **miscellaneous letters sent ("general letter book"), June 1789–November 1877** (107 vols., 25 ft.), but thereafter there is an increasing number of replies, mostly routine, to women relatives and friends inquiring about men who were in the Navy or who were trying to enlist. The series has been filmed as M209 (43 rolls). Similarly, the Secretary's **miscellaneous letters received ("miscellaneous letters"), January 1801–December 1884** (823 vols., 157 ft.), have been filmed as M124 (647 rolls). Some letters from women are accounts of poverty and neglect or desertion by men in the Navy or attempts to persuade the Secretary that some friend or relative was worthy of rapid promotion. **Letters from officers below the rank of commander ("officers' letters"), April 1802–December 1884** (845 vols., 231 ft.), filmed as M148 (518 rolls), sometimes contain descriptions of homelife by officers who requested leaves of absence or resigned their commissions. **Letters from officers commanding squadrons ("squadron letters"), February 1841–November 1886** (309 vols., 77 ft.), filmed as M89 (300 rolls), occasionally contain enclosures from subordinates including some personal information such as the condition of wives and families.

45.3. Among fiscal records, 1794–1893, **weekly statements of purchases by bureaus, January 1883–June 1890** (7 vols., 1 ft. 3 in.), arranged chronologically, some records identify women who had business dealings with the Navy.

45.4. In the spring of 1862, Union forces captured C.S.S. *Red Rover* and fitted it out as the first U.S. Naval Hospital Ship. Names of a matron and a laundress appear after those of male nurses on a "list of officers and men" in the Doctor's Department of the ship. The document is in a series of **muster rolls and payrolls of vessels, 1779–1885** (36 ft.).

45.5. From 1815 to 1842 the Board of Navy Commissioners procured naval stores and materials and arranged for the construction, armament, equipment, and repair of U.S. naval vessels. The **journal of the**

Board of Navy Commissioners, April 1815–September 1852 (19 vols., 3 ft.), is arranged chronologically. The board's **miscellaneous letters sent, May 1815–August 1842** (8 vols., 2 ft.), and its **miscellaneous letters received, January 1812–July 1842** (64 vols., 9 ft.), deal with businessmen bidding for or holding Navy contracts. A few of the contractors were women, usually widows of businessmen, and records about them can be located by using name indexes and registers to the journal and the correspondence.

45.6. Logs and journals kept by U.S. naval officers, 1789–1938 (248 vols., 24 ft.), give occasional glimpses of their families. For example, comments by an officer's daughter about the Mexican War were entered into the "Journals of Lt. Tunis Augustus M. Craven, 1846–49" (2 vols., 1 in.), which also include several poems Craven wrote to his wife. The "Journal of Stephen Trenchard commanding the U.S.S. *Rhode Island*, July 31, 1861–August 17, 1865" (3 vols., 3 in.), contains descriptions of social engagements ashore. Women are mentioned briefly as passengers on prize ships or as refugees in the "Journals of Comdr. (later Capt.) George F. Emmons Commanding the U.S.S. *Hatteras*, *R.R. Cuyler*, *Monongahela*, *Brooklyn*, *Lackawanna*, and *Pensacola*, November 1, 1861–March 31, 1866" (4 vols., 5 in.). "Journals of Midshipman (later Lt.) Henry Wise, July 1837–November 9, 1860" (12 vols., 2 ft.), describe the social life of a bachelor in antebellum Philadelphia in the early volumes and his affection for his wife and family in some of the later volumes.

45.7. Like the logs and journals, **letters sent and received by U.S. naval officers, ca.1798–1908** (434 vols., 47 ft.), were donated to the Naval Records Collection. Among these are "Fair and press copies sent by Lt. (later Chief of the Bureau of Ordnance) Henry Wise, August 1851–April 1868," which include references to his own wife and family and the families of some of the men who served under him. One volume contains poems about love and friendship. "Letters sent and received, telegrams received, and orders issued by Rear Adm. David D. Porter while comanding the Mississippi Squadron on board the U.S. Flagship *Black Hawk* (September 1862–October 1864) and the North Atlantic Blockading Squadron on board the Flagship *Malvern* (November 1864–May 1865)" (81 vols., 15 ft.), contains indexed letters from women who wrote to Admiral Porter about men who served under him. "Letters sent and received by Commodore Andrew A. Harwood Commanding the Washington Navy Yard and Potomac Flotilla, July 1862–December 1863" (11 vols., 2 ft.) mention some Washington women who were involved in the Civil War or victimized by it. "Letters sent by Acting Master William R. Browne commanding the U.S.S. *Restless* in the East Gulf Blockading Squadron, January–July 1864" (1 vol., ½ in.), mention women as refugees, contraband (i.e., former slaves), prostitutes, and naval wives requiring rations.

This World War I poster reminded women of three ways they could exercise their patriotism. 45-WP-1008.

45.8. The 1775–1910 part of the **area file, August 1648–December 1910** (ca. 123 ft.), has been filmed as M625 (414 rolls). These records are possible sources of material for family and social history of the cities where naval installations were located. It is a collection of letters, reports, and other records arranged according to geographical areas. The records were taken from other series, most of which cannot be identified, and relate chiefly to occurrences or conditions in particular places. There are a few records about women. For example, there are a few copies of contracts with women to supply goods to the Continental Congress, and there is a letter about fitting out the *Red Rover* as a hospital ship that notes the assistance of the women of the St. Louis Sanitary Commission.

45.9. The **subject file, ca. 1775–1910** (332 ft.), arranged by an alphabetical filing scheme, consists of files that are of considerable bulk. In the NL-Living conditions (Personnel) section is "Living Conditions of Officers and Their Families, 1858," by Mrs. H. A. Wise, 258 pages, and a folder marked "Society for the Relief of Families of Officers Killed While in Service, 1820." The folder contains a 17-page history of the Navy Relief Society incorporated in 1904 to provide relief for indigent widows and orphans of Navy officers and enlisted men. Another folder contains a notebook of the "Navy Wives Club, Navy YMCA, Norfolk, Va." for 1930–40. It includes photographs, lists of officers, and minutes of meetings. Section OA-Organization and Administration is an 1838 draft of an order requiring approval of the Secretary of the Navy for taking the families of officers aboard ship as passengers or residents.

45.10. Originally a part of the subject file described above, the **subject file of the Confederate States Navy, 1861–65** (33 ft.), filmed as M1091 (61 rolls), is also arranged according to the alphabetical filing scheme. It includes Confederate women's names under "ML Medical Personnel" as nurses and under several other categories as signers of receipts for payment for lodging, meals, and labor of slaves provided to naval personnel.

45.11. The work of yeomen (F), and female assembly line workers during World War I is documented in another **subject file, 1911–27** (several hundred feet). In addition, the file includes some records about nurses and volunteers in relief organizations. The principal subdivisions containing records about women are:

MR.   Red Cross, YMCA, and K. of C. [Knights of Columbus] Organizations

NA.   Personnel

    1. Officers, Navy [includes records about yeomen (F) and Navy Nurse Corps in folders marked "Regulars and Reserves"]

    3. Enlisted, Navy [includes records about women in folders marked "General Information" and "Women in the United States Naval Reserve Force—Employment as Yeomen F"]

NC.   Casualties

    1. "Naval Personnel Losses, 1919–26"

ZN.   Commission on Training Camp Activities

ZNP. Wartime Histories of Naval Districts (8 ft.)

The index includes terms "Women," "Yeowomen," and "Yeomanettes." Records (1 ft.) for the 1st Naval District include a chapter on the District Enrolling Office providing information on the admission of women into naval work and containing photographs of clerical staff; lists of employees; and copies of the magazine *The Navy Salvo*, edited for a time by a yeoman (F), containing articles about employees' social life, promotions, assignments, and awards at the Boston Navy Yard, as well as photographs of "yeowomen" in uniform. Histories for the 9th, 10th, and 11th Naval Districts are bound together and include responses of naval contractors to a questionnaire about war industries. Among the questions were percentage of women among employees, their wages, their efficiency, and social welfare work among employees. There is also a report of the conviction of a woman under the Espionage Act.

45.12. Thirteen **World War I posters, 1914–18** (WP, 783 items), show women in war work. They were collected by the Navy Department from Government agencies and organizations and placed in the Naval Collection.

Records of the Bureau of Medicine and Surgery

Record Group 52

52.1. The Bureau of Medicine and Surgery was created in the Department of the Navy by an act of August 31, 1842. It was responsible for the administration of naval dispensaries and hospitals, caring for the Navy's sick and injured, ensuring the adequacy of health facilites on Navy ships and stations, and other medical matters. The Bureau was abolished in October 1982; its functions were assigned to the Naval Medical Command. The principal records relating to women deal with the Navy Nurse Corps, the health and welfare of Waves, and the care of families of Navy personnel.

52.2. Replies to women inquiring about relatives in the Navy and other matters and to widows of Navy personnel seeking information needed for pension applications are in **letters sent ("letter book")**, **September 1842–February 1886** (47 vols., 7 ft.), arranged chronologically and indexed in the front of each volume, and in **indexes to letters sent, May 1848–December 1849, December 1875–March 1877** (2 vols., 5 in.), arranged alphabetically by name of addressee and thereunder chronologically.

52.3. Letters from women on the same subjects are in **letters received ("letter book"), September 1842–December 1856** (114 vols., 22 ft.), arranged by year and thereunder by class of sender, and in **letters received ("letters from all sources"), January 1857–February 1885** (298 vols., 59 ft.), arranged chronologically. Both are indexed in the front of each volume.

52.4. General correspondence, February 1885–April 1912 (445 ft.), and **general correspondence, March 1912–December 1925** (142 ft.), are partially indexed in **index to general correspondence, 1896–December 1925** (8 ft.), which contains entries for subjects and the names of naval facilities arranged alphabetically and thereunder chronologically. After Congress created the Navy Nurse Corps in August 1908, some of the correspondence of Lenah Higbee, the second superintendent of the Corps, was filed in these correspondence series. Files 125686 and 115738 contain records relating to two controversies involving Corps performance in its early years. Useful index terms referring to women are "Base hospitals," "Bureau, War Risk Insurance," "Dietitians," "Families of officers," "Families of enlisted men," "Nurse" (which includes references to Sisters of Charity, nurses who served the Navy in the Spanish-American War, and volunteers), "Red Cross Society," "Woman's Army and Navy League," "Woman's Christian Temperance Union," "Women dentists," "Women doctors," "Women patients," "Women Section, Navy League," "Women's Industrial Conference," "Women's National Service School, Navy League," "Women's Oversea Hospital," and "Yeomen." Records relating to the Navy Nurse Corps can be located under the names of naval facilities in the index.

52.5. The **general correspondence, January 1926–51** (210 ft.), arranged in three chronological subseries (1926–41, 1942–46, and 1947–51) and thereunder according to the *Navy Filing Manual*, contains records about women in file A18-1/EN "WAVES," OG "Navy Nurse Corps," P7 "Domestic relations," P14-2 and P14-2/OG "Appointment/employment," and P20-2/OG "Matters of performance." It is served by an **index** (35 ft.), arranged in the same chronological subseries, in which some of the entries that refer to records relating to women are "American Board of Obstetrics and Gynecology," "American Medical Women's Association, Inc.," "American Nurses' Association," "Applications for position" (including dietitians, librarians, anesthetists, stenographers, and teachers), "Coast Guard Women's Reserve," "Flight nurses," "Librarians," "Nurse Corps, USN," "Nurse Corps, Army," "Nurses Aides," "Nurses National Memorial," "Nurse(s), Nursing General," "Occupational therapy," "Prostitution," "Spanish War veterans" (including nurses), "Woman(en)—Women's Auxiliary Corps for Navy," "Women," "Women's Industrial Conference," "Women's Medical Specialist Corps," "Women's Oversea League," "Women World War Veterans," and names of naval facilities. Specifically in the 1942–46 subseries of the index, the following entries relate to women: "Employees, civilian," "Enlisted personnel," "Families," "Keller, Helen," "Laundries," "Legislation," "Maid," "Maternity," "Nurses Aides," "Nurses Corps, Army," "Nurses Corps, Navy," "Nurses Corps, U.S. Naval Reserve," "Nurse(s), Nursing General," "Nurses National Memorial," "Red Cross, American National," "Uniforms (General)," "Women," "Women's Army Auxiliary Corps," "Women's Auxiliary Corps of the Navy," "Women's Auxiliary, Disabled American Veterans," and "Women's Patriotic Conference on National Defense."

52.6. **Letters sent by the superintendent of the Nurse Corps, 1909–December 1911** (3 vols., 4 in.), are arranged as follows: volume 1, letters marked "Personal" and "Semi-official," sent by the first superintendent, Esther V. Hasson; volume 2, Hasson's official letters; and volume 3, letters sent by Lenah Higbee, second superintendent. They concern appointments to the Corps, explanation of administrative procedures, discussion of social relations of nurses, and disciplinary action within the Corps.

52.7. The Navy Nurse Corps traces its beginnings to the nurses who volunteered for service to the Navy during the Spanish-American War. In **records relating to the history of naval medicine, 1775–1945** (6 ft.), arranged according to a numerical classification scheme, there is a small amount of material concerning nurses in this period in file .300 "Female nurses," and file .500 "Civilians."

52.8. **Records relating to the history of the Navy Nurse Corps, 1908–75** (2 ft.), arranged alphabetically by subject, include miscellaneous series of records consisting largely of processed studies and pamphlets.

Included are histories and biographical sketches of former superintendents of the Corps and relating to nurses held as prisoners of war during World War II. Also included are records pertaining to legislation affecting the Navy Nurse Corps, awards and medals, personnel policies, the utilization of black nurses, World War II demobilization, and involuntary recalls during the Korean war.

52.9. The National Research Council, composed of prominent civilian scientists, was organized within the National Academy of Sciences in 1916 to coordinate the scientific resources of the country in the interest of national defense. During World War II its Division of Medical Sciences addressed questions of rationing, needs of working mothers, and health facilities at defense plants and military facilities. In **formerly security classified minutes, publications, reports, and correspondence of subcommittees of the Division of Medical Sciences of the National Research Council, 1940–43** (7 ft.), arranged by name of subcommittee, are records relating to "Food habits," "Food and Nutrition," and "Health and Welfare Services," demonstrating the work of home economists, child development specialists, public health officials, and anthropologists (including Margaret Mead). The Council's subcommittees also considered "Venereal Diseases (Treatment)—Prostitution," under which are filed reports on surveys in particular geographic areas, a copy of a 31-page pamphlet, *Prostitution and the War* (Public Affairs Pamphlet No. 65) by Philip S. Broughton (New York: Public Affairs Committee, Inc., 1942), and papers prepared during World War I proposing authorized houses of prostitution. Under "Federal Security Agency Advisory Committee on Social Protection" are filed minutes of meetings where there was discussion of prostitution and Federal aid to defense areas for rehabilitation and social services for those involved. The Division of Preventive Medicine of the Bureau of Medicine and Surgery maintained a few related records such as "Historical Records—WAVE" and "Venereal Disease (Treatment)—WAAC, WAVE, British, Canadian," which are filed with the National Research Council records.

52.10. Among the Bureau's audiovisual records are **prints and transparencies of Navy Nurse Corps uniforms, 1908–70** (52-NNU, 304 items), arranged alphabetically by subject (for example, dress uniforms, insignia, and accessories).

Records of the Bureau of Yards and Docks

Record Group 71

71.1. The Bureau of Naval Yards and Docks was established in 1842 and renamed the Bureau of Yards and Docks in 1862. It designed, constructed, and maintained all naval public works, such as drydocks, harbor structures, storage facilities, power plants, and buildings at shore establishments. The Bureau was abolished in 1966, and its functions were transferred to the Naval Facilities Engineering Command. Women appear in the Bureau records as civilian employees and, during World War I, as yeomen (F).

71.2. General correspondence, 1925–42 (923 ft.), is arranged according to the *Naval Filing Manual* (NFM),in which records relating to civilian employees are filed under classification "LL." Under QR8 "Women's Auxiliary Reserve in the Navy," records relate to the construction of administration and training buildings and housing for enlisted women. The **index to the general correspondence, 1925–42** (249 ft.), consists of cards that contain abstracts of letters and other documents under each NFM category. In the LL category, cards are arranged alphabetically by employees' names. Most women employed by the Bureau were clericals. On QR8 cards are entries for correspondence relating to the detail of Waves to the Bureau of Yards and Docks, qualifications for enlisted women, and appointments to and employment in the Merchant Marine Reserve. Entries under LL classification (6 in.) in **formerly security classified history cards for confidential correspondence, 1918–46** (31 ft.), refer to investigative reports, espionage, and other matters concerning individual employees, men as well as women.

71.3. Chronological **monthly reports of officers and employees at the Naval Asylum, 1869–72, 1884–85** (½ ft.), show women as scrubbers, laundresses, and cooks.

71.4. It is not known why **cash books of private merchants, 1784–85, 1803–11, 1817–20** (10 vols., 1 ½ ft.), are among the Bureau's records. However, purchases of household goods by women in northern Virginia and Washington, DC, are recorded.

71.5. Photographic **panoramas, 1917–19** (71-PA, 7 items), include two groups of yeomen (F), one photographed on White House grounds in February 1919, and the other in front of the Navy Building in May 1919 with Secretary of the Navy Josephus Daniels and Assistant Secretary Franklin D. Roosevelt, a few months before all yeomen (F) were discharged from service in the Naval Reserve on July 15, 1919.

Records of the Bureau of Aeronautics

Record Group 72

72.1. The Bureau of Aeronautics was established in the Navy Department in 1921 with functions involving construction and equipment of naval aircraft testing materials, and outfitting bases and other shore establishments. During World War II its functions were expanded, but it was abolished in 1959, and its functions were transferred to the Bureau of Naval Weapons.

72.2. The **general correspondence relating to aviation, 1914–21** (210 ft.), arranged by three different filing schemes, and the **formerly security classified correspondence relating to aviation, 1917–19** (5 ft.), arranged numerically, are both served by an **index, 1917–19** (12 ft.). Material relating to yeomen (F) in both correspondence series are indexed under "Employees," "Female," "Women," "Yeomen and reservists," "Yeomen," and "Yeowomen."

72.3. The **general correspondence, 1925–42** (2,416 ft.), arranged according to the *Navy Filing Manual* (NFM), includes in file QR8 planning documents, April–December 1942, for the utilization of Waves. Subjects covered are the establishment of training schools and living quarters for Waves. There is correspondence with officials at Navy and Marine Corps air stations about possible types of jobs that women might fill and estimates of the number of Waves that each station might require. The file is continued in **general correspondence, 1943–45** (2,340 ft.). **Record cards, July 1941–June 1944** (176 ft.), also arranged according to the NFM, contain abstracts of letters in parts of both general correspondence series, including 339 cards, front and back, for QR8, beginning on April 20, 1942. In addition, there are record cards for correspondence under QR10 (2 items) for records relating to the Rigger Battalion (Parachute), under QR11 (2 items) for the WAC, and under QR12 relating to the Women's Marine Corps Reserve.

72.4. A few memorandums in **formerly confidential correspondence, 1922–44** (719 ft.) filed under QR8 relate to the need for Waves with engineering, radio, or electrical backgrounds in the office of the Inspector of Naval Aircraft at Columbus, OH.

72.5. The Classification Section of the Civilian Branch conducted a **survey of civilian personnel in the bureau, January–August 1944** (2 ft.). The records, arranged alphabetically by name of division within the Bureau, include a job description sheet for each employee, many of whom were women, showing employee's name, organizational unit, job title, name of supervisor, and other information about duties, hours, assessment of the utilization of his or her abilities, and other information. An interview sheet is attached to each job sheet. It is possible to determine what kinds of jobs were held by women, their grades, and their relative positions on the organization charts that are also a part of the series. There is also a report of the recommendations made as a result of the survey.

72.6. Formerly confidential correspondence, 1945 (165 ft.), includes records in a QR8 file relating to plans for a women's reserve in the postwar Navy. The same file designation in **unclassified correspondence, 1946** (165 ft.), and QR8 and OO files in **unclassified correspondence, 1947** (260 ft.), both include a few records under the QR8 classification relating to plans for a woman's reserve in the postwar Navy. File OG in the 1946 series contains unclassified issuances relating to legislation to establish the Navy Nurse Corps as a staff corps of the Regular Navy.

Records of the Bureau of Ordnance

Record Group 74

74.1. The Bureau of Ordnance and Hydrography was established in the Navy Department in 1842. Its name was changed to Bureau of Ordnance in 1862 when its duties relating to Hydrography were transferred to the Bureau of Navigation. It was responsible for the design, manufacture, maintenance, and issuance of naval armament and for the operation of naval gun factories and other naval ordnance plants. It was abolished in 1959 with its functions transferred to the Bureau of Naval Weapons. In records after 1926 that are arranged according to the *Navy Filing Manual* records about women appear under classifications QR8 (WAVES) and LL (civilian employees).

74.2. Filed under QR8 in **formerly security classified general correspondence, 1885–1944** (6,147 ft.), arranged in four segments with differing arrangement schemes, are records relating to WAVES training, assignments, quarters, and courts-martial. In sizable LL annual files there are scattered memorandums, letters, and reports about the employment of women in naval and contractor ordnance plants and navy yards.

Records of the Office of the Chief of Engineers

Record Group 77

77.1. The Corps of Engineers, U.S. Army, was established by an act of March 16, 1802, to organize a military academy at West Point. In 1818 the Office of the Chief of Engineers (OCE) was established in Washington, DC, and the Army topograpical engineers were placed under the Chief's supervision. The responsibilities of the Office have included producing and distributing Army maps, building roads, and maintaining fortifications. Its civil responsibilities have included inprovement of inland waterways and harbors, planning for flood control, and approving plans for the construction of bridges and other works over navigable waters. There are a few textual records relating to women as employees of the agency and some cartographic records relating to women as landholders.

77.2. The OCE **general correspondence, 1894–1923** (3,041 ft.), is arranged numerically in general chronological order and is accompanied by an extensive **name and subject index** (322 ft.). The correspondence includes consolidated files relating to some women employees. The records show the gradual increase in the number of women employed until

World War I when there was a sharp increase, followed by a postwar reduction-in-force that not only reduced the number of women but also the percentage of women in the total number of employees. In file 116924/1 there is a copy of "Storage Bulletin No. 9 on the Employment of Women in the Storage Warehousing Depots of the United States Army" (21 pp., rev. 1917) by Mary van Kleeck for the Storage Committee of the War Industries Board of the Council of National Defense. Headings in the **name and subject index** (322 ft.) include "Womens Clubs, General Federation of" and "Women's club, federation of" under State names. The letters relate largely to women's concern for natural resources near Army engineering projects.

77.3. The **Civil Works (Headquarters) map file, 1800–1935** (32,438 items), was accumulated during the period before 1890 when the OCE was the central repository for maps prepared or acquired by Army units. It is arranged by a geographic alpha-numeric system. Many maps scattered throughout the series identify rural property by name of landholder. The names of women landholders appear frequently on military campaign maps of the Southern States during and after the Civil War, but some women's holdings are noted on maps as early as 1820. Other cartographic files containing maps that in rare cases show land ownership are the **fortifications file, 1790–1941** (57,000 items), and the **miscellaneous forts file, 1840–1920** (7,000 items), a collection of manuscript maps of military reservations, ground plans of forts and other military posts, and plans and views of individual buildings. In discharging its responsibility for flood control projects on the Mississippi River and its tributaries, the Mississippi River Commission created **cartographic records, 1876–1954** (1,333 items), consisting of manuscript and published river charts that often show features of adjacent shore areas along the rivers, including towns and settlements in which property and businesses, some owned by women, are occasionally identified.

General Records of the Department of the Navy, 1798–1947

Record Group 80

80.1. The Department of the Navy was established by an act of April 30, 1798. Control of naval affairs had previously been exercised by the Congress under the Articles of Confederation and later by the Secretary of War. In 1947 the Department of the Navy became part of the National Military Establishment, which in 1949 was renamed the Department of Defense. The principal tasks of the Department of the Navy are policy control, naval command, logistics administration and control, and business administration. Most records of the Secretary's Office before

1885 are in the Naval Records Collection of the Office of Naval Records and Library (RG 45).

80.2. Except as friends and relatives of Navy servicemen and as members of patriotic and welfare organizations, women had little contact with the Navy until they began to serve as nurses in the latter part of the 19th century. A small number of women served in the Navy during World War I as yeomen (F), but in World War II women became an important part of the Navy as members of the Women Appointed for Voluntary Emergency Service (WAVES).

Records of the Office of the Secretary

80.3. The Navy Department's **general correspondence ("general file"), January 1897–August 1926** (3,000 ft.), is the chief single source of information regarding the activities of the Navy and the Navy Department during the period covered. On April 1, 1908, the general correspondence of the Judge Advocate General (JAG) was added to the series, and when the Office of the Chief of Naval Operations (CNO) was created in May 1915, the general correspondence of that Office, too, was incorporated into this same series, although particular areas of the CNO's responsibilities were given series of their own. The series is arranged by a complicated numerical system.

80.4. This general correspondence can be accessed by means of a **general index to the general correspondence** (202 ft.) and **special indexes to organizations and activities** (12 ft.), both of which have been filmed as M1052 (119 rolls). A record of a family living on board ship in 1912 is can be located under "Women" in the general index. There are subentries for "Woman's Aid Society," "Woman's Christian Temperance Union," "Woman's Missionary Society," "Woman's Naval Reserve," "Women's American Club of Utah," "Women's Army and Navy League," "Women's City Club (D.C.)," "Women's Cooperative Committee of Denver," "Women's Independent Voters Association," and "Women's International League for Peace and Freedom." There are also entries in the general index for "Clothing factory," "Dependent relatives," "Nurse Corps, female," "Nurses, civilian (female)," and individual women's names. Housing, uniforms, and privileges of female enlisted personnel, and investigations of their misconduct and complaints are indexed under "Yeomen" and "Yeowomen." Among the special indexes under "Bureau of Supplies and Accounts," there are subentries for "Woman's Relief Committee," "Women's Committee of the Council of National Defense," and "Women's Naval Service."

80.5. For example, the index term "Clothing factory" leads to a June 1898 exchange of letters between the president of the Women's Patriotic Industrial League of America and the Navy Department. She enclosed leaflets describing league efforts on behalf of working women and the wives of volunteer servicemen. The Secretary's reply pointed out that women had long been employed in the Navy's clothing factory in Brooklyn, NY.

80.6. A **register ("history cards"), July 1897–August 1926** (275 ft.), arranged numerically, contains abstracts of the 1897–1926 correspondence. These may occasionally be the only record of a transaction because some of the correspondence was dispersed by Navy recordkeepers into other series and cannot be located. For example, an abstract of a miscellaneous file (13673-4136) contains information about the Navy League and garments knitted for distribution to sailors by its Comfort Committee. Circular letters and memorandums relating to Mother's Day, 1921–26, are abstracted on cards for file 13673-5097. There are no records corresponding to either of these subjects in the general correspondence.

80.7. Examples of records about women in the general correspondence include file 26543, which deals with the issuance of 6-month pensions to the wives and mothers of servicemen killed in action. Document 203 in the same file deals with the question of the eligibility of a husband or dependent mother for benefits related to the service of a yeoman (F). File 28550-402 contains the August 2, 1918, letter from the Commandant of the Marine Corps, Gen. George Barnett, to the Secretary of the Navy requesting authority to enroll women in the Marine Corps Reserve, and Secretary Josephus Daniels' response. In file 28553-510 there are memorandums documenting the 1923 decision that Marine and Navy ex-servicewomen would be eligible for hospitalization in the National Home for Disabled Volunteer Soldiers. Files 7940-467, 7940-475, and 7940-485 concern women working at the Portsmouth, NH, Navy Yard. Bonuses for civilian employees and yeomen (F) is the subject of file 4488-677 (2 ft.). File 4488-678 contains reports of men and women who needed money to return home from Washington at the end of World War I. Names of employees who participated in a beauty pageant and flower carnival in 1921 appear in file 13673-5139. File 3809-870, dated 1919–25, contains letters from Franklin D. Roosevelt and others about the work of Emma (Mrs. William H.) Hamilton for the Navy and her ideas about a Navy Day and a Navy club for enlisted men.

80.8. The records in the **formerly secret and confidential correspondence of the Chief of Naval Operations and the Office of the Secretary of the Navy, 1919–27** (58 ft.), have been filmed as M1140 (117 rolls). Indexes and a card register to the series have been filmed as M1141 (9 rolls). An investigation at the Boston Navy Yard in the spring of 1918 involved yeomen (F)-officer relations, naval intelligence, and the welfare work of officers' wives. A summary of principal statements in several affidavits is in file 104-10.

80.9. After 1926 much of the Navy correspondence is filed according to the alpha-numeric filing scheme prescribed in the *Navy Filing*

Manual (NFM). The **general correspondence, 1926–40** (1,762 ft.), of the Secretary of the Navy, the JAG, and the CNO, is filed according to the NFM. File EG12/P13-6 (3 in.) contains letters of outrage about conditions for families of naval personnel stationed in Honolulu. The conditions were said to have contributed to the "Moana Loa Incident" involving the rape of a naval officer's wife. In file EE (32)/A9 (360609) is a processed June 1936 report to the President, "The Prison Labor Problem in Maryland: A Survey by the Prison Industries Reorganization Administration," in which Chapter 5 is entitled "The Employment of Women." Records about Navy nurses are filed as follows: OG (names, records about individuals relating to such matters as misconduct, claims, and deaths), OG-A (legislation about the Navy Nurse Corps), OG-L (pay and benefits on board ship), OG-P (separation, requests for appointment and assignment of individuals, including letters sent to Eleanor Roosevelt and forwarded by her for reply), and OG-P19-2 (regulations about the retirement of disabled nurses). There are records about Amelia Earhart in file A4-5(5)-(361030-4), which contains correspondence about preparations for her 1937 attempt to circumnavigate the globe and a 97-page "Report of Earhart Search by U.S. Navy and U.S. Coast Guard, July 2–18, 1937" submitted by the Commandant of the 14th Naval District at Pearl Harbor to the CNO.

80.10. Another series of **general correspondence of the office of the Secretary of the Navy, the Chief of Naval Operations, and the Judge Advocate General, 1940–42** (490 ft.), arranged according to the NFM, contains under file designation QR8 correspondence at the highest Navy levels about the founding of a women's auxiliary or reserve in the Navy. Included are copies of letters sent by Secretary of the Navy Frank Knox to Senator David I. Walsh; a letter from Eleanor Roosevelt forwarding a letter from Virginia C. Gildersleeve, Dean of Barnard College; and applications from women, including a former yeoman (F), wishing to join any women's auxiliary that might be formed.

80.11. An index that serves these last two general correspondence series has been filmed as *Name and Subject Index to the General Correspondence of the Office of the Secretary of the Navy, 1930–42* (M1067, 187 rolls). Many entries for "Dependents" refer to files concerning pension and hospitalization legislation, private bills, and transportation for families to and from the United States. Jacqueline Cochran's letter to Eleanor Roosevelt suggesting an organization of women pilots is referenced under "Women."

80.12. The **formerly secret and confidential correspondence, 1927–39** (110 ft.), of the CNO and the Office of the Secretary are arranged by type of security classification and thereunder according to the NFM. Under "ND14" for Naval District 14 in both the secret and the confidential sections there are several reports, some correspondence, and newspaper clippings concerning the "Moana Loa Incident." A few documents relating to Earhart's last flight are in file A21-5. **Subject cards to**

secret and confidential correspondence, 1927–39 (20 ft.), consist of abstracts of the documents. There are **name and subject indexes** (1 ft.) and more detailed **indexes to the incoming communications** (6 ft.) as well as **indexes to outgoing communications** (9 ft.).

80.13. Full officer rank, marriage, and resignation are subjects abstracted under "Nurse Corps" in a miscellaneous subject section of the **name and subject index** (21 ft.) to the **general correspondence of the Executive Office of the Secretary of the Navy, 1946–47** (30 ft.), arranged according to the NFM. The index is divided into several subseries. Under "Miscellaneous" there is an entry for "Women's Reserve, Marine Corps." Under the term "Women" there are entries for the Woman's Christian Temperance Union, the Women's Patriotic Conference on National Defense, and records about the employment of women in shipyards.

80.14. Formerly top secret, secret and confidential correspondence, 1940–47 (1,244 ft.), of the Office of the Secretary and the CNO is arranged by year, thereunder by level of security classification, and thereunder by the NFM. Among the formerly confidential records are the following examples of records relating to women: a P16-1/ND file for 1943 containing reports on communications personnel complements and the potential use of women service personnel in that field, a file P16-2/QR8 for 1945 containing the JAG's opinion regarding an injury sustained by a Wave, and a P16-1/NY3 file of 1943 containing some information about the Navy Manpower Survey in specific locations, including some material about women. In the confidential section for 1944, file P8-5/ND13 deals with the rights of Navy wives in Oregon, and file P14-2/ND10 notes requirements of Navy wives in Bermuda. Some records filed under P14-2 relate to civilian women working in navy yards and other naval installations; file PG-1/OG4 deals with an injured nurse, and file P11-1 contains records about flight nurses. The series is accompanied by separate indexes for incoming and outgoing letters. These indexes are complex, consisting of yearly sections for personal names and subjects; naval districts and other geographical locations; bureaus of the department; and other executive agencies, boards, and committees.

80.15. The **general correspondence of the Office of the Secretary of the Navy, 1942–46** (154 ft.), arranged according to the NFM and thereunder by year, includes QR8 files that consist mainly of cross-reference sheets to documents, some about women, filed under other designations. File A-18 "Legislation and congressional action" for 1942–43 concerns bill S.720, to authorize the appointment of women doctors and surgeons in the Army and the Navy. File OG "Navy Nurse Corps" includes records about the civilian U.S. Cadet Nurse Corps. Records relating to travel for dependents is usually filed under L20-4. File P3-2LL (1944) contains memorandums about the Navy's night nursing service for military and civilian personnel in Washington, DC, and P3-2LL (1942) contains records about the Women's Aid Service for employees. Files P3-2/P7 for all years include legal opinions and other records about the hospitalization of dependents, including maternity cases. Legislation affecting the wives and mothers of Navy, Marine Corps, and Coast Guard personnel and other matters relating to the personal lives of Navy families are filed under P7 in several yearly segments. Under P14-2 there are frequently records relating to the employment of women. The **index** (124 ft.) to this correspondence is complex, consisting of yearly sections for personal names and subjects; naval districts and other geographical locations; bureaus of the Navy department; and other executive agencies, boards, and committees. In the name and subject section there are entries for "American War Mothers," "Women," and "Women's Military Service Club." Under the entry for "Walsh-Healey Public Contracts Act" there are several references to letters relating to applications by Navy contractors for an exemption to permit the employment of girls between 16 and 18 years of age.

80.16. The **office file of Secretary of the Navy Frank Knox, 1940–44** (25 ft.), arranged largely by a subject-numeric scheme, includes letters from women seeking to enter the Navy or requesting medical or other waivers for a commission (file 23). Women appear in some reports of labor unrest and strikes at defense plants in file 42. Item 42-1-23 is a copy of a transcript of a hearing before Labor Secretary Frances Perkins about a woman economist at the Bureau of Labor Statistics accused of being a communist. Entries in the name and title **index** (6 ft.) include abstracts of the documents indexed. The few entries under "WAVES" include abstracts of documents about the enlistment of blacks, recruitment of women into the WAVES, and appropriate barracks for them in the Washington, DC, area.

80.17. A campaign to raise money for a national nurses' memorial is the subject of letters in **formerly classified general correspondence of Secretary of the Navy James V. Forrestal, 1944–47** (55 ft.), arranged according to a numerical scheme, which also contains records about plans for a postwar WAVES progam, anniversary celebrations of the Women's Reserve, voluntary retention of enlisted Waves through June 1948, the wearing of civilian clothing by Waves, legislation for a permanent Women's Reserve, and the reenlistment of personnel in a volunteer reserve. There is also a transcript of hearings at which Capt. Jean Palmer, Director of the Women's Reserve, testified. In file 54-1 there are letters from the national director of the Sweethearts of Servicemen protesting that too many black nurses were being commissioned in the Navy Nurse Corps and letters from Mary McLeod Bethune hailing the admission of black women into the WAVES. Transcripts of testimony before the Senate Armed Services Committee, March 17–May 3, 1948, about universal military training include several depositions of women representing women's organizations. Several items relating to the Navy Nurse Corps are cited in a name and subject **index** (4 ft.) to this series.

Issuances

80.18. *Navy Regulations*, 1865–1948 (17 vols., 2 ft.), arranged chronologically with an index in each volume, affected the lives of women in Navy families as well as civilian and military personnel. For example, regulations in the 1865 volume required commanding officers to urge their men to make pay allotments to their families and prohibited women from residing or traveling regularly on naval vessels. The 1893 regulations restricted marriages on board ship. "Families," not an index term in 1865, appears in the 1909 index. The 1909 volume includes regulations for the Navy Nurse Corps, established in 1908. Regulations for the Corps are indexed under "Female" and "Nurse." The 1920 regulations provide conditions of medical care for families of naval personnel, restrict the travel of officers' families to new permanent stations, and define "dependents" of Navy men.

80.19. *Navy Department General Orders*, 1863–1948 (14 vols., 1 ft.), arranged chronologically, have been filmed as M981 (3 rolls). Indexes in the volumes indicate that orders sometimes referred to Navy families and nurses.

80.20. Circulars issued to the naval establishment in general ("Alnav" circulars), January 1918–December 1943 (1 ft.), arranged chronologically, include several relating to dependents during World War II. The circulars have been filmed as M984 (3 rolls).

Records of Units and Officials Attached to the Secretary's Office

Records of the Assistant Secretary

80.21. Coordinating the Navy's wartime civilian personnel and shore establishment matters was in large part the responsibility of the Assistant Secretary. The **office file of Assistant Secretary Ralph Bard, 1941–43** (3 ft.), is arranged by year and thereunder by subject. Files under "Civilian personnel" contain information about women's training, names of women holding jobs in the Division of Personnel Supervision and Management, absentee rates, ratios of men to women employed at naval establishments, and the utilization of Waves in civilian billets. A 1944 "WAVES" file includes records about admitting black women into the Women's Reserve and statistics of the numbers of Spars, Women Marines, and enlisted and officer Waves among headquarters personnel.

Records of the Office of the Under Secretary

80.22. In the **formerly classified general correspondence of Under Secretary James V. Forrestal, 1940–42** (3 ft.), arranged by subject, a file labeled "Women's Auxiliary" contains published transcripts of hearings and committee reports on House and Senate bills to establish a Women's Reserve in the Navy, a legal opinion on the types of Navy positions that could be filled by women, and a processed circular letter (5 pp.) from Waves at the Northampton, MA, Naval Training School at Smith College, describing events there. Other records pertain to the philanthropic work of the women in the Navy League, including Mrs. James V. Forrestal.

80.23. In 1942 the Industrial Incentive Division was established in the Office of the Under Secretary. The division monitored defense plants and awarded the Army-Navy Production Award and the Navy "E" for excellence to successful companies. The **general correspondence, 1942–45** (62 ft.), is arranged according to the NFM. In the Army-Navy "E" Award Section under L24-1 (1), records arranged alphabetically by name of company include a few about women workers. Other files documenting women's work are A13-7 "Beneficial suggestions" and P6-7 "Condolences." File P20-1 "Morale" includes documents on Ens. Jane Kendeigh, a Navy flight nurse who, after evacuating wounded from Iwo Jima and Okinawa, toured war plants and spoke to workers. An index to the series is filed under A6-6.

80.24. Scrapbooks, 1942–45 (16 ft.), documenting the work of companies that received awards include programs and photographs of awards ceremonies. Newspaper clippings and photographs of plant tours show the participation of women and the wives of company officials in the programs.

Records of the Office of General Counsel

80.25. Filed under "Allotments" in the **office files of the executive director, 1941–46** (6 ft.), are records about legislation to extend allotments to Navy dependents during servicemen's absences from post.

Records of the Office of Budget and Reports

80.26. The **general correspondence, January 1943–March 1947** (12 ft.), is arranged according to a subject-numeric filing scheme. Filed under "VII Military Personnel" are correspondence and circulars dealing with the Navy's demobilization plan, including a formula for determining discharge eligibility for women and men. There are also statistics of the number of officers and enlisted personnel by sex as of June 3, 1945. In the same subject category, a file marked "Family allowances" (2 in.) contains correspondence pertaining to the Servicemen's Dependents Allowance Acts of 1942 and statements of disbursements under the acts for enlisted men's families and for allotments and insurance for the support of dependents. There is an alphabetical **subject card index, 1943–47** (5 in.).

Records of the Office of Procurement and Material

80.27. The **general correspondence, 1942–46** (140 ft.), of the Office of Procurement and Material, arranged by year and thereunder according to the NFM, includes a few documents pertaining to women employees. For example, in records for 1944 under NFM designation "P" are records relating to wages for women. An **index, 1942–46** (60 ft.), is arranged by year and thereunder by activity, subject, or name.

80.28. During World War II many small businesses worked for the Federal Government under contract. **Photographs of small businesses contracted to supply the Navy with war materials, 1943** (3,045 items), prints arranged by State, negatives arranged numerically, include many pictures of women working in the plants (80-PM). Information about the plants are recorded on the backs of the prints. The Navy Department prepared "A Pictorial Display of the Navy Department's Use of the Smaller War Plants of the Nation as a Source of Supply in Promoting the War Effort," November 23, 1943. Four volumes (4 in.) of photographs of the display and items in it are arranged by State.

Records of the Office of Public Relations

80.29. This office was established in 1941. Earlier publicity records are frequently filed with the records of particular offices. **Press releases and transcripts of press conferences and speeches of the Secretary of the Navy, January 1917–December 1936** (20 ft.), arranged chronologically, include a few stories about yeomen (F). The **subject file of the Office of Public Relations, July 1937–July 1943** (2 ft.), includes a heading, "Policy—Navy Relief Society," under which there are records about Navy wives who volunteered to help widows and wives of Navy personnel. To raise money for their work, the women sponsored "Victory Garden Harvest Shows."

80.30. Among the records of the Radio Section **radio scripts, 1944–45** (16 ft.), arranged by year and thereunder alphabetically by title, name of performer, or subject, include full-length programs, spot commercial announcements, and Navy broadcasts that were reviewed for security clearance. "The Kate Smith Show" and "Fun Canteen" are among the shows featuring women entertainers. A Betty Crocker script emphasizes women's work and patriotic attitudes. Spot announcements promote Navy and Marine Corps women's reserve programs. Filed under "Red Cross" are scripts including interviews with Mrs. George A. Garrett, chair of the Red Cross Volunteer Special Services, and Mrs. J. Douglas Jones, chair of the Production Corps of the District of Columbia Red Cross. Eleanor Robson (Mrs. August) Belmont, chair of the National Council on Red Cross Nursing, was mistress of ceremonies for a program about Jane A. Delano. Other script titles relating to women are: "Something for the Girls," "Lt. Col. Ruth Cheney Streeter, USMC," "Seventh War Loan Drive

Spots," "Navy Day," "WAVES on Parade, June–December 1945," "WAVES, Miscellaneous Recruiting," and "Women in Navy Blue."

80.31. The **correspondence, 1942–45** (3 ft.), of the Special Activities Section of the Office of Public Relations is arranged by year and thereunder by subject. A 1944 file on the Naval Aid Auxiliary documents the participation of the women members in the President's War Relief Control Board. There are a few 1944 communications about the use by the "March of Time" of the music and script of "Operation Petticoat," which was written by Waves. A 1945 file is labeled "Nurse Corps, Public Relations Program." Another file, labeled "Navy Mothers' Club," includes a letter from Emma Jones, its founder and national commander, describing its purpose and activities.

80.32. Publicity photographs (80-PR), 1921–43 (ca. 4,000 items), arranged numerically, includes pictures of nurses on hospital ships and at shore installations, seamstresses at the Navy Clothing Depot in Brooklyn, NY, and a seaman modeling knitted clothing made by women according to Navy instructions. An incomplete **subject index** (80PRL, 2 in.) includes entries under "Uniforms" for Navy nurses' outfits.

Records of the Office of Industrial Relations

80.33. The Office of Industrial Relations was established in 1945 by renaming the Division of Shore Establishments and Civilian Personnel, which was the successor of the Division of Shore Establishments.

80.34. The **general correspondence, 1943–44** (35 ft.), of the Division of Shore Establishments and Civilian Personnel, arranged by year and thereunder according to the NFM, is accompanied by an **alphabetical file** (19 ft.) of cross-reference sheets and copies of letters sent that serves as an index to the correspondence. A subseries of 1944 correspondence arranged by naval district and geographical location of shore establishment follows the main correspondence files for that year. Records about civilian women assigned to drydocks and depots include complaints concerning hours and the employment of returning veterans, minors, and women as personal assistants. There are also questions about the use of Waves in the division. Under the term "Women" in the alphabetical file is a 1943 reply to a racial discrimination complaint regarding the application of a nurse for a job in a Navy hospital.

80.35. The **general correspondence, 1945–46** (41 ft.), of the Division of Shore Establishments and Civilian Personnel and the Office of Industrial Relations (OIR) is arranged by year and thereunder by the NFM. A **name and subject index** (26 ft.) is arranged by year and thereunder in six subseries. In the "Miscellaneous" subseries, entries under the terms "Women" and "Female" usually refer to routine personnel actions for individuals. Filed under NFM designation P1-4 "Race and Citizenship" (3 in.) in the correspondence are scattered documents concerning women grievants in 1945. Other 1945 correspondence on grievances is filed under P8-1 "Labor and Labor Unions" (6 in.), P8-1 (2) "Grievance Procedures" (1 in.), and P8–5 "Complaints" (9 in.). Other records about women employees appear under P14-2 "Appointments and Employment" and P14-2(5) "Recruitment of Personnel." P16-1 "Personnel Strengths and Distributions" includes records about Waves as well as civilians. Records about women are also found under the following headings: L24-1(1) "Housing for Employees," P7 "Domestic Relations," and P19 "Separations." The immediate postwar adjustments for women employees are documented under P8-5 "Complaints," P16-1-(5) "Reductions in force," P19 "Separations," and P20-1 "Matters of Performance."

80.36. The Industrial Manpower Section of the Shore Establishments Division was created in 1942 to determine personnel policies for civilian employees not only in Navy installations but also in contractor facilities. It also served as the Navy's liaison with other agencies concerned with industrial management problems, such as the War Manpower Commission. The section's **general correspondence, 1942–44** (30 ft.), is arranged according to a subject-numeric system. The following subject categories relate to concerns of women employees: Community Facilities: 1–2 (Housing Area Studies), and 3 (Day Care); Conservation: 4 (Hours of Work); and 12 (Women). The series is served by a **name and subject index** (6 ft.). In the last months before it was abolished the section's **general correspondence, June–August 1945** (24 ft.), was arranged according to the NFM with a **name and subject index** (8 ft.). Correspondence filed under P16-1 for Willamette Iron and Steel Corporation, Portland, OR, includes a report entitled "Manpower Utilization and Organizational Survey" in which one chapter concerns women's counselors. Both indexes are subdivided into the Navy's six index categories.

80.37. The **general correspondence , 1923–43** (14 ft.), of the Shore Establishment Division's Safety Engineering Section is arranged numerically. File 308 "Protective clothing for women" contains a letter from the Donnelly Garment Sales Company, maker of "action clothes for American women," promoting "Nelly Don defense uniforms." File 1510 "Employment of women (policies)" contains a report entitled "General Recommendations Made after Visiting Certain Naval Industrial Establishments with Special Attention to Women Employed on Naval Production" (7 pp.) prepared by Cornelia LeBoutillier on contract. Attached to the report are a summary sheet of statistics for employees at shore establishments entitled "Women Worker Survey, August 1, 1942 file 2304" and similar statistics for other periods.

Early Personnel Records

80.38. Press copies of letters of appointment sent by the Secretary of the Navy to civilian job applicants, March 1893–December 1899 (25 vols., 3 ft.), arranged chronologically and indexed by name, include many letters to women describing available jobs and salaries. Similar information for a later period is in **press copies of lists of Navy Department civilian employees and positions and related records, March 1889–December 1901** (1 vol., 2 in.), partially indexed by navy yard. Unsuccessful applicants are recorded in **press copies of letters sent by the Secretary of the Navy and the appointment clerk to civilian job applicants ("applications"), June 1890–December 1899** (35 vols., 4 ft.).

80.39. **Reports from chief clerks relating to clerical personnel in response to a circular letter of June 23, 1904** (1 vol., 1 in.), arranged in order of receipt of replies, consist of lists of clerical personnel, including women, in each bureau or office of the War Department and the class and percentage of the work in that class performed by each clerk.

Records of the Chief Clerk

80.40. The duties of charwomen in the Navy Department are outlined in **press copies of letters and memorandums sent by the chief clerk, May 1891–July 1907** (2 vols., 3 in.), arranged chronologically with an index. A list of more than 100 seamstresses at the Marine Clothing Factory in Philadelphia, June–July 1901, is also in the series.

80.41. In the chief clerk's **record of memorandums sent by the Secretary of the Navy to chiefs of bureaus and officers, December 1882–December 1934** (11 vols., 1 ft.), arranged chronologically with indexes, there are references to women working for the Navy, especially in the World War I period. One memorandum provided that clerical vacancies were to be filled by women. Another transmitted a letter from the National American Woman Suffrage Association inviting new women war workers in Washington, DC, to social events at "Suffrage House." There are also letters about the participation of women workers in parades and celebrations.

Records of Boards and Committees

Records of the Submarine Board

80.42. This Board was established in 1928 to evaluate the suggestions for improvement of submarines submitted by many persons, including some women, after a submerged Navy submarine was rammed and sunk by a Coast Guard vessel off Provincetown, MA. The board's **letters sent, July 2, 1928–May 21, 1929** (3 in.), arranged chronologically, include letters to two women about their improvement suggestions and a few about women clericals working for the Board. The **correspondence of members of the board, 1928–29** (6 in.), is arranged alphabetially by name of member. In the records filed under the name J.R. Strauss there is a copy of the America-Japan Society's Special Bulletin No. 7, "Presentation of the Relics of Commodore Matthew Calbraith Perry by his Descendents to the People of Japan through the American Ambassador" (40 pp.), which contains copies of letters from two Perry granddaughters offering items to be presented to Japan.

Records of the Top Policy Group

80.43. Minutes of the Top Policy Group, 1940–47 (4 ft.), arranged chronologically, contain, in the minutes of an August 10, 1945, meeting, the record of a brief discussion of the continuation of a women's organization in the Navy after the war.

Records of the Manpower Survey Board

80.44. This Board was established in November 1943 to study the distribution and utilization of manpower, women as well as men, civilian and military, at all Navy shore establishments. Its **minutes, November 1943–June 1944** (3 in.), arranged chronologically, deal principally with the requirements of the survey. **Records related to the minutes, November 10, 1943–July 4, 1944** (2 in.), include a "Historical Report on the Navy Manpower Board, November 12, 1943–June 30, 1944" (½ in.). In the **correspondence of members of the board, December 1943–July 1944** (5 ft.), arranged by names of members and thereunder by bureau, naval district, or subject, there are a few records about women in files labeled "WAVES" and "Civilians—Views and Suggestions" (2 in.).

80.45. Replies to a questionnaire of December 3, 1943 (2 ft.), from commanding officers at the shore establishments include responses to questions about replacing male officers and enlisted men with Waves, Spars, and civilian women. **Summaries of replies, 1944** (2 ft.), are arranged by district number, with Coast Guard and Marine Corps summaries separate from those of Navy installations.

80.46. Reports of shore establishments, December 1943–May 1944 (93 ft.), arranged numerically, include statistical and narrative reports and correspondence. "General Summary" forms completed by survey groups show the number of women employed as officer, enlisted, and civilian personnel and the number recommended by the Board's surveyors to replace men and to fill additional requirements. The **index to reports from shore establishments, December 1943–May 1944** (4 ft.), is arranged by naval district and thereunder alphabetically by activity.

80.47. Summary personnel lists, n.d. (3 in.), record the numbers of officers, enlisted men, and civilians at naval air stations and recommend the replacement of some men with women. The **final report of the Navy Manpower Survey, June 28, 1944** (3 vols., 1 in.), recommended the assignment of Waves overseas and discouraged the use of trained nurses in linen rooms.

Records of the Board of Decorations and Medals

80.48.   Letters to the Secretary of the Navy relating to recommendations for awards, 1945–47 (2 ft.), arranged alphabetically by name of award nominees, recommended both approval and disapproval of awarding decorations or medals to men and women of the Navy.

Records of the Civilian Advisory Committee

80.49.   Women appointed to this committee in April 1946 included Margaret Culkin Banning, author; Grace M. Morley, director of the San Francisco Museum of Art; and Mildred McAfee Horton, president of Wellesley College (and under her maiden name, Mildred McAfee, former head of the WAVES). Charged with advising the Navy on "matters and progam dealing with the nonmilitary phase of a serviceman's life," the Committee was disbanded at the end of 1946. The **minutes, reports, and other records of the Civilian Advisory Committee, 1946** (3 ft.), arranged generally by type of record, include uncaptioned photographs of the Committee members and files of individual members arranged alphabetically by name.

Records of the Navy Board for Production Awards

80.50.   This board recognized outstanding performance of industrial plants working for the Navy. Its **general correspondence, 1941–45** (46 ft.), is arranged alphabetically by name of firm or subject. Files for "Absenteeism" and "Accident Rates" include specific information about women. A file for a particular company would include, among other things, the number of men and women employed, production statistics, and remarks, which sometimes provide information about individual women. Filed with records about the Pratt Whitney Aircraft Corporation is "Estimated Operating Ratios in the Engine and Propeller Industries, February 1945, Restricted WS-387E prepared by the Manpower Office, Management Control; Air Technical Service Command (Army)." In it are statistics on labor turnover by sex in specific plants. The series also contains copies of the shipyard newsletter *Full Speed Ahead* published by the Navy Industrial Incentive Division to raise workers' morale. It has occasional articles about women workers.

Audiovisual Records

80.51.   The **decimal classified photographic file** (80-CF), 1916–45 (20,000 items), is arranged according to the **photograph library's classification list** (2½ in.). Classifications most likely to include references to women are 80-CF-83745 "Entertainment, USO Clubs"; 80-CF-

86642 "Navy Relief Drive"; and 80-CF-86660 "Red Cross, Gray Ladies." The file of photographs includes likenesses of actresses Loretta Young and Josephine Baker, wives of Navy officers, and numerous Red Cross volunteers. Photographs documenting some of the types of occupations to which Waves were assigned are in categories under file 80-CF-881 "Special Groups in Navy—Waves."

80.52. The Navy Department's **general photographic file (80-G), ca. 1900–58** (700,000 items), is served by a **subject and name index, 1900–61** (80-GX, 776 ft.). Among entries relating to women in this index are the following: "Aircraft—hospital planes," "American Red Cross," "Col. Florence Blanchfield," "Josephine Beatrice Bowman" (Superintendent of Navy Nurses, 1922–34); "Amelia Earhart"; "Sadie Flay" (yeoman [F]); "Gray Ladies"; "Lenah Sutcliffe Higbee" (Superintendent of Navy Nurses, 1911–22); "Myrna M. Hoffman" (Superintendent of Navy Nurses, 1935–38); "Hunter College"; "Holyoke"; "Marines, women"; "Navy Nurses"; "Northampton"; "Nurses, American"; "Nurses, Korea"; "Recruits and recruiting"; "Reserves"; "WACs"; "Women"; "Women in aeronautics," including the "first woman hired as a learner-mechanic at U.S. Naval Station, Quonset Point, R.I., April, 1942"; "Women ordnance workers"; "Women workers"; "Women war workers," and "Yokosuka, Japan." The "WAVES" section of the index is lengthy. Under "Washington, D.C.—Awards" is a photograph of Lt. Comdr. Faye E. White, USN, the first Navy nurse to receive the Bronze Star. One sequence of photographs (80-G-355545 to 355572, with gaps) represents different types of naval assignments made to women.

80.53. There is a **catalog of subject headings used in the subject index to the Navy's general photographic file, 1943–61** (80-GXAA, 1 vol., 1 in.).

80.54. **Photographs from the Navy's color photographic file (80-GK), 1943–56** (ca. 7,000 items), include a few pictures of Waves, Women Marines, and Navy nurses in uniform.. This series is also served by the 80-GX index. In the subseries of the index for personal names are the following: Capt. Sue Dauser, Comdr. Joy Bright Hancock, Ens. Jane L. Kendeigh, and Capt. Mildred McAfee.

80.55. **Photographs of personnel, 1917–45** (80-PA, ca. 7,500 items), arranged alphabetically by name, include pictures of Amelia Earhart, showing her at an aerial review at Lindbergh Field, July 28, 1932.

80.56. **Photographs of women in the Marine Corps, Navy, and Army Air Corps, 1943–45** (80-PSW, 18 items), are captioned with names of all women pictured and some information about their duties. **Photographs of aircraft, personnel, and facilities at the Naval Air Station, Lambert Field, St. Louis, MO, 1943–45** (80-LSM, 39 items), show Wacs, Waves, Women Marines, and Army nurses modeling old and new uniforms. **Photographs taken at Headquarters, 7th Naval Dis-**

trict, **Miami, FL, 1943–46** (80-MF, 286 items), arranged numerically, include pictures of Lt. (j.g.) M.M. McFarquhar, M.D., the first woman doctor assigned to the district (80-MF-148 through 152); unidentified Waves at work and play (80-MF-157-through 171); and some Spars (80-MF-172 through 176).

Records of the
Office of the Quartermaster General

Record Group 92

92.1. The first quartermasters were appointed in 1775, but until 1818, when Congress created a Quartermaster's Department under a single Quartermaster General, they were regarded as field staff officers appointed in time of war to serve with the principal armies. The Quartermaster General ensured efficient systems of supply, movement of the Army, and accountability of officers and agents charged with money or supplies. An act of August 24, 1912, combined the Subsistence, Pay, and Quartermaster's Departments to form the Quartermaster Corps of the Army, headed after 1914 by the Quartermaster General. Although a number of special organizations were established to serve the Army during World War I, the National Defense Act of 1920 restored to the Quartermaster Corps most of its former functions, including those of transportation and construction. The former pay function of the office was placed in a separate finance department.

92.2. The transportation and construction functions were permanently removed from the jurisdiction of the Quartermaster General during World War II. In 1961 most of the other responsibilities of the Quartermaster General were transferred to other agencies, and Department of the Army General Order 44 of July 23, 1962, abolished the Office of the Quartermaster General. The Quartermaster General employed women, used their services in carrying out its responsibilities, and handled supply and transportation for the Army Nurse Corps and the Women's Army Corps (WAC), once they were established in the Army.

92.3. Like most military organizations, the Quartermaster General received many inquiries from women about the whereabouts of male relatives believed to be in the Army. Women's names appear in indexes to **letters sent by the office of the Quartermaster General, main series, 1818–70** (107 vols., 24 ft.), filmed as M745 (61 rolls), arranged chronologically. Letters about other matters such as transportation for families of military personnel are included, as well as a copy of a letter to "Mrs. A. Lincoln," from a woman who apparently wanted to help a friend sell Kentucky horses to the Union Army.

92.4. Women's names also appear in the **name indexes** to **press copies of miscellaneous letters sent relating to such matters as the assignment of personnel, property and supplies, transportation, and the organization and administration of the Quartermaster Department, December 1861–December 1870** (121 vols., 18 ft.), and in indexes in volumes of **press copies of reports and letters sent to the Secretary of War, February 1862–December 1870** (69 vols., 9 ft.). The letters to women in these two series deal primarily with women as servants to and as claimants against the Army.

92.5. The Quartermaster General's **letters received, 1819–70** (166 ft.), are arranged according to registry numbers assigned in **registers of letters received, 1818–70** (142 vols., 31 ft.), which are arranged by time period and thereunder alphabetically by initial letter of the name or title of the correspondent. The letters for the Civil War period contain the greatest number from women including requests for passes for nurses under Supt. Dorothea Dix, discussions of providing supplies and assistance to women of the U.S. Sanitary Commission, and claims for remuneration for services and supplies furnished the Army and for reparations for damages sustained during the war.

92.6. Some letters entered in the registers described in **92.5** have been removed and filed in the **consolidated correspondence file, 1794–1890** (276 ft.), which is arranged alphabetically by subject or surname of correspondent and contains a few letters dated as late as 1915. A few letters in the series are from women inquiring about employment as seamstresses, copyists, and nurses for the Army. There are also employment statistics, lists of employees, and employee record cards filed under the following headings: "Civil Service Commission," "Civil Employees," "Claims," "Employees," "Poor women," "Schuylkill Arsenal," "Women—employed in the QM Dept," and "Woman's Hospital, Washington, D.C." Under the heading "Philadelphia" are record cards (1 in.) for seamstresses, dated 1912. Letters relating to seamstresses also appear under geographic file headings such as "St. Louis." There are also files for Clara Barton and for Josephine S. Griffing (2 in.). Griffing was active in freedmen's relief after the Civil War.

92.7. The Quartermaster General's **general correspondence, 1890–1914** (8,613 ft.), arranged numerically and thereunder chronologically, can be accessed by using the accompanying **subject and name card index** (1,152 ft.). Entries under "Army nurse" and "Nurse" relate to a consolidated file about the burial of nurses in military cemeteries, including congressional bills on the subject, and to other matters relating to the service of nurses in the 1890s. Other letters cited under these entries deal with quarters and travel for members of the Army Nurse Corps, including transportation to the Philippines at the turn of the century. There are also citations to Army regulations and opinions of the Judge Advocate General and the Comptroller General about the corps as it was being established. Applications for positions as civilian employees and in the "Army Nurse Corps (female)," as the corps was called until 1918, can be found using the heading "Female." Other headings relating to women are "Charwoman" and "Seamstress." Entries for "Wives" refer to letters mostly about meals and lodging provided to the Army and to the transportation or burial of deceased wives of servicemen.

92.8. Officers of the Quartermaster Corps made periodic **reports of persons and articles hired, 1818–1905** (1,526 ft.), arranged principally by year and thereunder alphabetically by surname of reporting officer. Because of this arrangement, it is difficult to find records about women. There are, however, several series that serve as finding aids to the reports. For example, there is a **card index to names of persons mentioned** for the 1898–1902 part of the series (29 ft.) and **a list of Indian scouts mentioned** (1 vol., 1 in.), some of whom were women. Among oversized reports for the Civil War period are a few lists of seamstresses who produced uniforms, showing employee's name, rate or amount of pay, dates of service, and remarks.

92.9. Women were among citizens from the "States in rebellion" who claimed after the Civil War that they had been loyal to the Union and had sustained damage resulting from Union activity during the war. Many **letters sent relating to claims, 1871–89** (116 vols., 24 ft.), were addressed to the Southern Claims Commission, the Court of Claims, claimants, and attorneys in Southern Claims cases after an act of 1871 allowed Union loyalists in the South to make such claims. There is a **name index** (20 vols., 4 ft.) to the series.

92.10. There are several other series of claims files relating to rent, supplies, and services to the Union Army as well as losses of crops, farm animals, equipment, and real estate due to actions of the Federal Government's agents. They are all indexed in **name indexes to various registers of series of claims files, 1839–94** (2 vols., 6 in.), which can also be used as a finding aid to **correspondence relating to claims submitted to Gen. J.C. McFerran and Col. James Ekin, investigators of claims authorized under the act of July 4, 1864, at Louisville and Jeffersonville, 1870–82** (99 ft.), arranged alphabetically by name of claimant, a number of whom were women.

92.11. In **general correspondence ("subject" file), 1922–35** (306 ft.), arranged according to the War Department decimal classification scheme, file 210 "Dependents" and file 210 "Relatives" deal largely with moving servicemen's families from one permanent station to another.

92.12. During World War II the Quartermaster Corps was extensively concerned with women's clothing and personal equipment because of the number of women in military service. A formerly security classified file, 400.112 "Clothing, Protective—Women's" in the 1946–52 section of **classified and unclassified general correspondence ("subject file"),**

1936–61 (2,075 ft.), contains a photostatic copy of correspondence and reports relating to a 1943 project to determine the effect of mustard and lewisite gases on underwear to be worn by WAC and Army Nurse Corps personnel and to establish sizes and functions of garments for these women.

92.13. Uniforms, service pins, and burial rights for Army personnel are subjects of **classified and unclassified general correspondence relating to organizational units ("miscellaneous" file), 1939–54** (311 ft.), arranged by name of unit with folders for WASP, WAAC, and WAC (3 in.) arranged thereunder by the War Department decimal system. File 320.2 "WAC" (¼ in.) in the 1946–52 part of the series contains information regarding the numbers of women in the WAC stationed in the United States and overseas, information needed by the Quartermaster General for planning levels of stocks of clothing and equipment in Army depots.

92.14. The Quartermaster General's Office was heavily involved in the Gold Star Mothers' and Widows' Pilgrimage to Europe in 1930–33. Laws passed by Congress in 1929 and 1930 made possible a federally funded pilgrimage to the cemeteries of Europe by mothers and widows of deceased American soldiers and sailors who were killed during World War I and buried overseas. **Correspondence relating to the Gold Star Pilgrimage, 1930–33** (20 ft.), includes copies of reports listing the names of the pilgrims, their relationship to the deceased, reports of the office in charge of each trip, of those in charge of embarkation from New York, and of observers sent with each group. Two volumes (4 in.) of photographs document the trips. There are separate folders (2 in.) of records of the journeys of black mothers and widows.

92.15. In addition, there is **general correspondence of the New York Office, Gold Star Mothers' and Widows' Pilgrimage to Europe, 1930–33** (32 ft.), and of the **Paris Office, 1930–33** (10 ft.). The letters of nurses and clerks who applied for jobs to the New York Office are in a 201 file (4½ ft.) in the records of the New York Office. Among the records of the Paris Office are copies of officers' reports, pilgrimage regulations, and party files for each trip, which usually include a list of pilgrims, a chronological history of the pilgrimage, medical reports, and daily schedules of events. The **register of Gold Star Mothers and Widows, 1930** (1 vol., 3 in.), is arranged alphabetically by State or country and thereunder alphabetically by women's names. Each entry shows the relationship of the Gold Star woman to the deceased serviceman, his military unit, the cemetery where he was buried, and the date when the widow or mother wished to make the trip.

92.16. In special reports, 1916–23, a **history of the Quartermaster Corps, AEF, during World War I, ca. 1919** (2 in.), includes a chapter on the Garden Service of the Quartermaster Corps, AEF, that mentions American women as civilian employees of the Garden Service at Versailles in the spring of 1918. Another chapter tells of activities at the ports of embarkation as the Quartermaster Corps supervised the return to the United States of Army nurses, welfare workers, civilians employed by the War Department, and war brides and other wives of American servicemen at the end of the war.

92.17. Another special report, **"A Summary Comparison of Labor Emergency Legislation in Great Britain and the United States," written by the Section on Cooperation with States, Council of National Defense, ca.** 1917 (1 in.), deals with 8-hour laws, "dilution of labor," and registration of the labor force, all of which affected women of the period.

92.18. Papers relating to the burial of some Army nurses and welfare organization volunteers as well as to soldiers who died during or shortly after World War I are in **correspondence, reports, telegrams, applications and other papers relating to burials of service personnel ("burial case files"), 1915–39** (2,270 ft.), of the Cemeterial Division. Arranged alphabetically by name of the deceased, the files contain correspondence and completed forms relating to a proposed or existing burial place for each individual. In a number of cases, the documents are from women family members of the deceased men or women or contain information relating to female relatives. The names of those who died in Europe are also in an alphabetical **card register of burials of deceased American soldiers, 1917–22** (136 ft.), maintained by the Graves Registration Service.

92.19. The records of field offices of the Quartermaster Corps were maintained separately for each installation. Philadelphia was the site of a depot of clothing and equipage for the Army from the early days of the Republic. Among the early records inherited by the Quartermaster General under later reorganizations are the **bound volumes of the Philadelphia supply agencies, 1795–1858** (600 vols., 70 ft.). An inspection book, 1804–9 (1 vol., 1 in.), is a chronological record of the work finished by each "sewing woman," giving the name of the seamstress or tailor, the number and kind of articles produced, and a comment on quality. The same information appears in a clothing register, 1809–11 (1 vol., 2 in.), and a record of articles of clothing and equipage received from seamstresses, 1813–15 (2 vols., 1 in.), which also includes the kind and quantity of cut cloth issued to each worker.

92.20. Historical studies of selected quartermaster depots and other field installations, 1943–52 (7 ft.), are arranged alphabetically by name of installation. Among those for the Philadelphia Quartermaster Depot are "A Wardrobe for the WAAC," March 1943; "Clothing the WAC, September 1943–February 1945," May 1945; and "The Army Nurse and Her Wardrobe," January 1944.

92.21. Applications, assessment of work quality, hiring policy, and production statistics are among the subjects of correspondence concerning

Army contract seamstresses in the **correspondence and record cards, 1911–16**, of the Philadelphia Quartermaster Depot. The **name and subject index cards** (94 ft.) to this correspondence contain a great number of entries for "Seamstresses" and a few for "Women, sewing."

92.22. Among the records of the Schuylkill Arsenal are similar series concerning women hired as seamstreses. A few of the **press copies of personal reports and letters sent by Capt. William H. Gill, military storekeeper, relating to personnel, 1882–89** (1 vol., 1 in.), relate to seamstresses. A series of **press copies of letters sent relating to seamstresses and other employees, May 1900–July 1905** (7 vols., 10 in.), is arranged chronologically with indexes in the volumes. The arsenal also maintained a list of **females employed, ca. 1865** (1 vol., ½ in.), that is arranged alphabetically by surname of employee giving for each employee her name, address, a class number, and remarks. A **register of work performed by seamstresses, August–October 1873 and January–June 1874** (2 vols., 4 in.), arranged by time period and thereunder alphabetically by surname of seamstress, shows the number of each type of garment sewn and the date.

92.23. Among the records of the port of embarkation (POE) Hoboken, NJ, the demobilization of nurses and other women at the end of World War I is documented in the **general correspondence, 1917–20** (219 ft.), arranged by the War Department decimal classification scheme. File 080 contains the names of the following organizations: Army Girl's Transport Tobacco Fund, Army Relief Society, Ambulance Corps of America, American Red Cross, Motor Corp. of America, Women's Army and Navy League, War Camp Community Service, and the YMCA and YWCA. These organizations either had women members or were active in welcoming returning servicemen or women. Accompanying the correspondence are **record cards (consolidated reference sheets) 1917–20** (81 ft.), and **record cards (consolidated reference sheets "closed files"), 1917–19** (35 ft.). There are references to women under such headings as "Women," "Wives of enlisted men," "Wives of officers," "Wives of Army field clerks," "Nurse corps," "Hostess house," and "Hotel Albert, New York City." The files include letters of complaint and praise as well as information about conditions on Army transports and at Army installations and the assignment of nurses to the POE. Reports of morale units aboard transport ships sometimes mention welfare workers, many of whom were women, serving on the ships.

92.24. Among other POE Hoboken records is a series of **formerly confidential special orders and troop movement special orders, 1917–19** (7 ft.), arranged by year and thereunder numerically. A **name card index** to the series includes, for example, names of Army nurses ordered to return to the United States. There are similar records for POE Newport News, VA.

92.25. Panoramas of Quartermaster Corps facilities and personnel, 1918–24 (92-PN, 57 items), include five group photographs of personnel at Jeffersonville, IN, showing employees in the Accounting Branch and in the Uniform Manufacturing Branch. A photograph of those who participated in a Defense Day Parade at the Philadelphia Depot in 1924 includes a number of uniformed women. Women photographed at anniversary celebrations may be wives of Quartermaster Personnel rather than employees.

War Department Collection of Revolutionary War Records

Record Group 93

93.1. Most of the records of the Continental Army in the custody of the War Department were destroyed by fire on November 8, 1800. The War Department Collection of Revolutionary War Records was begun in 1873, when Secretary of War William Belknap made the first of several purchases of Revolutionary War records in private hands. By acts of July 27, 1892, and August 18, 1894, Congress directed other Executive departments of the Federal Government to transfer to the War Department military records of the Revolutionary War in their possession. A final major addition to the collection was made in 1914–15, when photographic copies of records in the possession of individuals and institutions were made by the War Department to supplement the original records.

93.2. About 6 percent of the records are bound, of which roughly three-quarters are in volumes numbered sequentially 1–197 and known as **numbered record books, 1775–98** (199 vols., 13 ft.), filmed as M853 (41 rolls). The descriptive pamphlet prepared by the National Archives to accompany the microfilm publication greatly simplifies access to these records. The volumes contain orderly books and rosters of military units, and include records concerning military operations and service, pay and settlement of accounts, and other records relating to the Quartermaster General's Department and the Commissary General of Military Stores. Two indexes, the "catalog and subject index" and a two-part index to 70 orderly books, have been filmed on roll 1 of M853. In addition, 46 separate indexes (most of which refer only to names that appear in 46 of the orderly books) have been filmed thoughout the microfilm publication, just before the appropriate orderly book. There are a few subject references in some of these indexes that point to records about women, such as "Rations" and "Women with the Army," in addition to personal feminine names. The names of Mrs. George Washington and Mrs. Timothy Pickering appear in the name indexes to personal memorandums included among the orderly books. The names of other women appear in the indexes, albeit infrequently, as matrons or nurses. The "Record of Disbursements by Samuel Hodgdon, Deputy Commissary General of Military Stores, March 22, 1780–March 8, 1781," for supplies purchased for the Army and the "Ledger of Samuel Hodgdon, 1777–98" (both on M853, roll 35), for his personal accounts show that corn and silk were purchased from women and that some women were paid rent for land and wages for services as scribes and spinners. "Letters sent by Joseph Howell [War Department accountant], January–December, 1794" (M853, roll 19), contain copies of communications to widows of officers attempting to settle amounts of wartime subsistence and pay still owing to them for their husbands' services.

93.3. Miscellaneous numbered records ("manuscript file"), 1775–84 (38 ft.), filmed as M859 (125 rolls), contain diaries, receipts, reports, memorandums, and returns, many of which provide evidence of female entrepreneurship and patriotism. The records under the heading "Miscellaneous Troops, Organizations, Persons, and Subjects" (documents numbered 28,637–30,074 on rolls 99–104) and "Records Pertaining to Continental Army Staff Departments" (documents numbered 20,421–28,636 on rolls 65–98 and 30,463–30,849 on rolls 106–108) include account books kept by officers and other persons to record lodging and goods supplied, some of which were obtained from women. The records show that women furnished musket balls, cartridges, blankets, beeswax, candles, clothing, fine linen, buttons, and thread to the Continental troops. Some of the returns in this file include the names of wives, mothers, and even children of enlisted men who traveled with the troops and drew rations. Some women are identified as cooks. There are occasional instances in which women witnessed payment of military pay to their husbands or requested back pay due relatives who had been killed.

93.4. An alphabetical name index, called the **"special index" to the numbered records, 1775–83** (80 ft.), filmed as M847 (39 rolls), and a **subject index** (2 ft.) serve both the numbered record books and the manuscript file.

93.5. Records showing women as consumers even before the Revolution appear in **miscellaneous unnumbered records, ca. 1709–1913** (9 in.). A "journal of supplies and accounts kept at Albany, NY, 1758–60" is the record of a local merchant who sold food and clothing to women of the area as well as to military officers encamped nearby during the French and Indian War.

93.6. The series *Revolutionary War Rolls, 1775–1783* (M246, 138 rolls), includes muster rolls, payrolls, and returns of company and regimental personnel. Hospital Department records (roll 35) carry the names of a few women. Listed with medical officers at the General Hospital in Albany, NY, are several female nurses and a matron, a few of whom received rations for their children as well as for themselves. A return of the sick and wounded at Danbury, CT, lists two pregnancies among the conditions treated. The Revolutionary War rolls were used extensively by the Record and Pension Office to compile service records for individual soldiers as a basis for establishing pension eligibility, among other things.

93.7. *Compiled Service Records of Soldiers Who Served in the American Army During the Revolutionary War* (M881, 1,096 rolls) arranged by military unit, were also created for use as the basis for awarding pensions. The information in them comes from many of the muster rolls, returns, payrolls, and other records in this record group The *General Index to Compiled Military Service Records of Revolutionary War Soldiers* (M860, 58 rolls) includes the names of a few women. The name of "Margt. Johnson," for example, is listed as one that "appears on a mess roll," and Cpl. Samuel Gay, in whose file there are no personal papers, is recorded as being a woman. Civilian women employees are documented in *Compiled Service Records of American Naval Personnel and Members of the Departments of the Quartermaster General and the Commissary General of Military Stores Who Served in the Revolutionary War* (filmed as M880, 4 rolls). Pay, length of service, and duty station are given for each employee.

Records of the Adjutant General's Office, 1780's–1917

Record Group 94

94.1. The Adjutant General's Office (AGO) was established by an act of March 2, 1821, and, except for a brief time in 1904–7, was in continuous existence throughout the period covered by this record group. The Adjutant General was charged with matters relating to command, discipline, and administration of the Military Establishment and was responsible for communicating the orders, instructions, and regulations of the Secretary of War to troops and individuals in the U.S. Army. He issued commissions, compiled and issued the *Army Register* and the *Army List and Directory*, consolidated the general returns of the Army and militia, and managed recruitment. The AGO handled Army orders, correspondence, and other records and received final custody within the War Department of virtually all records concerned with the Military Establishment, including records of discontinued commands, noncurrent holdings of bureaus of the War Department, and special collections.

General Records

94.2. Letters received, 1805–89 (620 ft.), have been copied on five microfilm publications: 1805–21 (M566, 144 rolls), 1822–60 (M567, 636 rolls), 1861–70 (M619, 828 rolls), 1871–80 (M666, 593 rolls), and 1881–89 (M740, 1 roll). The letters are arranged in annual segments and thereunder alphabetically by surname or office of correspondent or numerically. The series is served by **indexes, 1812–89** (6 ft.), parts of which (1846 and 1861–89) have been filmed as M725 (9 rolls). There are numerous entries in the index for Dorothea Dix. There are also **registers of letters received, 1814–89** (133 vols., 34 ft.), filmed as M711 (85 rolls), that contain an abstract of each letter registered. The principal references to women in the letters received during the pre-Civil War period are reports of payments to laundresses, the employment of officers' wives as laundresses, and, during the Mexican War, limitations on the number of laundresses that could be employed for each unit. The letters can be located in the index under such headings as "Laundry" and "Medical attendance, enlisted men."

94.3. References to women are more numerous in the letters received in the 1860's (M619). For example, Special Order 36, Headquarters, Department of the East, March 15, 1863, created a committee to investigate the management of a hospital for sick and wounded soldiers established by a women's association in New York City (file 275-E-1863). Records relating to an investigation of conditions at Hammond General Hospital at Point Lookout, MD (file 96-Q-1862), contain statistics on the number of nurses, matrons, and black women laundry workers employed at the hospital. In file 96-W-1862 there is a request from a surgeon at Headquarters, 16th Army Corps, in Memphis, for authority to employ black women nurses because he thought they were better suited to the work than men. The proceedings of a board of inquiry about the management of Allegheny Arsenal near Pittsburgh (file 426-A-1862) contain testimony regarding procedures for hiring employees, most of whom were women, and a description of the operations of the arsenal where 156 of the 186 women workers died in an explosion in September 1862. Letters relating to the investigation of the alleged mismanagement of the Watertown, MA, arsenal by Maj. Thomas J. Rodman from September 1864 to July 1865 (file 2293-W-1865) also include testimony of women munitions workers. Another investigation dealt with camps that were established by the Federal Government but often administered by civilians to house slaves who fled to the Union Army. Such persons were known as "contraband." An investigation of the conditions in one contraband camp was conducted by a Freedmen's Inquiry Commission that reported to the Secretary of War. Commission records (file 328-O-1863, 9 in.) include interviews with freedwomen who gave their personal histories—some even reporting early years in Africa, and the testimony of Government officials and of women such as Laura Towne, who taught freedmen in schools in the South.

94.4. Among the AGO letters received, 1871–80 (M666), are letters relating to an attack by the U.S. Army on a village of Comanche Indians in which Indian women and children were captured (file 4882 AGO 1872). File 1405 AGO 1878 concerning the Lincoln County Controversy in New Mexico contains at least one document (no. 5633) that deals with problems of women in need of protection from two armed factions of settlers and the Army intervention in behalf of the women.

94.5. In the final segment of letters received (1881–89, M689) letters relating to a yellow fever epidemic in Key West, FL (file 3832 AGO 1887), indicate that a sergeant's wife was the first victim. The letters also deal with volunteer and hired women nurses in Key West.

94.6. The **War Department collection of post-Revolutionary War manuscripts, 1784–1811** (1 ft.), filmed as M904 (4 rolls), includes a "List of Payments Made to the Widows of Officers by the Office of the Accountant, War Department." The list gives the name of each widow, the name of the deceased officer, the date, rate of pay, amount paid, and occasionally the date and place where the officer last saw action in the War of 1812.

94.7. Post-Revolutionary War Papers, 1784–1815 (200 ft.), include records showing that, although most military nurses in this period were men, a few women were employed as nurses, matrons, and laundresses. Several documents relating to Polly Gordon, who apparently was a nurse in the military hospital near Natchez in 1798, are in the correspondence of the War Department accountant (3 ft.), a subseries of the papers. Paymaster records in the same series, arranged in rough alphabetical order by name of paymaster, also contain some women's names. Annie Oakley's April 1898 letter to President William H. McKinley offering to recruit 50 women sharpshooters in the event of war is in file 33879/2441.

94.8. Letters sent and received beginning in 1890 were filed together in the **general correspondence ("document file"), 1890–1917** (10,000 ft.). Consolidated files dealing with a particular subject are common. The **index** (2 vols. and 585 ft.), filmed as M698 (1,269 rolls), and summaries of or extracts from the letters on **record cards, 1890–1917** (3,672 ft.), provide access to the series. Among entries in the index relating to women are the following:

Barton, Clara

Boardman, Mabel T., Miss [chair of the National Relief Board, American Red Cross]

Hasson, Esther V. [Army nurse and first superintendent of the Navy Nurse Corps]

Hospital, Matrons

Jones, Clarissa F. [Civil War nurse]

Langdon, Ollie [woman who wished to enlist as a soldier]

Laundry, Misc.

McGee, Dr. Anita Newcomb [founder of the ANC]

Medical Attendance, Misc.

Nurses, Corps of, Misc.; Female; Misc.

Prostitution

Rations, Commutation of, Nurses

Red Cross, Society of, Nurses

Relief

Wives

Woman's Christian Temperance Union

Woman's Homestead Association

Woman's League for Self Defense

Woman's National Defense Conference

Woman's Patriotic and Industrial League

Woman's National War Relief Association

Woman's Peace Party

Woman's Relief Corps

Woman's Republican Club

Woman's Suffrage Association

Woman's Veteran Auxiliary Corps

Woman's Veteran Relief Union

Women

Women Soldiers

File PRD 5416 in the same series has been microfilmed as *Reports and Correspondence Relating to the Army Investigations of the Battle at Wounded Knee and to the Sioux Campaign of 1890–91* (M983, 2 rolls). A major concern of President Benjamin Harrison, who ordered the investigation, was whether or not noncombatant women had been killed indiscriminately by the U.S. Army.

94.9. In addition to references in correspondence, information about women may appear in orders. Orders transmit instructions or commands from the War Department or from commanders of military units. Before the Civil War, few orders relating to women or families of military personnel or to women contract employees were issued by the War Department. A few are cited in the *Subject Index of the General Orders of the War Department from January 1, 1809 to December 31, 1860* (Washington, DC: Government Printing Office, 1886) under the following headings: "Chaplains—posts (record book of marriages, baptisms, and funerals)," "Hospitals—matrons," "Laundresses," "Medical attendance," "Pensions," "Quarters—officers, families of," "Widows," and "Women (reducing the numbers of, allowed to a company)." The index and the orders were filmed as *General Orders and Circulars of the War Department and Headquarters of the Army, 1809–1864* (M1094, 8 rolls). They are arranged in two subseries, manuscript and printed; both are arranged by year and thereunder numerically. Typical of orders relating to women was General Order 39 issued on December 29, 1862, by Headquarters, Army of Kentucky, that required a woman to hold a permit to enter a Union Army camp. Special orders concerning personnel actions, such as transfers and assignments of Army nurses, are also in this series.

94.10. Muster rolls of Regular Army organizations, 1784–October 31, 1912 (1,278 ft.), document the presence of women with units of the U.S. Army. A muster roll is a list of all personnel present on parade or otherwise accounted for on the day of muster or review of troops under arms. In a folder filed under "Posts—Legion Period" are six hospital rolls dated 1792–96 showing that there were women nurses and matrons at all six hospitals in that period. Muster rolls for the fall and winter of 1812 show that the majority of nurses serving in the Hospital Department at Greenbush, NY, were women, and the number of persons hired as nurses, cooks, and laundresses were reported separately on weekly returns from the General Military Hospital at Greenwich, NY, in 1813. The rolls are filed under "Hospitals and Casualties." Many matrons' names appear in the records of the 1840s for "Hospital Corps in the United States." Muster rolls for the Hospital Corps during the Civil War (100 ft.) also show the names of many matrons.

94.11. Women were also carried on **muster rolls of Volunteer organizations: War of 1812, 1812–15** (300 ft.), as nurses, matrons, or hospital attendants.

94.12. Muster rolls of Volunteer organizations: Civil War, Mexican War, Creek War, Cherokee Removal, and other wars, 1836–65 (4,784 ft.), arranged alphabetically by State, thereunder by arm of service, regiment number, and name of war, show women serving as matrons, attendants, and wardmasters. Even in Vera Cruz, Monterrey, and Tampico during the Mexican War, attendants and matrons were women. The segments of this series covering the Hospital Corps in the Civil War years (ca. 150 ft.) also list the names of matrons and women attendants. At the end of the series are muster rolls for "Hospitals Afloat," including women's names.

94.13. Some women assisted the military during the War of 1812 by allowing the Army to employ their servants or rent their property. **"Miscellaneous records," [1812–15]** (78 ft.), include documents showing payments to women for services and land use. There is a **special index** (55 ft.) to the series.

94.14. **"Generals' papers and books"** (140 vols., 51 ft.) are principally for the Civil War period and were collected by the War Department from its own records and from the families of generals for use in the compilation of *Official Records of the Union and Confederate Armies.* In the papers of Ambrose E. Burnside there are references to women including one woman's offer of service to the Union and another woman's complaint that a most dangerous female rebel was "walking free" about the city of Cincinnati.

94.15. Numerous women's disloyal acts are described or alluded to in "Baker-Turner" records, 1862–66 (28 vols., 33 ft.), filmed as *Case Files of Investigations by Levi C. Turner and Lafayette C. Baker, 1861–1866* (M797, 137 rolls, with an index on roll 1). Major Turner was Associate Judge Advocate, and Baker was a special agent for the War Department and a special provost marshal. They accumulated evidence of conspiracies, contraband trade, and other actions potentially harmful to the Union as they investigated, apprehended, and brought to trial before a military commission those men and women whose actions allegedly threatened the Union during the war. The quantities of records vary from case to case. Some files simply contain requests from women to visit or write to a relative in prison. A few others document some women's work as informants, other women's fraudulent business practices, and still other women's attempts to obtain the restitution of confiscated property. The files for Belle Boyd and Anna Ella Carroll are small despite their notoriety, but there are larger files for unknowns like Frances Abel, a Union informant accused of robbery and dissolute behavior.

94.16. Not all of the Baker-Turner records have been microfilmed. In **records of prisoners, 1861–65** (28 vols., 32 in.), the volume labeled "Record of Prisoners, March 1863–July 1864," contains statements of a few women concerning the facts supporting the charges against them. The names of women in the District of Columbia's Old Capitol Prison are among lists and registers of prisoners, some showing the dates and other details of confinement. The names of women who signed an oath of allegiance to the Union appear in **drafts of letters, flags of truce, and boat papers** (1 ft.).

94.17. Some women were among those who filed pardon petitions in response to President Andrew Johnson's Amnesty Proclamation of May 29, 1865, because they were excluded from the provisions of the proclamation at the end of the Civil War. Their files are in **"Amnesty Papers," 1865–67** (30 ft.), filmed as M1003 (73 rolls). Arranged by State, the files include statements of age, family connections, and property holdings of the petitioners.

94.18. During the Spanish-American War and the Philippine Insurrection, **correspondence relating to applications for discharges and furloughs, n.d.** (2 ft.), contains some letters from soldiers' wives and mothers that contain many personal details.

94.19. By the 1880s, the AGO was employing women in clerical positions. The names of women who were AGO employees are indexed in **registers of letters received and endorsements relating to civilian employees, December 2, 1882–June 30, 1894** (1 vol., 2 in.). Some women's names that appear in employees' files are not indexed; for example, landladies or women creditors who complained of debts owed by AGO employees. **Registers of clerks, 1863–64, 1881–82** (4 vols., 6 in.), usually give for each man or woman listed the date of appointment, birthplace, residence when appointed, and person(s) who recommended the employee.

Reference Aids and Other Special Files

94.20. The AGO was responsible for maintaining the historically significant records of the Army before a National Archives was established. To solve its own problems of locating hard-to-find items in military records, the AGO created reference aids and special files that are still useful. For example, a **"special file,"** 1790–1945 (6 ft.), consists of materials that were separated from various War Department files and were kept in the safe of the Old Records Division of the AGO. Among records relating to famous persons like Abraham Lincoln and Robert E. Lee is a file (1 in.) about a relatively unknown woman named Annie E. Jones who was accused of spying for the Confederacy.

94.21. In the same subgroup is a **"general information index,"** **1794–1918** (41 ft.), which indexes many series in a number of different military record groups. An individual jacket in this index may include information about its subject or even records pertaining to it. The index contains entries for the following women and organizations in which women worked:

Barton, Clara

Bickerdyke, "Mother" Mary Ann [Ball]

Boyd, Belle

Carroll, Anna Ella

Christian Commission, U.S.

C[ommission] on T[raining] C[amp] A[ctivities]

Cushman, Pauline

Dix, Dorothea

Greenhow, Rose

Negro women employed in hospitals

Nurses

Pittman, Mary

Sanitary Commission, U.S.

Smith, Elizabeth

Surratt, Mary

Tubman, Harriet

Walker, Dr. Mary E.

Wittenmyer, Annie

Women, soldiers

In the "R" section of the index is an entry for "Roswell Factory" where several hundred Confederate seamstresses were taken prisoner.

94.22. After the Civil War, the AGO established precedent files, first in bound volumes and later on cards and envelopes. Ideally such a file would contain a card or envelope for every type of problem that arose in the office with information about (or copies of or extracts from) any document that dealt with each type of problem. These often included opinions of the Judge Advocate General and the Comptroller General, memorandums and decisions from the President and Cabinet members, laws, court decisions, orders and correspondence from other War Department offices, and even excerpts from newspapers, magazines, and textbooks.

94.23. One such file is the **administrative precedent file ("Frech file"), 1775–1917** (81 ft.), which contains references to the work of and benefits for contract nurses, AGO employees, families of military personnel, and the Army Nurse Corps. Among the woman-related alpha-numeric subject headings found in an accompanying subject card index (8 in.) are the following:

3B2e.	Furnishing record information concerning age, birthdate, and birthplace
3F4.	Kinship, heirship, etc.
3H3b.	Women with or in the Army
3I2.	Human physiology
24K4b3(c)	Conditions entitling women to burial in national cemeteries
30N6	Women's Societies
92	Conduct of employees
283D6	Health Committee for Benefit of Employees
283D7	Volunteer nurses aides and emergency health organization
283L	Visiting nurses, welfare committee, and U.S. Employees Compensation
283M	American Red Cross—Home Service Section
457D	Certain classes of employees—female (A.E.F.)
477	Medical, surgical, and dental treatment and attendance
477I5	Civilians Employed under Contract Nurses Matrons, Attendants, Cooks, and Wardmasters a. General b. Female nurses
477P	Medical, surgical, and dental treatment and attendance

94.24. A **precedent file: Correspondence Division, 1775–1917** (919 ft.), includes under the heading "289— Medical Records Relative to Births and Marriages" material about the great number of civilians who were treated in Army hospitals or attended by a military physician including women family members of officers and enlisted personel, civilian employees, visitors, and nearby residents who were without other medical assistance.

94.25. Similarly, there is material about wives and other family members of Army personnel in **precedent file: ACP Division and Officers' Division ("Kohr file"), ca. 1775–1925** (13 ft.). Among its subjects are:

Beneficiaries

Bills introduced in 1922 and 1923

Clerks, female

Commutation of quarters for dependents

Husband

Legislation

Nurse, Army

Passports to wives and others of officers and soldiers

Pensions

Remains

Red Cross, American

Red Cross, auxiliary

Transportation

Wives of officers in Germany

94.26. Another **precedent file: "Driscoll file," n.d.** (3 ft.), is accompanied by a **subject index** (1 ft.) and is arranged according to the War Department decimal classification scheme. It contains copies of several letters prepared after World War I in response to questions about women's service in that war. Some of the letters of inquiry about the wartime status of a particular person or class of persons were written by former servicewomen. In file 293 "Misc.-A," a letter outlines the policy and precedents in regard to the burial of wives of enlisted men and officers.

94.27. In **reference file: Old Records Division, ca. 1775–1917** (5 ft.), there is a folder entitled "Women Soldiers—Revolutionary War." Another folder labeled "Pensions" provides information about veterans' widows and consists largely of carbon copies of letters written in reply to inquiries, clippings, etc. The **reference file: Old Records Division ("Tarr file"), ca. 1775–1917** (2 ft.), includes a folder labeled "American Red Cross" that deals with Clara Barton's work, and one labeled "Widows

Clara Barton cared for the wounded during the Civil War. 111-B-1857.

(Remarried)," which relates to pensions. Under "Nurses" in both of these files are copies of correspondence with Anita Newcomb McGee, the Judge Advocate General, and nurses' associations as well as copies of bills, acts, legal opinions, orders, and annual reports relating to the postwar veteran status of the nurses who served during the Spanish-American War.

Records of Administrative Units

94.28. The Commission Branch of the AGO was established in 1863 to handle personnel matters for officers and relations with some civilians such as veterinarians and post traders. In the branch **letters received, 1863–94** (725 ft.), the 1863–70 part of which was filmed as M1064 (527 rolls), are many letters from women recommending male relatives or friends for promotion or other recognition. In 1871 the branch became the Appointment, Commission, and Personal Branch (ACP). In the ACP **letters received, 1871–94** (1,500 ft.), there are a number of letters relating to women post traders. They are indexed under "post traders," "women," and individual names in the **name and subject index** (M1125, 4 rolls). Other information about women sutlers appears in **registers of post traders, 1821–89** (4 vols., ½ in.), which also include the terms under which post traders received the exclusive privilege to sell to military personnel in a particular post.

94.29. The Colored Troops Division was established in 1863 to handle matters relating to the recruitment, organization, and service of black soldiers. In the division's **letters received, 1862–88** (700 ft.), and its **letters received relating to recruiting, 1863–68** (12 ft.), there are a few letters from soldiers' female relatives, mostly about routine matters.

94.30. The Enlisted Branch was established in 1862 to do for enlisted men what the ACP Branch did for officers. Before 1862 personnel records for enlisted men were in "Addison's files." In **letters received relating to soldiers, 1848–62** (26 ft.), among the Addison files and **letters received, 1862–December 1889** (1,433 ft.), by the Enlisted Branch, most of the letters received from women are requests for special attention for particular enlisted men.

94.31. Records relating to the establishment, occupation, maintenance, and abandonment of military posts and reservations in a **reservation file, early 1800's–1916** (30 ft.), include some letters from women protesting the location or closing of particular forts and reservations. In the file for Fort Gaston, San Francisco, for example, letters from the Allegheny and Pittsburgh Women's National Indian Association object to the location of the fort on the Hoopa Reservation.

94.32. The Volunteer Service Division had charge of Volunteer units and officers. The records of at least two women are filed in the division's **letters received, 1861–89** (640 ft.). Correspondence about Ella E.G. Hobart, who was apparently elected chaplain of the First Wisconsin Heavy Artillery, makes up consolidated file VS 3370 W 1864. Dr. Mary E. Walker's consolidated file, VS 2068 W 1863, includes letters commending her for her work and others questioning her competence as a physician.

94.33. Dr. Walker received the Congressional Medal of Honor, but her citation, along with many others, was rescinded in 1917 when Congress estalished new retroactive guidelines for the medal. In 1977 she was posthumously reinstated as a Congressional Medal of Honor recipient. Her file (4 in.) in **case files relating to requests for correction of records of the Adjutant General's Office, 1961–79** (1 ft.), created by the Army Board for the Correction of Military Records (ABCMR), includes copies of her military personnel records, her pension application file, the application of her grandniece to the Board, and the Board's proceedings on the case. Included also are a case summary, transcripts of the hearing, and the recommendation of the ABCMR.

Records of the Record and Pension Office

94.34. The **general correspondence ("document file"), 1889–1904** (1,650 ft.), of the Record and Pension Office is arranged by numbers assigned in arbitrary sequence and consists chiefly of correspondence about Volunteers' military service on which federal benefits could be based. Women most frequently mentioned were camp followers, relief workers, and telegraph operators. A large consolidated file for Anna Ella

Carroll (R and P file 454155) documents her claim to have served as a military strategist and propagandist during the Civil War. Also among the general correspondence are files relating to women's groups that wrote to request pensions for Civil War nurses. The **index** to this correspondence (160 ft.), filmed as M686 (385 rolls), contains entries for "Women," "Female soldier," "Woman's Relief Corps," "Woman's Veteran Relief Union," and individual women's names. **Record cards, 1889–1904** (1,168 ft.), contain abstracts of each inquiry and response and note whether a letter was referred elsewhere in the War Department or placed in a particular consolidated file.

94.35. Also for the purpose of handling pensions based on military service, the Record and Pension Office prepared compiled military service records for Volunteers in the post-Revolutionary War period, the War of 1812, Indian Wars, the Mexican War, the Civil War, the Spanish-American War, and the Philippine Insurrection by extracting information from muster rolls, payrolls, and other original records of service and copying it onto cards that were filed in jackets for individual soldiers. There is one card in a serviceman's jacket for each entry on a muster roll. Whether an individual was black or a member of a religious order is noted. For most of the compiled military service records there are indexes, many of which have been microfilmed. Some women's names appear in the indexes.

94.36. A few women claimed to have disguised their sex to serve in the Union Army. There is little chance of locating records about them in **carded records, volunteer organizations: Civil War** (13,268 ft.) unless the researcher has a good deal of information about each claimant. The records are arranged by State, thereunder by branch of service, thereunder numerically by regiment, and thereunder alphabetically by soldiers' surnames. The **general index** to the series is arrangd by State and thereunder alphabetically by soldiers' surnames. For instance, in the files for Company G of the 95th Illinois there are papers for a woman named S. Emma Edmonds Seelye who was disguised as "Albert D. J. Cashier" from September 1862 through February 1865. To find her records, the researcher would have to know her male alias and the State from which she served even to locate her name in the index.

94.37. Records of a few contract nurses appear in a **"miscellaneous file, medical and military," of carded records, Spanish-American War and Philippine Insurrection** (3 ft.).

94.38. In **carded service records of hospital attendants, matrons, and nurses, 1861–65** (40 ft.), the majority of those listed are women. There are 14 cards referring to 14 files or muster roll entries for "Mother" Mary Ann Ball Bickerdyke at seven hospitals. On each card is personal name, occupation, station, dates of service, remarks about personnel actions taken, and references to the original records from which the information was compiled. There is a similar series for **female matrons, nurses, cooks, and laundresses, n.d.** (22 ft.).

94.39. Medical statements of service, n.d. (1½ ft.), arranged alphabetically by name, consist largely of cards for persons who appear to be all women. Also included are occasional original records, as in the case of Annie T. Wittenmyer's initiatives regarding diet kitchens.

94.40. Reports and correspondence regarding contracts for nurses, n.d. (3 ft.), arranged numerically, include names, dates, and terms of employment. The correspondence concerns the annulment of contracts, final payments, and some indication of the performance or behavior of the nurses. **Card indexes to reports and correspondence** (2 in. for women's names, 5 ft. for men) are arranged in separate alphabets for men and women. Actual **contracts** (about 10 in. for women, 20 ft. for men) show that nearly all the men were contract nurses, whereas most of the women were black cooks.

94.41. Letters received by Dorothea Dix concerning nurses, 1863–65 (8 in.), consist primarily of letters from women applying for appointments and for particular assignments. There are also letters from male surgeons requesting that more women nurses be sent to the field. There is a name index (1 ft.) to this series.

94.42. Among Spanish-American War records there are some records of members of the ANC. At the outbreak of the war, Dr. Anita Newcomb McGee, a physician and a national officer of the Daughters of the American Revolution, proposed that a D.A.R. Hospital Corps composed of nursing school graduates be recruited. These nurses were contract nurses during the war, but in 1901 they became the nucleus of the "Army Nurse Corps (female)" in the Regular Army pursuant to the Army Reorganization Act of 1901.

94.43. Carded medical records: Regular Army, 1894–1912 (602 ft.), include records (ca. 40 ft.) for the Hospital Corps, including the nurses recruited by Dr. McGee. A few entries for women nurses on hospital staffs are among the registers of sick and wounded in **field records of hospitals: Spanish-American War and Philippine Insurrection, 1898–1902** (4,000 vols., 130 ft.), for which there are separate geograpical indexes. In the index for the District of Columbia are many entries for women's names. A few lists of civilians admitted to hospitals, especially to the smallpox hospitals, include women's names.

94.44. Women, mostly wives of servicemen, account for at least one-third of the **carded medical records of civilians, 1894–1912** (40 ft.), arranged alphabetically by name of patient, which give personal and medical information about the patient and rank and organization of the person whose military connection entitled the patient to medical service in an Army hospital. Other carded medical records of civilians, 1884–1912, are in a separate series each for birth, death, and marriage records.

94.45. Several series of records of and pertaining to medical installations contain records about women employees and women in military families. **Field records of hospitals, 1821–1912** (11,000 vols., 1,120 ft.), contain occasional medical records of Army families. **Medical histories of posts, 1868–1913** (905 vols., 110 ft.), monthly reports to the AGO from post surgeons concerning the facilities, grounds, personnel, and nearby civilian communities, include reports of births, marriages, and deaths, including those of civilian women and children. There are similar records in the **"papers file," 1895–1912** (9 ft.). The **index to hospital papers, muster and pay rolls, returns of hospital corps, and "papers file," 1886–1912** (2 ft.), indexes several series of the period. **Hospital papers: Spanish-American War and Philippine Insurrection, 1898–1903** (80 ft.), which is arranged in numerical sequence by post and includes some correspondence about nurses, has its own index.

94.46. In records concerning medical personnel, 1839–1914, a series of **personal papers, medical officers and physicians, prior to 1912** (360 ft.), is arranged alphabetically by name and includes files for some women nurses who served during the Spanish-American War, one for "McGee, A.N.," and one for Dr. Mary E. Walker. In the same subgroup are **monthly returns of nurses, 1861–65** (40 ft.), showing that only 20 percent of the nurses in the period were women; and **miscellaneous medical record books, 1861–1903** (35 vols., 4 ft.), contain "Chaplain's Records of Marriages, Births, and Funerals" at Fort Keough, Montana Territory, 1880–90, and registers of medical personnel with an index in which the names of women contract nurses are placed together at the end of each alphabetical division. There are also **Medical Department registers, 1861–84** (20 vols., 1½ ft.), including records of "colored contract nurses," 1863–64; and **contracts with female employees, Bureau of Refugees, Freedmen, and Abandoned Lands, 1865–69** (1 ft.). **Reports of attendants, Bureau of Refugees, Freedmen, and Abandoned Lands, 1868–71** (3 ft.), are arranged by State and list monthly complements of cooks, nurses, laundresses, and matrons. There are also **returns of matrons, 1876–87** (9 ft.); **returns of the Hospital Corps, 1887–1911** (31 ft.), arranged in subseries, one of which is "female nurses"; and other registers and returns, all of which contain some information about women.

94.47. Among reports of diseases and individual cases, 1841–95, **"File A" and "bound manuscripts," 1861–65** (16 ft.), consists of surgeons' narrative reports, one of which (A388) is entitled "Reports on Prostitutes in Nashville."

94.48. The U.S. Christian Commission (USCC) was a private organization formed at a meeting of the local YMCA in New York City in 1861, but its staff and volunteer workers worked very closely with Union chaplains and surgeons during the Civil War, and the AGO kept some of its records after the organization was disbanded in 1866. Although most USCC workers who ministered to the religious needs of soldiers were men, women were involved in some of its activities. Ladies' auxiliaries raised money and made hospital supplies, and women worked in diet kitchens that supplied Army field hospitals with specially prepared meals for the sick and wounded.

94.49. USCC **letters sent, central office, 1862–65** (15 vols., 1½ ft.), include letters of thanks to ladies' auxiliaries and requests for more hospital supplies. A good many were addressed to Annie Wittenmyer, who was both the Superintendent of the USCC Diet Kitchen Service, and a representative of the Soldiers Aid Society. Wittenmyer's 83-page summary report describing the diet kitchen program is in **communications received, central office, 1862–66** (1½ ft.), which also contains letters from women and women's groups volunteering their services and transmitting donations. One section in a **register of commission letters, 1864–65** (1 vol., 1 in.), is composed of entries for letters from women's groups.

94.50. Record of inquiries, Bureau of Information, Washington, DC, 1864 (1 vol., 1½ ft.), and the Individual Relief Department's **register of letters received, 1864–65** (1 vol., ½ in.), **letters received, 1864–65** (1 in.), and **record of inquiries, 1864–65** (1 vol., ½ in.), all contain information about women wanting to learn the whereabouts and condition of individual soldiers. Male USCC workers who wrote letters for disabled soldiers in hospitals kept a **record of letters written for soldiers, Army of the Potomac, 1865** (3 in.), and **reports of letters written for soldiers, individual relief department, Nashville, Tenn., station, 1864–65** (3 vols., 3 in.), both of which cite or contain many letters written to women.

94.51. Evidence that the USCC was reluctant to permit women to organize ladies' auxiliaries is in the **minutes of the executive committee, 1861–65** (3 in.), along with some documentation of Wittenmyer's activities.

94.52. Registers of delegates, 1863–64 (3 vols. and 3 index vols., 2 in.), and **memorandum of commissions sent to agencies, 1863–64** (1 vol., ¼ in), both show the names of a few women, principally in Chicago and St. Louis, who worked mainly in diet kitchens, offices, or reading rooms, and a few who worked as nurses. **List of agencies and agents, n.d.** (1 vol., ¼ in.), and **record of branches and agencies, n.d.** (1 vol., 1 in.), include the names of officers of ladies' auxiliaries or other groups associated with USCC in Buffalo, San Francisco, and several towns in Pennsylvania.

94.53. Invoices, 1862–65 (1½ ft.), **invoice books 1862–65** (9 vols., 1 ft.), and **receiving books, 1862–65** (7 vols., 6 in.), all document the flow of supplies from women and women's organizations to the USCC.

94.54. Invoices of money received from soldiers and forwarded, 1864–65 (2 vols., 1 in.), **record of money expressed, 1864–65**

(11 vols., 1½ ft.), and **express books, 1864–65** (11 vols., 1½ in.), document another service of the USCC. Many recipients of money so "expressed" were women.

94.55. A **record of ladies' auxiliary Christian commissions, 1864** (1 vol., 1 in.), and a **record of contributions, ladies' auxiliary Christian commissions, 1864–65** (1 vol., 1 in.), give both the name of the church each auxiliary was associated with and some information about fairs and financial drives to support the work of the commission. Women's names are scattered throughout **memorandum books, 1863–64** (11 vols., 6 in.), with lists of donations from various locations, mainly in Pennsylvania. The records show that piece goods were sent to women by the USCC central office in Philadelphia to be used in making hospital gowns. The women also sent jam and other delicacies to relieve the tedium of hospital diet. A series of **scrapbooks, 1862–65** (5 vols., 1½ ft.), includes a few notices of women's meetings and at least one diet kitchen menu.

94.56. Twelve women were included in the USSC **cartes-de-visite photograph album, 1864–65** (CC, 377 items). Among the autographed portraits of USCC officials and workers are those of Mary E. Keeney, president of the Ladies' Christian Commission of the Pacific in San Francisco; Mrs. E.H. Humbert, a diet kitchen manager who died during the war; and "Mother" Mary Ann Ball Bickerdyke, who worked with both the USCC and the U.S. Sanitary Commission.

Records of U.S. Army Commands, 1784–1821

Record Group 98

98.1. In 1784 the U.S. Army consisted of one infantry regiment. After a considerable increase at the time of the War of 1812, by 1821 the Army consisted of seven infantry regiments and two regiments of light artillery. In 1813 a War Department general order divided the Nation into nine military districts. Although geographical designations fluctuated thereafter, as did the number and designations of units, the concept of decentralized command was established. The few references to women in these records are largely incidental.

98.2. In **letters sent by Maj. Thomas Cushing, Commanding Troops on the Mississippi, July 1799–March 1800** (1 vol., ½ in.), and in his **letters received, April–November 1799** (1 vol., ½ in.), both arranged chronologically, Mrs. James Wilkinson, wife of the brigadier general who was Cushing's superior, is mentioned several times, and the marriage of Susan Pearsey to a Lieutenant Semple is noted. The 6th Military District with headquarters at Charleston, SC, was under the command of Maj. Gen. Thomas Pinckney during and shortly after the

War of 1812. In the first volume of the District's **letters sent, March 1813–June 1815** (2 vols., 3 in.), arranged chronologically, there are instructions for the protection of women unable to leave the city during the British blockade of Charleston. Amounts of rations and rates of pay for laundresses attached to the garrison were prescribed in orders of the period such as the **orderly book for the Company of Capt. Jonathan Heart, September 1785–May 1788** (1 vol., ½ in.), arranged chronologically.

Records of the Office of the Paymaster General

Record Group 99

99.1. A Pay Department, headed by a Paymaster General, was first established by an act of April 24, 1816. The general system of paying the troops instituted at that time continued until an act of August 24, 1912, abolished the Office of the Paymaster General and transferred troop payment to the Office of the Quartermaster General.

99.2. Payments to women who were witnesses or court reporters at courts-martial are among those recorded in **registers of payments to acting assistant surgeons, clerks, messengers, additional paymasters, citizen witnesses and others, 1874–1917** (9 vols., 2½ ft.).

99.3. A **register of payments to hospital stewards and matrons, 1849–1905** (7 vols., 13 in.), is arranged chronologically. The volume for 1849–55 lists hospital matrons by position only and gives the period for which each was paid, by whom, and the name of post.

99.4. There are also **records of payments to hospital nurses, 1859–1913** (4 vols., 1 ft.), and **lists of civilian employees, 1861–1911** (9 vols., 1 ft.), which both contain women's names.

Records of the Bureau of Refugees, Freedmen, and Abandoned Lands

Record Group 105

105.1. The Bureau of Refugees, Freedmen, and Abandoned Lands (Freedmen's Bureau) was established in the War Department on March 3, 1865, to supervise all activities relating to refugees and freedmen in the South at the end of the Civil War and to assume custody of all abandoned or confiscated lands or property—functions previously shared by military commanders and Treasury Department special agents. The Bureau, which operated in former Confederate States, border States, the District of Columbia, Delaware, and parts of Kansas, was headed by

Commissioner Oliver Otis Howard with headquarters in Washington, DC. He supervised assistant commissioners in the States, who in turn supervised subordinate officials usually responsible for Bureau affairs in one or more counties. The Bureau was abolished by an act of June 10, 1872, and its remaining functions, relating chiefly to the settlement of claims, were continued by the Freedmen's Branch in the Office of the Adjutant General (see RG 94). After 1879 the claims work was assumed by the Colored Troops Division of the Office of the Adjutant General.

105.2. Officers of the Bureau issued rations, clothing, and medicine to destitute refugees and freedmen; operated or leased abandoned or confiscated land; established hospitals; and cooperated with benevolent societies in establishing schools. Families scattered by wartime conditions turned to the Bureau for help with locating relatives and for transportation to reunite them. Transportation was also needed to get persons to jobs. Beginning in 1866 the Bureau helped black soldiers and their dependents collect claims for bounties, pay arrearages, and pensions. Freedwomen and Southern white women figured in the work of the bureau as recipients of its assistance; Northern women worked with the Bureau as teachers and benefactors who ministered to the suffering people in the South.

Records of the Washington Headquarters

105.3. Two National Archives Microfilm Publications contain a good many of the records of the Commissioner and the agency's Washington headquarters. *Selected Series of Records Issued by the Commissioner of the Bureau of Refugees, Freedmen, and Abandoned Lands, 1865–1872* (M742, 7 rolls), includes **letters sent, May 1865–June 1872** (7 vols., 1 ft.), arranged chronologically with **name and subject indexes** (7 vols., 5 in.); **special orders, May 1865–June 1872** (1 vol., 2 in.), arranged generally by year and thereunder numerically with a name index in the front of each volume and a subject index in the back of each volume; **circulars, May 1865–July 1869** (1 vol., 1 in.), arranged by year and thereunder numerically; and related records. As was customary in this period of military recordkeeping, a response to a letter received was frequently written on the letter, which was then returned to the sender or forwarded to another office, but the response was also copied into an endorsement book. **Endorsements sent, 1865–71 with gaps,** (6 vols., 1 ft.), arranged chronologically, with accompanying **name and subject indexes** (6 vols., 5 in.), also filmed on M742, are therefore important series.

105.4. The registers copied on *Registers and Letters Received by the Commissioner of the Bureau of Refugees, Freedmen, and Abandoned Lands, 1865–1872* (M752, 74 rolls), are useful in the same way, indicating other offices of the Bureau to which some letters were referred. In addition, the registers contain summaries of incoming letters and are useful as finding aids to the contents of the letters received.

105.5. The indexes on both of these microfilm publications contain the names of women prominent in the work of the Bureau, such as Laura Haviland, Jane Swisshelm, and Josephine S. Griffing. Other entries in these indexes that often point to letters relating to women are "Asylums," "Clothing," "Marriage," "Orphan," "Property, restoration of," "Syphilis and pregnancy," and broader terms such as "Schools," "Rents," "Loans," "Destitution," and "Homes." Many of the letters sent and received deal generally with the condition of freedmen and freedwomen and the conditions and attitudes of whites in the former Confederate States. There are letters from blacks, Southern whites, and Northern volunteers. Some of the letters from private citizens are requests for black female servants.

105.6. Headquarters records that were not filmed on M742 or M752 also contain records about women. The Bureau's **letters of appointment, reappointment, and revocation of appointment, October 1867–June 1872** (11 vols.), arranged chronologically with name indexes, include records about women who worked as agents of the bureau. For example, Josephine S. Griffing worked through the District of Columbia field office, and Elizabeth Van Lew became a clerk for the Freedmen's Bureau in Virginia. Records for each of them appear in this series. The records consist of form letters that show name, position, salary, State assignment, and effective date for each personnel action. In addition, clerks in the Commissioner's office compiled **synopses of letters and reports relating to conditions of freedmen and Bureau activities in the States, January 1866–March 1869** (3 vols., 5 in.), arranged chronologically. They provide some guidance as to which incoming letters and reports relate to women.

105.7. The Commissioner also received **monthly reports of the assistant commissioners on rations, clothing, and medicine issued to refugees and freedmen by bureau officers, 1865–69** (5 ft.), arranged alphabetically by State and thereunder chronologically. They contain separate reports for freedmen and white refugees that provide information about women, black and white, in the South. The printed forms provide separate categories for the dependent or destitute, those in Government employ, and those who gave a lien on their crops in exchange for rations. The reports show separate statistics for men, women, and children receiving rations; for the sick and well; and for gains and losses by birth and by death, subdivided by gender.

105.8. Rosters of employees in the States, some of whom were women, were maintained in the Commissioner's office in **station books of civilians on duty in the States, 1867–68** (2 vols., 2 in.), arranged by year, and a **station book of officers and civilians on duty at Bureau headquarters and in the States, 1869–70** (1 vol., 1 in.), arranged by year and thereunder by State with bureau headquarters listed first.

105.9. Among other records received in the Office of the Commissioner are **freedmen's marriage certificates, 1861–69** (2 ft.), arranged alphabetically by State in which the marriage was performed and thereunder generally alphabetically by initial letter of bridegroom's surname. Bureau personnel in the field were instructed to register legitimate marriages between freedmen when local authorities refused to do so. Some Bureau personnel also conducted marriage ceremonies. The series includes marriage licenses and monthly reports of marriages registered or performed. They are arranged alphabetically by State and thereunder most frequently alphabetically by the surname of the bridegroom. Information provided in the certificates varies. Mississippi and Tennessee personnel used forms that included name, residence, age, and color of each partner; color of each parent; previous cohabitation and number of children therefrom; and reason for separation from former partner.[1]

105.10. Letters requesting the return of confiscated and abandoned land and buildings are in the Land Division's **letters received, July 1865–August 1870** (5 ft.), arranged as they were entered into the **register of letters received, July 1865–August 1870** (1 vol., 2 in.). The register is arranged alphabetically by initial letter of surname of correspondent and thereunder chronologically. Some files contain detailed records about circumstances during and resulting from the war. **Monthly reports of abandoned and confiscated lands, 1865–70** (5 ft.), arranged alphabetically by State and thereunder chronologically, submitted to the Land Division by assistant commissioners show the former owner's name; location of property by county and boundaries; whether the property was abandoned or confiscated; acreage total and acreage cultivated, cleared, and wooded; the number and kinds of buildings; and the use made of the property by the bureau. **Registers of abandoned and confiscated lands and property, 1865–86**, give much the same information but also include the estimated value of the property, date of seizure (if confiscated), and date of restoration.

105.11. Also in the records of the Land Division are **orders issued by the assistant commissioners authorizing the restoration of property, 1865–68** (4 ft.), arranged alphabetically by initial letter of the property owner's surname. Each order includes the name of the former owner and the address and description of the property. About 20 percent of these property owners were women.

105.12. The Claim Division at the Bureau's headquarters tried to help black soldiers and sailors or their widows or other heirs file for and collect bounties, pensions, and pay arrearages. Among the records of the Division's Prosecution Branch are **letters received, January 1866–June 1872** (23 ft.), arranged as entered in its register. Included are many letters of widows and other female relatives of deceased black soldiers requesting

[1]See Elaine C. Everly, "Marriage Registers of Freedmen," *Prologue* 5 (Fall 1973): 150-54.

such assistance. Partially indexed **registers of claims for pensions, March 1866–October 1872** (2 vols., 4 in.), arranged alphabetically by initial letter of claimant's surname and thereunder chronologically, serve as a finding aid to case files of **claims for pensions, March 1866–February 1872** (3 ft.), arranged numerically. Many of the claimants were black widows.

105.13. Several series were filmed as *Records of the Education Division of the Bureau of Refugees, Freedmen, and Abandoned Lands, 1865–1871* (M803, 35 rolls). **Letters received, September 1866–January 1871** (4 ft.), arranged by time period, include many applications from women seeking teaching positions. Because teachers' salaries were often paid by benevolent societies, there are also letters from society officers regarding administrative procedures and the conditions in which teachers found themselves. **School reports from State superintendents, June 1865–December 1870** (14 ft.), arranged alphabetically by name of State, thereunder by type of report, and thereunder chronologically, contain narrative progress reports and statistical reports giving information about the race of teachers; the numbers, ages, and sex of pupils; and the financial support of the schools. Approximately half of the names on **lists of teachers employed by benevolent societies, n.d.** (1 vol., ¼ in.), arranged alphabetically by name of teacher, are those of women. Most of the lists are arranged alphabetically by initial letter of teachers' surnames and show the employing society and the State in which the person was teaching.

105.14. The records of the Bureau's Chief Quartermaster also contain records about women teachers. The **letters sent, October 1866–June 1872** (7 vols., 2 ft.), arranged chronologically, and **unregistered letters received relating to transportation for teachers and goods, October 1866–March 1869**, arranged chronologically, document the movement of teachers, most of whom were white women, to the South to educate freedmen.

105.15. Also among the records of the Bureau's Chief Quartermaster is a series of **unregistered letters received requesting transportation for refugees and freedmen, January–April 1867** (1 ft.), arranged chronologically. The series provides details about the work of the Washington headquarters office in sending former slaves, many of whom were women, to Northern cities. The requests for freedmen's services, often submitted on printed forms, give the name and address of the future employer and the names and ages of the members of his or her household.

105.16. Correspondence and other records maintained at State Bureau offices provide the greatest amount of information about the Bureau's activity as it related to women. Records of assistant commissioners for all Southern States and the District of Columbia have been microfilmed. Records of the District of Columbia and of Tennessee described below are examples of such records.

Records of the District of Columbia

105.17. In the correspondence series in *Records of the Assistant Commissioner for the District of Columbia, Bureau of Refugees, Freedmen, and Abandoned Lands, 1865–1872* (M1055, 21 rolls), for instance, the names of several women who participated in more than one freedmen's aid project appear frequently. They worked in industrial schools and diet kitchens and ministered to the destitute. They sought and received aid from local women's groups for bureau programs. The records also document the work of Josephine S. Griffing. As general agent of the National Freedmen's Relief Association of the District of Columbia, her activities were supported by private donations. On two occasions, however, she was employed by the Bureau. For several months in 1865 she was an assistant to the assistant commissioner for the District of Columbia, and in 1867 she served as an employment agent. Her extensive work in helping freedmen to find employment and to relocate in other cities as well as her relations with the Bureau staff are well documented in the records.

105.18. Correspondence consists of **letters sent, June 1865–December 1868** (5 vols., 1 ft.), arranged chronologicially with **name indexes, September 1865–November 1968** (4 vols., 4 in.), and **letters received, September 1865–August 1869** (7 ft.), arranged as entered in **registers** (5 vols., 1 ft.) and served by **name and subject indexes** (7 in.). **Special orders issued, June 1865–December 1868** (1 vol., 2 in.), arranged by year and thereunder chronologically, record personnel actions in the District of Columbia assistant commissioner's office and the restoration of abandoned property in parts of Virginia and Maryland to former owners, some of whom were women. The great majority of **monthly narrative reports of operations from visiting agents in the District of Columbia, August 1865–February 1866** (½ in.), arranged chronologically, are those of Josephine S. Griffing and other women associated with benevolent societies who were authorized by the assistant commissioner to determine the number of destitute freedmen and to recommend rations to be issued. Other records of the assistant commissioner for the District of Columbia include **monthly narrative reports of operations of industrial schools sponsored by the bureau, December 1865–December 1868** (1 in.), arranged chronologically, including those from Freedmen's Village in Alexandria, VA, and Howard Industrial School in Cambridge, MA. Many reports were prepared by women or discuss the work of women, and they provide statistics of attendance and numbers of garments produced as well as accounts of incidents and conditions. **Trimonthly and monthly reports of operations of employment offices, 1865–68** (4 in.), arranged chronologically, also document Josephine S. Griffing's work.

105.19. Monthly reports of persons and articles hired, 1866–67 (1 vol., 1 in.), arranged chronologically, are also among the assistant commissioner's records, showing that women served as school superintendents, nurses, matrons, cooks, clerks, and charwomen. The Special Relief Commission for relief of destitute persons in the District of Columbia was funded by a special appropriation of Congress. **Weekly reports on the operations of the Special Relief Commission, May 1866–October 1868** (1 ft.), arranged chronologically, include the names of a great many women. Each report contains a list of names and addresses of the destitute accompanied by information on race, cause of destitution, supplies needed, and the name of the agent recommending the relief. Several other similar series pertaining to the many women who came to Washington after the war are among the selected series copied on M1055. A small series of **miscellaneous reports, 1865–66**, includes a report on the laws of Southern States relating to freedmen. Those particularly affecting women include laws about marriage, cohabitation, intermarriage, and apprenticeship.

105.20. Records of the Bureau's local field offices, which operated below the State level, are generally not available on microfilm. Among records of the District of Columbia's local field office for Washington and Georgetown, for example, is the series **labor contracts, August 1865–March 1867** (8 in.), arranged numerically. The contracts are mainly on printed forms and detail the wage rates, types of work, and periods of service. Wives are sometimes mentioned in men's contracts and occasionally put their marks on the contracts. In **letters sent, July 1865–September 1868** (2 vols., 2 in.), **endorsements sent and received, August 1865–August 1868** (2 vols., 1 in.), **letters received, October 1866–August 1868** (1 ft.), and **unregistered letters received, August 1865 and February 1866–August 1868,** all arranged chronologically, there are communications about particular assignments to Josephine S. Griffing and other women, such as sending a child to a particular matron at an orphan asylum in another jurisdiction, searching for a girl en route to a job in another city, or reporting troubles at freedmen's institutions.[2]

Records of Tennessee

105.21. *Records of the Assistant Commissioner for the State of Tennessee, Bureau of Refugees, Freedmen, and Abandoned Lands, 1865–1869* (M999, 34 rolls), also contains records about Kentucky for the period from July 1865 to June 1866, when Kentucky was part of the Tennessee field operation. Although fewer women were employed by the Bureau in the former Confederate States than in headquarters and the District of Columbia, records from these field offices include many series that relate to women. For example, **narrative reports of operations and conditions,**

---

[2]For other RG 105 records that have been published on microfilm, see *Microfilm Resources for Research.* For a broad discussion of the various reports created by the Bureau at different administrative levels, see Elaine C. Everly, *Statistical Records of the Bureau of Refugees, Freedmen, and Abandoned Lands, Reference Information Paper No. 48* (Washington, DC: National Archives and Records Service, 1973).

February 1866–April 1869 (2 ft.), arranged chronologically, and **inspection reports, September 1865–March 1869** (5 in.), arranged chronologically, include accounts of economic and social conditions and the quality of education in Tennessee. Women who were accused of crimes or were its victims are mentioned in a few items in **reports of outrages, riots, and murders, April 1865–December 1868** (8 in.), arranged chronologically, from subordinate officers throughout Tennessee. Among **miscellaneous reports received, February 1866–October 1868** (2 in.), arranged by type of report, are reports relating to the conduct of agents and officers, including affidavits relating to an agent accused of rape.

105.22. Detailed information about teachers and their pupils is in records of the Bureau's State superintendents of education. For example, *Records of the Superintendent of Education for the State of Tennessee, Bureau of Refugees, Freedmen, and Abandoned Lands, 1865–1870* (M1000, 9 rolls), includes **registered letters received, September 1866–July 1870** (3 ft.), arranged in general chronological order, many from teachers seeking advice and support. **District superintendents' school reports, January 1866–June 1870** (10 in.), arranged chronologically, give for each school the usual teacher and pupil statistics but also report on literacy and status of the pupils before the war. **Agents' school reports, May 1867–June 1870** (6 in.), arranged chronologically, are on printed forms, but information in narrative form is provided in reply to 19 questions. In most cases, several schools are included in each report. A few of the questions deal with public sentiment and the need for further aid from Northern charities. **Teachers' monthly school reports, October 1866–June 1870** (3 ft.), arranged chronologically, give information on printed forms about teachers in Tennessee by race, showing that in addition to volunteers from the North, some freedmen and local whites became teachers in schools.

105.23. At the local level, series such as **records and affidavits relating to Memphis riots, May 1866** (6 in.), arranged by type of record, provide accounts of the incidents and lists of persons killed, wounded, or mistreated that show that many women were involved.

105.24. Similar records of other State superintendents of education are available as National Archives Microfilm Publications as follows: Alabama (M810), Arkansas (980), District of Columbia (M1056), Georgia (M799), Louisiana (M1026), Texas (M822), and Virginia (M1059).

Records of the Office of the Secretary of War

Record Group 107

107.1. The Office of the Secretary of War was established in 1789 to head the Department of War. The Secretary was directly responsible for most military matters. Gradually separate bureaus were established to discharge various functions until, by the middle of the 19th century, the Secretary's office was largely concerned with matters of policy and general administration. Under the National Security Act of 1947, the War Department became the Department of the Army within the National Military Establishment, which was renamed the Department of Defense in 1949. Most of the records about women in this record group relate to civilian War Department employees and women in the military services.

General Records of the
Office of the Secretary of War, 1791–1900

107.2. In the correspondence of the Secretary of War, 1791–1889, **letters received (main series), 1801–89** (387 ft.), consist of three chronological segments, each arranged differently: 1801–70, filmed as M221 (317 rolls); 1871–81; and 1882–89. The accompanying **registers of letters received, 1800–1889** (50 ft.), are also variously arranged. Those for 1800 to 1870 have been filmed as M22 (134 rolls). The contents of each registered letter is abstracted, and if a letter was referred by the Secretary's Office to another bureau, the name of the bureau is given. There are also **name and subject indexes to registers of letters received, 1861–89** (32 vols., 9 ft.), which serve some of the registers of the main series and a few other series of registers. Of these the first 14 volumes, covering 1861–70, have been filmed as M495 (14 rolls). In the indexes, subjects relating to women include "clerks," "nurses," and "women"; "Columbia Female College," "National Woman Suffrage Association," "Woman's Christian Temperance Union," "Women's Relief Association," and "Union Ladies"; and "Annie T. Wittenmyer," "Josephine S. Griffing," and "Mrs. E.M. Harris."

107.3. Letters received by the Secretary of War (unregistered series), 1789–1861 (27 ft.), are arranged largely by year and thereunder alphabetically by name or title of correspondent. They have been filmed as M222 (34 rolls). File R-Misc-1814 filmed on roll 13 is a "Receipt Roll of Women Employed in the Ordnance Department, September and October 1814." It contains the names of 39 women who were paid for "sewing cartridges."

107.4. Letters received ("irregular series"), 1861–66 (7 ft.), are arranged in two chronological subseries, March–December 1861 and July 1861–March 1866. They have been filmed as M492 (36 rolls). The letters are varied in source and subject matter. For example, filed under T-22 for 1863 in the second subseries (roll 35) are some letters forwarded by the Commissioner of the Office of Internal Revenue on May 10, 1863, reporting the pursuit and harassment of a "lady copyist" in the Treasury Department by James Cooke Richmond, an Army chaplain who had been asked to leave Washington. The evidence submitted in the case includes love letters, poems, and sketches.

107.5. Brief accounts of the lives of private citizens appear in **records concerning the conduct and loyalty of certain Union Army officers, War Department civilian employees, and U.S. citizens during the Civil War, 1861–72** (8 in.), arranged alphabetically by name or subject. About a third of this series consists of personal letters intercepted by the War Department. Some women's letters describe their difficulties in keeping families together and fed and express their opinions on the nature of the war. Some documents taken from Rose O'Neil Greenhow are in cipher. In the file for Gen. Judson Kilpatrick there are sworn statements given by Southern blacks about alleged immoral conduct of certain Union generals with women.

Records of the Appointment Division

107.6. The number of women's names in the chronologically arranged volumes of **registers of applications for civilian and military appointments, 1847–92** (16 vols., 3 ft.), increases toward the end of the 19th century. For each applicant the place of birth, position sought, names of references, and bureau to which the application was referred are given. Entries in the registers refer to **applications for Regular Army commissions and civilian appointments, 1847–87** (97 ft.), arranged alphabetically by surname of applicant. Women occasionally submitted calling cards or photographs with their letters of application and occasionally included descriptions of family circumstances. Letters of recommendation filed with many of the applications provide additional information.

107.7. After the Civil War, loyalty to the Union was no longer taken for granted. Applicants for Federal jobs were required to file oaths of allegiance, which appear in **case files of applicants for positions as clerks and copyists, January 1872–February 1875** (7 ft.), arranged by numbers assigned in the order in which the applications were received. A typical case file also includes the applicant's answers to examination questions, personal and job experience history, and a physician's statement about the applicant's health.

107.8. Applications for unclassified civilian positions in the War Department, 1898–1902 (14 ft.), are arranged by type of position requested. Many of the applications are on printed forms. About half of the applications under "Stenographers and typists" are from women. Under "Miscellaneous" (which constitutes over half the series) are more applications for clerical jobs, many from women.

107.9. Also on printed forms are **applications for positions as laborers and charwomen, 1901–03** (3 ft.), arranged in two subseries, one for laborers and one for charwomen. A good deal of personal information is provided, including whether the applicant used alcohol. A successful applicant's name was placed on a list of charwomen eligible to be called when the Department required their services.

107.10. There are eight series of registers of civilian employees of the War Department dated between 1863 and 1917, all of which include women's names. Each register was designed for a different purpose and provides various items of information about each employee. There is also a **list of civil service appointments in the War Department, 1883– 1904** (1 vol., ½ in.), arranged chronologically by date of appointment, which includes a few women's names.

107.11. Memorandums and statistical reports relating to civilian employees of the War Department, 1898–1908 (1 in.), arranged chronologically, include percentages of men and women employed in each War Department bureau, in Washington, DC, and in the position of "clerk."

Records of the Secretary of War and the Assistant Secretary of War, 1913–42

107.12. During this period, most of the Secretary's correspondence on important policies and major issues was filed with records of the Adjutant General's Office.

107.13. Correspondence concerning the relief of Americans in Europe, August 1914–January 1915 (3 in.), arranged alphabetically by name of correspondent, contains information about several women who were in Europe at the outbreak of World War I.

107.14. The **general correspondence, 1932–42** (83 ft.), arranged alphabetically by name or subject, includes copies of pre-1932 letters as well as original correspondence for the period 1932–42. Filed under "Citizens" (8 in.) are records regarding the work of Anita Phipps as War Department liaison with national women's organizations in 1927–29 and copies of letters sent to the wives of employees who were missing in the Philippines after the outbreak of World War II. Under "Nurse Corps" there are copies of 1899 letters from Elizabeth Mills (Mrs. Whitelaw) Reid about auxiliary nurses in the Spanish-American War and the Philippine Insurrection as well as Secretary Henry L. Stimson's correspondence regarding legislation concerning benefits for nurses. Under a separate file "Nurses" there are records about the appointment of married women to the Army Nurse Corps and of women as doctors and occupational therapists. "Women's Activities in Time of War" includes correspondence relating to legislation to provide benefits to women who served with the AEF in World War I, to establish a Women's Army Auxiliary Corps, and to authorize the appointment of women in the Medical Department of the Army. The file "Women's Relations" also includes records about Phipps' work and about the consideration in 1929 of the appointment of civilian women as aides.

107.15. The **appointment books of the Secretary of War, 1917–34** (24 vols., 3 ft.), show meetings with representatives of women's groups as diverse as the World War I Gold Star Mothers and the Women's Bureau of the Republican National Committee.

107.16. The **papers of Emmett J. Scott, special assistant to the Secretary of War, 1917–19** (10 in.), arranged in two alphabetical subseries, one by name and the other by subject, relate to the "interests of colored soldiers and citizens" during World War I. A file labeled "Reports on Conditions in Negro Training Camps" includes a few references to women.

107.17. A July 1918 proposal that women employees of the War Department wear uniforms is documented in item No. 135 of **memorandums and miscellaneous records of John B. Randolph, 1908–29** (1 vol., 1 in.), arranged and numbered chronologically. Randolph was assistant to the chief clerk at the time.

Records of the Office of the Secretary of War, 1940–47

107.18. During World War II the Office of the Secretary of War was chiefly concerned with major policy considerations. The few records relating to women, therefore, deal largely with proposed legislation for the war and postwar periods.

107.19. There is a file labeled "Nurses" in **formerly top secret correspondence of Secretary of War Henry L. Stimson ("safe file"), July 1940–September 1945** (7 ft.), arranged alphabetically by subject. Filed under "War Mobilization Office" is material on the Austin-Wadsworth Bill to conscript civilians, including women, for essential wartime service.

107.20. The **correspondence of Secretary of War Henry L. Stimson ("official file"), 1940–45** (5 ft.), is arranged alphabetically by subject or name of correspondent. A file "Army Emergency Relief Red Cross" includes 1943–44 correspondence with Lt. Gen. Brehon Somervell and Gen. Henry H. Arnold about the work of women's volunteer organizations under the leadership of Mrs. Somervell and Mrs. Arnold for relief and welfare of Army personnel and their dependents. Venereal disease and prostitution are mentioned in memorandums filed under "Morale (Special Services)," and under the heading "National Service Act" are correspondence and drafts of bills proposing that all able-bodied persons, including women, be required to work during wartime. A few items under "Universal Military Training" indicate women's strong support for that proposal.

107.21. The Secretary's **general correspondence, January 1943–January 1946** (111 ft.), arranged according to the War Department decimal classification scheme followed by project files at the end of the series, includes records about women in the following files: 291.3 "Women," 321 "Nurse Corps," and 334 "WASP Training Program." A "WAC Project" file, 1946–47, contains drafts of bills and proposals for the creation of a permanent body of women in the Army and procedures for transferring the women in the wartime WAC to a new permanent WAC.

107.22. From December 1941 to September 1945, Goldthwaite H. Dorr was adviser to the Secretary of War on manpower utilization. The **general correspondence of Special Assistant Goldthwaite Dorr, 1942–45** (9 ft.), arranged according to a numerical scheme, includes records relating to civilian women employees and to women in military service. The files cited below are examples.

107.23. In file 200.09-03 "Civilian personnel," there is a list of Army installations that gives the primary function of each and the numbers of men and women employed at each as of February 28, 1943. Memorandums written by Ann R. Taylor, Dorr's assistant, discuss the chief of training for women in the Civilian Personnel Division (CPD). During Representative Robert Ramspeck's investigation of Federal employment practices, Dorr's office prepared the War Department position papers to be presented before Ramspeck's Committee on the Civil Service. Among them is the draft of a statement to be presented by James P. Mitchell, Director, Industrial Personnel Division, Headquarters, Army Service Forces (ASF), which includes material about women in the civil service. Hearing transcripts are filed under 200.09-03b "Ramspeck Hearings, ASF," which includes material about training women, rates of employment, clerical and assembly line employees, and civilian personnel administration within the ASF. There is also a copy of the Committee's "Interim Report on Investigation of Civilian Employment, October 13, 1943." Records filed under 1000.01-05 "Walsh-Healey Act" document consideration of relaxing labor laws to permit the employment of 16-to-18-year-old girls. There are several headings for records about the labor supply on the West Coast as well as a general one, "Available Labor Supply." A high-level memorandum is filed under "Draft of Women for Military Service." In a file labeled "WAAC—Miss Taylor's" is a November 25, 1942, "Report on Suitability of Military Occupations for WAAC Auxiliaries" (19 pp.) prepared by the Classification and Enlistment Branch of the Adjutant General's Office. Other material relating to women is filed under "Joint Army-Navy Personnel Board."

107.24. File 200.04-29 "Report of the Commanding General of the AAF to the Secretary of War," marked "For public release January 4, 1944" (54 pp.), is in two sections. "Section Two: Building an Air Force" includes chapters entitled "Women Airforce Service Pilots," "Women's Army Corps," and "Aviation Medicine," which includes documents about Army nurses.

107.25. A few professional women are recognized for their war work in **letters recommending individuals for the Medal for Merit or the President's Certificate of Merit, July–September 1947** (5 in.).

107.26. Attached to the Office of the Assistant Secretary of War, the Office of the Civilian Aide to the Secretary of War was established in 1940 and in 1942 was made the official War Department liaison with the President's Committee on Fair Employment Practices. William H. Hastie was the first Civilian Aide. The **general correspondence ("Judge Hastie File"), 1940–48** (35 ft.), arranged alphabetically by subject, contains press releases, memorandums, letters, and telegrams relating to complaints of discrimination against black military personnel, women as well as men. Filed under "Women's Army Auxiliary Corps" (3 in.), "Women's Army Corps" (2 in.), and "Nurses (A.N.C.)" (3 in.) are records including letters from Mary McLeod Bethune and the directors of the women's Army services. **Formerly security classified reports and memorandums concerning race relations at home and overseas, August 1944–January 1946** (2 ft.), arranged by type of report, are periodic reports from various geographical locations. The racial incidents discussed involved some women among military personnel, civilian employees, and citizens of communities near Army installations.

Records of the Office of the Under Secretary of War, 1918–47

107.27. The Under Secretary of War was primarily responsible for materiel procurement, but his Office dealt with the women of the WAC and from military families. Filed under "Women" in the **general correspondence ("misc. and subject" file), December 1940–March 1943** (58 ft.), arranged alphabetically by subject, are charts for proposed training of WAAC personnel to replace enlisted men by occupation, correspondence about rights for Waacs, and legislation prohibiting an extended work day for Waacs and the hiring of women under 18 years of age. Under "Housing" there are records relating to facilities for War Department civilian employees and families of military personnel. There is a June 8, 1942, record of the number of men and women employees at each Government-owned ordnance and aircraft plant who needed dormitory accommodations.

107.28. In the **general correspondence of Under Secretary of War Robert Patterson, March 1943–November 1945** (120 ft.), arranged according to the War Department decimal classification scheme, files 291.3 and 292 contain a few records about women in industry. Under 211 "Nurses" (1 in.) there is correspondence with Members of Congress, the public, and other War Department officials relating to a 1945 bill to draft nurses.

107.29. Statistics relating to recruitment and other material about Army nurses in 1945 are filed under "Nurses" and "Medical Department" in **formerly security classified records of Julius H. Amberg, Special Assistant for congressional activities, 1941–45** (33 ft.), arranged alphabetically by subject or name of congressional committee. Records relating to the Ramspeck hearings include statistics showing the distribution and grades of men and women employed in each division of the War Department.

Records of the Planning Branch

107.30. The Planning Branch **general correspondence, 1920–34** (ca. 54 ft.), arranged alphabetically by subject, contains several files relating to women. Correspondence with Maude Wetmore, chair of the National League for Women's Service (NLWS) and with Mrs. Coffin Van Rensselaer, executive secretary of the National Civic Federation's Woman's Department is in file 555 "Labor, 1922–29." A report, dated September 28, 1923, in file 556 includes a chapter entitled "Creative Impulse in Industry" by Helen Marot, former executive secretary of the Women's Trade Union League. File 557 is labeled "Labor—Studies Prepared by: National League for Women's Service" (2 in.). Among these, a 1924 report to the Industrial Planning Division includes chapters on the labor market during World War I, the availability of women in the workforce, the character of labor required for specific industries where women might be employed, and statistics on numbers of men and women employed in various war industries during 1918. Another report, "Resume of Such Results of Survey of Woman Power of America (Sponsored by the National League for Women's Service) as Bear on Labor Mobilization for War Emergency," was submitted on February 27, 1931, by Van Rensselaer. In addition, in file 1432 a report by Col. J.D. Fife, March 26, 1923, on "American Labor in War" contains a chapter on "Women in War Work" and an April 20, 1922, memorandum from Fife discussing the possibility of drafting labor in wartime, possibly including women.

107.31. The **general correspondence, 1934–42** (78 ft.), arranged alphabetically by master subject headings and thereunder by the War Department decimal classification scheme. It contains additional material about women in the workforce before 1941 filed under 116.6 "Plan for Industrial Mobilization" and file 175.5 "Labor—Women" (1940–42).

Records of the
Office of the Assistant Secretary for Air

107.32. In 1926 Congress authorized an additional assistant secretary to foster military aeronautics. The first assistant secretary served until 1933. After that the position was vacant until Robert A. Lovett was appointed to it in 1941. The **general correspondence, 1926–33** (31 ft.), is arranged according to the War Department decimal classification scheme. In file 080 is documentation on the Betsy Ross Flying Corps, including newsletters and a report on the Corps. There is also some correspondence with Amelia Earhart, filed under her married name, Putnam, and records relating to the award of her Distinguished Service Cross. Filed under 201 is correspondence with another woman flyer, Lillian Gatlin.

107.33. A bill (HR 3358) introduced on September 30, 1943, to permit women pilots to become Army officers received strong support from Gen. Henry H. Arnold in a memorandum filed under 324.5 "WASP" in the **formerly security classified correspondence of Robert A. Lovett, 1940–45** (60 ft.), arranged according to the War Department decimal classification scheme. Copies of letters referring to Jacqueline Cochran and cross-references to documents relating to her in other series are filed under her name in file 095.

Records of the
Office of the Assistant Secretary of War, 1941–47

107.34. John J. McCloy was Assistant Secretary throughout World War II. Among his responsibilities was administration of Executive Order No. 9066, which authorized the Secretary of War to designate military areas from which any and all persons could be excluded. Under a specific exclusion order, 110,000 West Coast Japanese Americans were moved into relocation camps. The **formerly security classified correspondence of John J. McCloy, 1941–45** (21 ft.), is arranged according to the War Department decimal classification scheme. In file 014.311 are letters from women protesting the relocation of the Japanese Americans. In the same file are exclusion orders, work permits for excludees, and investigative reports that name individual men and women.

107.35. The **general correspondence of John J. McCloy, 1941–45** (28 ft.), also arranged according to the War Department decimal classification scheme, contains in file 021 "Personal Affairs Division (Red Cross-A.E.R. Relations)" memorandums, reports, and opinions about avoiding duplication of relief and welfare activities. Another file under 021 concerns the Office of Dependency Benefits. Under 292 "Families of Enlisted Men and Officers" there is correspondence about amendments to the Servicemen's Dependents' Allowance Act of 1942 and the Sailors' Civil Relief Act of 1940, transportation of dependents in wartime, war brides, birth control, policy regarding families at duty stations, and notifying next of kin of casualties. In file 334 there is a memorandum of a meeting of the Advisory Council to the Women's Interest Section, which was originally set up in the Bureau of Public Relations to provide information about living conditions to soldiers' wives and mothers. Records in file 021 (4 in.) about black and Japanese-American Wacs and in file

211 about black and Japanese-American nurses document charges of discrimination in both cases. In the 211 file there are letters from Mary McLeod Bethune, Representative Edith Nourse Rogers, and Eleanor Roosevelt. Letters from women in file 201 "Gen. J.L. DeWitt" support his position favoring Japanese relocation.

Records of the Civilian Personnel Division

107.36. Records of the Civilian Personnel Division, known before 1919 as the Appointments Division, document broad policies of personnel administration. Its **general correspondence, 1913–40** (44 ft.), contains several files that relate specifically to women. Part of file 150 relating to rules for employees' conduct in offices pertains to women's complaints about the smoking of male employees. File 392 (2 in.) includes discrimination complaints, letters of inquiry, and lists of women employees, some of whom held responsible positions. File 392.1 concerns the employment of married women and the reduction in force after World War I.

107.37. Records of the Employee Relations Branch, 1941–44 (4 ft.), are arranged alphabetically by subject. Among the subject headings under which there are records about women employees are the following: "Absenteeism," "Child Care," "Government Girl Campaign," "Housing," and "Recreation."

107.38. Mrs. Warwick B. Hobart was adviser to the Civilian Personnel Division on the employment of women and in 1945 was made the chief of its Placement Branch. **Records of the Placement Branch, 1941–45** (4 ft.), arranged alphabetically by subject, document her work. There are files for various war plants and arsenals. Among subject headings for records relating to women are: "Huntsville, Arsenal, Alabama"; "Labor—Minors and Women in Hawaii"; "Placement of Women," "Pregnant Women, Employment of"; "Training"; "Utilization of Women, Shown in Inspection Reports"; "Women (General—Women's Health Maintenance)"; "Women—Jobs for Women"; and "Women—War Department."

107.39. Registers of appointments and changes in status of civilian employees of the War Department,1914–34 (13 vols., 2 ft.), arranged chronologically, documents the surge in the employment of women during World War I and the postwar decline in the number of women employees.

Records of the Bureau of Public Relations

107.40. The Bureau of Public Relations (BPR) was established in the Office of the Secretary in February 1941. The BPR News Division **correspondence relating to motion pictures, 1941–45** (18 ft.), deals largely with the review of films and scripts for accuracy of military information and clearance for security purposes. Scripts in the series that relate to women are "Cadet Girl," "Bride by Mistake," "Army Wives," "Janie,"

"In the Meantime, Darling," "Maisie Goes to Reno," "Marriage is a Private Affair," "Reveille with Beverly," "Six Girls and a Pilot," "Three Little Sisters," and "A WAVE, a WAC, and a Marine."

107.41. Motion picture film released to the newsreel room, 1942–46 (191 reels), arranged numerically, includes footage documenting American military activity in all theaters of operation. Wacs, Army nurses, and women Red Cross workers are shown in a few of them. Descriptions of the contents of each reel are available at the National Archives.

107.42. The News Division records also include **radio scripts, 1942–45** (19 ft.), for programs sponsored by the Radio Branch, such as "WAC on Parade," January–April 1945; "Army Hour," March 1942–October 1945; "Command Performance," March–December 1942); "Tokyo Calling" (later called "Pacific Serenade"), June–October 1945; and "Army Service Forces Presents," May 1943–September 1944.

107.43. Recordings of "The Hour of the Victory Corps" and "The Victory Hour," radio series designed to enlist high school students in the war effort, are filed with **radio broadcast recordings, 1942–43** (37 items). Included are speeches by several prominent persons, such as Arlene Francis, on the role of women workers in the war effort. Some women workers are also interviewed.

107.44. The Industrial Services Division of the BPR was responsible for publicity designed to improve labor morale, provide work incentives, and discourage absenteeism in war plants. **Correspondence concerning industrial incentives programs, 1943–45** (9 ft.), arranged alphabetically by subject, includes two files that relate to women. Filed under the heading "Picatinny Arsenal Recruitment" are newspaper clippings, memorandums, photographs, and a poster pertaining to a drive to recruit 1,000 women workers. Because the nearest available labor source was the Harlem district of New York City, much of the material is about black women. There are photographs of black women workers filed under "Quartermaster Corps."

War Department Collection of Confederate Records

Record Group 109

109.1. The War Department Collection of Confederate Records consists of the records of the Confederate States of America acquired by capture or surrender at the close of the Civil War or acquired later by donation or purchase. On July 21, 1865, the Secretary of War established a unit in the Adjutant General's Office for the collection, preservation, and publication of the "rebel archives." The records were used to protect the Federal Government against claims arising from the war, to establish pension claims, and to be made available for historical purposes. Certain Federal records relating to Confederate soldiers were maintained with the Confederate records and in part interfiled with them. Since most of the records are those of the Confederate War Department, most document the activities of women who in some way served or were involved with the Confederate Army. There are very few records about women in pursuits not related to military activities.

109.2. Among the official records of the Confederacy are a few papers of individual officers, including the **Jefferson Davis papers, 1861–65** (7 in.), arranged alphabetically by name of correspondent and accompanied by a name and subject index. The papers include a number of offers of help from Southern women, records of the arrests of a few of them, and a few papers of Mrs. Jefferson Davis.

109.3. Many of the series described below are parts of the **collected record books of various executive, legislative, and judicial offices, 1860–65** (2,750 vols., 300 ft.), for which there is a published *Index of Books in the Confederate Archives Division, Adjutant General's Office* compiled by the U.S. Adjutant General's Office. The volumes are arranged numerically by chapter number according to a rough approximation of provenance and thereunder by volume number. The chapter and volume numbers are useful in identifying and locating the records and are cited in this guide when bound volumes are described.

Records of the Secretary of War

109.4. The Secretary's **letters received, February 1861–April 1865** (48 ft.), filmed as M437 (151 rolls), are arranged numerically by number assigned on date of receipt until 1862 and thereafter by year and thereunder alphabetically by initial letter of the name of correspondent. There is an **index** (40 ft.), filmed as M409 (34 rolls) and arranged alphabetically by correspondent, and a companion series of **letters sent, 1861–65** (19 vols., 5 ft.; ch. IX, vols. 1, 2, 2½, 3, 4, and 6–19) with an index in each volume, filmed as M522 (10 rolls). Women who corresponded with the Secretary were principally concerned about exemptions from military service for male relatives and friends and about joining husbands who had deserted to Canada or who were living in Union territory. There are also a few letters from Confederate spies Belle Boyd and Rose O'Neal Greenhow.

109.5. In the **record of applications for appointment in the Army, 1861** (1 vol., 1 in.; ch. IX, vol. 89), arranged alphabetically, there are records for Lt. Harry T. Buford, whose real name was either Loreta Velazquez or Laurretta P. Williams, a woman who disguised herself as a man to serve in the Army, as well as for women who applied for positions as clerks. **War Department payrolls, July 1862–March 1865** (2 vols.,

2 in.; ch. IX, vols. 87–88), arranged by month and thereunder by office, bureau, or department, show that female clerks were hired in almost every bureau and department of the Confederate War Department. **Requests for salary funds and lists of persons to be paid, 1861–65** (1 in.; ch. IX, vol. 98), include for each employee the period of service and the amount paid.

109.6. **Records of passports issued, 1862–64** (90 vols., 8 ft.; ch. IX, vols. 101–109, 111–129, 131–137½, 139, 140, 140A, 140B, 140C, 141–151½, 152–173, 173½, 174, 174½–181½, 182, 182½, 183, and 183½), were created at various points within the Confederate lines but were accumulated in rough chronological order in the records of the Department of Richmond, a Confederate military command. Several volumes are labeled "Ladies." Each entry shows the date of issue and the name, destination, and sometimes the purpose of the journey of the person to whom the passport was issued.

Records of the Adjutant and Inspector General's Office

109.7. **Letters received, 1861–65** (26 ft.), arranged by year, thereunder alphabetically by writer's name, and thereunder numerically, are accompanied by an **index to letters received, 1861–65, by the Adjutant and Inspector General's Office and the Quartermaster General's Office, n.d.** (32 ft.), filmed as M410 (41 rolls). The index contains references to the names of many women, including Buford/Velazquez/Williams.

109.8. Reports on military organizations, posts, hospitals, prisons, and other offices and installations were filed with **inspection reports, 1863–65** (5 ft.), filmed as M935 (18 rolls), and arranged according to an alpha-numeric scheme. An incident in which a Mrs. A. Ackland was suspected of transporting cotton from her Mississippi plantation to Northern sympathizers in New Orleans is described in file 15-H-19. Among the institutions inspected were several hospitals in Richmond. Inspectors commented briefly on the responsiilities of matrons for diet and for supervising laundry and kitchen work done by soldiers or male employees. One woman named Sally Tompkins is especially praised for her work at Robertson Hospital.

109.9. Confederate War Department policies relating to pay and responsibilities for matrons, laundresses, female nurses, and other hospital attendants are set forth in **general orders, 1861–65** (9 vols., 2 ft.; ch. I, vols. 1, 2, 2A, 3–5, 202, 203, and 215½), arranged by year and thereunder numerically. All nonduplicated orders for 1861–65 have been filmed as M901 (1 roll).

Records of the Medical Department

109.10. Among the records of the Surgeon General's Office, **hospital muster rolls, 1861–65** (10 ft.), arranged by State and thereunder by hospital name or location, list the names of stewards, wardmasters, cooks, nurses, and detached soldiers serving at hospital as well as patients, and show the duties and wages of each employee, many of whom were women. Another series of **hospital rolls, 1861–65** (10 ft.), arranged by location and hospital name, consists of the clothing receipt rolls and payrolls of attendants and patients, which also indicate that women were employed in Confederate hospitals.

109.11. In addition to the hospital records maintained in the Surgeon General's Office, there are records of many separate hospitals throughout the Confederacy. Examples of series that contain records about women in Richmond hospitals are: **morning reports of patients and attendants, General Hospital No. 21, 1861–63** (3 vols., 2 in.; ch. VI, vols. 120, 327, and 331); **record book, General Hospital No. 24, 1862–65** (1 vol., 1 in.; ch. VI, vol. 122); **lists of employees, Chimborazo Hospital No. 2, 1863–65** (1 vol., 1 in.; ch. VI, vol. 85); **letters, orders and circulars issued and received, Jackson Hospital, 1863–66** (3 vols., 4 in.; ch. VI, vols. 376, 406, and 407); **lists of employees, Divisions No. 1–4, 1863–64** (1 vol., 1 in.; ch. VI, vol. 187), which are arranged by type of employee with "female" as one type; and **register of patients and lists of employees, Smallpox Hospital, 1862–64** (1 vol. 1 in.; ch. VI, vol. 247). Most of these series are arranged alphabetically by personal name. Among records of other hospitals in Virginia are **weekly reports of patients and attendants, General Hospitals No. 1–3, Camp Nicholls, Ladies Relief, Pratt and Way Hospitals, at Lynchburg, 1862–65** (1 vol., 2 in.; ch. VI, vol. 724), arranged by hospital, thereunder chronologically, and thereunder by State of patient's military organization.

Records of the Ordnance Department

109.12. Women were employed extensively in ordnance establishments, and their work is documented among records of ordnance establishments at Macon, GA. **Letters sent, Superintendent of Laboratories, May 1862–April 1864** (2 vols., 3 in.; ch. IV, fols. 24 and 28), include a few items relating to the use of slave women. Enclosed in one letter is a newspaper clipping describing a fire at the Jackson, MS, ordnance laboratory, where 19 of the 21 women employees were killed. A **time book, Richmond Arsenal, January 1863–April 1865** (1 vol., 2 in.; ch. IV, vol. 99), contains information about women employed in its various shops.

Records of the Quartermaster Department

109.13. Many Confederate women had business transactions with the Confederate Army. Name indexes in some volumes of **letters and telegrams sent, March 1861–January 1865** (20 vols., 5 ft.; ch. V, vols.

13–31 and 42), arranged chronologically within each volume and filmed as M900 (8 rolls), refer to a number of women who had donated supplies or whose property had been confiscated. Other letters deal with back pay for a widow's deceased husband, suspicious activities, and the services of slaves.

109.14. Lists of persons employed by the Quartermaster Department are found in civilian **payrolls, 1861–65** (30 ft.), and **slave payrolls, 1861–65** (8 ft.), both arranged numerically. The **index to slave and other payrolls, 1861–65** (34 ft.), includes entries for free persons employed and for the slaveowners who signed the payrolls; women's names appear in both categories. The number of women employed was greatest in urban areas like Richmond, VA, and Montgomery, AL, where women worked in arsenals and made clothing for members of the Confederate armed forces.

Records of Confederate Military Commands

109.15. Confederate women who suffered hardships due to the war petitioned their government for relief. In a small series of **orders and circulars, Gen. Nathan B. Forrest's Cavalry, 1853–65** (3 in.), Army and Department of Tennessee, is a letter signed by 10 women who complained that competing with the government for available provisions put them at a disadvantage in providing for their children (40 altogether).

109.16. Problems with local women in Southern towns that were suddenly flooded with soldiers as Confederate and Union Armies moved through or occupied them are documented in the special orders of various Confederate commands. For example, the **orders and circulars, Trans-Mississippi Department, 1862–65** (1 ft.), include a copy of Union Gen. Benjamin F. Butler's order to Union troops concerning "ladies of New Orleans" and the Confederate response ordering Southern troops to defend "the chastity of your wives, your mothers, your sisters, your sweethearts. . . ."

Records of the Department of the Treasury and Congress

109.17. In Treasury records there is a **register of applications for office, ca. 1862** (1 vol., 1 in.; ch. X, vol. 156), arranged alphabetically by initial letter of applicant's name, that includes an occasional reference to a woman's request for a position as "housekeeper" or simply for employment. More numerous are the women's names that appear in the index in the back of a **register of applications for clerkships in the Treasury Department, 1861–65** (1 in.), arranged numerically.

109.18. Among **miscellaneous records of the Treasury, 1861–65** (24 ft.), there are individual tax returns including some for women confectioners and liquor dealers.

109.19. Among the Confederate **congressional bills and resolutions, 1862–65** (7 ft.), arranged chronologically, is a bill relating to pay and allowances for female employees of the Confederate government.

Miscellaneous Records of the Confederate Government

109.20. Women's applications for employment appear in **Confederate papers relating to citizens and business firms, 1861–65** (1,240 ft.), filmed as M346 (1,158 rolls). Filed under women's names are vouchers, receipted bills for articles purchased or rented by the government, and papers relating to claims for damages. Many other files relate to Southern women who rented slaves, buildings, farm equipment, and animals to the Confederate Army and sold crops, domestic products, and farm animals as well. Information relating to women can also be found in files for men. For example, the file of S.B. Lamar contains a reference to a "Georgia Ladies gunboat or floating battery."

109.21. The series, **manuscripts, 1861–65** (28 ft.), is a collection of papers, mainly Confederate but containing some Union materials, brought together after the papers were in U.S. War Department hands. In the **index to manuscripts, n.d.** (2 ft.), terms such as "clothing bureau, payroll, sempstresses," "hired," and "employees" refer to a few documents about Southern women.

109.22. **Intercepted letters, 1861–65** (3 in.), are personal letters seized by the Confederate government for possible intelligence information and include several letters for one woman.

Records of the
U.S. War Department Relating to Confederates

109.23. The War Department prepared for Confederate soldiers **"carded" military service records**, 1861–65 (5,474 ft.), which have been filmed in several National Archives Microfilm Publications, arranged mainly by State. Few women's names can be expected to appear among them, but in the **consolidated general index** (360 ft.), filmed as M253 (535 rolls), there is an entry for a Mrs. S.M. Blaylock, whose service record with the 26th North Carolina Infantry contains the following information: "This lady, dressed in men's clothes, volueteered, received her bounty, and for two weeks did all the duties of a soldier before she was found out, but her husband being discharged, she disclosed the fact, returned the bounty, and was immediately discharged April 20, 1862."

109.24. *Unfiled Papers and Slips Belonging in Confederate Compiled Service Records* (M347, 442 rolls), arranged alphabetically, includes letters of Rose O'Neal Greenhow on roll 156.

109.25. Records of Confederate prisoners of war in Union prisons have been filmed as *Selected Records of the War Department Relating to Prisoners of War, 1861–65* (M598, 145 rolls). Included on roll 96 is a **register of prisoners, Fort McHenry, MD, 1861–62** (1 in.), on which the name of one woman appears. Careful examination of the registers of other prisons may also reveal names of women prisoners. An entry in a prison register usually includes prisoner's name, date of confinement and by whose order, rank and organization for soldiers, residence, and disposition.

109.26. Personal letters to prisoners at Point Lookout, MD, 1865 (1 ft.), consist of letters that were undeliverable at the end of the war and never reached the addressees who had been set free from prison. Many were written by women and describe events and conditions at home.

109.27. A **general information index, n.d.** (2 ft.), was evidently compiled as searches were made in Confederate records by War Department staff in response to specific questions, so it must not be regarded as complete. "Female lieutenant" is the entry for records about Lt. Harry T. Buford, alias Loreta Velazquez, alias Laurretta P. Williams. An entry for "Richmond" refers to a report by a Board of Inquiry about an explosion allegedly caused by the carelessnesss of a woman employee killed in the blast. An entry for "Southern mothers" refers to Memphis women's charitable organizations for the care of sick and wounded Confederate soldiers. Under "Women" are references to "ladies" employed in the Ordnance Department, the Surgeon General's Office, and the Office of the Quartermaster General.

109.28. Records of Union provost marshals who protected freedmen and kept Southern whites under surveillance as Union armies occupied Southern territory were accumulated into one large file, the **"Union Provost Marshal Citizens File," 1861–67** (479 ft.). Records relating to one person are filed alphabetically by name of person in the "single-name file," which has been filmed as M345 (300 rolls). Records relating to more than one person are filed numerically in the "two-or-more-name file," which has been filmed as M416 (94 rolls) with an incomplete subject index on roll 1. If a name in the single-name file appears in the two-or-more file, a cross-reference was entered in the single-name file.

109.29. Among the transcripts of examinations, oaths of loyalty, transportation permits, claims, orders, and correspondence in the single-name file is a copy of an order regarding the imprisonment of Belle Boyd (M345, roll 32), In the same file (roll 218) are a number of reports, statements, and other records relating to Mary Ann Pitman or Pittman, alias "Lt. Rawley," alias "Mary Hays." In the index to the two-or-more name file (M416, roll 1) there are references to "Nashville—roll of citizen prisoners, male and female."

Records of the Provost Marshal General's Bureau (Civil War)

Record Group 110

110.1. The Provost Marshal General's Bureau was created by an act of March 3, 1863, to be headed by the Provost Marshal General and to be responsible for enrolling, recruiting, and drafting men for military service and detecting and arresting deserters. These functions were principally carried out by acting provost marshals in State and district offices. The Bureau and Office of the Provost Marshal were discontinued on August 20, 1866.

110.2. Correspondence with women seeking exemptions or special consideration for husbands, sons, or brothers is found in central office records in **press copies of letters sent, November 1863–August 1866** (17 vols., 2 ft.), arranged chronologically with name indexes in most volumes, and in **letters received, 1863–65** (86 ft.), arranged alphabetically by writers' names and thereunder by register number.

110.3. Correspondence, reports, appointments, and other records relating to individual scouts, spies, and detectives, 1862–66 (6 ft.), arranged alphabetically by surname of writer, include records relating to women employed by the U.S. Government in intelligence work, including Pauline Cushman. An alphabetical **list of scouts, guides, spies, and detectives showing stations to which assigned, n.d.** (1 vol., 1 in.), also contains the names of women.

110.4. Among financial records of the central office a **register of accounts forwarded to the Provost Marshal General's Office and other offices for payment, 1864–65** (1 vol., ½ in.), shows accounts in women's names for officers' lodging and rental of space for recruiting offices. There are similar records in a **register of contracts made in various States for the volunteer recruiting service, 1862–65** (1 vol., 1 in.).

110.5. Among **applications for passes to travel to and from rebel States, 1862–63** (7 in.), arranged alphabetically by name of applicant, are a number submitted by women.

110.6. A **list of employees in the Deserters' Branch, May 1864–October 1866** (1 vol., ½ in.), shows that women took jobs in Bureau offices during the Civil War. Several series of records relating to employees of the Disbursing Branch also include records about women.

Records of the Office of the Chief Signal Officer

Record Group 111

111.1. War Department General Order 18 of July 9, 1860, added to the Army's Staff a Signal Officer who was to establish a signal system for the Union Army. The Signal Corps became responsible for military telegraph service, meteorological observation, and early aeronautics. The War Department library was also under the Chief Signal Officer from 1894 to 1904, during which time the Signal Corps acquired photographs and negatives of historical value. This laid the basis for the Corp's responsiblity for ground photography (still and motion pictures) during World War I and later. In 1925 the Signal Corps was made responsible for the pictorial publicity work of the Army. It retained its communications function during World War I and engaged in greatly expanded activities during World War II. In 1964 the Chief Signal Officer became the Chief of Communications—Electronics. The principal Signal Corps records relating to women are in a few of its communications records and in its audiovisual records.

Textual Records

111.2. Intercepted letters, 1864–65 (2 in.), were written by private persons and apparently intercepted by the Union Army and examined either for possible hidden cipher code messages or for information on conditions behind the Confederate lines. More than half of the letters were written by soldiers to wives, sisters, and mothers. Others are private letters to soldiers, many from women.

111.3. Entries under "Telephone operators" in the **name and subject index, 1897–1917** (122 ft.), to the **general correspondence, 1889–1917** (540 ft.), arranged numerically within chronological segments, document the expanded use of women as telephone operators around the beginning of World War I. **General correspondence, 1917–40** (799 ft.), arranged according to the War Department decimal classification scheme, includes records about women telephone operators overseas under 231.3 "Telephone operators," and contains information about their uniforms, salaries, qualifications, performance, and demobilization, as well as photographs and biographical information about many of them. Under the same decimal classification there is a 1926 War Plans and Training Division "Study of the Service of Women Telephone Switchboard Operators of the A.E.F." (37 pages), which includes photographs, rosters, transcripts of cables, and letters about Gen. John J. Pershing's requests for women overseas. There is also information about the rules and regulations relating to and the organization of units of female switchboard operators and conclusions regarding the experience. Other 231.3

files deal with civilian clerical workers, many of whom were women. Appointment and pay records for charwomen are in file 231.4. Army nurses serving between World War I and World War II are mentioned in file 210 "Personnel."

111.4. Among the **annual reports of the Chief Signal Officer, 1898–1916, 1918–19** (21 vols., 1 ft.), arranged chronologically, the one for 1918–19 includes information about the number of women employed as operators and a chapter about their work, primarily their service with the American Expeditionary Force (AEF) in France.

Audiovisual Records: Still Pictures

111.5. In 1874–75 the War Department purchased a collection of the work of Civil War photographer Mathew B. Brady to form the **photographic prints and negatives of the Brady collection, 1861–70** (111-B, 111-BA, 111-BZ, 8,737 items), arranged numerically. The largest group of these (111-B) were filmed as T252 (4 rolls). They include views of the Civil War and portraits of eminent persons, among them Clara Barton, Confederate spy Belle Boyd, Union spy Pauline Cushman, and Dr. Mary E. Walker. Portraits of wives and daughters of prominent men include those of Mary Todd Lincoln and Mrs. Robert E. Lee, and the families of Ulysses S. Grant, George A. Custer, and other generals. In addition, women appear in some military camp scenes as domestics or visitors. A name and subject card index is available; pictures of women are listed under headings such as "camp scene," "contraband [ex-slave] school," "hospital," and "officers, groups of, with ladies," or "officer's family on visit to quarters."

111.6. A reference print file, arranged alphabetically by subject, was established by the National Archives staff to facilitate research. "Portraits" are arranged alphabetically by sitter in one section of this file, but many women's pictures are also filed in a section on "Women," which includes Brady photographs. Other headings under which pictures of women are found include "Blacks," "Houses," "Medical care and services," and "Ships." A card index to the numerically arranged prints and negatives contains an entry for "Persons," which includes all portraits and a reference to the execution of Mary Surratt. "Personnel—women," "Women," and "Women—groups" are sections of the finding aids for Brady photographs. Entries under "Women—activities" refer to works by photographers other than Brady. Additional useful headings in the card file are "Civilians—female," "Medical," and "Negro activities."

111.7. The Signal Corps **historical file of photographs, 1860–1954** (111-SC, 500,000 items), is arranged numerically in the World War II section and by broad subject for the World War II–Korean war period. Cards and lists for "Western and frontier subjects" and for "Indian Wars" include references to pioneer and Indian women and wives of

Mathew Brady or one of his associates photographed this unidentified woman at a Civil War encampment. 111-B-5295.

soldiers. This series is especially rich for the World War I period. The following headings from a "Signal Corps American Subject List (World War I)" document the variety of women's activities on the home front during that war:

American Red Cross

Army Nurse Corps [modeling uniforms]

Ceremonies
    Patriotic—Public Gatherings
    Parades

Demobilization—Arrivals Home

Disarmament Conference
    President and Mrs. Harding

Gold Star Mothers

Industries of War
    Farm Products
    Women

Liberty Bonds, Parades

Recruiting
    Recruiting Service—Draft Drawings

War Relief

War Camp Community Service
  American Girls Aid (housing in Washington)
  YMCA
  DAR
  Liberty Theaters
  Camp Fire Girls

Women's Activities
  Farming ["Farmerettes" in training]
  Food Conservation
  Nurses
  In Industry
    Aeronautics
    Munitions
    Uniforms
    Miscellaneous
  In Public Service [general]
    Laundrying [sic]
    Motor Corps
    Policing
  In Public Service
    Telephone Operators
    Miscellaneous

Public Buildings
  Capitol Hqtrs., S.C. Arcade Building
  Miscellaneous

The historical file also documents the experience of American women serving overseas with the AEF. There are several ways to gain access to this extensive collection of prints and negatives (which includes over 75,000 items for 1917–21 alone). A *Catalogue of Official A.E.F. Photographs* (War Department Document No. 903; Washington, DC: Government Printing Office, 1919), 577 pp., provides an alphabetical "Index by Person" and an index of major subjects. Some helpful subject headings for overseas views are:

American Red Cross
  Canteens, Stations, Outposts
  Christmas Boxes and Gifts
  First Aid
  Relief Work
  Warehouses
  Miscellaneous Activities
  Executive
  Headquarters
  Groups and Committees

Medical Department
  Base Hospitals
  Camp Hospitals
  Evacuation Hospitals
  Field Hospitals

War Relief
    Salvation Army
    YWCA

Women's Activities

111.8. "A List of U.S. Official Photographs Showing American Women with A.E.F.," prepared by the Signal Corps, contains brief captions and file numbers for 102 photographs, many of which also appear in the published catalog, highlighting some postwar activities in Europe. A few other women are in photographs listed for Siberia. A card index to the AEF photographs also contains brief captions and file numbers under numerous subject headings and names of persons and places. Photographs listed in the published catalog under a particular heading do not always appear under the same heading in the card catalog, making it worthwhile to consult both finding aids in the search for pictures of women during and after the war.

111.9. Subjects in the card catalog for the AEF that are of interest for overseas activities include:

Actors and actresses

Arts and artists

Army Nurse Corps

Barracks
    Women

Bedding
    Beds and bedding—T. of O.[theater of operation facilities for telephone operators]

Buglers

Ceremonies
    Military weddings—T. of O.

Cigars and cigarettes

Clerks—T. of O.
    Female

Convalescents
    Soldiers—T. of O.

Dances

Doctors

Entertainment

Indians

Kitchens
    Welfare—T. of O.

Libraries

Magazines

Nurses—American
  Nurses' quarters
  Nurses' uniforms

Operators
  Operators—telephone—female

Organizations
  Women's War Relief Corps, ARC
  American Committee on French Wounded
  American Volunteer Motor Ambulance Organization in
  France
  Miscellaneous

Red Cross
  Nurses

Salvation Army

Secretaries

Signal Corps
  Telephone
    France
    Germany

Telephones
  Operators—female—T. of O.

Victims of war

Weddings, military T. of O.

Women's Activities
  YMCA—T. of O.
  ARC—T. of O.
  Salvation Army
  Nurses—T. of O.
  QMC [Quartermaster Corps]—T. of O.
  Signal Corps—T. of O. [telephone operators]
  Miscellaneous—T. of O.
  Women—well-known [Americans]
    Belgium
    England
    France
    Italy
    T. of O.

YMCA activities
  T. of O.
  Personnel
    France
    Germany

111.10. While he was Chief Signal Officer, Adolphus W. Greeley placed particular emphasis on creating a photographic record of the corps. In the **Adolphus W. Greely Collection of photographs, 1882–1906**   109

(111-AG, 2,000 items), those taken in 1902 during the construction of military cable and telegraph lines in Alaska and a survey of the Valdez, Copper River, and Yukon Railroad Company show many white and Indian women and their families.

111.11. A few photographs of women appear in **photograph albums of maneuvers of the 1st, 2d, 3d, and 4th Armies, 1935–44** (111-SCA, vols. 6630–6704), arranged by number of Army and thereunder by year and subject. A woman war correspondent is shown at a microphone under "Broadcasting" in 1st Army photographs, 1940. In 3d Army 1943 photographs are pictures of nurses dressed in field attire, a nurse in a convalescent tent in a "Life of the Soldier" sequence, and a woman installing a radio in a bomber at Barksdale Field, LA, under "Aviation." Other headings for women's photographs are "Red Cross," "Medical Department: Nurses," and "Medical." Photographs of women for the World War II and Korean war periods appear in the previous 6,628 volumes of this series of prints.

111.12. Photographs of Wacs in Italy, England, and North Africa appear in **scrapbooks of illustrated newspaper clippings of World War II military activities, 1943–44** (111-NC, 17 vols., 14 ft.), arranged by month and year. Also included are a few pictures of women entertainers and civilian women hired as clerks, warehouse workers, and employees of the Aircraft Warning Service.

Audiovisual Records: Motion Pictures

111.13. During World War I Signal Corps cameramen were assigned to military units and volunteer organizations. Among **historical films, 1914–40** (600 items) are many dealing with women. "Patriotic Activities," 1918 (2 reels), includes footage of women in war gardens, activities at the Women's National Service Training Camp, and the construction of Government hotels for women war workers in Washington, DC. "Liberty Loan Drives" (5 reels) features actresses Mary Pickford, Marie Dressler, and Eloise Mann. Relief workers and personnel of the YMCA, Red Cross, and Salvation Army, many of whom were women, are shown in a number of films in **miscellaneous films, 1917–42** (700 items), a series of AEF unit histories. The American Women's Hospital Unit is featured in "Charitable Hospital and Ambulance Units in the AEF, 1918–19." Both series are described in *List of World War I Signal Corps Films, Special List 14* (Washington, DC: National Archives, 1957), which is available from NEPS, National Archives and Records Administration, Washington, DC 20408.

111.14. Among War Department films relating to women during World War II are the following from the Signal Corps **miscellaneous series:**

111-M-653 -   "Women Ambulance Drivers," 1941, 5 minutes, silent, b&w, 35 mm.

111-M-801 -   "Hail and Farewell," 1943, 7 minutes, sound, b&w, 35 mm.

111-M-933 -   "Calling All Dietitians," 1943, 10 minutes, sound, b&w, 35 mm.

111-M-958 -   "It's Your War, Too," 1944, 10 minutes, sound, b&w, 35 mm.

111-M-1000-   "We're in the Army, Now," 1943, 14 minutes, sound, b&w, 35 mm.

111-M-1030-   "To the Ladies," 1944, 15 minutes, sound, b&w, 35 mm.

111.15. Substantial film coverage of women's military service and work in welfare and factory work is available in the **Army Depository Copy** series (111-ADC, ca. 9,000 reels), a file of 35mm unedited documentary footage. Card catalog entries to films about women's activities include the following:

American National Red Cross

Army
  Military dependents

Marine Corps

Navy

Nurses and Nursing

Red Cross

Salvation Army

Women
  Employment

Women Marines

Women's Army Corps

Women's Auxiliary Ferrying Squadron

WAVES

World War, 1939–1945: War Work: Red Cross

An entire reel is devoted to Helen Keller's trip to Tokyo and Yokohama in 1948. Other women for whom ADC film clips are cataloged include Ambassador Eugenie Anderson, Mrs. Henry A. Arnold, and Marguerite Higgins (a war correspondent in Korea). Film 111-ADC-5331 is a September 20, 1945, interview with Iva Ikuko Toguri (Tokyo Rose). There is a continuation of this series covering 1950–64 (5,000 reels, 111-LC).

111.16. In the **Army-Navy Screen Magazine** (50 issues) produced by Frank Capra is "Soldiers in Greasepaint," 1946, the Signal Corps tribute to the show people who brought patriotic performances to the men at the front during World War II. It features the Andrews Sisters. Other performers in the series are Lucille Ball, Judy Garland, Lena Horne, and Dorothy Lamour.

Records of the Office of the Surgeon General (Army)

Record Group 112

112.1. An act of April 14, 1818, regulating the staff of the Army, established the Office of the Surgeon General (SGO) and for the first time provided a central organization for surgeons who served at posts or with regiments. The office is the headquarters of the Army Medical Department of which the Army Nurse Corps (ANC) is a part. Records about women in this record group include those about hospital matrons, nurses, civilian employees of the SGO, members of welfare organizations, and relatives of service personnel.

112.2. Long before the establishment of the ANC, women served as nurses and matrons in Army hospitals. References to these and other women are scattered throughout the early 19th-century records, although there is no large body of records dealing specifically with women until the period of the Spanish-American War.

Records of the Central Office

Correspondence

112.3. In the records of the central office, there is some mention of matrons in hospitals in the volume covering 1844 of **letters and endorsements sent, April 1818–October 1889** (90 vols.), which are arranged chronologically. Separate entries for "Matrons" and "Nurses" as well as for "Ladies' Union Relief Association of Baltimore" appear in the **name and subject indexes** (6 vols., 4 in.) to **letters and endorsements sent to the Secretary of War, March 1837–May 1866** (6 vols., 1 ft.).

112.4. In **letters received, 1818–89,** arranged alphabetically by surname of the correspondent, a May 8, 1862, letter to "Mrs. A. Lincoln" from a group of women in St. Louis offering to establish a hospital there is filed under "W." Numerous entries for Dorothea Dix in the yearly **name and subject indexes to part (1862–89) of letters received, 1818–89,** indicate that there is evidence among these letters of her work as Superintendent of Army Nurses during the Civil War.

112.5. The **name and subject indexes** (1 vol., 3 in.) to the SGO **general correspondence, 1890–94** (52 ft.), also contain entries for "matrons."

112.6. The **name and subject indexes** (435 ft.) to the **general correspondence, 1894–1917** (830 ft.), include entries referring to women employed by the Medical Department indexed under such headings as "Washing," "Female," and "Women." Women who served as contract nurses, American Red Cross nurses, and other volunteers are referred to under entries for "American Red Cross" and "Red Cross." Under the term "Contract nurses" there are numerous references to women for whom there are individual files. References to records about Dr. Anita Newcomb McGee, the founder of the Army Nurse Corps, can be found under the general heading "contract surgeons." Records about the work of women's volunteer relief and welfare organizations are referenced by the names of the organizations in the name and subject index. **Record cards, 1894–1917** (460 ft.), provide abstracts of documents in consolidated files and single document files in the 1884–1917 correspondence series.

112.7. A number of files in the 1894–1917 correspondence concern hospitals for women and women as patients, employees, and volunteers at Army hospitals. For example, in file 42300 there are letters from "Army women" (the wives of military personnel) taking stands for and against the sale of alcoholic beverages in Army canteens. Files 58829 and 61643 contain records relating to administrative policy in regard to contract nurses. In file 38641 there is voluminous correspondence with the American Red Cross and other volunteer and religious organizations that were major sources of military nurses at the turn of the century. In the same file are letters from a woman seeking a contract to supply grape juice; letters from Elizabeth Winslow Shippen, chair of the Cuban Relief Committee of Chicago; and letters from the Minnesota Volunteers Auxiliary Association concerning conditions in Manila in 1898 and the need for nurses there. File 56797 contains records relating to an investigation of mismanagement that involved a nurse in the Medical Department in the Philippines. In file 56186 there is an 1899 letter describing private medical research on syphilitic women and men in an attempt to produce a vaccine for venereal diseases.

112.8. The 1894–1917 general correspondence covers the period in which the Army Nurse Corps was established, so there is correspondence of the Surgeon General and of successive superintendents of the corps about its administration, including assignments, duties, complaints, and regulations of the first nurses in the corps. In addition, there are individual files for each of the superintendents of the corps and for individual nurses. There are files in this series documenting the pre-1917 careers of Jane A. Delano, who served as superintendent from 1909 to 1912, chaired the National Committee of the American Red Cross Nursing Service, and recruited nurses for the Army and the Navy during World War I until her death in France in 1919; Dora Thompson, superintendent from 1914 to 1919; and Julia C. Stimson, superintendent from 1919 to 1937, who had served as Chief of Red Cross Nursing Service in France early in World War I and later as Director of Nursing Service, American Expeditionary Forces in France.

112.9. General correspondence, 1917–46 (515 ft.), is arranged in six chronological subseries: 1917–27, 1928–37, 1938–40, 1941–42, 113

1943–44, and 1945–46, and thereunder according to the War Department decimal classification scheme. Below are descriptions of selected files relating to women:

112.10. Records relating to women in file 211 appear in all chronological segments of the correspondence and include administrative correspondence and statistics of the Nursing Division of the SGO and service records of individual nurses. Subjects documented in the files include the basic course of study for members of the Army Nurse Corps and eligibility of nurses for membership in the American Legion. There are cross-references to other files in the series about bills in Congress concerning the Army Nurse Corps, the retirement of nurses, the detailing of Army nurses for duty on Army transports, and the use of the Red Cross in mobilization plans.

112.11. The Army Reorganization Act of June 4, 1920, authorized officer status for Army nurses. Julia C. Stimson, Superintendent of the Army Nurse Corps, was given the rank of major at that time. After World War I, she was Dean of the Army School of Nursing from 1919 to 1931. Much of her correspondence in both capacities is in file 211 "Nurses" in successive segments of the SGO general corespondence.

112.12. Documents relating to women are also found under file 211 in specific chronological subseries. For example, 211 "Nurses, 1917–18" (10 in.), contains nurses' letters, memorandums and reports, and records concerning the service of individual nurses, overseas duty for nurses, and the arrangements for the return of nurses from Europe after World War I. File 211 "Physicians, women, 1940" in the 1938–40 segment contains a letter of July 2, 1940, from Dr. Julia M. Donahue to Maj. Gen. E.S. Adams stating that there were 55 female contract surgeons in World War I. In the 1943–44 segment of the series, file 211 "Dietitians" contains the administrative correspondence of Maj. Helen C. Burns, Director of Dietitians, at the time when dietitians were made members of the armed services rather than civilian employees of the Army. In the 1941–42 and 1943–44 segments there is correspondence about black and Japanese-American women in the Army and the new phenomenon of flight nurses. In the 1945–46 segment, shortages of nurses, wartime legislation to draft nurses, recruiting qualifications, and overseas duty are the subjects of correspondence. There is also a small amount of material on occupational therapists. In the same segment, a 211 file labeled "Nurses, Negro," contains petitions (3 in.) for the removal of restrictions on the use of black nurses in the Army and Navy.

112.13. In file 231 for 1917–27 there is correspondence (1 ft.) between Marguerite Sanderson, Supervisor of Reconstruction Aides, and Army hospitals and schools concerning the qualifications, training, and physical examinations of such aides, most of whom were women. Applications from women for positions as maids, hospital assistants, nurses aides, and social directors are in the same file. File 321 "Student Nurses,

October 1918–1927" (6 in.), pertains to the training, placement, benefits, and earlier service of nurses attending the Army School of Nursing.

112.14. Foreign war brides of U.S. servicemen and the families of returning servicemen are subjects documented briefly in file 292 (1917–27). Wartime travel by dependents, passports for wives and sisters, and other service to women relatives of Army personnel are in file 292.1 for that period.

112.15. Correspondence and reports of officials in the Medical Department concerning the Women's Army Corps (WAC) are in file 321 in the 1945–46 segment. Topics documented in this file include effects of fatigue on women in the WAC, women assigned to hospital units, a health survey, pregnancy, provost marshal procedures regarding Wacs, separation from service, and postwar policy about women in a reserve corps. File 321.6 contains several reports of the Special Planning Division on the "Medical Department in the Post War Army," which include discussions of the Army Nurse Corps and a proposed Women's Medical Specialist Corps.

112.16. The U.S. Cadet Nurse Corps was established in July 1943 under the administration of the Public Health Service (PHS) to alleviate the critical nursing shortage, and cadets served in both Federal and non-Federal hospitals. File 322.5-6 "U.S. Cadet Nurse Corps" in the 1945–46 segment contains circulars distributed by the Army Service Forces, of which the SGO was a part; PHS publications; a report interpreting nursing statistics for the war years; correspondence of the Nursing Consultants Division and of the Army Nurse Corps with hospitals and nurses' associations; and sheet music for the "United States Cadet Nurse Corps March." File 322.7 in the 1945–46 segment contains records dated as late as 1950 about plans for a Women's Medical Specialist Corps.

112.17. File 081.1 "Assistance from Societies and Associations, General, 1941–44," in the 1941–42 and 1943–44 subseries contains letters about the placement of psychiatric social workers and the status and condition of service of volunteer nurses aides. Included is correspondence with female officials of the American Red Cross and lists of names of social workers, recreation workers, and secretaries provided by the Military and Naval Welfare Service of the American Red Cross.

112.18. Records relating to Lt. Col. Margaret D. Craighill, M.D., who became the first woman Medical Officer and was appointed director of the Women's Medical Unit established in January 1944, are in file 333 in the 1943–44 and 1945 segments of the general correspondence of the SGO. The director was instructed to "develop policies and coordinate all activities within the Surgeon General's Office relating to the medical care and welfare of women in or connected with the Army." Among her reports are: "Conditions Affecting Women Personnel in China," "Health Conditions of Nurses and WACs in Middle East," "Health Conditions of Nurses in MTO [Mediterranean Theater of Operations]," "History of Woman's [sic] Medical Unit," "Medical and Social Conditions of Women in the Military Service, India-Burma Theater," and "Nurses and WACs in the ETO." In file 024.10-11 (1943–44) there are reports and correspondence for the Women's Health and Welfare Unit, which replaced the Women's Medical Unit in August 1944.

112.19. During World War II, the Army restricted information concerning Army Nurse Corps morale, nurses who were prisoners-of-war, nurses' illnesses, and changes of location of Army Nurse Corps members. Much of that information is in **formerly security classified general correspondence, 1938–48** (85 ft.). There are investigative reports, statistics, inspection reports, reviews of officer assignments, and correspondence in file 211 "Nurses," for the World War II years (6 in.). Included is a good deal of material on the utilization of black nurses. One report recommends military training for nurses because they were found to be poorly prepared for the war experience. Several communications concerning the assignment of women to posts overseas and in the United States are also in files 211 "Physical therapy aides" and 211 "Dietitians." In a folder labeled "NB161" is a 25-page report of July 24, 1945, titled "What Returnee Nurses Say About Their Overseas Experience"; it was prepared by the Information and Education Division, Headquarters, ASF. Among the few formerly security classified documents relating to Wacs is a seven-page report in file 322.5-7 concerning the incidence of venereal disease, mental illness, physical breakdowns, and pregnancies among Wacs.

112.20. Correspondence with military installations, commands, and units, and with civilian organizations ("geographic file"), 1917–46 (1,765 ft.), is arranged in four chronological segments: 1917–27, 1928–37, 1938–44, and 1945–46, each arranged by a subject-alphabetical classification scheme and thereunder by the War Department decimal classification scheme. In the 1917–27 segment is a 211 "Nurses" file (3 in.) for General Hospital No. 1 at Williamsbridge, NY, including administrative records relating to Army Nurse Corps and reserve nurses, psychiatric nurses, and laboratory technicians. In the same segment, a draft of a bill to create the Army School of Nursing, annual reports of the school, correspondence about it with the American Red Cross and the Council of National Defense, and wartime correspondence of its dean, Annie W. Goodrich, are filed under GG "Institutions—Army School of Nursing." Correspondence of Dean Julia C. Stimson in the early postwar period is filed under the same file heading. Students at the school studied and worked in medical facilities at Army training camps and served in permanent Army hospitals. In the same GG file, records of "cantonments," arranged alphabetically by name of camp, document some of their experiences. For Camp Hancock in Augusta, GA, in file 231 "Student Nurses" (½ in.) there are efficiency reports, letters from the chief nurse and other hospital officials about personnel and administration of base hospital schools, training of students, conditions at the camps, and the World War I influenza epidemic. Correspondence and reports about cooperative efforts of the Army and the American Social Hygiene Association to deal with prostitution and to offer health education are in a folder for the association filed under T "Societies and Associations." Also under "T" is documentation of many civilian organizations that provided goods and services to the Army. The Temple Sisterhood of Nashville, TN, made articles for soldiers. There are records from religious orders relating to real estate transactions. Records relating to the American Red Cross, 1917–19 (5 in.), include correspondence with and cross-reference sheets for letters from Mabel Boardman and other Red Cross officials about such subjects as women of the Motor Corps, Red Cross dietitians and nurses, assistance to military families, and canteen service for hospital trains.

112.21. In the 1928–37 segment a 211 "Nurses" file (2 in.) for Letterman General Hospital, San Francisco, includes records of promotions, transportation, and transfers. There is similar information in at least three 211 files for Hawaii for the interwar years. File 211 "Contract Surgeons" contains several references to women doctors. Reports of Red Cross military hospitals including photographs of nurses and narratives about their work are filed under "Red Cross" in file 314.7 "Military histories." File 319.2 "Annual Reports" mentions Army Nurse Corps personnel, American Red Cross hostesses at convalescent houses, and unusual medical cases involving women.

112.22. The Medical Department of the Army employed 20,000 Wacs during World War II, one-fifth of all women in the WAC, who served in many parts of the world. Therefore, there is considerable information about women in the **general correspondence of the Surgeon General's Office with military installations, commands, and units, 1940–49** (872 ft.), arranged geographically by Army area (for example, ZI, for Zone of the Interior, refers to the United States), and thereunder by War Department decimal classification. In file ZI 211 "Dietitians" there is documentation of the problem that dietitians and physical therapists had with qualifying for postwar benefits when part of their World War II service was rendered as civilians. "WMSC [Women's Medical Specialist Corps] Historical Statistics" (2 pp.) is also in file ZI 211. In file ZI 250.1 "War legislation on alcoholism and prostitution" is a manuscript prepared in 1918 for publication concerning regulations established under Sections 12 and 13 of the Military Establishment Act of 1917 regarding "control of vice and liquor selling in the extra cantonment areas throughout the United States." In file ZI 726 "Hygiene of Diseases and Diagnosis" is a subfile, ZI 726.1 "Genito-urinary, venereal, prostitution, and sex vices," which contains posters, correspondence, and studies that often relate to women. File ZI 353 "Training" (1 ft.) contains correspondence, manuals, reports, and newspaper clippings concerning such subjects as female medical and surgical technicians, hospital orderlies, and Sanitary Corps officers; a school for enlisted technicians at Wakeman General Hospital; Camp Atterbury, IN; and the Ballard School of Practical Nursing. Photographs and the text of remarks made at a conference of WAC hospital companies in May 1945 and a report on the meeting are filed under ZI 322.5 (5 in.). File ZI 024.10-11 "WAC Liaison Branch" contains records of WAC activities in the Medical Department.

112.23. Nursing histories with photographs were produced and filed with other manuscripts in file 314.7. Among the titles of the manuscripts are the following relating to women:

Mattie E. Treadwell, "WACS (Medical Department Utilization)"

Col. Florence A. Blanchfield, "The Army Nurse Corps in World War II"

Blanchfield, "Organized Nursing and the Army in Three Wars" (2 vols.)

Lt. Col. Alfred Mordecai, "A History of the Procurement and Assignment Service for Physicians, Dentists, Veterinarians, Sanitary Engineers, and Nurses"

Maj. Anne M. Baran, "Nursing Care of Casualties in Long Distance Air Evacuation"

Capt. Grace H. Stakeman, "Air Evacuation Nursing"

Lt. Col. Elsie Schneiver, "History of Nursing in the Middle Pacific"

Capt. Christine Chisnik, "History of the Army Nurse Corps, Central Pacific Base Command"

1st Lt. Ruth B. Kelly, "History of the Nursing Service in the South Pacific, World War II"

Maj. Minnie B. Schell, "The History of the Army Nurse Corps in Subordinate Units, Western Pacific Base Command"

2d Lt. Anne G. Oakley, "History of Nursing in SPA [Southern Pacific Area]"

In addition, there are histories and nurses' narratives of their experiences with evacuation, field, station, and general hospitals in the U.S. Army European Theater of Operations (ETOUSA). There are also accounts by others of nurses' war activities, such as "The Medical History of Anzio" by Brig. Gen. J.L. Martin, Army Surgeon. "History of the ANC [Army Nurse Corps] in MTOUSA," is volume 6 of a 12-volume "Administration of the Medical Department in the Mediterranean Theater of Operations."

112.24. Also in the ZI part of SGO correspondence with Army commands are Colonel Blanchfield's statistical reports of nurse trainees moving through basic training centers (file ZI 343, 4.in.). In file ZI 730 a folder is labeled "Neuropsychiatry Training, NP Nursing Courses." File ZI 322.5 "Army Nurse Corps, 1941," contains memorandums concerning budget, recruiting, and training. A ZI 210.31-33 file (4 in.) consists of personal history questionnaires completed by nurses, dietitians, and physical therapists to comply with officer qualification requirements, and a ZI 210.2 "Nurses and Promotions" file for 1945 lists the names and locations of those recommended for promotion. File ZI 291.2 "Race" contains material on the utilization of black officers, doctors, nurses, and enlisted men, and file ZI 293 "Nurses Buried in Arlington Cemetery" is filed in this series, even though it was prepared in 1964. It contains accounts of service of some nurses who served as early as the Spanish-American War. There is also a ZI 421 "Uniforms, Nurses (1941–45)" file.

112.25. Some of the ZI files are not restricted to events in the United States. For example, file ZI 211 "Nurses Awards, Casualties, etc.," deals with overseas activities and file ZI 211 "Nurses-NATOUSA" concerns the 11th Evacuation Hospital in the Sicily Campaign. Under ETO, file ZI 370 concerns employment, operation, and movement of troops. In it are folders labeled "Continental Operations, Nursing Division" and "Mounting the Operation—Nursing Division." A ZI 211 "Nurses" file contains copies of "Nurses' Newsletters," narrative and statistical reports, and investigative records. There is also a file ZI 421 "Nurses Clothing." For the Southwest Pacific area, file ZI 211 "ANC" documents the liberation of nurses from Japanese POW camps in the Philippines, and file ZI 014 contains records about the role of the Army Nurse Corps in civil affairs. Daily office diaries are filed under ZI 314.81 or ZI 024 for the Army Nurse Corps in sections for several geographic areas. Correspondence with women field workers of the American Red Cross about their work at St. Dunstan's Hospital for Men and Women Blinded on War Service is scattered throughout ZI file 730 "Ophthalmology—England."

112.26. Correspondence relating to persons and firms, 1917–37 (12 ft.), arranged alphabetically by name of correspondent, provides documentation about prostitution. An August 12, 1916, letter from Secretary of War Newton D. Baker to Maj. Gen. Frederick Funston, Commander of the Southern Department at Fort Sam Houston, cites a report written by Raymond B. Fosdick, Baker's special representative on the Mexican border, on the relation between prostitution and liquor sales at Army posts. A copy of the letter and several later reports by Fosdick are in a folder bearing Fosdick's name. In the same series are letters to and from Jane A. Delano and some records created after her death about the Army School of Nursing and the American Red Cross Department of Nursing.

Reports

112.27. The efficiency of matrons was one item given consideration on Medical Department **inspection reports of medical facilities of Army posts, 1890–94** (2 ft.). The forms are arranged alphabetically by name of post. Similarly arranged, but for letters S–V only, are **special sanitary reports, June 30, 1893** (6 in.), which describe in some detail the living and working conditions for matrons at their posts. One of the **inspection reports of sanitary conditions during the Spanish-American War, 1898–99** (6 in.), describes Mrs. Livingston Mason's Convalescent Home at Newport, RI. Other reports in the series mention women nurses briefly. Medical Department **reports to the Secretary of War relating to office activities, personnel, and expenditures, 1818–94** (9 vols., 2 ft.), list the names of women employees most often as matrons, but occasionally as clerks or in other positions. Information about pay, birthplace, and place of employment is given for each employee.

112.28. Annual reports of the divisions of the Surgeon General's Office, 1942–49 (15 ft.), arranged by division and thereunder chronologically, contain information on nursing including annual reports of the Nursing Division, 1942–45, a special report (8 pp.) on the Nursing Service by Col. Florence A. Blanchfield concerning morale and recruitment of nurses and legislation affecting them, and a 1945 report of the Nursing Policies Branch. Among the records of the Reconditioning Division are reports of the Occupational Therapy Branch, of which Winifred Kahmann was chief, November 1943–August 1944. In the records of the Civilian Personnel Division beginning in early 1942 is documentation of the physical therapy program under Maj. Helen C. Burns and Emma E. Vogel, a dietitian. In 1943 physical therapists and dietitians were transferred to the Military Personnel Division when they were given military rank in the Medical Department for the duration of World War II and 6 months thereafter. Some records pertaining to Wacs and other women are in the files of the Venereal Disease Control Branch of the Preventive Medicine Division. The 1944 annual report of the Women's Medical Unit, prepared by Lt. Col. Margaret D. Craighill, is filed under "Hospitals and Domestic Operations—Hospital Division Operations Service." The 1945 report of the unit, with its name changed to Women's Health and Welfare Unit, was prepared by assistant director Maj. Margaret Janeway and filed under "Professional Administrative Services." A 10-page historical report by Colonel Craighill is filed under "Army Services—Professional Administrative Service."

112.29. Reports relating to living conditions at Army posts in North Carolina, South Carolina, Georgia, Florida, and Alabama, 1868–69 (1 vol. 1 in.), arranged by post with an index to posts, contain scattered references to both black freedwomen and white women in the South after the Civil War. Prostitution, illness, disease, and quarters for married soldiers are among the subjects of the reports.

112.30. Medical problems encountered by women at Army posts are noted by post surgeons in **reports of epidemics, rare diseases, and vaccinations, 1888–1917** (3 ft.). Among them are a case of "triple birth," a miscarriage, and a few reports of venereal disease.

112.31. Annual reports of components of the Army Medical Department, 1940–49 (310 ft.), are arranged geographically by Army command, thereunder alphabetically by component (for example, arsenal, hospital, station, etc.), and thereunder numerically by unit designation or alphabetically by unit name. Separate quarterly and annual reports, 1942–45, are available for the Nursing Division in the records of the

Office of the Chief Surgeon, ETO, ETOUSA, and Headquarters, U.S. Forces, European Theater (USFET). The reports describe the activities of the division, list organizational and personnel changes, and include forms and trip reports of the director of the Nursing Service, ETO. American Red Cross club services and statistics for nurses are reported, as well as notes about the morale, training, health, and deployment of nurses.

112.32. Command reports deal with women other than nurses and therapists, including women in black WAC detachments, Gray Ladies (hospital volunteers), and prostitutes. The reports, which sometimes include photographs, cover venereal disease control, surgical procedures by type performed on women (including members of servicemen's families), social services, and convalescent programs. For example, the reports of the 804th Medical Air Evacuation Transport Squadron include accounts of flying nurses to Leyte, P.I., and other places, and quarterly reports of flying time for each nurse. The following specific reports are included:

Annual report, Medical Care of WAC, ETO, 1944, by Capt. Marion C. Loizeaux

Health and Status Report of WAC Personnel, December 3, 1945 (based on special consultants' reports of ETO for 1943–44 and the first half of 1945)

Quarterly Medical Historical Reports Concerning Headquarters Far East Air Forces WAC Detachments (APO 925), January and April 1945. (Includes references to women in New Guinea and the Philippines.)

Issuances and Forms

112.33. A few items in **office orders of the Surgeon General's Office, 1917–45** (3 ft.), relate to the women in the Army's Medical Department during World War I. There are 1918 orders about the Army School of Nursing and its Advisory Council, the Army Nurse Corps, and reconstruction aides. A history of the ANC is cited in the 1919 index to the series. Issuance F-915, December 4, 1920, contains a consolidation of Army reports on venereal disease for a month. Statistics are included for the number of men solicited by prostitutes, the number of cases of venereal disease contracted in houses of prostitution and the number contracted elsewhere, the number of "men who stayed all night," and the total amount paid by men for sexual services.

112.34. Employment and other concerns of women are further documented in **circulars and circular letters of the Surgeon General's Office, 1861–85** (7 vols., 1 ft.). These directives were issued to personnel of the Medical Department, usually to commanding officers and surgeons in charge of hospitals. There are numerous entries under the name of Dorothea Dix in the **subject index** to the 1861–80 part of these circulars and other index entries for "laundress," "nurse," and "matron." **Circulars and decisions of the Surgeon General, November 1887–April 1892** (1 vol., 1 in.), and **circulars of the Surgeon General's Office, July 1889–January 1905** (2 vols., 2 in.), contain directives on such matters as the use of registers of births, marriages, and deaths for pension application documentation; the hospitalization of civilians, including women; contracts for nurses; offers of assistance from "patriotic ladies" (1898); and regulations about the duties of the ANC members. One of the **circular letters of the Surgeon's Office, 1919–44** (2 ft.), required reports on cases of venereal disease. Among these same circular letters is Circular Letter No. 80, "Individual Venereal Disease Prophylactic Packets." The letter notes that embarrassment caused to soldiers by the increased number of women clerks in post exchanges "requires that further study of the method of distributing prophylactic materials should be undertaken." The prescribed Army Nurse Corps uniform is described in Circular Letter No. 150 (1942). Another 1942 circular is entitled "Hospitalization of Mental Cases Among the WAAC."

Personnel Records

112.35. The Army Nurse Corps traces its origins to the proposal of Dr. Anita Newcomb McGee, a physician and a national officer of the Daughters of the American Revolution, that a D.A.R. Hospital Corps of trained female nurses be organized for service in the Spanish-American War. The corps was made a part of the Regular Army in 1901. Letters in the **historical files of the Army Nurse Corps, 1900–47** (6 ft.), document McGee's work in support of HR 11770 (1899) and S. 5353 (1900), bills in Congress to establish an Army nurse corps. The series also includes a copy of McGee's *Standard for Army Nurse*; correspondence of the first superintendent of the corps, Dita Kinney, a former contract nurse; copies of orders and circulars relating to the corps; publicity materials; reports; copies of official correspondence; historical notes about the work of the Sisters of Charity of Emmitsburg, MD; and drafts of historical articles. There are also correspondence and publications about the first years of the American Red Cross after its incorporation in 1900 and about its founder, Clara Barton. Records relating to the dedication of a memorial to Jane A. Delano in 1934 include correspondence, copies of speeches, and a program. An extensive file containing correspondence, briefs, and petitions relates to the 1934 test case, *Edith C. Thorsen v. United States*, in which the U.S. Court of Claims decided that reserve nurses were entitled to disability retirement pay. Reports of nurses on duty, usually prepared monthly by the Army Nurse Corps superintendent, July 1923–June 1943, constitute approximately one-third of the series. Carded records, 1920–41, note the deaths of nurses during each year, while other records relate to their efficiency, uniforms, and awards. Historical summaries and miscellaneous reports of the superintendent show distribution of nurses at posts and on hospital ships through June 1943. In addition there are radio scripts designed to recruit nurses and press releases about the corps. There are reminiscences of nurses who served during World War II, including some in the form of poetry. Also in the series are records relating to the requirements for the postwar Army Nurse Corps; implementation of "Regular Army Nurse Corps Integration Program, 16 April 1947–16 April 1948"; and the possible integration of a Women's Medical Specialist Corps into the Regular Army.

112.36. Nurses are among the types of Regular Army personnel covered by records relating to military personnel, 1775–1947. **Case files of candidates seeking appointments as Army nurses, 1898–1917** (34 ft.), were filed in two subseries, successful and rejected applications. Applicants submitted training school certificates, physical examination reports, and application forms that included the question, "What do you consider the most important duties of a trained nurse?" For each candidate appointed, the file contains a copy of the appointment papers and the letter giving the nurse her first assignment. A **register of military service of members of the Army Nurse Corps, 1901–2** (1 vol., 1 in.), arranged alphabetically by initial letter of surname and indexed, includes the names of many women who had been contract nurses. **Monthly strength returns of nurses, 1899–1903** (7 ft.), and **station books of nurses, 1899–1903, 1911–16** (2 vols., 4 in.), show where and when nurses were assigned and the name of the chief nurse at each Army post. Other records about nurses in this period include **annual efficiency reports on nurses, 1898–1917** (9 ft.), arranged chronologically by year and thereunder by station, which give information on health, conduct, habits, professional work, duty assignments, and transfers of individual nurses, and **list of nurses who served with the Army Nurse Corps during World War I, 1917–21** (1 vol., 1 in.).

112.37. Monthly post returns of personnel and equipment of the Hospital Corps, 1887–1902 (31 vols., 2 ft.), arranged alphabetically by name of post, provide information about matrons at the posts, including place of birth for each. There is similar information in **returns of personnel and equipment of the Hospital Corps, 1887–96** (78 vols., 10 ft.).

112.38. Records of contract nurses are included among records relating to civilian personnel, 1862–1939. **Correspondence relating to Spanish-American War contract nurses, 1898–1910** (2 ft.), is largely that of Dora Thompson, who later became the first Regular Army nurse to be named superintendent of the corps. It contains letters from woman physicians, Red Cross Aid Societies, and other relief groups relating to Dr. McGee's military nursing program; McGee's correspondence about nurses for Maj. William Gorgas and others during the occupation of Cuba, 1900; reports of women contract nurses on the American hospital ship *Relief*, 1899–1900; and lists of nurses at various Army posts, 1898–99. There are also letters from and about individual nurses seeking medals for their service and verification of service required to qualify for other benefits. Among the more historically significant letters are those documenting the career of Esther V. Hasson, who served as a contract nurse in the Spanish-American War and on the *Relief*, as a member of the Army Nurse Corps in the Philippines, as the first superintendent of the Navy Nurse Corps when it was established in 1908, and later as an Army Reserve nurse with the American Expeditionary Force, 1917–19. Her file in this series documents her entire career, including letters dated after World War I requesting further assignments and her eventual burial in Arlington Cemetery. Also in this correspondence relating to Spanish-American War contract nurses are efficiency reports on nurses' service from which ratings and comments of medical officers were taken and recorded on **personal data cards of Spanish-American War contract nurses, 1898–1939** (6 ft.). Attached to each card is a questionnaire filled in by each nurse applying for a contract, including name, address, name of nursing school, hospital experience, other occupation, age, birthplace, and physical characteristics including skin color, health, and marital status. There are cards for Dr. McGee and Dita Kinney, including both their Spanish-American War service and later Army Nurse Corps service. For Isabelle McIsaac, the third superintendent of the corps, and some others, only corps service is recorded. Each card bears a number corresponding to entries in **registers of service of Spanish-American War contract nurses, 1898–1900** (8 vols., 2 ft.). The registers contain chronologically arranged entries giving for each nurse—men as well as women—the dates of contracts, pay, hospital assignments, and the name of the ship on which the nurse was transported to duty station. **Correspondence relating to the service of Spanish-American War contract nurses, 1898–1939** (6 ft.), are arranged alphabetically by surname of nurse.

112.39. Laundresses and other women laborers are listed in a **register of civilian employees of the Surgeon General's Office and of the medical supply depots, 1891–97** (1 vol., ½ in.), and in a **register of civilian employees in the field offices of the Medical Department, 1865–1904** (1 vol., 1 in.), which also contains names of charwomen. Each register is arranged by place of employment and thereunder chronologically by date of employee's entry into service and has a name index. Information recorded includes rate of pay, date of termination, remarks, and occasionally, place of birth and residence. There is also a **list of female nurses, cooks, and laundresses employed in Army hospitals during the Civil War, n.d.** (½ in.).

Fiscal Records

112.40. In SGO records relating to fiscal matters, 1822–1928, **abstracts of disbursements made by medical officers, 1862–1916** (87 vols., 18 ft.), note women in a variety of jobs during the Civil War. Women working in the U.S. Laboratory at Philadelphia were listed in the following jobs: forewoman, operator, folder, putter-up of medicine, bottle washer, cutter, and bandage roller. Women also washed towels for the Surgeon General. The name of the chief nurse or forewoman of each facility of the Medical Department continues to appear in later records in the series as well. For example, records for the military hospital in Vigan, P.I., show that Esther V. Hasson was in charge of nurses there in 1900.

112.41. Also documented among the SGO fiscal records are claims of private citizens and of officers for reimbursement for Civil War service. In **registers of claims settled by the Second Auditor of the Treasury Department (daybooks A1 and A2), 1849–64** (2 vols., 3 in.), and in **registers of accounts and claims referred to some other officer or department for approval (referred accounts), 1863–1914** (8 vols., 2 ft.), are entries for women's claims for boarding soldiers, tending the sick, and washing clothes. **Registers of approved claims for services and supplies, February 1883–July 1909** (11 vols., 2 ft.), record similar services by women, including members of religious orders.

Records of Individual Medical Officers

112.42. Some individual Medical Department officers reported on women's wartime work. The **letterbook of Surgeon Thomas F. Azpell, 1862–76** (1 vol., 1 in.), and **letters received by Surgeon Lincoln R. Stone, U.S. Volunteers, in charge of the general hospital at Gallipolis, OH, 1864** (1 vol., 1 in.), both contain letters and circulars about the work of nurses and other women in Union Army hospitals. Dr. McGee was the only woman Medical Department officer who left records with the SGO. The **journal of Dr. Anita Newcomb McGee, 1898–99** (2 vols., 2 in.), contains copies of her proposals to the Surgeons General of the Army and the Navy that both services employ women nurses trained in the nursing schools that had been established since the Civil War. Also included are the responses of the two offices, details of establishing a method of screening applicants for contract nursing positions, and McGee's day-to-day contacts with officers in the Medical Department and officials of private relief organizations. Over 1,000 nurses served in the Spanish-American War, and the **correspondence of Dr. Anita Newcomb McGee, 1898–1936** (2 vols., 2 in.), contains many of their letters to her reminiscing about wartime experiences. The series also contains her letters for 1898–99, which are arranged by military post or station (including the hospital ship *Relief*), and a 1908 essay, "Facts about the Army Canteen." Some of the records clarify the relationship of the contract nurses to the American Red Cross nurses. There are also copies of other articles, newspaper clippings, reports, and records about the Society of Spanish-American War Nurses that McGee founded. Also among her records is a journal of a 1904 trip to the Far East to attend meetings of the American Red Cross and other women's overseas groups, conferences with Japanese officials, and tours of hospitals and operating rooms in Japan.

U.S. Army nurses were training in Wales and waiting to be sent to European field hospitals when they formed this mass salute on May 7, 1944. 112-SGN-P-1.

Reference Aids

112.43. Several series among the SGO reference aids are helpful in locating records about women. **Abstracts of U.S. statutes and Army regulations relating to the Medical Department, 1790–1898** (1 vol., 1 in.), include copies of laws and regulations that affected women nurses and employees and the families of medical personnel. An incomplete (letters "L" to "Z" only) **reference book to letters received ("index to letters filed, Surgeon General's Office"), 1861–70** (1 vol., 2 in.), contains entries for "Ladies," "Sister [name]," "Wittenmyer [Annie]" and the names of women's organizations. Under the heading "Nurses" are references to records about camp followers, cooks, and matrons as well as nurses. Subject-indexed **decisions of government officials relating to the Surgeon General's Office, 1866–92** (1 vol., 2 in.), include summaries of information in statutes, circulars, regulations, and correspondence relating to the Sisters of Charity of Emmitsburg, MD, and their treatment of paupers after the Civil War in Providence Hospital, Washington, DC. There are references to hospital matrons and other women employees, medical attention for military families, and women nurses during the Civil War in **abstracts of decisions of the War Department relating to contract surgeons, 1872–86** (1 vol., 1 in.), and in the subject index to various items of War Department and Surgeon

General's Office information ("policy and precedent book"), 1871–79 (1 vol., ½ in.).

112.44. The **reference file ("policy and precedent file"), 1887–1948** (104 ft.), consists of copies of correspondence and issuances and reference cards arranged alphabetically by subject and thereunder chronologically. Records relate to a variety of topics about which frequent future reference was expected, including such subjects as the status and benefits of matrons and laundresses and even subjects as unusual as baby cribs and baby carriages. The file "Army Relief Association" (2 in.) documents the work of charitable organizations, including the Red Cross, the Sisters of Charity, and Red Cross Societies, as well as prominent persons and contract nurses, both men and women, during the Spanish-American War. A lengthy 1905 memorandum from Supt. Dita Kinney on the subject of servants for Army Nurse Corps quarters and housekeeping duties of nurses is in a file on the "Nurse Corps" (2 ft.). The file also includes records relating to the status, benefits, clothing, duties, demobilization, discharge, and marriage of Army nurses; Army Reserve nurses; and officer status for Army nurses, which was granted under the Army Reorganization Act of 1920. The file also contains records about the improving status of Army nurses after 1920, including their eligibility for retirement. Other records about retirement for both nurses and contract employees are filed under "Pensions" and "Employees, retirement." Course announcements; memorandums about students, employees, and regulations at the Army School of Nursing; and documents relating to the eventual decision to close the school are also in this file. There are records about hostesses under "Hospitals—Army management—service clubs"; about health care for families of servicemen and civilian employees under "Medical attendance," "Hospital management—patients," and under "Married men" as a subheading under "Enlisted men"; about visiting nurses under "Welfare service"; and about women welfare workers and destitute widows of servicemen under "Welfare work." Other records about women are filed under "Hospital fund—moral division," "Mother's Day," "Red Cross," "Venereal disease," "WAAC," "War Camp Community Service," and "Women." The series also documents the expansion of the kinds of jobs women were assigned to during World War I under "Employees" (8½ ft., arranged by type of employment) and "Hospitals—Management—Army reconstruction." The jobs include anesthetists, laboratory technicians, telephone operators, and dietitians in addition to the traditional positions as matrons (sometimes referred to in the World War I period as servants), student nurses, and reconstruction aides, including physical and occupational therapists. Records about the post-World War I nurses' mess are filed under the heading "Hospital fund."

112.45. Also among the reference aids are **decisions and opinions of the Judge Advocate General relating to the Medical Department, 1904–9** (3 in.). Subjects that relate to women include "Obstetrics and gynecology" and "Large families."

112.46. The many ways in which women were affected by World War I are documented in **clippings from medical journals and newspapers relating to the Medical Department, 1904–19** (2 vols., 5 in.). Included in these scrapbooks are a few articles and photographs showing women doctors with the Army and the American Red Cross in France and the United States; women working in medical laboratories; the Girl Scouts' messenger service for the SGO; and Army wives doing volunteer work. Other clippings concern the vanguard of American Red Cross nurses who served with British Expeditionary Forces near Verdun before the United States entered the war, women YMCA representatives at the front, and women as welfare workers and assistants in rehabilitation work as the war drew to a close. The health of women in war industries and the expansion of the Army Nurse Corps are also subjects of clippings.

Records of Subordinate Offices

112.47. The records of the Personnel Division of the Medical Department include **semi-official letter books of the officers in charge, October 1906–October 1909; May 1912–September 1915** (7 vols., 1 ft.), which include letters to Red Cross officials such as Mabel T. Boardman, Jane A. Delano, and Mrs. William K. Draper.

112.48. Of the records of the SGO Nursing Service (so called until 1942) or the Nursing Division that supervised the application of professional policies governing the Army Nurse Corps and established procedures and training of the U.S. Cadet Nurses, few have survived. The **records of the Army School of Nursing, 1918–33, 1951** (3 ft.), include documentation of the establishment and history of the school, announcements, pay and allowances for students, uniforms, reports, daily service records of the nurses, and some papers of Annie W. Goodrich, the first dean of the school, and of Julia C. Stimson, dean of the school until it closed in 1931; a roster of student nurses; and a folder labeled "Graduates of the Army School of Nursing on Duty in the Army Nurse Corps, February 1951."

112.49. The Women's Health and Welfare Unit, Professional Administrative Service, developed policies and coordinated all activities relating to the medical care of women in the Army during World War II. Also known as the WAC Liaison Branch, the unit created and collected a variety of records in the course of preparing a basic field manual on physical training for Wacs. **Records relating to the preparation of field manual 35-20, 1942–44** (1 ft.), arranged by subject, consist of correspondence, reports, publicity material, working papers, and draft copies of the manual prepared by the WAAC Training Center in Des Moines, IA. Some folder titles in the series are: "Policy," "Physical fitness conferences," "Elizabeth Arden," "Menstruation," "T/centers—schools: Officer candidate, Des Moines, Oglethorpe," and "Weight study."

Col. Julia Stimson of the Army Nurse Corps led Red Cross nurses in a parade through Paris at the end of World War I. 112-SGN-P-2.

112.50. The SGO Inspection Branch, Mobilization and Overseas Operations Division, maintained records of overseas inspections by SGO personnel during World War II, interviewed military and civilian experts on medical and sanitary matters on their return from overseas, and prepared reports on their findings. A geographical inventory of the transcripts of interviews and reports of meetings in **interviews with officers visiting S.G.O. installations, 1943–45** (3 ft.), lists numerous reports by Army nurses in the ETO, the southwest Pacific area, on hospital ships, and elsewhere. An April 14, 1944, report on conditions at Roberts Field in Liberia closed with recommendations concerning nursing assignments. In the "POWs (Philippines)" section of the list is a June 7, 1945, report on "Conditions at Santo Tomas" by a field director with the American Red Cross Hospital Service who was in the Philippines before Pearl Harbor. She describes life during the bombing and the subsequent occupation of the islands by the Japanese.

112.51. Scattered throughout **formerly security classified diaries, 1943–48** (4 ft.), of the SGO Operations Service are records relating to the WAC including such subjects as venereal disease, physical standards, conditions of confinement after court-martial, and appropriate uni-   129 forms for women working in the southwest Pacific. The diaries are weekly reports recording the daily operations and activities of the subdivisions of the service, including the Hospital Division, the Training Division, and the Technical Division. A summary precedes the report for each week, highlighting events so that those that involved women are easily noted.

112.52. Among the records of several general hospitals are **medical case files of patients ("clinical records")**. The series for Walter Reed General Hospital in Washington, DC, 1909–12 (40 ft.), for example, includes many files on the wives and daughters of military personnel. Files for women have either "Army Nurse Corps" or "Civilian" stamped on the jackets. There are also hospital records for other general hospitals, station hospitals, and infirmaries.

112.53. Photographs of Army Nurse Corps nurses on duty with the Army and Army Air Force units in the ETO include scenes of their living quarters both near the front and in the rear. Among the **prints of activities of the Medical Department in ETO, 1943–46** (SGA, 1,149 items) there are about 15 photographs of nurses. **Photographs of the celebration of the 48th anniversary of the Army Nurse Corps, 1949** (SGN, 149 items), are also available.

Records of the American Expeditionary Forces (World War I)

Record Group 120

120.1. The American Expeditionary Forces (AEF) originated on May 26, 1917, when Maj. Gen. John J. Pershing assumed the duties as its commander in chief under General Order No. 1, General Headquarters, AEF, after the United States entered World War I. Following the armistice, AEF occupation troops in Germany were designated the American Forces in Germany. AEF troops remaining in other countries were placed under the American Forces in France, which were returned to the United States as rapidly as possible. The AEF was dissolved in January 1923 when U.S. troops in Germany returned to the United States.

120.2. There are documents about American women in many series of AEF records. After the United States entered the war, the first Americans sent overseas were personnel for six base hospitals, including more than 400 nurses, who sailed for France in May 1917 for service with the British Expeditionary Forces. In addition to Regular Army nurses who served with the AEF, there are records in this record group for nurses and volunteers who served overseas with the American Red Cross, the Salvation Army, the YMCA and YWCA, and other service organizations.

Series in this record group are arranged according to the War Department decimal filing system and thereunder chronologically unless otherwise noted.

Records of the Office of the Commander in Chief

120.3 The work of women who served as nurses, welfare workers, and telephone operators is documented in the **general correspondence, 1917–19** (550 ft.), of the Office of the Commander in Chief, which is arranged according to a numerical filing scheme. An **index**, filmed as T900 (132 rolls), includes abstracts of the documents cited. Under the heading "Hospitals," abstracts for U.S. Base Hospital No. 10 include a request for identity cards for 120 nurses stationed in Le Treport, France. This hospital was one of the first American hospitals organized for service with the British Expeditionary Forces before U.S. troops were sent overseas. Under "Jane A. Delano," who was Superintendent of the Army Nurse Corps when war broke out, are entries for her work inspecting AEF evacuation hospitals with Julia C. Stimson and for records about the removal of her body from France after her death to be interred in Arlington Cemetery. There are also headings for "Civilians" and for welfare organizations that had women working as volunteers, such as the American Red Cross, Jewish Welfare Board, Knights of Columbus, Salvation Army, YMCA, and YWCA. Under the heading "Nurses" are abstracts about American Red Cross nurses, Army Reserve nurses, and Army Nurse Corps nurses, including demobilization plans at the end of the war, the proposed trial of a nurse for associating with an enlisted man, and requests for German-speaking nurses for welfare work. Abstracted under "Wives" and "Women" is information about policies relating to the transportation of wives of military personnel to Europe and war brides to the United States. Under "Women" and "YWCA" are references to the morals of women associated with the U.S. 3d Army. Material under "Hospitals" in a separate **index** (11 ft.) deals with medical treatment for civilian employees overseas.

120.4. Civilians working for welfare organizations in U.S. and overseas military installations were required to wear uniforms or some other form of identification. The development of this policy and detailed descriptions of uniforms for each organization are in file 11706 of the correspondence. The new status of telephone operators and clerical personnel as uniformed civilian employees on foreign soil was the subject of numerous memorandums in file 13404. Records about telephone operators, including those about chief operator Grace Banker, contain documents about their transport to Europe, supervision, organization, pay, accommodations, and their eligibility for military benefits for hazardous duty. The feasibility of employing women in certain jobs, procedures for requesting female clerks, and escorts for clerks are all subjects of documents in this series.

120.5. Reports of the commander in chief, AEF, staff sections, and services relating to the history of the U.S. Army in Europe during World War I, 1919 (19 ft.), are manuscript drafts of reports that became volumes 12–15 of *U.S. Army in the World War, 1917–1919*, 17 vols. (Washington, DC: Historical Division, Department of the Army, 1948). In the following list of report titles, the numbers of the volumes in which they were published have been placed in parentheses.

"Report on Activities of G-1" [Personnel], with appended reports made to the division by the American Red Cross, Salvation Army, YMCA, and YWCA. (Vol. 12)

"Report of Commanding General, Services of Supply" (SOS), including a chapter on the Medical Department and one on welfare work, both of which involved women (Vol. 15)

"Report of the Chief Surgeon" (Vol. 15)

"Report of G-4 [Coordinating Section] on Hospitalization, Evacuation, and Medical Supply" (Vol. 14)

There is a **subject index** (1 ft.) to the manuscript reports. General orders for the troops overseas and bulletins issued by the AEF appear in the published volumes 16 and 17 of the history including orders and bulletins on family allotments, allowances for civilian employees, war risk insurance, notification of families of servicemen and others killed overseas, passports for officers' wives, pay for civilian clerks, and accommodations, laundry, and leave for Army nurses.

Records of the General Staff, 1917–19

120.6. The AEF General Staff's G-1 Administrative Division conducted necessary oversight of various American welfare organizations and handled matters concerning women who were paid employees of the Army. In file 080 "Societies and Associations" (3 ft.) of the division's **general correspondence, 1917–19** (57 ft.), high-level correspondence and reports document decisions regarding the status and privileges of civilian organizations. Communications from Gen. John J. Pershing and Raymond B. Fosdick, Chairman of the Commission on Training Camp Activities (CTCA), mention the role of women in raising morale and aiding in relief work. A few folders in the file are labeled "Red Cross," "Salvation Army," "YMCA," and "YWCA." The records for each organization include strength reports by sex, descriptions of duties for different kinds of work, and letters about the marital status of women workers. In file 211.31 "Nurses and Matrons" is documentation of visits of Army Nurse Corps and Red Cross personnel to the front. Requests for women stenographers and typists are in file 231.3.

120.7. The Red Cross urged the women who served as searchers responding to inquiries about the whereabouts of servicemen to pay personal visits to the subjects of such inquiries if they were in Army hospitals. Instructions for searchers' work in collecting information about the condition of patients are in **correspondence of the American Red Cross representative at General Headquarters, 1917–18** (1 in.).

120.8. In the records of the G-1 Statistical Division is a series of **weekly statistical reports relating to personnel, supplies, and equipment shipped to France, 1918–20** (13 ft.), which includes medical reports (1 ft.) giving figures to show the discrepancy between the number of nurses required and the number supplied. A shortage of nurses was chronic.

120.9. A few women not attached to the military in any official way were investigated by the Secret Service Division of G-2 (Intelligence). Reports in the **correspondence of Assistant Chief of Staff Aristides Moreno relating to civilians suspected of enemy activities, 1917–18** (5 in.), give biographical information and information about romantic interests and influential contacts of suspects.

120.10. The Counterespionage Section (G-2-B-3) of the Secret Service Division (G-2-3) of the General Staff also reported suspicious actions of civilian as well as military personnel. File X06-5 of **correspondence relating to European civilians suspected of enemy activity or of German sympathy ("doubtful file"), 1917–18** (2 ft.), includes a memorandum for the Chief of Staff regarding the control of U.S. civilians in France. Attached to it is a list of persons, including women working for welfare societies, who were sent back to the United States as a result of investigations. There is a **name card index, 1917–19** (12 ft.), to this series and the **general correspondence, 1917–19** (13 ft.), of the Secret Service Division.

120.11. A letter of introduction for a woman making a film for the Committee on Public Information is among the records of the Censorship and Press Division (G2-D) at AEF General Headquarters. It is item 29 (Oct. 1918) in the "Photographic Censorship" folder in **correspondence of the Photographic Censorship Subsection, 1918–19** (3 ft.).

120.12. Many women correspondents covered the war for the U.S. press. Forms for each reporter or journalist appear in **correspondence relating to visitors ("personnel files"), 1918–19** (2 ft.), in records of the Visitor's Bureau (G-2-E). The files include letters about certain reporters who had been negligent about clearing articles through the censor. **Correspondence relating to visits by the press, American political and military leaders, and others in the area occupied by Allied forces, 1917–19** (10 in.), concerns the issuance of automobile passes. A **name index** (1 ft.) serves both series. Information on each card of the index includes the name of the newspaper or journal the correspondent served, the locations for which passes were requested, and the dates of the proposed visits.

120.13. Because soldiers complained about the YMCA, the Inspector General (IG) of the AEF conducted an investigation in December 1918. At the suggestion of the Secretary of War, the study was broadened to include the work of other U.S. welfare organizations as well. The **report of the Inspector General relating to the investigation of the Young Men's Christian Association in the AEF, 1917–19** (6 vols., 5 in.), filed with the records of the Historical Section of the General Staff provides brief administrative histories and detailed accounts of the functions of the American Red Cross, the American Library Association, the Jewish Welfare Board, the Knights of Columbus, the Masonic Overseas Mission, and the Salvation Army in addition to the YMCA. The first volume, devoted to the YMCA, contains a chapter on women workers, and there are other specific references to women throughout the report. Some of the major areas of concern were free distribution of goods, accounting systems, canteen service, entertainment and comfort personnel, discipline, cooperation with the Army and other organizations, popularity of services, and the conclusions drawn by the investigators.

Records of the Administrative Staff

120.14. Several series of cablegrams have been filmed as *Cablegrams Exchanged Between General Headquarters, American Expeditionary Forces, and the War Department, 1917–1919* (M930, 19 rolls). They are arranged by security level and thereunder by a numerical scheme that is essentially chronological. Related indexes were not filmed. Some of the cablegrams relate to women with the AEF during and immediately after the war and to others located at military camps in the United States. Other cablegrams relate to military families seeking to be reunited. There are entries in the subject indexes for nurses, telephone operators, wives, women entertainers, the women's hospital unit, the Women's Oversea Hospital, and YMCA and YWCA personnel.

120.15. General orders, 1917–19 (4 ft.), and **bulletins, 1917–19** (2 ft.), are in the records of the Adjutant General of the AEF Administrative Staff. They were published as volumes 16 and 17 of the *U.S. Army in the World War* noted in **120.5** and include such subjects as allotments for families of military personnel; allowances for civilian employees and their families; American Red Cross hospitals; regulation of various U.S. organizations; war risk insurance; family notification of deaths of servicemen; passports (often issued to wives of officers); and accommodations, laundry, and leave for members of the Army Nurse Corps. **Indexes** (9 ft.) to the manuscript for the *U.S. Army in the World War* are in the records of the Adjutant General, Administrative Staff.

120.16. Civilians with U.S. relief organizations attached to the AEF received worker permits that authorized them to work in certain areas and entitled them to certain military privileges. Most of these major organizations, including the Knights of Columbus, the American Red Cross, the Salvation Army, and the YMCA, employed American women, each of whom had to secure such a permit. Requests, authorizations, and acknowledgments of receipt of permits by name are in **correspondence relating to civilians attached to the AEF, 1918–19** (4 ft.), maintained by the Permit Division of the AEF Adjutant General's office.

120.17. The records on which the report cited in **120.13** was based are in the records of the Inspector General in the records of the Administrative Staff. The series **reports of investigations of welfare organizations, 1917–19** (1 ft.), arranged geographically, is a body of affidavits sworn by soldiers in response to questions about the quality and type of service provided, the character of the personnel, the number of women workers, names of persons in charge, and similar subjects.

Records of Tactical Units

120.18. There were three tactical units in the AEF. The 1st Army was organized in the summer of 1918, the 2d Army in October, and the 3d Army in November 1918.

120.19. Letters of thanks to telephone operators and other records about women are in file 221.35 of the **correspondence, 1918–19** (2 ft.), of the Chief Signal Officer of the 2d Army. Lengthy letters of commendation for nurses in mobile and evacuation hospitals, with descriptions of their working conditions, are in files 200 and 211 of the **general correspondence, 1917–19** (1 ft.), of the Chief Surgeon of the 2d Army.

120.20. Published histories of welfare organizations submitted by their representatives in the 3d Army and accompanied by additional summaries prepared by the 3d Army Welfare Officer for the Office of the Commander in Chief are in **reports, studies, monographs, and other records relating to the activities of the Third Army ("historical file"), 1918–19** (20 ft.). G-1 file 17 contains detailed information on the activities of the YMCA, which provided assistance and rest facilities for women employed in the war effort and later to the wives of newly married soldiers ("war brides"). The file also includes a report on "a unit of Signal Corps girls assigned to duty" at Advance General Headquarters. There are similar series in the records of other armies and for corps and base sections of the AEF.

120.21. Women who served as secretaries (official representatives) of welfare organizations and other women who worked with the organizations as entertainers for the army of occupation in Germany are mentioned in documents scattered throughout files 080 and 320 of the **general correspondence, 1918–19** (2 ft.), of the 3d Army General Staff.

120.22. Welfare organizations attached to the 3d Army were also investigated. **Reports of investigations of welfare organizations, No-**

vember 1918–July 1919 (10 in.), are in the records of the Inspector General of the 3d Army and contain information about some women who worked in such organizations in occupied Germany.

120.23. Much of the 3d Army Chief Signal Officer's extensive file on civilian personnel relates to women telephone operators and other American women employed with the army of occupation in Germany after the Armistice. Among the pertinent parts of file 150 (4 in.) in his **correspondence, 1918–19** (3 ft.), are the following:

150.1   Leave and passes

150.6   Citations [war decorations]

150.C   Civilian personnel—general [regulations, living quarters, dress, etc.]

150.C.1   Leave and sickness reports

150.C.2   Promotions

150.C.3   Discharges

150.C.4   Transfers

150.C.5   Requests and approvals of travel passes

150.C.6   Pay, commutation of rations

120.24. Several hundred Army nurses were stationed in Germany after the armistice. One of them was Grace E. Leonard, Assistant Director of Nursing Service, AEF. Her correspondence (5 in.), including letters demonstrating her handling of personnel transfers, travel, and the work of individual nurses, is in **correspondence, 1917–19** (1 ft.), of the Chief Surgeon, 3d Army. Large segments of this material are in file 200 "Personnel"; in file 211, "Nurses," in folders marked "Change of Status"; and in chronological correspondence, December 2, 1918–July 21, 1919. Letters of commendation for nurses and recommendations of several for the Croix de Guerre for bravery under enemy fire are in file 211 "Decorations." The rehabilitation work of reconstruction aides and therapists for the AEF continued through June 1919. Topics in file 230 "Aides" include duties and quarters for some of these women and lists of their names. Additional information about women with the 3d Army is in **correspondence, reports, and other records relating to the history of the Office of the Chief Surgeon, 1917–19** (2 in.).

Records of American Forces in Germany (AFG), 1919–23

120.25. Correspondence of the Adjutant General, AFG, in file 291.1 (1 ft.) of the **general correspondence, 1919–23** (99 ft.), of the Office of the Commander, AFG, relates to soldiers' marriages, including memorandums establishing policies and precedents for recently married enlisted men. Letters and translations written by the women who married them or by others on behalf of the women are in the file. Additional correspondence regarding requirements for physical examinations and lists of officers who had wives and children in Europe are in file 292, which also includes records of welfare society work, particularly that of Maud Cleveland of the YWCA. **Subject cross-reference cards** (3 ft.) to the correspondence and yearly **subject indexes** (1 in.) to interfiled telegrams complement the correspondence series. Most of file 080 in the same correspondence series deals with various welfare societies and includes letters, memorandums, reports, and issuances, several of which relate specifically to women's work in hospitals, canteens, hostess houses, and administrative positions.

120.26. "Militarized Societies" is the title of part II (13 pp.) of the "Annual Report of Operations, First Section, General Staff Headquarters, AEF, July 11, 1919–June 30, 1920" in file 1-11.4 of **reports, studies, monographs, and other records relating to the activities of the AEF in Germany ("historical file"), 1919–23** (2 ft.), in records of the Office of the Commander, AFG. In it are described activities of men and women representing the YWCA, YMCA, Salvation Army, American Library Association, and American Red Cross in providing welfare and hospitality services for U.S. troops in occupied Germany.

120.27. Decisions rendered by the Judge Advocate, AFG, about the citizenship status of German women who married U.S. soldiers are in file 014.33 of his **general correspondence, July 1919–January 1923** (16 ft.). Other marriage-related memorandums and directives on topics such as procedures for Army chaplains are in file 291.1.

Records of Headquarters, Services of Supply

120.28. Responsibility for procurement and transportation of supplies was assigned in March 1918 to the Services of Supply (SOS), which also for a short time after the Armistice supervised the repatriation of U.S. troops. Overseas, the Army Nurse Corps became a part of SOS.

120.29. File 332.2 of **general correspondence, 1917–19** (120 ft.), of the Office of the Commanding General, SOS, contains records about Grace Banker, the chief telephone operator who was awarded a Distinguished Service Medal. File 292, "Quasi-military Personnel," deals with families of military personnel seeking to join their relatives in Europe at the end of hostilities. A **name card index to correspondence relating to officers and enlisted men in the SOS recommended for medals and decorations ("locator file")** (5 ft.) includes names of women nurses and Salvation Army workers. There is also a **name card index of officers and enlisted men requesting transportation from the United States to Europe for their wives and families** (6 in.).

120.30. Special orders, 1917–20, relating to American women hired for service with the AEF are located in several series of records maintained by the Office of the Commanding General, SOS. In addition to an alphabetical **name index** (128 ft.) to these series, there is another entitled **name index relating to assignments and transfer** (2 ft.), arranged by arm or branch of service and thereunder alphabetically. Headings that relate to civilian women include "Ordnance," "Signal Corps," and "Telephone operators."

120.31. Reports prepared by American relief and welfare organizations after the war about their service with the AEF include descriptions of the work of various women in their ranks. They are located in G-1, file 17 (2 in.), of **reports, studies, monographs, and other records relating to the Services of Supply in France during World War I ("historical file"), 1917–19** (91 ft.).

120.32. The YWCA set up hostess houses at base ports in the United States for war brides on their way to new homes in America. Internal memorandums, copies of letters to the American YWCA in Paris, and lists of European women married to U.S. servicemen constitute the file "Wives" (3 in.) in **reports and studies relating to various personnel matters ("special files"), 1918–19** (3 ft.), in the G-1 records of the General Staff, SOS. The lists provide maiden and married names of the women, home country, and ultimate destination. Also in the G-1 records are telegrams asking for particular entertainers, including women, and reports on their performance in **correspondence of the entertainment officer, 1919** (10 in.).

120.33. The Inspector General on the Administrative Staff of Headquarters, SOS, kept files on American women overseas after the war. His **general correspondence, 1918–19** (10 ft.), includes letters, reports, notices, and memorandums and is served by a **name and subject index** (2 ft.). Useful index entries are "American Women's Clubs," "Families," "Nurses," and "Welfare Societies."

120.34. Correspondence of the Personnel Division, 1918–19 (2 ft.), in the Office of the Chief Ordnance Officer includes a good deal of information about routine personnel actions pertaining to women who worked mainly in clerical positions for that SOS unit. A **name card index to correspondence relating to civilian personnel** (5 in.) consists almost entirely of women's names, many of whom, however, were Europeans hired by the AEF/SOS.

120.35. The SOS Troop Train Meal Service, Graves Registration Service, and Remount Division of the Chief Quartermaster's Office hired women for overseas duty. They were assigned to positions as draftswomen, translators, indexer-catalogers, stenographers, typists, and clerks. Names and overseas and home addresses appear on lists of civilian employees in file 230 (1 in.) in **general correspondence, 1917–19** (126 ft.), of the Chief Quartermaster, SOS. Memorandums in the file cover topics such as the mobilization of women workers by the YWCA, requirements for women workers, logistical problems, and conditions experienced by the women upon returning home. The file includes descriptions of uniforms worn by stenographers and telephone operators and a copy of an agreement of temporary service in the Quartermaster Corps.

120.36. **General correspondence, 1917–19** (156 ft.), of the Chief Signal Officer, SOS, includes extensive information on women telephone operators and some information about clerks, the problems of demobilizing women, and the nature of women's work during the occupation period in files 221.35 (2 ft.) and 231.3 (½ in.). Information about telephone operators is included in **reports, summaries, photographs, and charts relating to the history of the Signal Corps in combat ("historical file"), 1917–19** (2 ft.).

120.37. Bessie Bell arrived in France in November 1917 to become chief nurse of the AEF. She was succeeded in the fall of 1918 by Julia C. Stimson, whose title was Director of the Nursing Service, AEF. **General correspondence of the Office of the [Chief] Surgeon, headquarters, Line of Communications (LOC), 1917–18** (12 ft.), arranged by subject number, contains Bell's reports (file 3.23) as chief nurse, AEF, about Army nurses with the British Expeditionary Forces. Army Reserve nurses, recruited by the American Red Cross to alleviate the Army's shortage of nurses in France, are the subject of several letters in file 11.13. File 12.22 concerns subsistence, welfare, and allowances for nurses. Additional material concerning nurses and civilian employees is in **correspondence of the Surgeon, Headquarters, LOC, 1917–18** (8 in.).

120.38. Abstracts of correspondence concerning Bell (file 211.28) and Stimson (file 211.43) are in the **subject index to correspondence of the Chief Surgeon** (1 ft.). The series is a finding aid for **general correspondence of the Chief Surgeon, 1917–19** (138 ft.). The Stimson abstracts, on 9 sheets, mention such other topics as the romantic involvement of nurses and Jane A. Delano's visits. File 319.129 "Returns of Medical Officers and Nurses," consists of documents placed in the series under that file designation with cross-references to similar items filed elsewhere in the series. File 211.312 "Nurses" and its subparts (4 ft.), is one of the largest bodies of material on Army nurses with the AEF. It contains applications for appointment as Army nurses and as matrons, copies of oaths of office, and records of assignments and of war-related deaths of nurses. Because of the thousands of nurses who served in World War I, service-related disability was a greater problem for nurses than in previous wars. File 211.29 "Chief Nurse," relates to pay, promotion, and duties of that position. The basic records about reconstruction aides are abstracted on 14 sheets in file 231.238. There are abstracts for other positions held by women in the following files: 231.311 "Secretaries and Dietitians," 211.56 "Anesthetists," 211.56 "Contract Surgeons," and 720.13 "Diet Kitchens."

120.39. The names of both Bell and Stimson are among those of Army nurses, Army Reserve nurses, and civilian women reconstruction aides that appear in **name indexes to telegrams and special orders of general headquarters, base sections, and the Office of the Chief Surgeon relating to personnel of the Medical Department (201 and**

alphabetical file), 1917–19 (7 ft.). The index sheets contain synopses of the personnel actions for each employee, including permanent assignments, temporary duty, and return to the United States.

120.40. Few of the nurses sent overseas were close enough to the front to be on surgical teams. Those who were, however, are mentioned in **records of evacuation hospitals nos. 1–60 and 114, 1917–19** (42 ft.), arranged by hospital number and thereunder by type of record. Nurses are mentioned in documents scattered throughout correspondence and reports and are noted in Army Nurse Corps returns and efficiency reports that record the number of nurses on duty and the quality of work, health, and conduct of each. These are accompanied by **returns of Army Nurse Corps at evacuation hospitals, 1918–19** (3 in.).

120.41. The records of the Chief Surgeon contain more than 500 feet of records for hospitals—camp, mobile, division, and base hospitals and American Red Cross military, nonmilitary, and convalescent hospitals. Typical of these hospital records is a large consolidated series, **records of base hospitals, 1917–19** (151 ft.), which is arranged by hospital number and thereunder by type of record. The correspondence in the series is arranged by subject or according to a decimal classification scheme. Monthly efficiency reports in this and similar series for other types of hospitals show the names and titles of nurses and women in related fields who had arrived for duty during each month, station from which each had come, and an assessment of the quality of work and general conduct and health of each woman.

120.42. From the beginning, the SOS serviced all of France and Great Britain; later it was also responsible for Italy and the Rhine area of Germany. For administrative purposes this territory was divided into geographical numbered base sections, an intermediate section, an advance section, and various independent sections. For each section, records are divided into records of section headquarters and section installations. The series described below are typical of many of these geographical base sections.

120.43. In the section headquarters records of Base Section No. 2, the **correspondence of the section Judge Advocate, 1918–19** (3 ft.), contains numerous requests in file 014.32 from soldiers for information on procedures for naturalization, mostly for their European wives. The hospital center at Perigueux, France, was an installation of Base Section No. 2. The **correspondence of the hospital center at Perigueux, September 1918–May 1919** (5 in.), contains a few documents about Red Cross women in file 080 and some concerning individual Army nurses in file 211.

120.44. Photographic and narrative coverage of nursing activities in Great Britain is provided in **history of the operation of Base Section No. 3, 1919** (7 vols., 10 in.). Volumes 6 and 7 (3 in.) contain a lengthy chapter entitled "American Welfare Societies in England." There are sections on each American Red Cross hospital, on the convalescent and nursing service, on the home communication service, and on the Red Cross Care Committee.

120.45. Also in the headquarters records of Base Section No. 3 is the series **correspondence, reports, and other records relating to the history of the Medical Department, 1917–19** (6 in.), which contains a history of the Army Nurse Corps at that base section. It provides an overview of the nursing personnel at U.S. Army hospitals in Great Britain, including nurses in the hospital train service from the front. Other correspondence and statistical reports regarding nurses are in the folder entitled "Historical Data." At the beginning of the series is a list of subjects found in that series and/or in **reports, returns, and rosters of the section surgeon, 1917–19** (1 ft.).

120.46. Fragmentary information about Army Nurse Corps personnel and Army Reserve nurses who served at hospitals in Base Section No. 4 are in files 200 and 211 of the section headquarters **general correspondence, October 1917–July 1919** (7 ft.). One of those, the U.S. Base Hospital No. 21 at Rouen, France, was among those attached to the British Expeditionary Forces but staffed with American personnel. Also in this series is file 080, which contains a few records about the postwar activities of women in overseas welfare organizations.

120.47. A few photographs of American civilian women serving overseas with the AEF are among **photographic prints: Army Air Service facilities, 1917–19** (AS, 824 items). In a folder labeled "Facilities, Paris Office of the Assistant Chief, Air Services," there are several group staff pictures including American civilians. Women working for the YMCA and American Red Cross are in interior views of entertainment facilities at a YMCA hut and Red Cross canteen.

Records of the Office of the Judge Advocate General (Navy)

Record Group 125

125.1. The Office of the Judge Advocate General was established in 1880 and in 1921 merged with the Office of the Solicitor, which had handled nonmilitary legal matters for the Navy Department since 1900.

125.2. The Office of the Judge Advocate General has authority over military, administrative, and applied law concerning the operation of the Navy. It administers military justice, prepares orders for enforcement of court-martial sentences, and administers a legal assistance program.

125.3. Many court-martial cases are filed in the Naval Records Collection of the Office of Naval Records and Library (RG 45). However, *Records of General Courts-Martial and Courts of Inquiry of the Navy Department, 1799–1867* (M273, 198 rolls), and **records of proceedings of general courts-martial, February 1866–November 1940** (794 ft.), are filed with the records of the Office of the Judge Advocate General. As in the proceedings of Army courts-martial in RG 153, the cases occasionally involve women. The two Navy series, however, are usually indexed and registered only by the name of the accused, most often a man. To discover whether women are involved, the researcher must use the indexes and registers to learn the nature of the charge in each case.

125.4. The **general correspondence file, January 1905–March 1908** (133 ft.), arranged numerically by numbers assigned in order of receipt of communication, contains copies of letters from the Surgeon General (Navy) to the Secretary of the Navy in 1906 and 1907 urging that a Navy nurse corps be created, along with copies of bills introduced in Congress to accomplish this. The selection and appointment of the first superintendent of the corps is the subject of file 26477-4. There is also a 1906 comment by the Secretary of the Navy about the possibility of employing women "in minor clerical positions, involving routine duty and offering little prospect of promotion" in file 3842. An additional few pieces of correspondence pertaining to the establishment of the Navy Nurse Corps appear in volumes 39, 43, and 45 of the Judge Advocate General's **letters sent, December 1879–December 1911** (48 vols., 5 ft.), arranged chronologically.

125.5. Memorandums, circulars, instructions, and regulations of the Office of the Judge Advocate General ("scrapbooks"), 1893–1918 (2 vols., 7 in.), are arranged chronolgically and include subject indexes. Records relating to women include family allowances and allotments under the War Risk Insurance Act, the employment of women during World War I, and demonstrations for woman suffrage.

125.6. Numerous bills introduced into the House and Senate, mainly in the years immediately after World War I, regarding benefits for military nurses and female relatives of military personnel are listed in the Judge Advocate General's **register of congressional bills affecting the Navy Department, February 1892–June 1934** (25 vols., 2½ ft.). Volumes in the latter part of the series are arranged by Congress, with sections for the House and the Senate, and thereunder by subject. An entry usually gives the bill number and date of introduction, the name of the legislator who introduced it, committee assignment, and subsequent legislative history. Other sections of each volume contain records of legislation referred to the Navy Department for comment, originating in the Department, or referred to the Bureau of the Budget. Pensions for widows of men killed in action in all previous wars, for divorced wives of servicemen, and for nurses are the subjects of several bills as well as laws authorizing pay to members of the Nurse Corps for time when they were prisoners of war, for retirement benefits, and for disability retirement. Also in the register is the legislative history of bills to finance visits of bereaved mothers to graves of sons and daughters buried in Europe ("Gold Star pilgrimages").

125.7. Several women who visited naval vessels, whose property was adjacent to naval facilities, or whose relatives were killed in naval action brought claims against the Navy for damages or personal injury. The claims are documented in **correspondence relating to claims, 1926–34** (1½ ft.), arranged alphabetically by claimant's name.

Records of the U.S. Marine Corps

Record Group 127

127.1. In 1775 the Continental Congress provided for the raising of a force of marines, which served throughout the Revolutionary War. The U.S. Marine Corps (USMC) was created by an act of July 11, 1798, which authorized the Commandant of the USMC to appoint an adjutant, a paymaster, and a quartermaster. Around these three staff officers and the commandant, the branches of Marine Corps Headquarters developed. Although the USMC was at first subject to both Army and Navy regulations, an act of June 30, 1834, placed it under exclusive naval control except for units detached by Presidential order for Army service.

127.2. The USMC provides amphibious forces for service with the Navy in seizing and defending advanced naval bases and conducts land operations essential to a naval campaign. Women served the USMC as nurses and menial workers in the 19th century and also as members of the Marine Corps Women's Reserve in the 20th century.

127.3. As is the case with each branch of the armed services, the Commandant's **letters received, 1799–1815** (3 ft.), arranged by time period and thereunder by subject, contain occasional letters from women seeking information about or special treatment for friends and relatives in the USMC. For example, in a folder under the heading "Discharge" there is an 1812 letter from a mother requesting a hardship discharge for her son. Other letters from women concern such matters as courts-martial, desertion, recruitment, pay, and leave. There are similar letters in a later series of the Commandant's **letters received, 1819–1903** (412 ft.), which is arranged alphabetically by initial letter of correspondent's surname or subject, and further arranged chronologically under each letter of the alphabet. **Letters and endorsements received ("case files"), January 1904–December 1912** (369 ft.), arranged in two complicated subseries and served by **synopsis cards for letters sent and received, January 1904–December 1912** (188 ft.), arranged in the same system, are also served by a **name and subject card index ("case index cards")** 143

(195 ft.) that is arranged in rough alphabetical order. Examples of files that relate to women in this last series of letters sent and received are: cases 11440 and 11029 concerning the USMC decision not to authorize transportation on a warship for the wife of an officer, and case 18123 concerning a woman's offer to sell a parcel of land on the York River in Virginia to be used as the site for a USMC camp.

127.4. During World War I, the USMC enrolled women in its Marine Corps Reserve component to release men from clerical and other noncombat positions for combat duty. Navy nurses served the USMC, and wives and dependents of marines are frequently the subject of records. The Commandant's **general correspondence, 1913–38** (279 ft.), is arranged in two subseries, 1913–32 and 1933–38, and thereunder numerically according to the ELLS-DRAN Filing System. In this system, the following numeric-subject classifications refer specifically to women in this correspondence series and others filed according to the ELLS-DRAN system:

1240-110-10	Women's Reserve [Uniforms]
1470	Dependents
1500-95-5	Discharge—Women's Reserve
1505-70	Discipline—Reserve Women
1520-35-25	Education—Navy—Female Schools
1535-55-10	Enrollment—Reserve—Women's Reserve
1945-50-20	Navy—Personnel—20—Nurses (female)
1965-90-10-5	Officer—Reserve officers—Female—Appointment & Commission
1975-60-20-10	Recruit training (Training Directive for Women 22 Dec 1948)
2185-65-10	History of the USMCWR
2185-95-10	Bulletin (Hdqtrs Bulletin)
2220-15-35	Quarters—Officers—Nurses
2295-100	Annual Reports—Women's Reserve
2455-30	Dependents—Children—Relatives—Wives

In these classifications for the early subseries are documents about qualifications for enlistment in the Women's Reserve, their pay and allowances, medical examinations, duties, uniforms, and the termination of the program. There are statistics of the number of women who served in the program and a postwar evaluation of the program. There is an occasional letter or memorandum in file 1155 about women's associations and societies, such as the Women's Auxiliary of the Navy Relief Society and the District of Columbia Chapter of the American Red Cross. Files 1850-10 and 1860-30 deal with the USMC policy regarding marriages of personnel, sea and shore assignments of married men, and discussions of postwar policy regarding marriage. Records relating to recreation (2255-80) include a folder (1 in.) on dances and shows. In it are memorandums, issuances, and invitations regarding the Navy Relief Ball, official receptions, and gala occasions to which officers and their wives were invited. Files 2455-30 and 1470 relate to the transfer of wives and other relatives as general policy and in particular cases. File 1215 contains information about prostitutes on Pennsylvania Avenue in the District of Columbia and the complaint of a Beaufort, SC, woman about the illegal manufacture and sale of intoxicants near Parris Island, SC.

127.5. In the USMC **general photographic file, 1775–1941** (127-G, 16,650 images), there are about 60 prints filed under "Women Marines." A photograph, taken about 1921, of Marine Bandmaster John Philip Sousa and his wife, Jennie Bellis Sousa, is among "Portraits."

127.6. The records of the USMC Historical Division contain a **card register of communications sent and received, 1798–1918** (10 ft.), arranged in two subseries: one alphabetical by subject and name of location and the other alphabetical by name of person. It serves as an index to several correspondence series. Information on each card includes the name of the correspondent, date, place, index terms, and a brief summary of the communication described. The cards present evidence of rations issued to wives and women "detailed" as nurses or laundresses in the Revolutionary War period, refer to letters of inquiry about men in the USMC throughout the period covered by the series, and under the subject heading "Wives of officers," include references to the lifting of restrictions in 1916 on officers having their wives with them in Haiti.

127.7. During World War II more than 20,000 women served in the Marine Corps Women's Reserve (MCWR), popularly known as "women marines." It was the last of the four women's military service organizations (WAC, WAVE, and SPAR) to be formed during the war. There are records relating to women marines in several files of the Commandant's **general correspondence, January 1939–June 1950** (816 ft.), also arranged by the ELLS-DRAN system. The records of the director, MCWR, were sent to this central file and were interfiled with records on similar subjects from other parts of the USMC. In addition to the ELLS-DRAN classifications that deal with women in the 1913–38 correspondence noted above, the following are useful for the World War II period:

1500-95-3	Qualifications for reserve [marital and family status, mental health, age]
1515-35	Duty [records about service for MCWR in Hawaii in 1944]
1520-30-65	Education [training of women and men as bakers and cooks]

127.8. Volumes of **muster rolls, 1798–1945** (1,285 vols., 353 ft.), that document the World War II years are arranged in two subseries: posts and stations, and mobile units. MCWR personnel records showing assignments, transfers, promotions, discharges, and training appear in the rolls for the following stations:

A Marine in the Training Aids Section wields an air brush in 1963. 127-GRA-69-A556154.

Northampton Naval Reserve Midshipman's School, March–July 1943

New River, NC, Women's Reserve Schools (organized July 2, 1943)

Oceanside, CA, Women's Reserve Battalion (Camp Pendleton), March 1944

Milledgeville, GA, Naval Training School, Georgia State College for Women, Marine Training Detachment, October 1943

Camp Lejeune, NC, Women's Reserve Battalion, March 1944; Women's Reserve Schools, March 1944–Fall 1945; and Women's Reserve Separation Company, October 1945

New Bern, NC, Reserve Districts—Women's Reserve Unit

127.9. Motion pictures, 1939–45 (21 reels), include one entitled "Lady Marines" (3 reels) showing officer candidates graduating from training at Mount Holyoke College, enlisted women at the completion of boot training at Hunter College, recruits' life at Camp Lejeune, NC, and a dramatization of women replacing servicemen in numerous office jobs.

127.10. Sound recordings, 1942–43 (8 items), include a USMC recruiting broadcast series called "It's the Tops" (16 programs) featuring popular singers Connie Haines and Kay Starr with the big bands of the era.

Lance Cpl. Felicia A. Lynch, a 19-year-old Marine, smiles during a 1971 ceremony. 127-GRA-70-A702309.

Records of the
Office of the Judge Advocate General (Army)

Record Group 153

153.1. A judge advocate of the Continental Army was appointed in 1775. Legal provision for a U.S. Army judge advocate was made in 1797, but the number and status of judge advocates varied during the following years. A Judge Advocate of the Army was appointed in 1849, and in 1884 after several administrative changes, the Judge Advocate General (JAG) became the head of the Judge Advocate General's Department. Since 1946 the Office has been an Army staff agency.

153.2. The Office of the Judge Advocate General (Army) supervises the system of military justice throughout the Army, performs appellate review of records of trials by court-martial, and furnishes the Army's legal services. The JAG serves as legal adviser to the Secretary of the Army and all Army offices, agencies, and personnel. Women's names appear in the records of this Office as suspects, plaintiffs, defendants, and witnesses.

153.3. During the Civil War, Southern women living in Union-oc-cupied territory were tried by court-martial for a variety of offenses. In **letters sent ("record books"), 1842–89** (57 vols., 15 ft.), arranged chronologically with a name and subject index in each volume, there are letters relating to such cases as an application for a pardon or mitigation of sentence from a woman convicted of murdering a former slave. In volume 21 (pp. 647–52) is a request from Dr. Mary E. Walker that she be given a commission or a brevet as surgeon in the U.S. Army in rec-ognition of her service during the Civil War, along with the Judge Advo-cate General's reply. Separate **indexes to letters sent, 1842–76** (4 vols., 9 in.), are divided into a subject index (1 vol.) and a name index (3 vols.). Among the headings in the subject index are "Marriage, enlisted," and "Prostitute, marriage to." The names of women who served as witnesses in general court-martial trials appear in the various indexes to the outgo-ing letters.

153.4. The **Index, 1894–1912** (23 ft.), to the JAG's numerically arranged **general correspondence ("document file"), 1894–1912** (61 ft.), contains the following headings relating to women: "Army Relief Association" (for widows and orphans of Army men), "Marriage," "Pros-titutes," "Widow," "Wife," "Woman," "Woman's Army and Navy League," and "Woman's Relief Corps." Documents indexed under "Nurses" relate to precedent-setting decisions furnished in response to requests for legal opinions from the Surgeon General of the Army relating to appointments, pay, rations, benefits, duties, and regulations governing both the nurses in the newly established Army Nurse Corps and those who served as contract nurses during the Spanish-American War. Considerable legal advice was also provided concerning the status of female employees and military dependents in **general correspondence, 1912–17** (60 ft.), ar-ranged according to the JAG decimal filing scheme, for which there is a **name and subject index** (50 ft.), primarily for 1917, and a **manual for the JAG "decimal" classification scheme, 1912–17** (1 vol., 1 in.), which provides a file number for "Army organization—Nurse Corps," "Gratuities—Army Nurse Corps," and "Gratuities—families of enlisted men." There are references to women in the index under headings such as "American National Red Cross," "Army Nurse Corps," "Employees," "Female," "Matrimony in the Army," "Nurse," "Pensions," "Prostitutes," "Revised Statutes 1116," "Woman suffrage," "Women" (which includes references to contract surgeons, industrial contract workers, and clerical personnel), "Women lawyers," and "Young Women's Christian Associa-tion."

153.5. The JAG **general correspondence, 1918–August 1942** (362 ft.), arranged according to the War Department decimal classification scheme, includes letters about such cases as that of a soldier's wife who shot another soldier with whom she was living (file 220.46 "Line of Duty"); officers and wives accused of desertion by their spouses (241.3

"Family Support," 6 in.); and similar problems with enlisted men (242.4 "Family Support," 4 in.). The 1932 alleged rape of an Army nurse at Fitzsimmons General Hospital, Denver, is documented in file 250.1 "Rape," which also includes opinions of boards of review in matters of discipline. Other file designations with records relating to women are 0.51 "Rape"; 251.1 "Prostitution"; 291.1 "Marriage" (8 in.) including State laws, individual cases and special studies, and a 1936 War Department study regarding the marriage of enlisted men; 292 "Families" (1 in.) including adoption, birth, marriage, divorce, desertion, nationality, and parentage; and 710 "Venereal Disease." Many letters in this series relate to nurses. File 211 "Nurses" (3 in.) deals with administrative policy and legal decisions in individual cases about such matters as pay and benefits, World War I service of the Army Nurse Corps, and lists of nurses with their Army serial numbers. Smaller files are 524.21 "Nurses' baggage" and 331.4 "Nurses' mess." A few references in file 354.01 "WAACS," dated 1941–42, relate to a proposed auxiliary force of civilian women, including the status of such an organization in the Military Establishment.

153.6. Registers of court-martial cases, 1809–90 (15 vols., 3 ft. 6 in.), filmed as M1105 (8 rolls), serve as finding aids to the case files and provide chronological and alphabetical lists of cases. A register entry gives for a case the defendant's name, rank and unit (where applicable), case file number, date and location of the trial, the verdict, sentence, and names of court officials.

153.7. Court-martial case files, 1809–1938 (5,133 ft.), are arranged according to an alpha-numeric scheme for the 1809–94 period, and numerically by date of filing during the 1894–1938 period. A case file includes the complete record of the trial, noting charges and specifications, arraignments and pleas, exhibits, proceedings, findings and sentences, action by the Secretary of War and the President where applicable, and related correspondence. Women's names appear in the records as defendants, witnesses, victims, accomplices, and sources of soldiers' predicaments. Case files E11 and E12 in 1814 both relate to trials of Dr. Samuel Akerly, hospital surgeon at Greenwich, NY, accused of mismanaging the hospital. The files include the testimony of several women who had served under him as cook, nurse, and washerwoman, all of whom described his temperament and ethics. Many cases for the Civil War period deal with women who were tried before military commissions for alleged treasonable acts and questionable loyalties. In file M 2867 relating to the military commission that investigated the Sand Creek Massacre of November 29, 1864, names of white women as Indian prisoners and Indian women as victims appear in the proceedings. Maj. Marcus Reno was the defendant in two cases (QQ 87 and QQ 1554) in which he was accused of taking liberties with women in the families of other officers. File QQ 52 is a similar case involving another officer, which took place in 1876 at Omaha Barracks, NE. Records of other military commissions or courts of inquiry also related to women, including the one that investigated the Lincoln assassination. (See 153.10.)

153.8. A copy of a special edition (12 pp.) of *Minnesota in the War*, February 15, 1919, devoted to the work of the Women's Committee of the Minnesota State Commission of Public Safety is filed in the **papers of Col. Mark Guerin, Judge Advocate of the 6th Corps Area, 1918–24** (3 in.).

153.9. Briefs of American Expeditionary Forces court-martial cases, 1918–20 (4 ft., 6 in.), arranged alphabetically by subject, provide access to court-martial case files for the World War I period. For each case the brief supplies the charge, name of defendant, date, and case number. Subjects relating to women include "Bastardy," "Bigamy," "Conduct," "Husband and wife," "Insurance," "Marriage," "Prostitute," "Rape," and "White slave law." Findings, opinions, or action on a sentence are noted on some cards.

153.10. Records of investigations include those of the military commission that met in Washington for several weeks after the assassination of President Abraham Lincoln and the attempt on the life of Secretary of State William H. Seward on April 14, 1865. Chief investigator was Col. H.L. Burnett, formerly Judge Advocate of the Northern Department of the Army. National Archives Microfilm Publication M599 *Investigation and Trial Papers Relating to the Assassination of President Lincoln* (15 rolls) reproduces the principal series related to the event, and an index to the witnesses called at the trial has been prepared by the National Archives and is printed in the descriptive pamphlet that accompanies the microfilm publication. The index includes a number of women's names, indexed to the page number of the records and to the roll number of the microfilm. Series filmed include several that relate to women. **Records relating to Lincoln assassination suspects, 1864–65** (1 ft.; rolls 4–6), arranged by page number of the "Military Commission Record Book," include statements from persons in Ford's Theatre when the President was shot, servants in nearby houses, and others, among them a number of women. The **register of records relating to Lincoln assassination suspects ("Military Commission Record Book"), 1864–65** (1 vol., 2 in.; roll 1), arranged chronologically by date of receipt (with a name index), consists of abstracts of letters, testimony, and reports regarding persons who were in any way suspected of involvement in the case. **Letters sent by Col. H.L. Burnett, April–July 1865** (1 vol., 2 in.; roll 1), are arranged chronologically with a name index that includes the names of Mary Surratt and of six other women who were arrested but released because of insufficient evidence. **Letters received by Col. H.L. Burnett, April–August 1865** (1 ft.; rolls 2–3), are arranged in numerical order as registered in a **register** (1 vol., 2 in.), which is indexed. Additional **unregistered and unnumbered letters received relating to Lincoln assassination suspects, 1864–65** (4 in.; roll 7), are arranged alphabetically by name of suspect or other person; there is an index. Filmed following the records of investigation and evidence is the record of the trial, court-martial case file MM 2251 (rolls 8–15), consisting of proceedings and exhibits. The defense of Mrs. Surratt is not filed with the proceedings but was widely published.

153.11. The War Crimes Branch in the International Affairs Division of the Office of the JAG was established during World War II to collect evidence for eventual use in trials of enemy war criminals. American women who were interned by the enemy included Army and Navy nurses and missionaries, nuns, and other civilians. When repatriated, their sworn statements were taken to create a record of their experiences. They are in **case files, 1944–49** (551 ft.), arranged geographically and include descriptions of attrocities observed or endured. The case files also include correspondence, trial records, transcripts, interrogation reports, exhibits, and newspaper clippings. A **Far East place-name index, 1944–49** (14 ft.), and a **Far East name index, 1944–49** (81 ft.), can be used to locate particular prison camps or individuals. Indexes are available for similar case files for European and Mediterranean Theaters of Operations, but most American women who were POW's were imprisoned in the Philippines. The following case files are among those that relate to women: 40 "Northern Luzon and adjacent islands"; 40-31 "Santo Tomas Internment Camp, Manila"; 41 "Southern Luzon, Mindanao, and adjacent islands"; and 41-6 "Los Banos Internment Camp." Other places in the place-name index where women served or were imprisoned are Bataan, Corregidor, Bilibid Prison, and Fort Santiago.

153.12. Interrogation reports on Americans held as prisoners of war, 1943–47 (65 ft.), relate principally to German prisons, but also included are lists of all prisoners liberated in the Philippines including reports on civilian internees.

153.13. Iva Ikuko Toguri (Tokyo Rose), Mildred Gillars (Axis Sally), and Rita Zucca, all U.S. citizens, became famous for broadcasts of enemy propaganda to American servicemen in attempts to undermine morale. There are records about Toguri and Gillars in the **war crimes case files,** (551 ft.). Both were convicted of treason in civilian courts after the war. Zucca renounced her U.S. citizenship and was not tried in the United States. There are records about her in **records relating to untried war crimes of European and Mediterranean Theaters of Operation and the Far East command, 1944–49** (169 ft.), in the War Crimes Branch, International Affairs Division. One index serves both series.

Records of the Office of the Chief of Ordnance

Record Group 156

156.1. The Ordnance Department was established as an independent bureau of the Department of War by an act of May 14, 1812. It was abolished, and its functions were transferred to the U.S. Army Materiel Command during a 1962 Department of the Army reorganization. The Ordnance Department was responsible for procurement, distribution, and maintenance of Army ordnance and equipment and the development and testing of new types of ordnance. Women were employed in arsenals and in various types of home piecework for the Bureau beginning during the Civil War period.

156.2. The **general correspondence, 1894–1913** (1,689 ft.), is arranged numerically. The **name and subject index** (354 ft.) to the 1904–11 part of the correspondence includes cards (7 in.) for "Employees—clerks" at Bureau headquarters and at arsenals in many parts of the country. The records demonstrate the increasing number of women in this employment category. There are also many entries under "Women." Entries for "Compensation for injuries to employees" and "Frankford Arsenal, Philadelphia, Pa." refer to a few documents about women working at the Frankford Arsenal.

156.3. There is information about women employed by the Ordnance Department headquarters and at arsenals, including the Frankford, Picatinny (Dover, NJ), Rock Island (Moline, IL), and Watervliet (NY) Arsenals, in the **general correspondence, 1915–41** (2,150 ft.), arranged according to the War Department decimal classification scheme. The **name and subject index** (96 ft.) is arranged in three chronological segments, 1915–24, 1925–31, and 1931–41. The first two segments contain many entries under "Women," particularly during the World War I period. In file 230.6/8704 Circular 31, Headquarters, 4th Army Corps Area, Charleston, SC, is entitled "Welfare of Women" and outlines requirements for teachers and stenographers and the duties of hostesses. Several reports in file 230.38 provide information about men and women employees separately. In files 342.4, 342.6, and 342.8–11 there is correspondence about a plan to enlist women. Most of the women were clerical personnel or factory workers, but there is some correspondence about women carpenters, chemists, and physicians. One officer wrote of the drill activities of a "military" organization of women employed in the Inspection Division (file 353.54/32). Items 3531–3588 and 7329 in file 381 (postwar defense planning) recall the World War I service of women in the Ordnance Department. Women employed as inspectors at Frankford were praised in 1924 records of postwar review (file 381./3664).

An American factory worker keeps the ammunition flowing overseas to troops fighting the First World War. 111-SC-31606.

156.4. Housing for Ordnance officers and their families is illustrated by **plans of officers' quarters at arsenals, 1876** (3 vols., 3 in.), showing floor plans and front elevations. The quarters included parlor, conservatory, dining room, bedrooms, fireplaces, piazzas, and servants' rooms.

156.5. In 1917 the Ordnance Department created a Women's Branch in the Industrial Service Section to provide industrial counseling for and about women employees. It became a part of the Production Division and was a forerunner of the Women's Bureau in the Labor Department. Records of the Branch (4 ft.) in the **collection reports and correspondence of the Ordnance Department and its divisions, 1917–20** (255 ft.), among the records of the Historical Branch of the Executive Section consist mainly of reports from women's representatives in the field and the final report (3 vols., 443 pp.) of Director Clara M. Tead dated December 1918. The report deals with women working in machine and crane operations and welding, inspecting, and engaging in other activities. It also discusses wages, working conditions, services for women employees, and strikes.

156.6. There is Tead correspondence in files 23.1 and 62.1 of the **general correspondence of the Administrative Section, 1918** (55 ft.), of the Production Division. There are also reports that were sent from the

Women's Branch representatives in field offices in file 319.12 (2½ ft.) and a special report on protective clothing for women machine workers in file 319.12/290. A **name and subject card index** (26 ft.) is helpful.

156.7. Information about the number of women employed in munitions work and the hourly rate of pay for "female help" at various war plants is found on completed **questionnaires sent by the Small Arms Section to contractors relating to labor, 1918** (3 in.), arranged alphabetically by name of ordnance district. The questionnaires are among the records of the Production Division.

156.8. In the 3d volume of a typewritten **"history of the industrial demobilization of the Ordnance Department," 1920** (3 vols., 3 in.), there are photographs of several types of work stations at Frankford Arsenal showing women wearing trousers, work aprons, or dresses depending on the nature of their tasks.

156.9. Besides records of headquarters of the Department of Ordnance, there are records of each arsenal. For example, the records of the Watertown (MA) Arsenal include **general correspondence, 1916–44** (102 ft.), which contains letters, mainly 1918–19, to and from women employees in files 230.3 "Clerical" and 230.82 "Discharge and dismissals." There are women's names in the January 1865–April 30, 1868, part of the Watertown Arsenal **monthly returns of civilian employees, October 1824–January 1903 with gaps** (9 vols., 2 in.), arranged chronologically. The names of women employed as seamstresses and in other capacities at Watertown are included in **timebooks of civilian employees, 1859–93** (2 vols., 2 in.), even though one volume is labeled "Report of Men Employed in the Laboratory." A woodcut entitled "Filling cartridges at the United States Arsenal, Watertown, Massachusetts," appeared in an issue of *Harper's Weekly* in 1861. A photographic copy of the picture, which shows a room full of women at work, is filed with a manuscript of the **history of Watertown Arsenal, 1816–1942, and related records** (2 in.).

156.10. In another example, the **general correspondence, 1915–39** (140 ft.), of the Watervliet (NY) Arsenal, arranged according to the War Department decimal classification scheme, contains letters about women employed there, mostly in clerical positions. In a **register of births and deaths, 1892–1909** (1 vol., ½ in.), for the hospital at Watervliet there are records of women who became patients while visiting the facility.

156.11. Folder 97 of headquarters records labeled "Ordnance Facilities" in **photographs collected by the Historical Branch, 1917–19** (156-H, 2 ft.), includes three photographs of women working on ordnance projects. The prints are in an album of views of the Winchester Repeating Arms Co., New Haven, CT, ca. 1919.

156.12. A few photographs of women at their work stations at the New York Air Brake Company are in one of the **albums: production of World War I ordnance, 1917–19** (156-OP, 112 items).

Records of the Office of the Inspector General (Army)

Record Group 159

159.1. The Inspector General's Department of the Army was created by an act of March 3, 1813. The Office of the Inspector General (IGO) became part of the personal staff of the Army Staff in 1972. The IGO inspects, investigates, and reports on all matters affecting the efficiency, discipline, and welfare of the Army. There are very few references to women in these records.

159.2. For the period 1863–91, some references to women can be found in inspection reports that are filed with **letters received, 1863–94** (60 ft.), arranged by year and thereunder by name of writer, 1863–76, and by year and thereunder numerically, 1877–94. The letters are accompanied by **registers, 1863–89** (11 vols., 2 ft.), and **name and subject indexes to the registers, 1863–91** (3 vols., 11 in.). Maj. William Painter's April 1864 report includes the investigation of fraud at Camp Cleveland, OH, where a hospital steward returned $300 after admitting that he had padded the rolls of matrons. In a report from Maj. E.H. Luddington, there is a letter of complaint from journalist Jane Swisshelm to Secretary of War Edwin M. Stanton complaining that an institution established on Federal property for the relief of destitute black women and children was badly managed. An 1879 report commented on the problem of marriages of enlisted men. For the same period there are **letters sent, 1863–89** (5 vols., 1 ft.), arranged chronologically with an index in each volume, and **letters sent, 1891–94** (12 vols., 1 ft.), also arranged chronologically with an index in each volume.

159.3. Inspection reports, 1898–1914 (74 ft.), are arranged by year and thereunder by subject (such as "hospitals") or by name of military command or post. They include a few comments on the quality of nursing service available and the condition of nurses' quarters. A 1913 report for Fort Leavenworth, KS, contains an offer from a soldier's wife to operate a dairy for the post.

159.4. Inspection reports, 1903–12 (12 vols., 1 ft.), arranged chronologically, are served by the **index to general correspondence, 1894–1914** (18 ft.). Among the reports are copies of reports of investigations of complaints of nurses at a large hospital at the Presidio of San

Francisco. In the **index**, an entry "Eligible females" refers to a Civil Service Commission circular regarding clerks and typists.

159.5. The **general correspondence, 1894–1914** (88 ft.), arranged numerically, contains a complaint on behalf of Jennie Roper, a private's wife whose admission to an Army hospital had been publicized in a local newspaper. A March 1898 letter from Elizabeth F. Hill expressing interest in becoming a government nurse presaged congressional authorization the following month to hire women as Army contract nurses during the Spanish-American War. Photographs of women working in the new steam laundry at Fort Leavenworth, 1904–5, are with a report on the operation and financial statement of the laundry.

159.6. The **name index to unclassified, confidential, and secret decimal correspondence files, 1917–54** (192 ft.), includes the names of accused and accusers as well as subjects. Each index entry includes the War Department decimal number, the date, and the original security classification of the file referenced. There is also a **subject index to unclassified, confidential, and secret correspondence, 1917–54** (85 ft.). Among the subjects are misconduct, subversion, misassignments, WAC unit inspections, and complaints of racial discrimination. Most references to women are to WAAC or WAC personnel, but there are entries for "Immoral," "Prostitutes," and "Women." The correspondence covered by the 1917–54 indexes is divided into several series by time segment (1917–34, 1935–39, 1939–47, and 1947–54) and thereunder by original level of security classification. The records for 1947–54 have not been declassified. The examples below were taken from the 1939–47 segment.

159.7. Most files concerning "immorality" were assigned War Department decimal classification 333.9 "Inspections and Investigations." One 1943 file under 333.9 in the **formerly confidential correspondence, 1939–47** (546 ft.), is labeled "The Tides Apartment Hotel, Daytona Beach, Florida," and deals with leasing the facility for WAC trainees against the owner's wishes.

159.8. Documents in decimal classification 333.9 and other classifications in **formerly secret correspondence, 1939–47** (33 ft.), arranged according to the War Department decimal classification scheme, provide a mixture of fact, gossip, and policy statements about daily life in the service. There are also complaints from civilian employees and embittered mothers. One 333.9 file, available with deletions of privileged information, relates to alleged homosexual activities at the 3d WAC Training Center, Fort Oglethorpe, GA, in 1944. Correspondence and reports about prostitution and the sale of alcoholic beverages near military reservations are scattered throughout this correspondence in files numbered 250.1 and 250.11, including letters from irate women citizens and women restaurant owners.

159.9. The **unclassified general correspondence, 1939–47** (468 ft.), arranged according to the War Department decimal scheme, consists mainly of 339.9 files relating to military units and departments, persons, and industrial plants. File 230.8 "Hostesses and Librarians" consists of complaints on behalf of women in those job categories.

Records of Headquarters Army Service Forces

Record Group 160

160.1. Headquarters Army Service Forces (ASF) was established by War Department General Order 14, March 13, 1943, as the successor to the Services of Supply to provide services and supplies to meet military requirements of the Army. It was abolished in June 1946. The records relate to women as civilians and as military personnel in World War II. Unless otherwise noted, the records in each cited series are arranged according to the War Department decimal classification scheme.

Office of the Commanding General

160.2. The **formerly security classified correspondence, 1942–45** (13 ft.), arranged alphabetically by subject in two chronological subseries, 1942–44 and 1945, includes a file, "Morale Services, 1941–44," that contains a March 1943 memorandum from Commanding Gen. Brehon B. Somervell relating to the low esteem for Waacs revealed by a survey of enlisted men and to plans for a publicity campaign to solve the problem. There is also a file labeled "Women's Army Corps, 1945."

160.3. Among the **speeches by General Somervell and General Styer, 1941–45** (1 ft.), arranged chronologically for each general, is one made by General Somervell to the National Advisory Council of the Women's Interest Section on June 25, 1943, seeking the support of women's clubs for WAAC recruitment.

160.4. The final report of a "Survey of Women's Services Among Young Men, Young Women, and Parents, November 1943" (73 pp.), is in **formerly security classified . . . miscellaneous records, 1942–45** (3 ft.), arranged by subject.

160.5. In the records of the Chief of Staff, the **formerly security classified correspondence of Lt. Gen. W.D. Styer, 1942–45** (7 ft.), arranged alphabetically by subject, includes a file labeled "Women's Army Corps" (1 in.).

160.6. The **formerly security classified general correspondence, 1943–45** (24 ft.), of the Deputy Chief of Staff for Service Commands contains in file 020 "W.A.A.C." cross-reference sheets referring to documents relating to housing, civilian schools for training, requests for

WAAC detachments, entertainment, recruiting, clothing, administrative jurisdiction, utilization, and discipline for the corps.

160.7. The records of the Public Relations Advisor contain **drafts and transcripts of Somervell speeches, articles, and press releases, 1942–45** (4 ft.), arranged alphabetically by subject. Included are two speeches to Wacs serving in the ASF under the heading, "WAC Film—July 29, 1943—Washington, D.C." Compulsory labor for women in Germany and the United States is considered in documents filed under "Independent Women—Article—Women at War." There are photographs of a WAC parade at the first WAC Training Center at Des Moines, IA, and other anniversary ceremonies in a **scrapbook . . . commemorating the third anniversary of the Army Service Forces on March 9, 1945** (1 vol., 3 in.). The scrapbook also includes newspaper accounts of an address at Topeka, KS, by Army Nurse Lt. Blanche Kimball, who had escaped after 3 years in a Japanese prison in Manila.

Directors and Divisions Under the Commanding General

160.8. The alphabetically arranged **general correspondence, 1942–43** (2 ft.), of the Director of Administration includes under "WAAC" (3 in.) correspondence relating to recruiting with references to advertisements in women's magazines, minimum age limits, the industrial-military manpower problem, and the reluctance of military men to accept a noncombatant women's auxiliary military service. Other subjects are proper utilization of Wacs, outfitting them, regulations relating to Wacs who married, and NAACP charges of discrimination against black women. **Formerly security classified correspondence, 1942–43** (1 ft.), contains in file 020 "WAAC" correspondence about using WAC companies in the European Theater of Operations (ETO) and includes a memorandum of WAAC Director Oveta Culp Hobby pertaining to black company assignments and assignment of WAC companies to particular areas of the ETO. There are also minutes of meetings in which Gen. George C. Marshall's plans to expand the WAAC were discussed. In the same file are records relating to the conduct of off-duty Wacs stationed near Daytona Beach, FL, allegedly including assault and rape.

160.9. A "History of the First WAC Special Services Company" (10 pp.) is in an alphabetic subseries at the end of a large series of **formerly security classified general correspondence, 1941–43** (164 ft.), of the Director of Administration, Army Exchange Service. The account describes the work of Wacs in managing athletics, handicrafts, theater, music, and library activities for military personnel in the ETO. The heading "Hostesses" identifies records about librarians as well as hostesses in Army service clubs. Filed under "S" is a copy of the *Women's Army Corps Song Book* (Washington, DC: Government Printing Office, 1944). In the decimal file section, file 353.8 includes records of entertainment tours. Among professionals who performed for troops at U.S. and overseas bases were Dinah Shore, Martha Raye, and Loretta Young and athletes Alice Marble and Mary Hardwicke. In the same file are records relating to women involved in Army recreational activities through the American Red Cross and the USO.

160.10. There is a file labeled "Women's Army Auxiliary Corps" in the Mobilization Division's Command Installation Branch **formerly security classified correspondence, 1942–46** (18 ft.), arranged alphabetically by subject or by number of service command (No.1–9). It contains records relating to housing for Wacs.

160.11. "WAC in the Postwar Military Establishment" (1 in.) is in the Planning Division's **formerly security classified correspondence relating to supply, logistic, and service planning for the Army, 1942–46** (30 ft.), arranged alphabetically by subject.

Control Division

160.12. The Control Division's **general correspondence, 1942–46** (147 ft.), includes correspondence with women's organizations in file 080. Among the organizations represented are the American Women's Volunteer Services, Inc., which provided trained and uniformed chauffeurs and drivers for a motor transport service at Army installations; the Bataan Relief Organization; the Citizens' Manpower Commission of the Crawford (NE) Women's Club; Daughters of the American Revolution; National Federation of Music Clubs; Women Commandos; YWCA; and the WAC National Civilian Advisory Committee. In file 211 there is a report based on questionnaires completed by nurses returning from overseas. In files 210.3 and 211 there is information about the assignment of Wacs. File 323.3 contains records about the difficulty of outfitting Wacs in clothing, either on base or in local stores, especially at Fort Dix.

160.13. Formerly security classified reports and studies relating to the organization, procedures, and operations of the Services of Supply and the Army Service Forces, 1942–45 (8 ft.), arranged numerically, include the following that relate to women:

13. Minutes of Meetings of the Committee to Study the Activities of the Medical Department (2 vols.)

28. Reports Prepared by the Machine Records Branch, AGO, October 1942

33. A Study of Typing Volume in the Services of Supply in Washington, December 1942

35. Effective Utilization of Personnel, February 1943

68. Report on Employee Questionnaire, February 1943

76. Reply to Deputy Chief of Staff on Manpower Utilization, January 1943

111. Surplus Military and General Service Personnel, April 1943

113. Report on Officer Assignment in the Army Service Forces, July 27, 1943

115. Supply Service Personnel Comparisons and Trends, April 1943

138. Report on the Program for More Effective Utilization of Personnel, August 1943

167. Survey of Notification of Condolences for Overseas Casualties, March 1945

170. Report on Assignment and Transfer of Military Personnel in the Army Service Forces, May 1945

160.14. Reports that include information about WAC activity in **formerly security classified monthly progress reports relating to the major functions of the Services of Supply and the Army Service Forces, 1942–46** (30 ft.), arranged numerically, are found under the following headings: 5 "Personnel" (which also includes nurses and civilian women employees), 9 "Military training," 12 "Progress charts," and 17 "Demobilization—Postwar Planning." Under 10 "Special Services" there is a survey of the servicemen's attitudes towards the Red Cross and service clubs. The survey also included questions about servicemen's leisure time activities (among them "dating a girl").

160.15. WAC recruiting, assignment, operating personnel, enlistments, and strength, and numbers of reserve nurses on active duty are subjects of narrative or statistical **formerly security classified monthly progress reports of the service commands, 1942–45** (15 ft.), arranged numerically by number of service command (No. 1–9) followed by the Northwest Service Command and the Military District of Washington.

160.16. Issuances relating to women in the alphabetically arranged **miscellaneous formerly security classified issuances of the Army Service Forces, 1942–46** (26 ft.), are filed under "Civilian Personnel." The following issuances are pertinent: "The First Six Months: A Report of the Activities of the Civilian Personnel Division, Headquarters, Service and Supply, March to September, 1942"; "Placement and Employee Relations of the Army Service Forces," April 1945; and "Basic Data: Civilian Personnel of the Services of Supply, September 30, 1942." In the same series there are Army Service Forces Civilian Personnel Information Bulletins. Two of them, both numbered "3," relate to women: "Guide to the Immediate and Maximum Utilization of Civilian Womanpower," November 10, 1943 (21 pp.), and "Guide to Training Women for Work with the Army Service Forces," April 5, 1944. In addition, there is "Reference Material on Civilian Workers," which includes sections on absenteeism and separations that specifically mention women, and a scrapbook filed under "Soldier Morale" that includes records about the "Maxey Command," a group of young single women who organized service club dances to entertain the men at Camp Maxey, TX.

160.17. The records of the Administrative Management Branch of the Control Division include **formerly security classified reports relating to the development and activities of the Army Service Forces,**

1941–45 (14 ft.), arranged by organization. Under "Women's Army Auxiliary Corps, 1942–44," there are copies of a publication about physical training for Wacs and another providing general information about enlistment, training, assignments, pay, and uniforms. "The ASF in World War II" contains a nine-page chapter on WAC problems. There are also copies of press releases noting the participation of the WAC National Civilian Advisory Committee and of women's clubs nationwide in recruiting for the WAC. The work of the Women's Volunteer Committee, which was chaired by Mrs. Brehon Somervell, wife of the commanding general, is also documented. An essay, "Battle Casualties and Their Welfare," contains information on benefits for servicemen's widows and wives, and a copy of *Demobilization and Readjustment* (Washington, DC: Government Printing Office, 1943), 106 pp., a National Resources Planning Board publication, includes a statement on women's postwar rights and privileges.

160.18. Also in the Administrative Management Branch records are **organization charts, statements of functions, and reports of activities of units of the Army Service Forces ("Administrative logs"), 1945** (5 ft.), arranged by ASF organization. There is some information about WAC activities in the logs of the nine numbered commands and the Military District of Washington and in other logs filed under "Headquarters, ASF, Control Division." The activation of WAC Hospital Companies and the discontinuation of WAC recruiting are documented. A draft history of the AGO, March 1942–August 1945, includes WAC-related accounts.

160.19. Material relating to the history of the WAC is collected in file 291.3 "Women's Army Auxiliary Corps" in the Statistics and Progress Branch's **formerly security classified correspondence, 1941–43** (9 ft.). Included are circulars, bulletins, equipment and clothing allowance documents, tables of organization, and memorandums, some of which suggest policies and plans for training. A "Report on Suitability of Military Occupations for WAAC Auxiliaries," is dated November 25, 1942.

Intelligence Division

160.20. Among the records of the ASF Intelligence Division, the **formerly security classified correspondence, 1943–46** (47 ft.), includes a section labeled "Communists" in file 000.5 with records about Elizabeth Gurley Flynn and other women who attended Communist Party meetings. File 095 contains records about the CIO; the One Canteen; the Peace Now Movement; the Sweethearts of Servicemen Club; the We, the Mothers Mobilize for America organization; and the WAC Mothers Organization. Filed in 320 "WAAC" and 322 "Corps—WAC" are records documenting the whispering campaign against the Wacs, including derogatory leaflets.

Office of the Director of Military Training (ODMT)

160.21. ODMT **formerly security classified correspondence, 1942–46** (180 ft.), includes records relating to the training of Army women. File 290 (1 in.) contains memorandums about the early phases of WAAC training and the curriculum for officer candidates at the Fort Des Moines, IA, WAAC Training Center. In file 352 (4 in.) there are records relating to the WAC Advanced Officer Training School at Purdue University and contracts with colleges for facilities and training courses for WAAC and WAC personnel. Records in file 353 (3 in.) relate to policy on the use of firearms by WAC personnel, the training of black Wacs, National Civilian Advisory Committee recommendations, and physical fitness training for Wacs. The closing of the WAC Training Center is documented in file 354.1 (4 in.) along with progress reports of training programs and training requirements.

160.22. In **correspondence relating to the Army specialized training program, 1942–46** (10 ft.), file 353.9 includes records relating to women's training in medicine. The correspondence is mainly with college officials and members of Congress about policy and eligibility for the program.

160.23. Correspondence, histories, reports, and studies relating to the training of the Women's Army Corps ("historical file"), 1942–45 (3 ft.), is arranged by subject. The records relate to the training of both officers and enlisted women conducted in various ASF service schools such as those for the Quartermaster Corps and the Chemical Warfare Service. The variety of job types that Wacs were trained for is also noted, including coding clerk, medical technician, cook, and physical therapist's aide. Among the reports in the series is "Manners for Military Women."

Office of the Director of Personnel

160.24. In the **general correspondence, 1942–46** (12 ft.), of the Office of the Director of Personnel a war project file (5 in.) relates to the utilization and assignment of Wacs. Folder "A" of file 080 contains correspondence with the Women's Voluntary Service, Inc., about its transport service and its offer to establish a canteen service for troop trains. There are also records relating to the Women's Volunteer Committee.

160.25. The director's **formerly security classified correspondence ("project files"), 1942–46** (2 ft.), is arranged alphabetically by geographic location or subject and thereunder by the War Department classification scheme. Under the subject heading "Units—Women's Army Corps" there are records relating to overseas assignment of Wacs, recruiting and assignment of black and Japanese-American Wacs, and the comparative rejection rate of male and female recruits.

160.26. The Industrial Personnel Division's **general correspondence, 1940–46** (57 ft.), is arranged in three chronological subseries: 1940–42, 1942–44, and 1944–46. The first subseries is arranged alphabetically by subject, and the last two are arranged according to the War Department decimal classification scheme. In its work with wartime contractors, the division accumulated some records about women. Correspondence with the Women's Bureau about State laws affecting women is filed under the subject heading "Women in Industry" in the 1940–42 segment of the series. In the 1942–44 segment, women's complaints are filed under "Discrimination" (8 in.) in file 291.2. File 291.9. "Women" (8 in.) consists of press clippings, reports, and correspondence. Report titles include "Training and Utilization of Women in Selected War Department Establishments," "Problems of Employment of Women at Selected Ports and Reconsignment Points," "Problems of Employment of Women at Chemical Warfare Arsenals," and "Report on Projects Started in the Womanpower Section." File 322 "Women's Army Corps" (1 in.) mentions WAC recruitment policy in areas where civilian labor was in critically short supply.

160.27. In file 004.9 "Labor Supply" in the Industrial Personnel Division's **formerly restricted correspondence, 1942–44** (1 ft.), there are comments on women's performance in technical and skilled work. Information Circular No.2, "Number of Civilian Employees of Each Sex, Services of Supply," March 2, 1943 (14 pp.), is in file 230 "Civilian Employees." File 291.9 "Women in Industry" contains a small amount of correspondence with the War Production Board's Chief Economic Advisor and includes a table showing the numbers of men and women working in Army arsenals and ordnance depots. There is also a memorandum of the "policy on wages for women" and a copy of the "Statement of War Policy with Reference to Labor Standards," January 27, 1942, a Labor Department issuance that called for equal rates of pay for men and women.

160.28. The Division's **formerly confidential correspondence, 1942–46** (7 ft.), is arranged according to the War Department decimal classification scheme in two chronological subseries (1942–44 and 1944–46). The 1942–44 subseries includes records about women in file 230.5 "Absenteeism" and file 291.9 "Women in Industry." A June 1944 AGO policy statement on the confinement and punishment of Wacs is in file 250.4 "Courts martial" in the same subseries.

160.29. The **formerly security classified correspondence, 1942–46** (12 ft.), of the Labor Branch, arranged alphabetically by subject, includes in a file labeled "Womanpower" (1 in.) material relating to consultant Ellen M. Davies, including her speeches, notes on her career, and a study of women's industrial health and safety issues. The file "West Coast Aircraft Reports" includes correspondence, reports, and tables on women employed in various manufacturing plants. Black women's complaints of discrimination in wartime civil service jobs are in the Labor Branch **formerly security classified correspondence of the Race Relations Analyst, 1942–46** (5 in.), arranged alphabetically by subject.

160.30. The **general correspondence, 1942–46** (77 ft.), of the Military Personnel Division includes in file 080 records relating to attempts by the Red Cross and the Army to work out differences that arose over volunteer activities. "Army Regulations and Supporting Evidence Prepared by Eleanor C. Vincent, February 1, 1945, for Conference Requested by American Red Cross of G-1 to be Attended by Medical Corps, Special Services, and Personal Services" and correspondence with Catherine Hough, Assistant Director of the Military and Naval Welfare Service of the Red Cross are among the records.

160.31. In the Division's **formerly restricted correspondence, 1942–46** (16 ft.), arranged according to the War Department decimal classification scheme, file 220.3 "Women's Army Corps—Assignment" includes material on the assignment of Wacs including tables of organization, statistical data and memorandums relating to the placement of the authority to assign Wacs. There is also material about Wacs under "Officer Procurement Projects" in file 210.3 "Officers Appointments" and file 210.3 "WAC" and in 320.2 "Organization of the Army" and 322.5 "WAC." The **formerly confidential through secret correspondence, ("project files") 1942–46** (15 ft.), is arranged alphabetically by geographic location, command, or subject and thereunder according to the War Department decimal classification scheme. A file relating to Wacs (2 ft.) is at the end of the series and includes "Development Plan, Women's Army Auxiliary Corps," October 9, 1942, prepared by Lt. Col. Harold P. Tasker, Executive Officer, WAAC, which contains a schedule of priorities, requests for personnel, activation and flow process charts for training centers, expansion plans, and correspondence. Also included is material on the assignment and change of duty station for officers, including a "Survey of Promotion of Negro Officers"; information on the development of policies of recruitment, assignment, and discharge of Japanese-American Wacs; processing and assignment of women for overseas duty, including blacks and Japanese Americans; personnel problems overseas; and the withdrawal of Wacs from overseas. There is also some material about nurses. The Wac file also includes copies of *Occupations Suitable for Women* (Washington, DC: Government Printing Office, 1942), 103 pp., a Social Security Board publication; "War Demands for Trained Personnel," the proceedings of a 1942 conference; and a brief report, "Current and Anticipated Civilian Employment within the War Department, August 1942–June 1943."

160.32. The safety of Wacs in Africa and the assignment of Wacs as nurses' assistants are the subjects of brief correspondence under the heading "WAC" in **formerly top secret correspondence ("project files"), 1942–46** (2 ft.), arranged by geographic location or subject and thereunder according to the War Department decimal classification scheme. The Military Personnel Division also prepared a **"History of the Procurement, Distribution, and Separation of Military Personnel, 1939–45** (9 vols., 10 in.), that includes material about Wacs and Army nurses.

160.33. The Army Information Branch of the Information and Education Division issued to the troops a weekly publication, *Newsmap,* **1942–46** (240 items), which included maps with related pictures and descriptive text illustrating military and civilian activities during the war. Among the illustrations are pictures of women making incendiary bombs for the Chemical Warfare Service, helping in savings bond campaign advertisements, and modeling WAAC winter and summer uniforms. There are pictures of Army nurses during air evacuations and, in issues published during demobilization at war's end, photographic histories of the Army Nurse Corps and the WAC.

Records of the War Department General and Special Staffs

Record Group 165

165.1. A War Department General Staff was authorized by Congress on February 14, 1903, to include a Chief of Staff, a General Council, and three divisions, which, after frequent reorganizations, developed into the Personnel Division (G-1), the Military Intelligence Division (G-2), the Organization and Training Division (G-3), the Supply Division (G-4), and the War Plans Division, which became the Operations Division after 1942. The General Staff was a separate and distinct staff organization with supervision over most military branches—both line and staff. It prepared plans for national defense and mobilization of military forces in time of war, investigated and reported on questions affecting Army efficiency and preparedness, and gave professional aid to the Secretary of War, general officers, and other superior commanders.

165.2. During World War II increased responsibilities necessitated the formation of several special staff divisions: the Bureau of Public Relations (BPR), which reported directly to the Office of the Secretary of War; the Office of the Inspector General; divisions named Legislative and Liaison, Civil Affairs, Budget, Special Planning, and New Developments; the War Department Manpower Board; and several other special sections and groups. The War Department General and Special Staffs were abolished by the National Security Act of 1947, when the War Department became the Department of the Army in the newly created National Military Establishment, which was renamed the Department of Defense in

1949. These records document the early years of both the Army Nurse Corps and the Women's Army Corps (WAC).

Office of the Chief of Staff

165.3. Among the records of the Office of the Chief of Staff, **general correspondence ("reports"), 1907–16** (65 ft.), are drafts of congressional bills concerning Army nurses and other records about their military status, hospital benefits, quarters, and regulations about their exercise of authority. It is arranged numerically and is accompanied by a **name and subject index** (13 ft.). The **general correspondence, 1917–21** (85 ft.), is arranged alphabetically by a subject-numeric scheme. Records relating to women can be found in the following files: "Civilian Employees," "Education and Recreation Branch," "Nurses," "Young Women's Christian Association," "W.C.T.U.," and "Women." Folders marked "Training Camp Activities" and "Societies" contain records that deal with the problem of prostitution near Army camps. The records cover overseas service for women, women's clubs, medals and memorials, and pending legislation affecting women and relate to the work of the Women's Relations Unit established to provide hostess houses in port cities for returning servicemen. They also document the work of librarians and supervisors of matters relating to women in military camps and stations in the United States and other places such as Panama and the Philippines. The **subject card index** (19 ft.) to this 1918–21 correspondence contains an entry for "Women," and the **name card index** (29 ft.) contains a few women's names.

165.4. Unfortunately, much of what must have been a very large series of **formerly security classified general correspondence, 1920–42** (8 ft.), of the Office of the Chief of Staff was lost before the records were transferred to the National Archives. Its index, microfilmed as T1013, *Department of the Army: Records of the General and Special Staff (Indexes and Tally Sheets), 1921–February 1942* (17 rolls), contains an entry for the proposed "American Women's Auxiliary Corps" and references to it under "Women."

165.5. The further development of the Women's Auxiliary Army Corps (WAAC), later the Women's Army Corps (WAC), is documented in the **formerly security classified correspondence, 1942–47** (121 ft.), of the Chief of Staff. The records are arranged in four chronological subseries and thereunder according to the War Department decimal classification scheme. Cross-reference sheets for 1942 and part of 1943 have been microfilmed as T1014. In records for 1941–43, file 080 contains information about the Women's Overseas Service League and the Women's Victory League. File 211 "Nurses" has records relating to Japanese Americans, blacks overseas, personnel actions, awards, and conditions overseas. File 291.3 "Women" includes records about women in the Army Air Force and legislation about women in the military services. File

291.9 "WAAC" contains information about recruiting, inclusion of blacks, women's organizations, and troop movements overseas. File 291.9 "WAC" deals with pay, training facilities, recruiting campaigns, uniforms, discrimination, compulsory training, and service assignments. File 324.5 "WAC" contains records about uniforms, allotments, staffing, investigations, pregnancy, Japanese Americans, the National Civilian Advisory Committee of the WAC, Mary McLeod Bethune, and Col. Oveta Culp Hobby, the first director of the WAAC. File 324.5 "WASP" (Women Air Force Service Pilots) includes material about the WAFS (Women Auxiliary Ferrying Squadron). There is also a file 324.5 "WAVES." In the 1944–45 segment, an 080 file deals with a proposed nurses' national memorial and the Women's Ambulance and Defense Corps. The 211 "Nurses" file deals with demobilization, shortage of nurses, personnel actions, proposals to draft nurses, and awards. A 291.3 file contains correspondence relating to universal military training, hostesses overseas, chaplains, legislation about World War I service, and a pregnancy assistance plan. There are records about the Army Nurse Corps in file 321. The 345.5 "WAC" file contains records about medals, overseas conditions, minorities, complaints, pregnancy, and Colonel Hobby's recommendations for the future of the WAC when she retired. Subjects documented in the 1946 file 345.5 "WAC" include the National Civilian Advisory Committee (NCAC), age limits for WAC service, volunteer reenlistment, social conduct regulations, and postwar utilization of the WAC. The 324.5 "WAC" file for 1947 contains records of investigations and the retirement of Col. Westray Battle Boyce, the second director of the WAC. The 211 "Nurses" files in the 1946 and 1947 segments relate to legislation, demobilization, nurse shortages, and black nurses.

Records of the
Director of Personnel and Administration (G-1)

165.6. Relations with civilian women employees, wives and families of military personnel, and women's organizations fell to the Office of the Director of Personnel and Administration (G-1), and it was to this office that the WAC Director was assigned when the Corps was established. Long before that time, Anita Phipps was Director of Women's Relations in the Personnel Division (G-1) of the War Department General Staff in the 1920's and continued as head of the Welfare Service for civilian employees into the 1930's. Much of her work is documented in the division's **formerly security classified correspondence, 1921–42** (83 ft.), arranged by a numerical subject classification scheme in which the following files contain records about women: file 7000 (1 in.), the utilization of women, including a Phipps report; file 8604, utilization of women fliers, Fifth Women's Patriotic Organizations Conference (1929), and Women's Industrial Conference; file 9835 (2 in.), "History of Women's Relations, 1920–27," by Phipps, postwar Hostess Service, "Participation of Women in War Work," by E.S. Hughes (1928), Phipps' annual report (1929), and another study of women in war work prepared in 1930; file 10791 (½ in.) annual report of the Director of Women's Relations (1922); file 15839 (4 in.),"WAAC historical file," including planning documents (1939–42), consideration of drafting women, selection of a director, and correspondence with the Women's Ambulance and Defense Corps of America.

165.7. There is a **subject card index** for the series, divided into 1921–38 (5 ft.) and 1939–42 (14 ft.) segments. In the earlier segment, entries under "Women" include references to women's organizations such as the Women's Overseas Service League and the Motor Corps of America. Entries under "Women's Relations" refer to records relating to that office, utilization of women, and the Hostess Service. Entries under "Nurses" contain references to nurses in the Civil and Spanish-American Wars and World War I. Index cards for 1939–42 include entries for "WAAC Pre-Planning Group," "Red Cross," "Dependents," "Waiver," and "Women."

165.8. The **formerly security classified general correspondence, 1942–48** (236 ft.), of the Personnel Division (G-1) is arranged in two chronological segments, 1942–June 1946 and June 1946–1948, and thereunder according to the War Department decimal classification scheme. In both chronological segments, file 291 "Marriage" includes records about women. Records relating to women in the 1942–46 segment can be found under the file numbers noted below. Under 211 "Nurses" are records relating to legislation for increased pay, satisfactory nurse coverage in Korea, and policy and procedures for demobilization. Under 291.2 records relate to Waacs and Wacs from racial minority groups. File 191.3 also includes records relating to racial minorities in the WAAC and WAC. In file 291.3 "ANC" there are records about the Army Nurse Corps, dietitians, and Wacs. The WASP and women physicians and surgeons are subjects of file 291.9. Records in file 292 relate to Army dependents, including their return from overseas, postwar care of dependents overseas, and proposed restrictions on their movement. Records in file 320.2 "WAC" document the transfer of the WAC Director from the Army Service Forces Headquarters to G-1, the use of Wacs in chemical impregnation companies, the progress of legislation to make WAC an integral part of the Army in 1943, physical examinations, Japanese Americans, proposed legislation for compulsory military service, Air Wacs, and uniforms for Wacs assigned to the Air Warning Service. File 321 "JAN" refers to the Joint Army-Navy Personnel Board, and file 321 "WMSC" contains correspondence with the Surgeon General and the Adjutant General in regard to the selection and appointment of officers for the Women's Medical Specialist Corps. There is a 321 "WAC Project" file in this segment. File 324.5 "WASP" contains records about the WASP Squadron, 6th Ferrying Group at Long Beach, CA. File 334 "National

Civilian Advisory Committee" documents the work of the committee of prominent citizens headed by Mrs. Oswald Lord, which was established to help improve the WAC image and to oversee the working conditions of Wacs. They visited separation centers, hospitals, and the European Theater of Operations. Correspondence in the file includes discussions of the possible continuation of the NCAC after the war. A separate "Project: WAC" section (2 ft.) is arranged according to the War Department decimal classification scheme. It contains a good deal of material about the formation of the WAAC, correspondence of the WAC Director with the Assistant Chief of Staff, and a list of numbers of court-martial case files with names of offenders and the sentence of each. There are also records about dependents, socialization between WAC officers and enlisted men, and black and Puerto Rican Wacs. Colonel Hobby's weekly reports, her final report upon retirement, and a trip report of her January 1945 overseas visit are also in this part of the series. In the 1946–48 segment of the series, file 080 includes records about several organizations, including the American Red Cross, the Young Women's Christian Association, the American Women's Volunteer Services, Inc., the Women's Overseas Services League, W.I.F.E., and Wives, Inc. There are also two reports: "A Good Leave Town: A Brief History of the War Hospitality Committee" submitted by the executive secretary of Recreation, Inc., in 1947, and "Information for Wives and Dependents Going Overseas to Join Servicemen in the Army of Occupation," May 15, 1946. File 210.3 "Assignment, Change of Station, Transfer" relates to Army and civilian women. File 211 "Nurses" deals with legislation about the Army Nurse Corps and training nurses in civilian institutions. Correspondence relating to proxy marriages between U.S. citizens and U.S. military personnel stationed overseas is in file 291.1. There is a copy of *Dependency Deferments: Special Monograph No. 8*, Selective Service System, 1947, in file 292. Records in file 321 "Army Nurse Corps" document procurement, appointment, commissioning, and promotion of Army Nurse Corps and reserve personnel, and changes resulting from the enactment of the Army-Navy Nurses Act of 1947 (Public Law 36, 80th Cong.). File 321 "WAC" contains the correspondence of Col. Mary A. Hallaren, who became WAC Director in May 1947, with the Judge Advocate, the AGO, the SGO, and the Quartermaster General relating to historical statistics of World War II, postwar budget estimates, continued overseas duty, plans for a WAC element in the Organized Reserve Corps, and administration of the WAC in the Regular Army. File 321.3 "Hospitals" includes a special inspection report about general hospitals in the United States with an enclosure on the nursing service. A record of "Proceedings of the Meetings of the Advisory Committee to the Women's Interest Section," September 22, 1948 (52 pp.), is in file 334 "National Civilian Advisory Committee." File 510 "Transportation of Persons" relates to both civilian dependents and Army personnel. The "Project: WAC" segment contains correspondence of the

Director of the WAC with the NCAC and staff advisers relating to activities and progress of the WAC.

165.9. The WAC Director's **formerly security classified general correspondence, 1942–46 and 1949–50** (63 ft.), is arranged in two chronological subseries (1942–46 and 1949–50). The correspondence covers the full range of WAC concerns, including recruiting, training, organization, public relations, and uniforms. The 1942–46 correspondence, further arranged according to the War Department decimal classification scheme, includes the following significant files: 000.7 and 000.77 (1 ft.) containing radio scripts; 080 (2 ft.) consisting of correspondence with various civic associations including the National Association of Women Lawyers, Women's Military Service, Inc., American War Mothers, American Red Cross, and the Women's Overseas Service League; 210.31 and 220.3 (3 ft.) relating to assignments, changes of station, and separations of officers and enlisted personnel and aviation cadets; 314.7 (8 in.) consisting of letters, memorandums, organizational charts, and copies of congressional legislation pertaining to the establishment and subsequent history of the WAAC and the WAC and to matters of organization, policies, and administrative practices; 319.1 (1½ ft.) consisting of reports such as "Medical Aspects of WAC," September 1945, by Lt. Col. Margaret D. Craighill, M.D.; and "Preliminary Report on Motivation in Joining the WAC," January 1943; 320.2 (9 ft.) consisting of correspondence and tables of organization relating to WAAC and WAC units' strength, assignments, utilization in European and North African Theaters of Operations and elsewhere, and disbandment; and 330.14 (1 ft.) documenting complaints and rumors of alleged instances of poor treatment, sexual harassment, racial discrimination, and moral dereliction among WAAC and WAC personnel.

165.10. Historical and background material relating to the legislation and administration of the Women's Army Auxiliary Corps and its successor, the Women's Army Corps, 1942–46 (14 ft.), includes the WAAC Planning Service files and records concerning the work of Col. Gilman C. Mudgett and Col. Harold P. Tasker, who were involved with the planning of the WAAC. The legislative history of the bill to establish the WAAC is included, as are rosters of enlisted women by State, newsletters and posters, regulations, and circulars. Colonel Hobby's desk file, daily journal, and speeches are in this series, in addition to reports, correspondence, press releases, and working papers on WAAC pay and allowances, benefits, appropriations, training centers, and other legislative and administrative matters. In the file is the general correspondence, 1942–43, of Eugenia Lies, civilian assistant to Colonel Hobby for planning, including Lies' May 1943 study on the utilization of women in the military. There are also correspondence and reports pertaining to the NCAC, 1942–46, and a Young and Rubicam study of public opinion of the WAC.

Records of the Director of Intelligence (G-2)

165.11. Women's names appear as both suspects and witnesses in correspondence and related indexes of the Military Intelligence (MID). The **formerly security classified correspondence and reports, 1917–41** (1,810 ft.), includes correspondence, reports, and newspaper clippings in files such as 10110 "Activities of the I.W.W., Socialists, Etc." and 10314 "Vicious Enemy Propaganda." There are also records about Amelia Earhart's 1935 goodwill flight to Mexico and her ill-fated 1937 attempt at a 'round-the-world flight in files 183-Z-292, 255-I-94145, and 2657-G-774. Documents in the file are abstracted on **record cards** (75 ft.). This correspondence series and two others, **correspondence relating to personnel investigations ("PF" file), 1917–19** (310 ft.), and **formerly security classified correspondence relating to personnel investigations ("PF" file), 1917–41** (18 ft.), are all indexed in a **formerly security classified name index** (378 ft.) that has been filmed as M1194 (162 rolls). A few of the names of women represented in these records are Jane Addams, Ella Reeve ("Mother") Bloor, Harriet Conner Brown, Louise Bryant, Carrie Chapman Catt, Dr. Marie Equi of the International Workers of the World, Sarah Bard Field of the Women's Committee for World Disarmament, M. Eleanor Fitzgerald, Elizabeth Gurley Flynn, Emma Goldman, Kate Richards O'Hare, Margaret Sanger, and Ida M. Tarbell. The International Ladies Garment Workers, the International League for Peace and Freedom, the League of Women Voters, the National Woman's Party, and the Women's Trade Union League are also represented. There is also a **formerly security classified subject index** (103 ft.), which contains about 20 index cards under "Women."

165.12. Also in the G-2 records is **formerly security classified general correspondence, 1941–48** (6 ft.), arranged alphabetically by subject, which contains a folder labeled "Travel of Dependents" in which correspondents question the desirability of having wives and children of service personnel at overseas posts in the immediate postwar period, 1945–46.

165.13. Agents of the Plant Protection Section (PPS) of the MID inspected private and Government-owned manufacturing plants that were engaged in war work and investigated suspicious persons. The records contain information about women labor organizers as well as organizations and persons suspected of sympathizing with or working for the enemy. **PPS correspondence ("general"), 1918–19** (10 ft.), arranged alphabetically by subject, includes a folder labeled "Women in Labor" (1 in.) that contains responses of agents and manufacturing executives to a 1919 PPS questionnaire about women's participation in the war effort. "Welfare in Plants" and "WWI" folders also contain documents about women. Another correspondence series, a **"plants file," 1917–19** (56 ft.), consists of correspondence with and reports from agents, and is indexed in a **name and subject card index** (9 ft.). Inspection reports in this file describe conditions in plants and sometimes provide the number of female employees and the names of persons considered by the agents to be troublemakers. There is correspondence with agents in most of the PPS district offices in 15 U.S. cities (88 ft.), much of which can be accessed by registers and indexes. For example, "Labor agitators" in the **correspondence of the Boston district office, 1918–19** (15 ft.), includes documents about Emma Goldman. **Reports on labor problems, 1918–19** (5 in.), arranged by PPS district number, contain related material including references to the Ladies' Shoe Stitcher Union.

165.14. Names of suspect women also appear in a **card register of names and subjects in the correspondence relating to postal censorship at Key West, 1918–19** (2 ft.), with entries pertaining to documents in **correspondence relating to intelligence information obtained through postal censorship at Key West and other Southern cities, 1918–19** (3 ft.). Women's names appear in the **card register of names and subjects in the correspondence relating to postal censorship at San Francisco, 1917–19** (1 ft.), which has entries for documents in **correspondence relating to postal censorship at San Francisco, 1917–19** (2 ft.).

Records of the Organization and Training Division (G-3)

165.15. Until May 1943 responsibility for supervision of military training programs rested with the Organization and Training Division (G-3) in the War Department General Staff. Between May 1943 and 1946 military training was handled by the Army Service Forces, but was returned to G-3 in 1946. The **formerly security classified general correspondence, 1942–47** (136 ft.), of the Office of the Director of Organization and Training (G-3), arranged according to the War Department decimal classification scheme, contains documents relating to the expansion and utilization of the WAC.

Records of the War College Division and the War Plans Division

165.16. During World War I a variety of women's organizations expressed concern to the War Department about the moral well-being of American soldiers. References to their letters and to the Director of Women's Relations appear in the **name and subject indexes** (9 ft.) to the **general correspondence, July 1919–October 1920** (15 ft.), of the War College Division and War Plans Division. Most of the letters can be found in the correspondence series, which also contains documents reflecting concern about the working conditions of hostesses at Army camps.

165.17. The **name and subject index to the general correspondence of the War Plans Division, 1921–42** (103 ft.), filmed as M1080

(18 rolls) contains the following entries: "Women's Republican Club," "Women" (including records about a conference proposed by several national women's organizations on the "Cause and Cure of War" and a 1926 study entitled "Utilization of Women in Military Service"), and "Women's Relations, Director of."

165.18. Four indexes of several important series of the records of the War Plans Division and its predecessors have been filmed as *Indexes to Records of the War College Division and Related General Staff Offices, 1903–1919* (M912, 49 rolls). The following indexes for women-related records appear: "Army Nurse Corps"; "Civil employees"; "Prostitutes"; "Red Cross"; "Women"; "Women's Auxiliary—Quartermaster Corps, U.S. Army"; Women's Auxiliary Army Corps, U.S.A."; "Women's Hospital Unit for Foreign Service"; and "Women's Service Corps." Since many of the records indexed are no longer extant, the synopses of the indexed records that were entered on record cards are very important. They were filmed as *Record Cards to the Correspondence of the War College Division, Related General Staff and Adjutant General's Offices, 1902–1919* (M1023, 37 rolls).

165.19 In the **general correspondence, 1903–19** (225 ft.), of the Army War College, arranged numerically, there are some files relating to women. In file 8552 "Contentment of Enlisted Men," enclosure 48 consists mainly of copies of September 1919 letters of appreciation from the Secretary of War for wartime welfare services furnished by the American Library Association, the National Catholic War Council, the Salvation Army, the War Camp Community Service, the Young Men's Christian Association (YMCA), and the YWCA. File 10730 (1 in.) includes high-level War Department correspondence, reports, and opinions on topics such as a proposal to enlist women, quarters for women employees, training of women college students, services of woman physicians, and benefits for war nurses and other women who served with the American Expeditionary Force. Enclosure 37 in this file includes biographies of several women who provided meritorious service in World War I.

165.20. The Historical Section of the Army War College collected documents from a number of sources to form the **records relating to the history of the War Department, 1900–41** (237 ft.), arranged according to a numerical scheme. Letters, pamphlets, and reports assigned to files 7-17 through 7-17.9 (1 ft., 9 in.) in the G-1 section of the series concern "Agencies and Societies" at home and abroad, 1917–19. The records selected for inclusion in the collection document provisions for the divorced and common-law wives of servicemen under the Bureau of War Risk Insurance, YWCA training for women workers, Red Cross uniforms and activities, the Commission on Training Camp Activities (CTCA), nonmilitary organizations serving with the AEF, and the Council of National Defense. Material about female nurses, volunteers, and civilian employees was pulled together in sections 7-43.1 through 7-43.9 "Medical" and 7-65.9 through 7.66.9 "Personnel."

165.21. A small amount of information about American women is in the **records of the "Thomas File" of the Historical Section, 1918–48** (37 ft.) and can be located by consulting an index under "Women" and "Nurses."

165.22. The Historical Section compiled records of the General Staff's nonmilitary service to the War Department during World War I in **records relating to wartime economic programs of the government, 1918–19** (48 ft.). A **subject card index** (3 ft.) prepared by the National Archives is arranged in six broad sections: (1) general, (2) finance, (3) food, (4) fuel, (5) labor, and (6) transportation. Among the entries in the index for women are: "Women, Clearing House for Wartime Training of"; "Women Workers, National League of"; "Women in Industry Service, Labor Department"; "Women's War Work Division, Committee on Public Information"; "Women's Land Army"; "Women's Liberty Loan Committee"; "Women Active in War Work, Biographical Sketches"; "Women's Branch, Industrial Services Section, Ordnance Department"; and "Women's Trade Union League." Entries for nurses are: "Nurse Corps, Army" and "Nursing, Committee on, Council of National Defense."

165.23. "Americanization," the term used to mean the education of immigrants and refugees about U.S. customs, language, and the accepted rights and responsibilities of citizenship, became an important concern of American women shortly after World War I. This subject, along with services and problems of women and refugees during the war is documented in the **general correspondence ("subject file"), 1918–21** (10 ft.), of the Army War College Morale Branch. Among headings in two alphabetically arranged subseries, those containing records about women include "Agencies," "Army Nurse Corps," "Red Cross," "Venereal Disease and Work of the Social Hygiene Division, C.T.C.A.," and "Y.W.C.A."

165.24. The CTCA under the chairmanship of Raymond B. Fosdick was set up in 1917 to coordinate the activities of various welfare organizations. Reports on community education, juvenile delinquency, and other concerns of the CTCA are in a folder (3 in.) labeled "Committee on Protective Work for Girls," in **correspondence of the Education Section, 1918–20** (14 ft.), in the records of the Education and Recreation Branch of the War Plans Division, which succeeded the CTCA in 1919. There is a significant quantity of records concerning numerous women-related topics in the CTCA's **general correspondence, 1917–20** (72 ft.), arranged numerically. A **subject card index** (22 ft.) to the series contains a large number of entries for "Hostess houses," "National League for Women's Service," "Overseas women," "Prostitutes," "Protective work for girls," "Vice," "Wives," "Women," and "YWCA." There are fewer entries for the "American Library Association," "American Purity League," "American Red Cross," "Camp Mothers Association," and "Nurses." An alphabetical **name and subject index, 1917–18** (9 ft.) lists additional topics:

"Bureau of Social Hygiene," "National Women's Trade Union League," "Venereal disease," "Woman's Suffrage Association," "Woman's Committee of the Council for National Defense," "Women's Foreign Missionary Council," "Women's Cooperative Alliance," and "W.C.T.U." Another **name index, 1918–20** (15 ft.), includes names of women prominent in these organizations. Among them are Mrs. John B. Casserly, Director of Women's Relations, G-1, War Department; Helen A. Davis, Secretary, YWCA; Dr. Katherine B. Davis, Chair, Section on Women's Work, CTCA Division on Social Hygiene; Dr. Anna Howard Shaw, Chair, Women's Committee, Council of National Defense; and Katherine Scott, YWCA War Work Field Secretary.

165.25. CTCA **reports relating to training camp activities, 1917** (3 ft.), are arranged alphabetically by State and deal largely with investigations of reports of vice and prostitution near Army camps. CTCA **correspondence with welfare agencies, 1917–19** (1 ft.), discusses the construction, salvaging, and functions of hostess houses in the effort to control vice. Field staff reports in CTCA **correspondence relating to special subjects, 1917–19** (35 ft.), arranged alphabetically by subject, describe burlesque shows, soliciting, and girls sent to reform schools.

165.26. A Committee on Education and Special Training, established in 1918, was composed of Army officers and a group of civilian educators. Its **correspondence with civilian schools relating to military training, 1918–19** (35 ft.), contains a brief recommendation to the Chief of Staff that a "Women's Service Corps" be created.

Records of the Operations Division

165.27. The Operations Division coordinated, planned, and developed current and planned operations in conjunction with the Joint Chiefs of Staff and the Combined Chiefs of Staff after the reorganization of the War Department in 1942. The **formerly security classified general correspondence, 1942–45** (537 ft.), of the Operations Division, arranged according to the War Department decimal classification scheme, can be accessed by using **subject card indexes and cross-reference sheets to formerly security classified and top secret correspondence, 1942–45** (32 ft.). File 095 of the correspondence contains records about women in civilian positions. File 211.31 "Nurses" relates to movement and return home of Army nurses, their incarceration as prisoners of war, and their marital status. File 322.999 WAC (4 in.) covers civilian employees as well as Wacs and includes records of the creation of the WAAC and early duty with the Aircraft Warning Service. File 513.4, Section I, Case 4 deals with the transportation of war brides to the United States.

165.28. Formerly top secret general correspondence relating to the location and leasing of Atlantic bases in British possessions,

Allied military conferences of World War II, and plans for strategic direction of operations of military forces in theaters of operation ("OPD executive file"), 1940–45 (38 ft.), arranged numerically in 17 files, is a collection of important documents prepared during World War II for the Assistant Chief of Staff. File 17 contains a folder of material relating to the numerical strength of Wacs and Army nurses in the "Troop Basis in re Conscription 5/22/43."

Records of the Civil Affairs Division

165.29. The Civil Affairs Division (CAD) of the War Department Special Staff was established on March 1, 1943, to formulate and coordinate U.S. military policy for the administration and government of captured or liberated territory. The CAD **formerly security classified general correspondence, 1943–July 1949** (181 ft.), is arranged in five chronological subseries and thereunder by the War Department decimal classification scheme and is served by **cross-reference sheets** (199 ft.). In each of four segments covering 1943–48, file 324.5 "Independent organizations" includes references to the WAAC/WAC; to overseas service, training for jobs in military government, and demobilization; and to correspondence with numerous organizations such as the American Red Cross, Girl Scouts, and church and business groups about relief and education in Europe and the Far East. Visas for wives of servicemen and marriages of U.S. personnel in Europe are documented under file 291.1 in segments for 1943–August 1945 and June 1946–December 1948; the same subjects for August 1945–June 1946 are in file 292.

Records of the Legislative and Liaison Division

165.30. The topic of Universal Military Training (UMT) was much discussed both during and after World War II. The **general correspondence, 1944–48** (11 ft.), of the division's Plans and Policy Office is arranged alphabetically by subject. A 201 file for "Woods, Mrs. Arthur" contains records about former Wac Helen Woods' service as a UMT consultant to the Secretary of War. Women's letters supporting UMT for men are in **the same office's formerly security classified correspondence, reports, memorandums, and other papers pertaining to Universal Military Training, 1944–48** (4 ft.), arranged according to the War Department decimal classification scheme. Communications about UMT from the following women's organizations are in file 080: Blue Star Mothers of America, Daughters of the American Revolution (Jan.–Apr. 1945), General Federation of Women's Clubs (May 1945), National Council of Parents and Teachers (Mar.–Dec. 1945), National Non-Partisan Council on Public Affairs (May 1945), Women's Citizen's Committee for Universal Training of Young Men (Dec. 1944–May 1945), Women's International League (Nov. 1944–Jan. 1945), and the Women's National Committee for Universal Training of Young Men (Apr.–Sept. 1945).

165.31. In the records of the Legislative Branch of this division are two series: **correspondence, reports, and other papers relating to proposed legislation affecting the War Department, January 1943–August 1946** (4 ft.), and a similar series **relating to pending and passed legislation affecting the War Department, January 1943–August 1946** (23 ft.), both arranged numerically by Congress. References in an **index** (55 ft.) to these records include "Womanpower, Selective Service"; "Women's Military, Naval, and Coast Guard Academy"; and "Women's Reserve." Subjects relating to women are age limits for recruitment, education, foreign service, and appointment of woman pilots.

Records of the Public Relations Division

165.32. In 1947 the War Department's Bureau of Public Relations was transferred to the General Staff's Public Relations Division, which later became the Public Information Division.

165.33. A 22-page report and some correspondence between Jacqueline Cochran and Gen. H.H. Arnold relate to the history of women pilots with the AAF. The report, which covers legislation, training, commendations, officer status, and demobilization, is in the 1944 reports section, file 319.2 (C), of the War Department Public Relations Division's **formerly security classified general correspondence ("BPR file"), 1939–46** (36 ft.). The records are arranged by year and thereunder according to the War Department decimal classification scheme.

Records of the War Department Manpower Board

165.34. The War Department Manpower Board was established early in 1943 as a Special Staff division to study the Army's need for and utilization of civilian and military manpower in the continental United States. Its **formerly security classified general correspondence, 1943–47** (4 ft.), arranged by year and thereunder by the War Department classification scheme, contains records relating to the administrative location of the Director of the WAC and the work of women in recreation in file 324 "WAC." The Board's **general correspondence, 1943–47** (39 ft.), is served by a **name and subject index ("cross-reference file"), 1943–44** (4 in.), arranged by year and thereunder alphabetically by name and subject, which contains headings for "WAAC," "WAC," and "Women's Professional Relations." Under "Civilian Personnel Administration" are references to records concerning the problem of child care service for female War Department employees.

Audiovisual Records

165.35. This record group contains over 110,500 still pictures, many of which show women's activities dating from the Civil War period.   177

165.36. Several series of photographs include formal portraits of ladies. **Civil War Photographs, 1861–74** (165-B, 2,770 items), are mostly prints made from Mathew Brady's original glass plate negatives that were purchased by the War Department. A set of photographs by Alexander Gardner for his 1866 *Gardner's Photographic Sketch Book of the War* includes a few women (165-SB, 100 items). There are also a small number of women's portraits among **cartes-de-visite: John Taylor album, 1861–65** (165-JT, 517 items).

165.37. Indians and whites are represented in photographs that record social activities and, to a lesser extent, family relationships, usually near military posts. **American Indian photographs, ca. 1881–85** (165-AI, 54 items), arranged by tribe, include a few images of Indian women and their families. In **American forts, ca. 1860–1914** (165-FF, 1,200 items), a few photographs of officers' wives and children are in sections for Kansas and Wyoming. Images of turn-of-the-century women at leisure appear in **stereographs: scenery, people, and industry in the United States, ca. 1865–1909** (165-XS, 393 items). A group of unidentified women, probably wives, stand in an 1894 group portrait of the Association of Military Surgeons of the United States in another series, **Army officers, ca. 1860–1918** (165-PF, 207 items).

165.38. The **American Unofficial Collection of World War I Photographs, 1914–19** (165-WW, 64,800 items), consists of photographs made by commercial firms, professional photographers, or agencies of the U.S. and foreign governments that were assembled by the Committee on Public Information to be used in an official history of World War I. They have been reproduced on microfiche as M1138 (2,396 fiche). Lists of subject headings are available. Some of the photographs filed in the "Service of the Interior" (homefront) sections that portray American women are found in the following categories:

American Library Association (fiche 122–149): Camp libraries, Hospital libraries, Library personnel

American Red Cross (fiche 150–224): Activities (Canteen service, Christmas boxes, Classes in Red Cross work [filed by State], Entertainment, Junior Red Cross, Motor Corps, Refreshments en route, Salvage, Soliciting funds [Entertainment, Personal appeal, Public gatherings, War work], Personnel, Uniforms)

Ceremonies (fiche 285–413): Patriotic, Peace demonstrations [i.e., Armistice], Street parades

Colleges and universities (fiche 431–585)

Council of National Defense (fiche 616–617): Woman's Committee

Drills (fiche 763–64): Civilian Groups—women

Enemy Activities (fiche 723–24): I.W.W. [including Emma Goldman and Crystal Eastman]

Food Administration (fiche 744–62): Anti-waste Campaigns, Personnel, Posters

A. F. Randall photographed the sister of Apache Chief Nalta in the 1880's, 165-AI-3.

Fuel Administration (fiche 763–64)

Girls' activities (fiche 770–71)

Industries of War [alphabetical by type of product] (fiche 814–999)

Liberty Bonds (fiche 1001–1098): Advertising methods, Parades, Personnel (fiche 1001–1046)

Medical Department (fiche 1047–1140): Dental Corps, First Aid, Hospitals, Army School of Nursing, Restoration work, Sanitary Service

Navy (fiche 1372–73): Recreation

Pacifist activities (fiche 1623–24)

Patriotic societies (fiche 1626–32)

Posters (fiche 1809–20)

Propaganda—motion pictures (fiche 1835)

Recreation—amusements (fiche 1842)

Recruiting Service and Draft Service (fiche 1880–1904): Draft drawings, Farewell scenes, Registration, Slacker raids

Signal Corps—apparatus (fiche 2044–52)

Uniforms and equipment (fiche 2180–2201)

War relief [numerous organizations in alphabetical order] (fiche 2249–2326)

War savings stamps (fiche 2331–35)

Women's activities (fiche 2337–2404): Farm and garden, In industry [by type of industry, including public service and sales], With the U.S. Army, In Marine Service, In Naval Service, Motor Corps of America, National League for Women's Service, Uniformed organizations, Vocational instruction

In the same series, photographs of American women overseas can be found under the following headings:

American Red Cross (fiche 177–216): Activities in the theater of operations, Ambulances, Baby dispensaries [including women doctors], Canteens, Christmas, Classes in Red Cross work, Construction, Headquarters and buildings, Recreation and sports, Refreshments en route, Refugees, Rehabilitation work, "Second aid" [a cigarette, a smile], Warehouses

Ceremonies (fiche 335–342). Peace demonstrations, Parades

Medical Department (fiche 1099–1139): Hospitals, Restoration work, Sanitary services

Women's Activities (fiche 2315–16)

165.39. Copies of Leslie's and Harper's illustrated weekly newspapers, 1898, contain some illustrations showing women in a variety of activities during the Spanish-American War (165-IWN).

165.40. Over 100 photographs showing women munitions workers and tool room and inventory attendants in Army ordnance plants; women working in factories of arms contractors; and dormitory, cafeteria, YWCA, and training facilities for women are in **prints of U.S. war industries: construction and use of military equipment and ordnance, 1917–19** (165-EO, ca. 800 items).

165.41. The voices of nurses recounting their experiences were recorded in **sound recordings, 1942–51** (ca. 1,000 items). On reel 165-4, interviews with two Army nurses who helped evacuate the beachhead at Anzio, Italy, were recorded. Representatives of the WAC, WAVES, WAF, Women Marines, and Army and Navy Nurse Corps addressing delegates of Girls Nation in Washington, DC, on August 25, 1949, about opportunities for women in the military are on reels 165-19 and 165-19A.

Records of the War Production Board

Record Group 179

179.1. The War Production Board (WPB) was established in the Office for Emergency Management by an Executive order of January 16, 1942, which transferred to it the functions of the Supply Priorities and

Allocations Board and the Office of Production Management (both established in 1941). The Office of Production and Management brought with it certain functions inherited from the Advisory Commission to the Council of National Defense.

179.2. The WPB exercised general direction over the war procurement and production programs of all Federal departments and agencies during World War II. It was terminated November 3, 1945, and its remaining functions and powers were transferred to the Civilian Production Administration (CPA). Finally, an Executive order of April 24, 1947, transferred all related functions to the Department of Commerce for liquidation.

179.3. During World War II 15.5 million women accounted for over 26 percent of the labor force, including the armed forces. Therefore, although there are few specific references to women in these records, much of what relates to the civilian labor force as a whole can be assumed to relate to women.

179.4. The **policy documentation file, 1939–47** (1,220 ft.), arranged according to a decimal classification scheme, constitutes more than half of the records in this record group. The **index** (300 ft.) to this series has been filmed as *Index to the War Production Board Policy Documentation File, 1939–1947* (M911, 86 rolls). Among entries under "Labor—women," are "Administrative problems [in production]," "Availability," "Employment [including analyses of State labor laws affecting women]," "Problems [of working women in Detroit]," and "Wage adjustment." Other index entries indicate the pervasiveness of the work of the WPB into every aspect of American life, affecting many decisions homemakers made daily. The following entries are illustrative: "Caskets"; "Chinaware"; "Church goods"; "Clothing, Children's, Men's, Women's"; "Lawn mowers"; "Nylon, Hosiery"; "Refrigerators, Domestic"; "Sewing machines, Domestic"; "Working conditions"; and "Zippers." The documents referenced by "Clothing, Women" relate to allocation of materials and to simplification of style to use the minimum of material. (WPB Order L-85, "Feminine Apparel, Outer Wear and Other Garments," exclusive of garments manufactured for the military, was the subject of much definition, interpretation, and amendment.) Entries for names of particular women, such as that of Harriet Elliott, who was appointed Consumer Commissioner on the Advisory Commission (NDAC) to the Council of National Defense in 1940, also appear in the index.

179.5. Records about Elliott are also in files not referenced under her name in the index. Her work is mentioned, for example, in WPB Study No. 3, "Relations Between the Armed Services and the Advisory Commission to the Council of National Defense," November 5, 1943, in file 033.308. Her work is also documented in file 012.2 relating to personnel of the NDAC. This file includes NDAC progress reports, July 24, 1940–May 28, 1941, which have been filmed as M186 (1 roll). In it are reports of divisions and offices, including Elliott's Consumer Division, where there are reports of the work of her women assistants with civic groups about children and health and welfare issues.

179.6. WPB Study No. 1, "Labor and Manpower Administration in War Production," by R. Burr Smith (May 1943) in file 033.308 R, discusses training, housing, recreation, wages and hours, community services, and labor disputes of wartime workers. In file 207 "Surveys and Investigations," there is a copy of *Production for War*, a March 1943 publication of the War Economics Division of the Research Institute of America that advised private industry on securing defense contracts, the kinds of positions women could fill, and ways of maintaining employee morale. File 241.11 includes the following documents: "Report to the House Committee Investigating National Defense Migration: Women in War Production," February 2, 1942 (69 pp.), by Thelma McKelvey; "The Child Care Program and Its Relation to War Production," October 30, 1943 (6 pp.), by Anne L. Gould; "Duties and Responsibilities of Women Consultants," February 14, 1944 (3 pp.), no author named; "Equal Pay for Equal Work for Women," Office of Labor Production Circular No. 2, September 24, 1942 (2 pp.); and "Employment of Women in War Work," 1943 (28 pp.), by the Statistics Division, Facilities Utilization Section.

179.7. Under file classification 900 "Demobilization and Reconstruction" there are records relating to speculation about a possible postwar depression and oversupply of labor when the men returned to civilian jobs now held by women. In file 960 "Reconversion to Civilian Economy," the section "Reconversion—Relation to Labor" contains a 1944 progress report of the Office of Labor Production in which field representatives from the Office of Women Consultants describe problems of women workers, such as fatigue, absenteeism, housing, and child care. References to women leaving the work force are in a folder, "Industrial Reconversion and Civilian Production," which contains a draft of volume 3 of "History of the Civilian Production Administration for July 1, 1945, to July 1, 1946"; the Report of the Chairman to the President, October 9, 1945, which is filed in a folder labeled "Reconversion Outlook and Wartime Achievements (J.A. Krug)"; and in a folder marked "War Production and Civilian Output—Post European War" in Part II of a Planning Division report of April 14, 1944, in a section titled "Reduction of War Programs and Release of Resources."

179.8. The **select document file, 1939–47** (347 ft.), arranged in rough alphabetical order by subject, consists of documents selected for inclusion in the policy documentation file but never placed in the file. Under the heading "Awards" in a folder entitled "Operations, Vice Chairman, Miscellaneous" is a small set of working papers of Anne L. Gould relating to questionnaires about the number of women, blacks, and black women in manufacturing plants and the extent of their participation in labor union activities. Under the heading "Civilian Economy" in folders labeled "Conservation," "Consumer Services," and "Requirements," there are records relating to consumer groups, consumer surveys, and ratios of consumption to production of household goods and wearing apparel, matters that often limited choices available to the average woman. A section marked "Civilian Economy Requirements" contains information gathered during WPB surveys of the needs of rural families from Texas to rural New England. Under "Nelson-Krug" a folder entitled "Administration-Labor" contains correspondence about part-time workers in the labor force, many of whom were women.

179.9. In **NDAC minutes of meetings, June 1940–October 22, 1941** (3 vols., 6 in.), Harriet Elliott's remarks on housing, retailers' organizations, the cost of living, and health and welfare problems are recorded. The effect of conservation programs on the civilian economy and consumers is a subject of **planning committee, minutes of meetings, February 1942–April 1943** (2 vols., 4 in.).

179.10. **Orders, regulations, directives, and related papers of the War Production Board and the Civilian Production Administration ("recording secretary's files"), 1941–47** (117 ft.), are arranged by type of issuance and thereunder numbered chronologically. "L" orders deal with the limitation of the production of durable consumer goods. Records under "L-85" (4 in.) include lists of meetings held with industry advisory committees before the issuance of orders as detailed as the regulation of the number of pockets and bows to be permitted on women's apparel. Included are copies of the *Federal Register* in which dress patterns appear as examples of the requirements. Bridal gowns and maternity dresses are noted as exemptions to the orders.

179.11. **Press releases, June 1940–June 1947** (31 ft.), with an **index, 1940–47** (34 ft.), have been filmed as M1239 (53 rolls). Included are not only WPB press releases but also those of the NDAC, the Office of War Information, the War Manpower Commission, and other wartime Federal agencies. In addition to references indexed under "Women," references to women appear under "Agriculture," "Civil defense," "Consumer," "Health and welfare," "Manpower, school teachers," "Manpower, women workers," "Nurses, shortages," and "United States Employment Service."

179.12. Informational and Educational Programs were an important aspect of WPB activities because the agency conducted many campaigns to persuade the American public to salvage such commodities as scrap metal and kitchen fat; to conserve paper, bottles, and clothing; and to convince civilians of the need for rationing consumer goods. WPB **scrapbooks, 1941–45** (1 ft.), contain newspaper clippings about the activities of the District of Columbia Salvage Committee. Accompanied by photographs of scrap collection and donation by District of Columbia area housewives and women's organizations, these stories cover social events and contests. Many articles were written by Katherine Smith, editor of the Woman's Page of the *Washington Times-Herald*. Numerous display ads show homemakers how to salvage kitchen fat and scrap metal.

179.13. Posters, 1942–43 (WP, 1,572 items), include many designed to recruit women for war work. Some **lantern slides, 1942–45** (S, C, 320 items), were used to encourage women to go to work by showing women in various clerical activities.

179.14. War Production Drive Division motion pictures, 1942–45 (70 reels), were shown by the WPB to private organizations to stimulate production. Women are featured in films as secretaries, factory workers, telephone operators, and in films about salvage, as housewives. The only Navy nurse who escaped from Corregidor appears in "Drive for Anthracite."

179.15. Some **sound recordings, 1942–45** (284 discs), used on radio programs, refer to women factory workers and include appeals to men and women to take war jobs. "Soldiers of Production" programs saluted a "War Worker of the Week" (sometimes a woman) and employees of companies receiving production awards. There are also spot announcements about salvage and conservation, speeches, interviews, dramatizations, and entertainment. Women were featured on WPB radio programs. Helen Hayes and Tallulah Bankhead hosted episodes of "Men, Machines, and Victory," and famous couples like George Burns and Gracie Allen and Fibber McGee and Mollie promoted WPB campaigns. A list of titles of the sound recordings is available.

179.16. Some of the special studies of the WPB that were written by staff members of the successor agency, the Civilian Production Administration, were published. In **historical reports relating to policies and operations of the War Production Board and predecessor agencies ("special studies"), 1946–47** (2 ft.), Special Study No. 20, "The Role of the Office of Civilian Requirements in the Office of Production Management and the War Production Board" (351 pp.), by Drummond Jones was issued on May 15, 1946. It traces the consumer interest beginning with Elliott's NDAC Consumer Division, through the WPB's wartime concern with rationing, prices, conservation, surveys, and investigations of shortages, to postwar reconversion problems. Another historical report, Special Study No. 6, "Resumption of Production of Domestic Electric Flat Irons, April 1943 to August 1944," by Drummond Jones and Maryclaire McCauley (113 pp.) was issued March 1, 1946. An unpublished administrative history of the Advisory Commission to the Council of National Defense, a predecessor of WPB, contains a chapter, "Industrial

Mobilization in Defense Period," 1940–41 (12 pp.), that deals with Elliott's work.

179.17. Marion Worthing was successively a staff analyst with the WPB, the Combined Raw Materials Board (CRMB), and the Civilian Production Administration. Evidence of her work in all three agencies is in **formerly security classified office files relating to commodities, particularly lead, 1943–46** (7 ft.). Enid Baird served in a similar capacity with the CRMB. Her **formerly security classified correspondence office files and cables, 1942–46** (7 ft.) reflect her expertise about graphite, mica, and rubber.

179.18. Records about personnel include a **survey of administrative personnel in regional and district offices, February 20, 1943** (2 in.), which is arranged by regional office and includes job descriptions and salaries of employees by name, many of whom were women. **The office file of Bernard L. Gladieux, Administrative Assistant to the Chairman, WPB, 1943–44** (3 ft.), is arranged by subject and contains references to women employees under "Administrative officers" and "Personnel."

179.19. Formerly security classified office files of G. Lyle Belsley, Executive Secretary of the War Production Board, 1941–46 (12 ft.), are arranged in three subseries: "Administrative correspondence file," "Official correspondence file," and "Reference file." In the reference file, which is arranged alphabetically, are documents that cite consumers' "readiness to sacrifice," with the general implication that most consumers were women. Statistics on population and the labor force by age and sex, narrative reports on women in war work, related concerns such as industrial health and safety and community facilities, a report on attitudes of and toward women in the labor force, and excerpts from union news sheets are in the file. Other pertinent folders in the reference file are: "Bureau of Intelligence—Office of Facts and Figures," which contains material on attitudes; "James F. Byrnes—Reports, etc., Director, War Mobilization and Reconversion"; "Miscellaneous Publications—G.L.B. Off.," which contains scattered references to women; "Office of Labor Production," which includes a "Brief Digest of the Labor Press" (2 in.); "War Production Program—1943–44—Bureau of Planning Statistics." It includes "Statistics in War Production," giving numbers of persons by sex in various industries; and copies of the *War Progress*, 1944–45, the WPB bimonthly.

179.20. In the **formerly security classified office file of Henry E. Edmunds, chief of the Historical Records Section, 1941–42** (3 ft.), is "War Agencies—World War I Source Material for Research," a bibliography prepared in 1942 by the Bureau of Labor Statistics, which includes references to articles in economics journals relating to women war workers in the World War I.

Records of
Naval Districts and Shore Establishments

Record Group 181

181.1. The Department of the Navy, soon after it was established in 1798, created navy yards and other fleet service shore establishments. A system of naval districts for the United States, its territories, and possessions was not formerly established until 1903. By the end of World War II the districts exercised almost complete military and administrative control over naval operations within their limits, including navy yards.

181.2. In the records of the Commandant's Office of the Washington, DC, Navy Yard, there are memorandums and endorsements relating to yeomen (F) in the 1917–18 segment of the **general correspondence, 1912–19** (70 ft.), arranged in five chronological segments and thereunder alphabetically by name or subject. Other records relating to women are under "Naval Reserve" and the names of individual women. Letters from the Women's Naval Service, Inc., formerly the Women's Secretary of the Navy League, invite enlisted men to participate in activities in the organization's recreation rooms, hostess rooms, and libraries. The Washington Navy Yard's **journals and daybooks of supplies and stores purchased and received at the yard, 1811–69** (22 vols., 3 ft.), arranged chronologically, include records dating from the mid-1840's and later of women who provided services such as quilting for the Navy. Each entry shows the type and quantity of goods furnished by a woman as well as the rate of payment and the total payment that she received.

181.3. Most of the records in this record group are in the National Archives regional archives. For example, the **general correspondence, 1914–39** (198 ft.), of the Great Lakes Naval Training Station, IL, which includes letters from women seeking or giving information about personnel stationed there, is in the National Archives–Great Lakes Region in Chicago. A list of the names and locations of the National Archives Regional Archives appears in Appendix D.

Records of the U.S. Joint Chiefs of Staff

Record Group 218

218.1. The U.S. Joint Chiefs of Staff (JCS) were originally the U.S. members of the Combined Chiefs of Staff (CSC), an agency established

Waves attending radio school follow the Stars and Stripes on a march through snow-covered Madison, WI, in March 1943. 80-G-471678.

in 1942 to ensure coordination of British and American war efforts. The National Security Act of 1947 established the JCS as a permanent agency within the National Military Establishment, now the Department of Defense. The JCS consist of the Chairman, the Army and Air Force Chiefs of Staff, the Chief of Naval Operations, and the Commandant of the Marine Corps. The Chairman is the principal military adviser to the President, the National Security Council, and the Secretary of Defense. The JCS determine policy relating to women in all U.S. military services.

218.2. A few documents in the CSC **decimal correspondence file, 1942–45** (231 ft.), arranged according to the War Department decimal classification scheme, relate to women in the U.S. military in general or to officers and enlisted women in the WAC, WAVES, and Women Marines assigned to the CSC. There are memorandums, circulars, and reports relating to women scattered throughout files 320.2 "Strength" and 320.22 "Enlisted Strength." In file 324.5 there are headings for "WAAC" and "WAC." The records relate to the assignment of WAC clerical personnel to kitchen duty for training, qualifications and allotments of WAAC personnel to the Office of Strategic Services, and the need for expert clerical help at Gen. Dwight D. Eisenhower's headquarters for the European Theater of Operations.

Records of
Temporary Committees, Commissions, and Boards

Record Group 220

220.1. Temporary committees, commissions, boards, and other bodies have been appointed from time to time by the President or created by an act of Congress to serve in factfinding or advisory capacities or to perform policymaking or coordinating functions with regard to the work of executive agencies. This collective record group includes the records of a number of such bodies whose records have not been assigned to separate record groups. Two commissions relating to military affairs include records about women.

Records of the Defense Manpower Commission

220.2. The Defense Manpower Commission was established by Congress in November 1973 to conduct a comprehensive study of the long- and short-term manpower requirements of the Department of Defense (DOD) and to devise policies to provide more effective utilization of manpower. One of the commissioners appointed by the President was Dr. Norma M. Loeser, who had been a Women's Air Force (WAF) officer from 1944 to 1966, rising to the rank of lieutenant colonel and serving as Director of Personnel Management, Headquarters, USAF, from 1964 to 1966. Maj. Gen. Jeanne Holm (Ret.), former WAF Director and the first woman to receive the Oak Leaf Cluster, served on the Commission's consultant panel while also serving as Director of the Secretary of the Air Force Personnel Council. Other women served on the professional staff of the Commission and wrote many of the reports published in *Defense Manpower Commission Staff Studies and Supporting Papers* (1973, 5 vols.). Among the subjects of the studies that relate to women are those on the role of women in the defense establishment, development and utilization of women, recruit screening, aptitude testing and selection, professional military education, the GI bill, manpower budgeting, and pay and retirement benefits.

220.3. The **minutes of meetings ("internal discussions"), April 19, 1974–March 26, 1976** (4 in.), arranged chronologically, include agenda items such as "minority women" and "women in the DOD." Filed with the minutes is a copy of the letter of appreciation from President Gerald R. Ford to Dr. Loeser, who left the Commission early to take a position as managing director of the Civil Aeronautics Board.

220.4. Minutes of public meetings, April 19, 1974–February 27, 1976 (10 in.), arranged chronologically, include correspondence, background and staff papers, lists of public attendees, and other records. They provide a record of discussions about the utilization of military and civilian women in the DOD (May 16, 1975) and a paper by a woman staff member on the topic (Feb. 13, 1976).

220.5. Transcripts of proceedings and other records of public hearings, November 1974–February 1976 (3 ft.), arranged chronologically by date of hearing, include testimony by representatives of several women's groups and a paper delivered by General Holm on July 17, 1975, entitled "The Role of Women in the All-Volunteer Military Force" (10 pp.).[3] At a hearing on January 28, 1975, a woman who was a strategic nuclear weapons analyst in the private sector presented her views.

220.6. Statements and other records of organizations on defense manpower issues, 1974–76 (1 ft.), arranged alphabetically by name of organization, include a statement from the Center for Women Policy Studies on "Admission of Women in the Service Academies," one from the National Organization for Women on "Women in the Military," and one from the Women's Equity Action League on "Women in Combat."

Records of the
President's Commission on Military Compensation

220.7. This Commission was established by President Jimmy Carter to study and analyze the then-current system of military compensation and make recommendations of needed changes. Jane C. Pfeifer, an executive with IBM and NBC, was the only woman on the nine-member Commission. They considered take-home pay, family allowances, military health care, and retirement and survivors' benefits. Letters, some as long as eight pages, from widows and wives of military personnel, active and retired, expressing views on the problems of military families are scattered throughout the Commission's **general correspondence, July 1977– March 1978** (3 ft.), arranged by subject. **Minutes of meetings, September 1, 1977–March 2, 1978** (8 in.), arranged chronologically, include a letter from Pfeifer stating her views and presentations by two of the four women on the professional staff. Partially indexed **transcripts of hearings, September 1977–January 18, 1978** (1 ft.), arranged chronologically by date of hearing, include testimony from Navy wives, a woman who was director of the Fort Eustis (VA) Service Club, a woman pilot, and the widow of an Air Force veteran. Summaries of interviews with personnel at selected military installations in **field trip reports, September December 1977** (negligible), arranged by name of post, touch upon widows' problems and retirement benefits for couples when both had military service. The **historical file, 1977–78** (1 in.), arranged by subject, includes information about Pfeifer's business experience.

---

[3]**Records of the President's Commission on an All-Volunteer Armed Force, 1969-70** (8 ft.), are also in this record group, but they contain little information about the participation of women in such a force.

Records of
Joint Army and Navy Boards and Committees

Record Group 225

225.1. The War and Navy Departments traditionally established joint boards and committees for interservice cooperation. The U.S. Joint Chiefs of Staff, created in 1942, became the principal agency for coordination between the Army and the Navy, but about 75 other interservice agencies existed during World War II.

225.2. One such committee was the Joint Army and Navy Committee on Welfare and Recreation, 1941–46, which was established to plan welfare and recreation activities. As a result of its studies and recommendations, the United Service Organizations (USO) was established. The Committee inspected facilities in the United States sponsored by the armed services and the USO and handled problems of these units and of the American Red Cross. The Committee dealt with women in the military, private and Government providers of services, "wayward women," young girls who might need protection, and the immediate families of service personnel.

225.3. The **general correspondence, 1941–46** (20 ft.), arranged alphabetically by name or subject, is accompanied by an alphabetical index in the form of **cross-reference copies of outgoing letters, 1941–46** (2 ft.). There is a file on Pearl Case Blough, director of USO services to women and girls. The correspondence covers such subjects as morale and official hostesses and librarians. The "pinup girl" as a morale builder is a subject under "Information and Reports" in the cross-reference sheets.

225.4. In addition, there are **minutes of committee meetings, 1941–46** (2 ft.), arranged chronologically. **Papers of committee members, 1941–44** (2 ft.), arranged alphabetically by name of member, include correspondence, reports, speeches, press releases, newspaper clippings, pamphlets, and related materials concerning the work of Sarah Gibson Blanding, a Committee member. The work of related organizations such as the Women's Interest Section of the War Department's Bureau of Public Relations, the American Red Cross, YWCA's for blacks and whites, the USO, and local citizens' groups in towns near military installations are also documented.

225.5. The **correspondence of Miss Florence Taffe, Director of Information and Reports, 1942–44** (1 ft.), arranged by subject, includes a file labeled "Social Protection Division." The series contains correspondence and reports about wartime housing and transportation and prostitution, mainly near military installations in Maryland and Virginia. The work of a women's advisory committee made up of representatives of women's organizations concerned about prostitution and venereal disease is documented. Other files pertain to servicewomen's use of leisure time.

Records of the Office of Strategic Services

Record Group 226

226.1. The Office of Strategic Services (OSS) was established in June 1942 when the Office of War Information assumed from the Office of the Coordinator of Information responsibility for the gathering of public information and disseminating it abroad in support of the war effort. The Office of the Coordinator of Information, redesignated the OSS, was left with responsibility for gathering information bearing upon national security and carrying out special operations that included sabotage, propaganda, transportation, and commando-type activities. William J. Donovan, the former Coordinator of Information, served as Director of the OSS until it was abolished in September 1945.

226.2. When the OSS was at its peak in 1944 with 13,000 employees, it is estimated that only about 10 percent were women. Few of these went overseas, and only a handful saw operations behind enemy lines. The women who held administrative positions and others with regional and linguistic knowledge were of great value to the OSS. Some women like Virginia Hall, Cora DuBois, Aune Irene Janhonen, Maria Gulovics, and Elizabeth MacDonald pursued colorful and dangerous careers.

226.3. At the end of World War II the OSS records were divided between the State Department and the War Department. The State Department assumed custody of the records of the Research and Analysis (R&A) Branch of the OSS. Of the 1,000 feet of R&A records transferred to the National Archives from the State Department in 1946, most are intelligence reports. Several indexes serve these records.

226.4. OSS records inherited by the War Department were those accumulated by some 40 OSS overseas field offices from Casablanca to Shanghai and by units in Washington, New York, and San Francisco. After the war, a Strategic Services Unit within the War Department organized the OSS files, identifying each file folder with a geographic point of origin, a branch at that location (Counterintelligence, Special Operations, Morale Operations, Secret Intelligence, etc.), and a category of record (administrative, operational, etc.). In 1947 the Central Intelligence Agency (CIA) assumed custody of these records, and in the 1980's approximately 3,000 cubic feet of OSS records in CIA custody were transferred to the National Archives. More than 30 years of continuing use of these records by the CIA has obscured their original arrangement. For all practical purposes the records are largely unarranged, but they are accessible to researchers through use of folder lists and indexes created by the National Archives. The indexes include the identifying information on each file folder and associate this identifying information with project names, personal names, and key words.

226.5. Researchers interested in locating OSS records about women should use the available indexes. These indexes do not include references to women in general, but they do include the names of specific women, such as those mentioned in **226.2**, who were either employed by or had contacts with the OSS.

Records of the U.S. Soldiers' Home

Record Group 231

231.1. The U.S. Soldiers' Home originated in an act of March 3, 1851, which provided for a "military asylum" with branches to support invalid and disabled soldiers. Temporary homes were set up at New Orleans, LA (1851–52), East Pascagoula, MS (1851–58), Harrodsburg, KY (1853–59), and Washington, DC. An act of March 3, 1859, changed the name of the asylum at Washington to the Soldiers' Home, which in 1947 began caring for Air Force as well as Army personnel. In 1972 the name was changed to Soldiers' and Airmen's Home. Records about women relate to those serving as nurses, other employees, and volunteers.

231.2. In **letters sent by the Governor, April 1869–June 1899** (2 vols., 5 in.), arranged chronologically with a partial name index in one volume, there are replies to women who offered to provide entertainment for the residents, usually in the form of plays, concerts, and lectures.

231.3. At first able-bodied residents handled nursing chores at the homes; later, nursing sisters had a nursing contract. This change is documented in **letters and endorsements sent by the Office of the Attending Surgeon, October 1881–June 1912** (23 vols., 2 ft.), arranged chronologically with a name index in each volume. They include correspondence with nuns from several hospitals and schools. **Press copies of letters sent by the Governor, 1902–6** (2 ft., 3 in.), arranged chronologically with name indexes in each volume, include a report that notes the introduction of women nurses and offers of volunteer visitation from women. There are protests against women nurses in **letters received, August 1899–June 1903** (1 vol., 2 in.), arranged chronologically. Nursing sisters are mentioned in **correspondence, reports, and orders . . . , 1851–1909** (2 in.).

231.4. Records documenting the concern of the board of the home about prostitutes on the grounds of the home appear in **administrative memorandums and orders, 1852–1923** (1 vol., 2 in.), arranged alphabetically by subject.

231.5. Orders issued by the office of the Governor, October 1892–September 1906; May 1915–December 1930 (2 vols., 6 in.), arranged chronologically, contain a few references to women who received permits to sell goods or services to residents.

231.6. Women hired principally as laundresses, charwomen, and dairy women in the 19th century are documented in **reports of civilian and inmate employees, December 1851–December 1852** (8 in.); **monthly reports of persons employed at the U.S. Military Asylum in East Pascagoula, MS, 1853** (¼ in.); and **monthly report of persons and inmates employed at the U.S. Military Asylum at Harrodsburg, KY, June 1853–September 1858** (1 vol., 2 in.). Later patterns of employment are documented in **register of employees showing transfers, discharges, absences, and resignations, July 1938–June 1941** (1 vol., 1 in.). All of these series are arranged chronologically.

National Archives Collection of World War II War Crimes Records

Record Group 238

238.1. After World War II the major German war criminals were tried before the International Military Tribunal (IMT) between October 1945 and October 1946. President Harry S. Truman provided that the Office of Military Government for Germany, United States (OMGUS), would handle the remaining trials of Nazi war criminals. In October 1946 U.S. military tribunals at Nuremberg began hearing cases against 12 indicted persons. These trials were known as the "subsequent proceedings" to differentiate them from the IMT cases. The names of a few American women attorneys and clericals appear in the records.

238.2. On January 19, 1946, Gen. Douglas MacArthur, Supreme Commander for the Allied Powers (SCAP) established the International Military Tribunal for the Far East (IMTFE). In the IMTFE records, more American women appear as witnesses because a number of them had been Japanese prisoners of war (POW's).

Records of German War Crimes Trials

238.3. In a **reference file** (52 ft.) there is a copy of "Women in Nazi Germany, Part IV, Readjustment Program," part of a five-part study prepared by Ruth Kempner, an American social worker, and her husband, Robert M.W. Kempner. The study is dated August 15, 1944. The authors recommended that American officials add "female liaison officers" to "the headquarters and units of G-5 [Military Government and Civil Affairs] and to all other forces which are active in operations, propaganda, public relations, etc." and that the American women should become "familiar 193 with the psychology of German women to help them readjust to Allied standards" during the occupation period at the end of the war.

238.4. Some of the Nuremberg trial records have been microfilmed, each case constituting one microfilm publication. For example, *Records of the United States Nuernberg War Crimes Trials: United States of America v. Josef Altstoetter et al (Case III), February 17, 1947–December 4, 1947* (M889, 53 rolls), contains **minutes of proceedings, February 17–December 4, 1947** (1 vol., 2 in.), on roll 1. On page 238 of the minutes (Aug. 28, 1947) is the statement, "Miss Arbuthnot continued the cross-examination of the defendant witness, Barnickle." In **English transcripts of the proceedings, February 17–December 4, 1947** (29 vols., rolls 2–11), the record for August 28 on roll 8 includes prosecution attorney Sadie Arbuthnot's cross-examination.

238.5. Barbara Skinner Mandellaub was Chief of the Court Archives, which consist of the records of Cases I–XII, official records of the military tribunals, and closely related administrative records. The Court Archives **correspondence, memorandums, reports, and other records, 1947–49** (1 ft.), include Mandellaub's administrative records and a history of the archives. Her signature and seal appear on **correction sheets for transcripts and document books, 1947–49** (5 in.), and documents in other series that required her certification.

238.6. Research analysts, several of whom were American women, screened German and other documents collected as evidence. The **staff evidence analysis forms (SEA's), 1945–48** (17 ft.), of the Document Control Branch of the Executive Counsel, arranged by document series with alphabetical identifiers, are summary analyses in English of the contents of original documents filed in other series. Most summaries are identified by name of author and date. The NG series of the SEA's (3 ft.) used in Case XI (the Ministries Case) contains the names of several women analysts. The NG series has been filmed as *Records of the Nuernberg War Crimes Trials: NG Series, 1933–1948* (T1139, 70 rolls). Also on film are the *Nuernberg Trial Records: Register Cards to the NG Document Series, 1946–1949* (M1278, 3 rolls). Lucille Petterson, a research analyst for Case XI, became director of the Berlin Document Center, 1963–68, after the center had been transferred to the State Department in 1953.

238.7. Memorandums regarding work assignments, copies of briefs, organization charts, and other papers in the **correspondence, reports, and other records, 1945–48** (3 ft.), of Trial Team No. 1 relate to women attorneys, research analysts, and clerical staff working on Case VI (*Carl Krauch et al*, known as the I.G. Farben case). Administrative records such as these were not microfilmed with the other records of this case on M892 (113 rolls).

238.8. A WAC prison officer, several women relatives of American personnel, and a woman teacher in the school for dependents are represented in **courthouse passes of civilians and military personnel, 1946–47** (4 ft.). Each pass contains a photograph of the person with his or her name, nationality, status, position or military rank, and information about the issuing agency.

238.9. The Berlin Branch of the Office of the Chief Counsel for War Crimes employed a number of women. Its **general correspondence, memorandums, and other records, 1946–48** (3 ft.), arranged by type of record, include correspondence relating to personnel and the work of divisions where women were employed. For the Economics Division there are lists of staff that include names of women with their special areas of expertise.

238.10. Photographs relating to minor Nuremberg trials, 1946–49 (238-OMT, 1,822 items), arranged by case number and subject followed by a section entitled "Palace of Justice," include in the Palace of Justice section documentation for the participation of women in the Nuremberg proceedings. There are photographs of women prosecution attorneys as follows: Case III (*Altstoetter et al*)—Sadie Arbuthnot; Case VI (*Krauch et al*)—unidentified woman; Case X (*Krupp et al*)—Cecilia Goetl; and Case XI (*von Weizsaecker et al*, or "Ministries Case")—Dorothea G. Minskoff. Women court reporters are identified in photographs in Case II (*Milch*), a research analyst in Case VII (*List et al*), and a United Press International woman correspondent in the Case XII (*von Leeb et al*). Pictures of a few other women journalists are among **photographs relating to major Nuremberg trials, 1945–46** (238-NT, over 800 items).

Records of the
International Military Tribunal for the Far East

238.11. Several series of the records of the IMTFE have been filmed as M1060 (253 rolls). **Transcripts of the proceedings, April 29, 1946– November 12, 1948** (74 vols., 31 ft.), arranged chronologically with pages numbered 1–49858, is accompanied by a **name and subject index** (1 vol., ½ in.) to pages 1–16997 of the transcripts ("General Index of the Record of the Prosecution's Case," and another **name and subject index** (1 vol., 1 in.) to pages 16998–24758 ("General Index of the Record of the Defense Case"). There are also **name indexes of witnesses** (1 vol., 1 in.). Wanda Werff was a witness for the prosecution, testifying about her experiences as a POW at Santo Tomas prison and the Los Banos Internment Camp in the Philippines.

238.12. Photographs relating to the trials by the International Military Tribunal for the Far East, 1946–48 (238-FE, 756 items), are arranged numerically in chronological order. Among them are well-identified pictures of Werff, women clerks and secretaries, a matron, and a teacher. Prominent visitors who were photographed include Col. Florence Blanchfield, Superintendent of the Army Nurse Corps; Mary A.

Hallaren, Director of the Women's Army Corps; Helen Lambert, a prosecution attorney; Mrs. H. V. Kaltenborn; Mrs. Douglas MacArthur; and the wife of Judge M.C. Cramer.

Records of the Office of the Chief of Chaplains

Record Group 247

247.1. The Office of the Chief of Chaplains was established in July 1920 as an administrative unit of the War Department. Previously, Army chaplains were assigned on a regimental basis and functioned only at that level. In 1950 the Office became an independent administrative service of the Department of the Army and is now an Army Staff agency. The Chief of Chaplains provides and supervises moral training and religious ministration for the Army.

247.2. The **general correspondence, 1920–62** (250 ft.), arranged according to the War Department decimal classification scheme, contains in file 080 "American War Mothers" references to that organization's annual Mother's Day service at Arlington National Cemetery. In file 231.3 (1 in.) there are letters from women who sought positions as hostesses or librarians at Army installations during World War II. File 250.1 "Morals and Conduct" contains a few items about women. Letters from members of Army families about baptisms, marriages, and funerals handled through the chaplains' offices are in file 291.1, as well as letters from women about pregnancies and breach of promises of marriage. There is a copy of a brief history of the Army Nursing School in file 321 "Nurse Corps."

247.3. Chapel registers, 1902–23 and 1939–April 1951 (29 vols., 5 ft.), sent from various Army installations to the Office of the Chief of Chaplains, are arranged alphabetically by the name of the installation, thereunder by type of service performed (baptism, marriage, funeral), and thereunder chronologically. There are registers for Fort Leavenworth, KS, dated as early as 1902. Chaplains' reports of baptisms, marriages, and funerals dating from the late 19th century through 1917 are filed in letters received and general correspondence of the Adjutant General's Office in RG 94, Records of the Adjutant General's Office, 1780's–1917. Weddings performed by Army chaplains were mainly those of civilian women to Army men, but the brides in some ceremonies were Army nurses or Wacs. Records of chaplains' activities before the establishment of the Office of the Chief of Chaplains are often filed with post records in RG 393, Records of U.S. Army Continental Commands, 1821–1920.

247.4. Chaplain monthly report files, 1917–50 (871 ft.), are arranged in four chronological segments, 1917–19, 1920–45, 1946–48, and 1949–50. The 1917–19 segment is arranged alphabetically by name of chaplain; the other segments are arranged by Regular Army or Army

Reserve and thereunder alphabetically by name of chaplain. They include records of services performed and lists of marital and premarital counseling sessions. Chronological **abstracts of information taken from chaplain monthly report files, 1923–50** (32 ft.), are also available.

Records of the Commissary General of Prisoners

Record Group 249

249.1. The Office of the Commissary General of Prisoners was established on June 17, 1862, although in October 1861 Lt. Col. William Hoffman was detailed as Commissary General of Prisoners under the Quartermaster General. The Commissary General of Prisoners was responsible for supervising Confederate prisoners of war and political prisoners confined in Federal prisons. On August 19, 1867, the Office was abolished, and its records and remaining duties were transferred to the Prisoner of War Division of the Adjutant General's Office. Most of the records of the Commissary General of Prisoners relate to Union prisoners in Confederate prisons, while records of Confederate prisoners in Union prisons are for the most part in the War Department Collection of Confederate Records, RG 109. Records deal with women as prisoners and as visitors to prisons.

249.2. Letters and telegrams sent, November 1861–May 1867 (16 vols., 4 ft.), arranged chronologically and generally numbered consecutively within each year, are accompanied by **name indexes, 1863–65** (9 vols., 8 in.). **Press copies of letters sent, 1861–67** (33 vols., 3 ft.), are also accompanied by **name indexes, March 1864–August 1867** (7 vols., 7 in.). Records in both series relate largely to prisoners of the Federal Government, some of whom were women. Entries in the **subject indexes, 1862–64** (7 vols., 7 in.), include "Female," "Ladies," and "Women." Most women incarcerated by the Federal Government were accused spies or suspected Confederate sympathizers.

249.3. There are hundreds of letters from women in **letters received, 1861–67** (140 ft.), which are accompanied by **registers, 1861–67** (27 vols., 6 ft.), with **name indexes** (22 vols., 2 ft.). Among names indexed are those of well-known prisoners like Belle Boyd (file B-3-1863) and less-known persons like Annie Nichols.

249.4. Letters received requesting information relating to the whereabouts of relatives serving the U.S. Army, 1864–65 (8 in.), are often requests for permission to visit or send packages to prisoners. There are about 100 telegrams to women on this subject in **press copies of telegrams sent, January 1863–January 1866** (5 vols., 6 in.), which are indexed by the name of the recipient in **name indexes** (4 vols., 3 in.).

249.5. In the **registers of rolls received showing the history of confinement of Confederate military prisoners of war, 1864–65** (2 vols., 4 in.), there are a few notes about imprisoned women, showing the places and dates of their imprisonment.

Records of U.S. Occupation Headquarters, World War II

Record Group 260

260.1. After the surrender of Germany in May 1945, Germany and Austria each were divided into British, French, Russian, and American occupation zones. The Office of Military Government for Germany, United States, known as OMGUS, was established in October to administer the American Zone.

260.2. After a period of military government in the Ryukyu Islands, the United States Civil Administration of the Ryukyu Islands (USCAR) took charge in December 1950. USCAR continued until the reversion of the Ryukyu Islands to Japan in 1972.

260.3. A number of American business and professional women, women educators, and leaders of American civic organizations went to Germany in 1945 to conduct studies and meet with the German people in an effort to establish a postwar rehabilitation program. Records relating to these women appear in the records of three of the branches of the OMGUS Manpower Division.

260.4. In the records of the Labor Management Technique Branch, **records relating to the Cultural Exchange Program, 1948–49** (6 in.), arranged alphabetically by subject, include correspondence relating to the visiting expert program and copies of two reports, "Women in German Industry," by Pauline Newman and Sarah Southall and "Workers['] Education in the U.S. Zone," by Alice Cook. The Newman-Southall report was based on a 1949 survey. Letters and memorandums from the Office of Labor Affairs, Hamburg, relating to the survey are in **subject files, 1945–48** (6½ ft.), of the Social Insurance Branch, arranged alphabetically by subject. The **visiting expert draft publication series, 1948–49** (8 in.), arranged alphabetically by last name of author, in the records of the Manpower Analysis Branch includes two reports by Eleanor Coit: "Recommendations on Workers' Education," and "Recommendations Growing Out of Contacts While in Germany."

260.5. Elizabeth Lam was Acting Chief of Group Affairs, which was redesignated the Community Education Branch of the OMGUS Division of Education and Cultural Relations. The branch was responsible for women's affairs, youth activities, and adult education.

260.6. The Women's Affairs Section of the branch emerged gradually out of volunteer programs designed to help German women after the war. Its director was Ruth F. Woodsmall. **Records relating to the work of the Women's Affairs Section, 1948** (15 in.), arranged by subject, include correspondence, memorandums, reports, cables, and periodicals pertaining primarily to the exchange of personnel and to the section's citizenship and political awareness educational programs for German women. Some subject headings in the series are: "Exchange Program," "U.S. Experts to Germany," "Manpower Branch—Berlin Sector," "Visiting Experts Reports," "Women's Clubs," and "Workshop Meetings," as well as personal names of officials of the section.

260.7. Records relating to the work of the Youth Activities Section, 1946–49 (8 ft.), arranged alphabetically by subject, document the work of WAC officers who were assigned to the Youth Activities offices in OMGUS field operations to serve as "big sisters" for 15-to-20-year-old German girls. There are also a few references to Elizabeth Lam and to women's affairs.

260.8. Records of L.E. Norrie, 1945–49 (7½ft.), arranged alphabetically by subject, were accumulated by Norrie in his capacity as chief of the Community Education Branch. Records under the heading "Women's Affairs, 1946–1948," refer to activities that predate the establishment of the Women's Affairs Section and deal mainly with youth activities.

260.9. Among the records collected by the Historical Branch of OMGUS are **records relating to the Personnel Division, 1946–47** (1 in.), consisting of the following two folders: "Procurement U.S. Civilian Personnel" (file 210.052) and "Civilian Employees Association" (file 210.53). Both files contain references to women, with the former including guidelines for women employees' dress.

260.10. The OMGUS *Weekly Information Bulletin*, **July 1945–49** (2 ft.), arranged chronologically, originally published by the Civil Affairs Division of U.S. Forces European Theater, was taken over by the Historical Branch of OMGUS. It contains news of the Special Consultant Program, which involved women.

260.11. Records of the Information Services Branch, Public Affairs Division, OMG Berlin Sector, include **press releases issued by the Public Information Office, 1945–49** (4 ft.), arranged chronologically. These records document the activities of the Cultural Exchange Program, including the inspection of WAC facilities by prominent advisers to OMGUS; visits from entertainers, including women; and meetings, training courses, and workshops conducted or attended by representatives of the Girl Scouts, International Ladies Garment Workers' Union, and U.S. leaders in the fields of religion, farm life, and social welfare.

260.12. American women were also employed in OMGUS field positions. Many women's names appear on "Rosters, July 1947," filed with **correspondence and related records, 1947–49** (8 ft.), of the Administration and Personnel Division, Office of Military Government (OMG) Bremen, arranged by subject. For each name on a roster there is information about position, title, grade, duty status, and date of contract expiration. The rosters cover several divisions of OMG Bremen. The **decimal files, 1945–49** (9 in.), of the Central Office, Bremerhaven Liaison and Security Detachment at Bremen, arranged according to the War Department decimal classification scheme, document the marriages of American soldiers to European and American women, including Wacs and civilian employees. Consent forms, military permission letters, affidavits, and marriage authorization forms are filed under 291.1 "Marriage of military personnel."

260.13. In the records of OMG Bavaria, **records of the Amberg Resident Office, 1945–49** (7½ ft.), arranged alphabetically by subject or type of report, include copies of a survey questionnaire distributed by the Women's Affairs Section and other records filed under the heading "Women's Affairs." "Dependents and Marriage 1949" contains information and regulations concerning marriage to alien nationals. There are also rosters of military personnel giving for each man his military status and residence, the name and nationality of his wife, and the names and sexes of his children.

260.14. The records of USCAR, 1945–71 (1,525 ft.), include the records of the predecessor military government. Only the audiovisual records have been declassified as of the date of this guide.

260.15. Photographs of commerce, industry, social services, and cultural affairs, 1949–72 (62,100 prints with negatives), are arranged according to a subject-numeric scheme and thereunder chronologically. Wives and daughters of American military personnel, nurses, teachers, consultants, and Wacs and Waves are among the women pictured. The series is accompanied by **photographic captions, 1957–72** (6 ft.), arranged chronologically. Some of the subject-numeric headings that may relate to women are: 010 General Education; 020 School Activities; 060 Scholarships; 070 Organizations; 110 Administration; 210 USCAR; 215 High Commissioner; 220 Civil Administration; 225 Women's Club; 290 Armed Forces; 550 Welfare; 560 Awards; 610 Public Health; 620 Hospitals.

Publications of the U.S. Government

Record Group 287

287.1. This record group was established to accommodate the record set of printed Federal documents formerly maintained by the Government Printing Office (GPO) as the library collection of its Public

Documents Division. Also in this record group are record sets of publications of other Government agencies that are not maintained as parts of the records of those agencies. What is presented below is essentially an annotated select list of the publications relating to women issued by military agencies of the Federal Government. No attempt has been made to cite every Government publication that relates to women.

287.2. Each GPO publication is assigned a number known as the "SuDoc No.," which is used primarily by the Superintendent of Documents, who directs the sale of Government publications and administers the depository library program. The publications cited below are arranged in SuDoc number order and are cited by SuDoc numbers. The placement of all military services under the Department of Defense in 1949 caused a change in the SuDoc numbering system. For example, a serial publication that began before 1949, may have two SuDoc numbers for the same title, one for the period before 1949, and one for issues dated 1949 and later. The publisher of each title is GPO unless otherwise indicated.

287.3. For an idea of the variety and quantity of Federal publications relating to women issued by both military and civilian agencies, one should scan the 19 pages of single-spaced entries under "Woman" through "Women's" in volume 15 of the *Cumulative Subject Index to the Monthly Catalog of United States Government Publications, 1900–1971*, a set that is available at any depository library, as are many of the publications cited in this chapter.

287.4. The *Official Register of the United States, 1907–59* (C3.10), is a biennial list of civilian employees of all Federal agencies. Between 1907 and 1911, it was a two-volume publication with postal employees requiring a separate volume. After 1911 the postal workers were excluded. For each permanent employee the register provides name; position; department, bureau, office or service; State, territory, or country of birth; congressional district, State, and county from which appointed; and place of employment. From 1925 until 1959, when the last edition was published, the register contains only the names of "persons occupying administrative and supervisory positions."

287.5. Important parts of the records of the 12 war crimes trials conducted by the U.S. military tribunals (see RG 238) were published in *Trials of War Criminals Before the Nuremberg Military Tribunals*, 15 vols., Department of the Army, 1949–53, (D102.8).

287.6. Wacs, Army nurses, and some women medical specialists are listed in the *Official Army Register for 1950* (D102.9:year beginning in 1950; previously M108:8:year and W3.11:year). An entry consists of name, serial number, date and place of birth, schools attended and degrees earned, ranks held, and promotion dates.

287.7. *Army Medical Specialist Corps, Department of the Army*, 1968 (D104.2:SP3), was edited by Col. Harriet S. Lee, USA (Ret.), and Lt. Col.

Myra L. McDaniel, USA (Ret.), with 15 additional contributing women authors including Col. Emma E. Vogel. It traces the history of dietitians, physical therapists, and occupational therapists who served with the U.S. Army from the World War I period through 1961. There is a later edition, *The Army Medical Specialist Corps, 1917–1971* (D104.2:SP3/917-71).

287.8. *Medical Department, United States Army, World War II* (39 vols.) includes material relating to American women in volumes described below:

Neuropsychiatry in World War II (2 vols.), *Volume I: Zone of Interior*, 1966 (D104.11:N39/v.1), edited by Col. Albert J. Glass and Lt. Col. Robert J. Bernucci, contains chapters written by or about nurses and women medical specialists and a chapter by Margaret Craighill about the Women's Army Corps.

Organization and Administration in World War II, 1963 (D104.11:OR3), by Blanche B. Armfield, covers the Surgeon General's Office and the various theaters of war.

Personnel in World War II, 1963 (D104.11:P43), by John H. McMinn and Max Levin, contains sections on the requirements, recruitment, and classification of members of the Medical Department, including nurses.

287.9. *The U.S. Army in World War II*, Office of the Chief of Military History, Department of the Army, includes several volumes that describe women's activities during that period. *The Women's Army Corps*, 1954 (D114.7:W84), by Mattie E. Treadwell in the Special Studies subseries is a history of the WAC through 1947. *The Medical Department: Medical Service in the Mediterranean and Minor Theaters* (D114.7:46/v.2) by Charles M. Wiltse in the Technical Services subseries includes numerous references to the Army Nurse Corps.

287.10. *Register of Commissioned and Warrant Officers of the United States Navy and Marine Corps*, 1950– (D208.12:950-977; previously M206.10 and N1.10) provides for each officer the serial number, date and place of birth, civilian and naval schools attended and degrees earned, ranks held and promotion dates, and languages spoken.

287.11. Three pamphlets recruited nurses for the Navy: *Navy Nurse Corps*, Bureau of Medicine and Surgery, 1958 (D208.2:N93) and 1960 (D208.2:N93/960); and *Navy Nurse Corps Candidate Program*, U.S. Navy Recruiting Aids Division, 1967 (D208.2:N93/967).

287.12. *Young Women Make Note of Your Future as a U.S. Marine Officer*, 1957 (D214.2:W84); *The Woman Officer in the United States Marine Corps*, 1967 (D214.2:W84/3); and *The Woman Marine Officer Candidate*, 1969 (D214.2:W84/4), are titles of USMC recruiting brochures.

287.13. The *Combined Lineal List of Officers on Active Duty in the Marine Corps*, 1956–57 (D214:Of3/4), and 1958–63 (D214.11:958-963).), includes reserve and retired officers and gives the occupational specialty of each person listed.

287.14. *Women Marines in World War I*, History and Museums Division, Headquarters, U.S. Marine Corps, 1974 (D214.13:W84), by Capt. Linda L. Hewitt, includes a partial alphabetical list of marine reservists (F) or "marinettes" in an appendix. Most photographs in the publication are available in series 165-WW, Records of the War Department General and Special Staffs, RG 165.

287.15. The *Marine Corps Women's Reserve in World War II*, by Lt. Col. Pat Meid, 1964 (D214.14/2:W84), contains extensive notes citing records in the National Archives.

287.16. U.S. Air Force publications about women include *Women Officers in the U.S. Air Force*, Department of the Air Force, 1969 (D301.2:W84/969), and *United States Air Force Hospital Nursing Service*, Department of the Air Force, 1970 (D301.35:160-2).

287.17. Three studies of the Women's Air Force (WAF) were prepared by Lois Lawrence Elliott of the Personnel Laboratory, Wright Air Development Division, Air Research and Development Command, USAF, Lackland Air Force Base, TX: *Prediction of Success in WAF Basic Training by Two Background Inventories*, 1960 (D301.45/13:60-216); *Factor Analysis of WAF Peer Nominations*, 1960 (D301.45/13:60-217); and *WAF Performance on the California Psychological Inventory*, 1960 (D301.45/13:60-218).

287.18. The *Air Force Register* (D303.7:year, after 1949; previously M302.7:year) provides name, serial number, date and place of birth, schools attended, degrees attained, ranks held, and promotions. Members of the WAF, Air Force nurses, medical specialists, and other USAF personnel are included.

287.19. *Medical Support of the Army Air Forces in World War II*, by Mae Mills Link and Hubert A. Coleman, Office of the Surgeon General, USAF, 1955 (D304.2:M46), includes material about nurses, Wasps, and Wacs.

287.20. *Women in the Military, November 1975: Special Bibliography Series, U.S. Air Force Academy* (D305.12:51) was compiled and edited by Betsy Coxe.

287.21. A publication of the Social Security Board that was much used by the military is *Occupations Suitable for Women*, 1942 (FS3.102:Oc1/2).

287.22. A predecessor of the *Official Register* described in **287.4.** was the *Official Register of Federal Employees* (11.25:862-905/2). Every Federal employee, down to janitors and charwomen, is listed, with his or her position, compensation, and geographical location.

287.23. The *U.S. Army in the World War, 1917–1919*, 17 vols., Historical Division, Department of the Army, 1948 (M103.9:1-M103.9:17), is a documentary publication consisting of excerpts of correspondence, reports, and general orders. (See **120.5** for manuscript of this publication.) Several chapters on personnel, welfare organizations, and the Medical Department contain references to women.

287.24. A U.S. Navy periodical, *The Naval Reservist*, October 1947–July 1949 (M206.9:date), includes information of interest to women as well as men reservists.

287.25. The *Marine Corps Manual*, 1949 (M209.9:949/.) and 1961 (D214.9:961), includes separate sections for women in Chapter 5 on recruitment and in Chapter 49 on women's uniforms. A section on personnel includes scattered regulations applicable to Women Marines in regard to detention, confinement, discharge, promotion, separation, basic training, and grooming.

287.26. *Annual Reports of the Secretary of the Navy*, 1823–1933 (N1.1:year), include the annual reports of the Navy Surgeon General, which include reports about the Navy Nurse Corps, particularly in 1908 and 1913. Reports for the World War I years include benefits for families of naval personnel, statistics and descriptions of the activities of Navy nurses and yeomen (F), and employment of women in the Naval Aircraft Factory.

287.27. *Lest We Forget*, 1943 (N1.2:L56), a pamphlet issued by the Navy Industrial Incentive Division, includes excerpts of a speech given at a war plant by Lt. (j.g.) Ann A. Bernatitus, a Navy nurse who escaped from the Philippines and was the first person in the Navy to receive the Legion of Merit.

287.28. In 1909, the year after the establishment of the Navy Nurse Corps, *Regulations for the Government of the Navy of the United States* (N1.11:year) included guidelines for the corps relating to appointments, assignments, pay and allowances, instruction, and special duty. There are a few regulations relating to families of naval personnel in the 1920 regulations, which was published under the title *Navy Regulations*. The regulations authorized medical treatment, restricted transportation of officers' families to new permanent stations, and defined "dependents" of male naval personnel.

287.29. *General Orders of the Navy Department* (N1.13/-) include General Order No. 65 dated May 4, 1910, which provides details relating to nurses' pay, and General Order No. 331 dated October 16, 1917, forbidding officers and men from boarding their families near the their vessels.

287.30. *Enlist in the Waves, Serve in the Hospital Corps*, 1943 (N10.2:W36), is a WAVES recruiting pamphlet.

287.31. *The Navy Nurse Corps*, 1943 (N10.2:93/2), and *White Task Force, The Story of the Nurse Corps*, 1945 (N10.2:93/4), are informational booklets.

287.32. *Navy Nurse Corps Relative Rank and Uniform Regulations,* 1943 (N10/13:N93/5/943), notes regulations applicable to Navy nurses at that time.

287.33. *Official Records of the Union and Confederate Navies in the War of Rebellion,* 1894–1922 (N16.6:2/3), is a documentary publication.

287.34. The names of Waves are included in the alphabetical listing in the *Register of Commissioned Officers, Cadets, Midshipmen, and Warrant Officers of the United States Naval Reserve,* 1943–44 (N17.38:943). Each entry includes name, file number, classification, rating, date of birth, and similar information.

287.35. *The Sea Clipper,* July 1945–September 1947 (N17.39), is a weekly and monthly newspaper issued by the Bureau of Naval Personnel. It features photographs and cartoons of men and women and pinup girls.

287.36. Under the Office of the Military Government of Germany, United States (OMGUS), American business and professional women made studies of postwar conditions in Germany. Articles by or about women consultants and women employed by OMGUS in public information and women's affairs jobs are listed in an appendix to *Women in West Germany,* 1952 (S1.95:W84), by Henry P. Pilgert for the Historical Division of the U.S. Hi ;h Commission for Germany.

287.37. *Annual Reports of the War Department,* 1822–1907, are available as National Archives Microfilm Publication M997 (164 rolls). Later reports were assigned W1.1:year. In the *Annual Report of the Secretary of War on the Operations of the Department,* 1875 (W1.1:875), there is a historical review of the employment of laundresses by the U.S. Army in the Inspector General's Report of October 11, 1875. Reports about Army nurses are found in the reports beginning about 1899. During World War I the reports give information about benefits for military families, telephone operators with the American Expeditionary Forces, American Red Cross workers, and efforts to control prostitution. Included in the report of the chairman of the Commission on Training Camp Activities, 1918, are reports on the Social Hygiene Division's Section on Women's Work and the Law Enforcement Division's Sections on Women and Girls, Reformatories, and Houses of Detention.

287.38. The *War Department Correspondence File (Revised Edition): A Subjective Decimal Classification with a Complete Alphabetical Index for Use of the War Department and the United States Army* (W1.2:D35/943) is the title of the 1943 revision of the War Department decimal filing scheme first issued in 1914 and frequently revised until it was abandoned in the early 1960's. A full account of its applications to subjects relating to women appears in the introduction of this guide.

287.39. *War Department Circulars* (W1.4:date/number) provided information to military personnel. Circulars in W1.4:943/125 and

Five Waves pose with their pistols during target practice at California's Treasure Island Naval Base in February 1943. 80-G-40594.

W1.4:943/245 include information relating to dependents' travel to and from points overseas.

287.40. *Regulations for the Army of the United States* (W1.6:year) are indexed by subject. Regulations relating to laundresses, hospital matrons, married men, and families of officers and enlisted men appear in 19th-century volumes such as the revision for 1863. Volumes for 1901, 1904, 1913, and 1917 contain regulations relating to the new Army Nurse Corps.

287.41. Each *Register of the War Department for Civilian Employees in Washington, D.C., 1885–1909* with gaps (13 vols.,W1:10:year), is arranged by War Department bureau, and there are lists of "female copyists" in various bureau listings. The entry for each person gives a synopsis of previous Federal employment and indicates place of birth. Registers for 1893, 1894, and 1896 list persons in the classified service such as laundresses or housekeepers employed in the offices of the depot quartermasters outside Washington.

287.42. *Correspondence Relating to the War with Spain and Conditions Growing Out of Same, Including the Insurrection in the Philippine Islands and the China Relief Expedition, Between the Adjutant General of the Army and Military Commanders in the United States, Cuba, Porto Rico, China, and the*

Philippine Islands from April 15, 1898, to July 30, 1902, 2 vols., 1902 (W3.2:C81/1 and W3.2:C81/2), contains some correspondence with and information about women.

287.43. *The WAC with the Army Ground Forces*, Recruiting Publicity Bureau, U.S. Army (W3.2:W84/10), is another recruiting brochure. There are at least 12 other pamphlets about the WAC under W3.2:W84.

287.44. The *Army List and Directory* (W3.10:date) was published every other month by the War Department. There are lists of personnel by hospital, depot, arsenal, or other facility as well as an alphabetical directory of all Army officers, giving for each his or her rank, position, service number, and current station assignment. Women contract surgeons are listed, and after 1921 when Army nurses achieved officer status, nurses are also included.

287.45. *General Orders and Bulletins*, War Department, 1861– (W3.22:date), were published and indexed annually and often included orders relating to the women who worked for the Army and the dependents of Army personnel. For example, General Order No. 70 (1919) lists those who were awarded medals with summaries of their meritorious service. Two members of the Army Nurse Corps reserve received the Distinguished Service Cross, and the Distinguished Service Medal was awarded to the Director of AEF nurses, a woman telegraph operator, and a woman American Red Cross worker.

287.46. The *Subject Index to the General Orders and Circulars of the War Department and the Headquarters of the Army, January 1, 1860, to December 31, 1880*, 1913 (W3.22:913), includes the following subjects that refer to printed issuances during the Civil War: "Chaplains—posts, record book of marriages, baptisms, and funerals"; "Clerks—female"; "Hospitals—nurses"; "Hospitals—general, cooks"; and "Hospitals—general, matrons"; "Laundresses"; "Medical attendance"; "Nurses—female"; "Nurses—Africans"; "Quarters—officers, families of"; "Pensions"; "Rations—commutation, title of widow." In the index for the period 1881–1911 (W3.22/881-911), entries that refer to records about women are: "Families of enlisted men"; "Families of officers"; "Hospitals—matrons"; "Medical attendance—Army nurses or Army Nurse Corps, families of enlisted men, families of officers"; "Nurse Corps (female)"; and "Nurse [contract, 1899–1900]." There is also a name and subject *Index to General Orders, Bulletins, and Numbered Circulars, War Department, 1917–26* (W3.22:927).

287.47. *General Court-martial Orders (GCMO), 1865–1942* (W3.32:year), are arranged by GCMO number rather than by case number. They state briefly the charges, specifications, findings, and sentence for each case, some of which involve women, but it is difficult to find pertinent orders except by reading through many records.

287.48. *Army Life and United States Army Recruiting News*, 1942–47 (W3.45:24/7-29/9), was published by the Adjutant General's Office and featured articles about nurses, medical specialists, Wacs, and cadet nurses in nearly every issue.

287.49. A *Digest of the Opinions of the Judge Advocate General of the Army* was published monthly and sometimes bound and indexed for several years. The bound volume dated 1912 (W10.7:912/3) covers opinions handed down between 1862 and 1912 and includes few that involve women. Those indexed under "Wives" refer to abuse of, evidence given by, and supplies purchased by them. There are also a few cases involving nurses. Later volumes (W10.8:year) include many more opinions relating to women. For 1918 (W10.9:2) there were decisions on the following subjects: "Allotments: compulsory, family allowances"; "Army Nurse Corps"; "Auxiliary agencies"; "Divorce"; "Marriage"; "Pay and allowances: Army Nurse Corps"; "Prostitution"; "White Slave Act"; "Witnesses: competence, wife"; "Women: employees at arsenals, officials of Red Cross"; and "Young Women's Christian Association: hostess houses." Among those for 1919 are: "Adultery"; "Army Nurse Corps"; "Army Transport Service: Navy Nurse Corps"; "Bigamy"; "Civilian employees: telephone operators"; "Divorce"; "Marriage"; "Medical Treatment"; "Nurses"; "Quarters"; "Widows"; and "Women's Land Army."

287.50. Editions of the *Manual for the Medical Department, United States Army* (W44.9:year) were published in 1902, 1911, and 1917. The 1902 edition refers to the usual subjects of Army Nurse Corps, hospital matrons, and laundresses, but also to the recording of marriages and illnesses at Army posts. The 1911 and 1917 editions refer to the employment of civilian women as nurses and the relationship between American Red Cross nurses and the Army Nurse Corps. One pertinent part of the 1916 volume is entitled "The Sanitary Service in the War."

287.51. *The Medical Department of the United States Army in the World War*, 15 vols., 1925–27 (W44.19:v. no.), includes a history of the Army Nurse Corps (volume 13, part 2). In volume 13, part 1, there is a history of physical reconstruction and vocational education and a chapter on welfare organizations. Volume 2 contains a section on the administration of the nursing section and reconstruction aides. Volume 5 deals with military hospitals in the United States with references to black nurses, and volume 10 on neuropsychiatry mentions women nurses.

287.52. *The Army Nurse* (W44.29:v. no) is a monthly magazine for members of the Army Nurse Corps, Medical Department dietitians, and physical and occupational therapists.

287.53. The *War of Rebellion: A Compilation of the Official Records of the Union and Confederate Armies*, 128 vols., 1880–1901 (W45.5), also published as National Archives Microfilm Publication M262 (128 rolls), includes, in Series III, vol. 1, a May 1, 1861, letter from the Acting Surgeon General for the Union Army stating, "This department, cheerfully and thankfully recognizing the ability and zeal of Miss D.L. Dix in her arrangements for the comfort and welfare of the sick Soldier in the present exigency, requests that each of the ladies who have offered their services as nurses would put themselves in communication with her before entering upon their duties, as efficient and well-directed service can only be rendered through a systematic arrangement. It is further suggested that the ladies exert themselves to the fullest extent in preparing or supplying hospital shirts for the sick; also articles of diet, as delicacies may be needed for individual cases, and such important articles as eggs, milk, chickens, etc. Miss Dix's residence is 505 Twelfth Street, between E and F. Respectfully, R.C. Wood."

287.54. From 1900, when the American Red Cross received its Federal charter, through 1947, *The American National Red Cross Annual Report* (W102.1:year) was submitted to the War Department. The reports include accounts of services performed by the ARC Nursing Division, other Red Cross personnel, and volunteers for Army and Navy servicemen and women and the families of service personnel. During World War II the American Red Cross furnished relief and assistance to POW's and to displaced persons.

287.55. The Defense Manpower Commission was created on November 16, 1973, to conduct a comprehensive study of the long- and short-term manpower requirements of the Department of Defense (DOD) and to devise policies to provide more effective utilization of manpower. **(See 220.2–220.6).** Women served on the professional staff of the Commission and authored and coauthored reports that are included in *Defense Manpower Commission Staff Studies and Supporting Papers*, 5 vols., 1976 (Y3D36.9). *Defense Manpower: The Keystone of National Security, Report to the President and the Congress*, 1976 (Y3.D36:1/976), is the final report.

287.56. Many letters and reports pertaining to women written during and after the Spanish-American War are published in *Report of the Commission Appointed by the President to Investigate the Conduct of the War Department in the War With Spain*, 1899 (Y3.W19:R29), and mainly relate to the management of the Army Medical Department. This volume is included as the first volume of an eight-volume set as Sen. Doc. 221 [serial nos. 3859–66], 56th Congress, 1st session, in the *Congressional Serial Set*.) The testimony of witnesses and scattered letters throughout the correspondence included in the report mention nurses, diet cooks, women physicians, relatives of the sick and wounded, and women among the residents of areas where military camps were located.

287.57. *Hearings Before the Committee on the Judiciary, United States Senate, Ninety-fourth Congress, Second Session, on S.1147 and S.2900 to Liquidate the Liability of the United States for the Massacre of Sioux Indian Men, Women, and Children at Wounded Knee on December 29, 1890*, February 5 and 6, 1976 (Y4.J89/2:W91) stressed the massacre of Indian women.

Records of the Army Staff

Record Group 319

319.1. The Army Staff, dating from 1947, is the military staff of the Secretary of the Army. Headed by the Army Chief of Staff, it prepares plans relating to the Army's role in national security, investigates and reports on Army efficiency and readiness, and supervises Army operations. This record group also contains the records of some predecessor offices. The records are arranged according to the War Department decimal classification scheme in yearly segments unless otherwise noted. They document the postwar period when the women's military organizations became permanent parts of the U.S. Armed Forces.

Records of the Office of the Chief of Staff

Records of the Secretary of the General Staff

319.2. The **security classified general correspondence, 1948–62** (368 ft.), of this office is arranged in seven chronological segments of varying length and accompanied by a **security classified index, 1948–62** (267 ft.), arranged in yearly segments; both are arranged thereunder by the War Department decimal classification scheme. Entries in the index summarize the documents indexed. Filed under 211 "Nurses" in various time periods are records about amendments to the Army-Navy Nurses Act of 1947 and investigation of alleged discrimination against Army nurses in occupied Japan. The proposed recall of nurses and women medical specialists in the organized Reserve Corps to serve in Korea is documented as well as later efforts to improve career opportunities and living conditions for nurses. A 1955 discussion of the possibility of commissioning male nurses and medical specialists is documented. President Dwight D. Eisenhower's concern for the quality of living for Army nurses was expressed in a letter to Gen. Maxwell D. Taylor, Chief of Staff, and prompted discussion of a proposed White House Conference on nurses in the armed services. There are records about the WAC in most segments under file 324.5 "WAC." For example, in 1949 there is correspondence about an officer procurement program at certain universities; training at Camp Lee, VA, for women in the Regular Army and the Officer Reserve Corps; postwar assignments in Europe; and modifications of the WAC uniform. Among 1951 records is a report on a study of homosexuality among Wacs primarily in the Military District of Washington. Subjects under file 291.1 for 1948 range from marital difficulties of individual military personnel to the expiration of the Alien Spouses Act relating to the transportation of war brides and husbands from overseas. Filed under 510 in 1949 are records relating to HR 6236, a bill in the 81st Congress to permit a pilgrimage similar to that of Gold Star Mothers after World

War I. In 1950 there are records under file 292 relating to military families in Europe and the Far East.

Records of the Office of the Comptroller of the Army

319.3. Monthly reports of civilian personnel, 1946–51 (4 ft.), are arranged in two subseries, personnel in the continental United States and those overseas, and thereunder chronologically by month. Although apparently not comprehensive, the reports include separate statistics for men and women hired and separated; statistics of women veterans, divided between those from World War II and those from other wars; and reports of the numbers of widows and wives of disabled veterans and the numbers of veterans of both sexes in absolute preference positions.

319.4. Monthly reports of operating personnel, 1945–50 (5 ft.), arranged chronologically by month, show the numbers of civilian and military operating personnel, their grades, and their positions in the organization of the Army.

319.5. Statistical reports relating to civilian employees of the Army, 1943–65 (2 ft.), are arranged in three subseries: War Department Monthly Statistical Bulletins on Civilian Personnel, 1943–51; Monthly Reports of Federal Civilian Employees (SF113), 1949–63; and Civil Service Commission Monthly Bulletins, 1965–52. Included are tallies of reasons employees gave for leaving their jobs in exit interviews. Most information is given by sex.

319.6. Among the **records relating to a statistical history of the Army in World War II, 1947–65** (2 ft.), arranged by subject, there is small file relating to women employed by the War Department, 1940–44. There are speeches of Mrs. Warwick B. Hobart, Chief of Training of Women, including one entitled "Tips on Training and Adapting Women Workers." There are also drafts of papers about women workers, publications of the War Department and other government agencies, and statistical information.

Records of the Office of the Chief of Legislative Liaison

319.7. Three series, **records relating to proposed legislation, 1947–54** (48 ft.), **records relating to Senate bills and resolutions, 1947–54** (70 ft.), and **records relating to House bills and resolutions, 1947–54** (130 ft.), are arranged by Congress. There are records about medical care for military families in the records of the 80th Congress in the series of proposed legislation. There is a sizable legislative file in the Senate series about Senate bill S.1641, which became the Women's Armed Services Integration Act in the 80th Congress. Among House bills important to women, HR 4090 (80th Congress) provided equal retirement benefits for Army and Navy Nurse Corps. HR 911 (81st Congress) to provide for the appointment of men as nurses, dietitians, and physical and occupational therapists in the Army, Navy, and Air Force was first introduced in 1951 by Frances P. Bolton. Bolton was also responsible for the enactment of PL 294 (84th Congress), which provided for the commissioning of men in the reserves.

Records of the Office of the Chief of Information

319.8. One of the responsibilities of the Office of the Chief of Information was the dissemination of information to Army personnel and military families. For example, in the 1957 segment of the **general correspondence of the Troop Information and Education Division, 1955–58** (13 ft.), file 247 contains correspondence, a pamphlet, and lecture material to clarify for military personnel certain features of the Dependents' Medical Care Act and the Servicemen's and Veterans' Survivor Benefits Act. In file 095 there are documents about an American woman journalist appointed by the French government to work with the Chaine D'Amitie, an organization sponsoring visits of American soldiers to French families. Earlier correspondence of the Troop Information Division is filed with the **general correspondence, 1949–59** (82 ft.), of the Chief of the Office of Information, which is accompanied by **name and subject indexes, 1949–56** (17 ft.). Many entries in the index relate to the WAC, to the accreditation of women journalists, and to film production and public relations campaigns. The **correspondence of the Command Information Division, 1963–64** (3 ft.), contains draft and published Army, Air Force, and Department of Defense (DOD) pamphlets on the Dependents' Medical Care Program and the Retired Serviceman's Family Protection Plan.

319.9. The Women's Interest Section was established in the Bureau of Public Relations (BPR) in July 1941 to provide information on the new defense Army to the women of the country. It continued to function until 1949, although the BPR was replaced by the Public Information Division. A national advisory council consisting of the presidents of most of the large national women's organizations attended meetings and conferences and helped disseminate information.

319.10. The **records of the Women's Interest Section, 1941–49** (4 ft.), arranged alphabetically by subject, consist primarily of correspondence between staff of the section and members of the advisory council. Among the organizations represented were the American Association of University Women; the American Legion Auxiliary; the American Social Hygiene Association; American Women of the American Farm Bureau Federation; the American Women's Volunteer Services; the Army Relief Society; the General Federation of Women's Clubs; the Ladies Auxiliary to the Veterans of Foreign Wars, Society of Daughters, U.S. Army; the National Woman's Christian Temperance Union; and the Young Women's Christian Association. Oveta Culp Hobby was director of the section before she became the Director of the WAAC in 1942. The records consist of minutes of meetings and conferences, reports, photographs, newspaper clippings, brief histories of the section, press releases, and copies of the periodical "Bulletin of Information." There is a large file labeled "Plan of Cooperation Between the W.A.A.C. and the Advisory Council."

Records of the General Staff

Records of the Office of the Assistant Chief of Staff, Personnel (G-1)

319.11. The G-1 **security classified correspondence, 1942–54** (700 ft.), includes only a few records about the WAC and the Army.Nurse Corps, but these consist of rather high-level policy-setting documentation. There is a 321 "WAC" file in almost every chronological segment. There are also records about other women. For example, segments for 1949 and 1950 include file 080 "Armed Forces Hostess" and 080 "Associations," which relate primarily to social services available to help military families settle in the Washington, DC, area; and files 291.1, 291.3, and 291.9, which include correspondence and reports about marriages of service personnel in Korea and Trieste and to foreign nationals, legislation about women in World War I, and the work of the Women's Medical Specialist Corps. File 292 "Dependents," includes a study of the effects on the morale of service personnel and on the international situation of sending military families overseas. The 1951–52 segment includes file 080 "American Red Cross," which contains statistics about the number of additional members of the Army Nurse Corps, Women's Medical Specialist Corps, and female medical officers that would be required as the Red Cross turned certain types of case work over to the Army. In the same segment, file 291.3 includes memorandums about the DOD Committee on Federal Manpower Policy on the Utilization of Female Military Personnel, and file 292 "Dependents" includes a booklet entitled *Ambassadors All* for military families going overseas and correspondence regarding legislation pending in Congress to assist dependents; file 323.3 "WAC Training Center" documents semiannual inspections. Also in 1951–52, file 334 "Working Group on Human Behavior Under Care of Military Service" is a report with Army officials' comments on subjects such as marriage of service personnel, sexual patterns, and women in the armed services; and file 720 "DOD Directive 6110.1" includes correspondence on physical examinations and physical and mental standards for women. Records for subsequent years follow similar patterns.

Records of the Office of the Assistant Chief of Staff, Intelligence (G-2)

319.12. There are two main series of correspondence for this office: **general administrative records ("decimal file"), 1941–56** (over 2,000 ft.), and records regarding military units, attachés, schools, and installations, and geographical entities ("project decimal file"), 1941–56 (1,404 ft.). Both are served by a **microfilmed cross-reference sheet index to the "decimal file" and other records maintained by the record section, 1941–45** (435 rolls); a **cross reference card subject index to the "project decimal file," 1953–56;** and a **cross reference card subject index to the "decimal file."** There are also **cross-reference sheets relating to persons, 1941–52** (26 ft.). In both series of correspondence files 324.5 for women in the military and 292 for dependents and families are sizable. Under 211 "Nurse" in the 1941–48 cross-reference sheets are references to stories of Japanese atrocities committed on Army nurses and the names of nurses who were investigated or who served as intelligence informants. Entries under 291.9 refer to women who worked in ordnance plants. Under 292 are references to reports about families of military attachés and their residential status. Documents pertaining to investigations of particular dependents were filed under 291.1. Under 322.5 "WAC" there are numerous entries on such subjects as the utilization of women, requests for WAC services, and homosexuality. References to Wacs assigned to Military Intelligence overseas appear under 324.5 "WAC."

319.13. In the Records Section of the Administrative Division, **records regarding miscellaneous organizations, associations, subjects, and titles ("impersonal name file"), 1941–56** (62 ft.), arranged alphabetically, include the names of women's organizations.

319.14. The **security classified intelligence and investigative dossiers, 1939–76** (111 ft.), of the Document Library Branch of the Collection and Dissemination Division are arranged alphabetically by name. The large dossier (3 in.) for Mildred Gillars (who broadcast as "Axis Sally") contains correspondence, copies of investigative reports, a microfilm copy of transcripts of interrogations, newspaper clippings, arrest details, and transcripts of Gillars' broadcasts from Germany. The series also includes records about a few other American women.

319.15. A smaller series with the same title, **security classified intelligence and investigative dossiers, 1939–76** (21 ft.), arranged by subject with a list of subjects at the beginning of the series, is in the Investigative Records Repository Files of the Counter Intelligence Corps. Included are dossiers for Madalyn Murray, a self-styled atheist, and Martha Stern, the daughter of a former U.S. ambassador to Germany, who was indicted as a Soviet spy and fled to Russia.

Records of the Office of the Assistant Chief of Staff, Operations (G-3)

319.16. In 1950 part of the Organization and Training Division was combined with the Plans and Operations Division to create the Office of the Assistant Chief of Staff, G-3.

319.17. WAC project files in each yearly segment of **formerly security classified correspondence, 1948–50** (154 ft.), of the Organization and Training Division document the planning and policy review functions of the division with regard to military women. The files contain weekly training schedules; course plans; memorandums, reports, and cross-references on a proposed WAC Reserve Section in the Organized Reserve Corps; Wacs as members of the active reserve; facilities for Wacs at service schools; and physical training for women. There is a copy of a 1950 report about an officer procurement trip to various colleges in file 322. A 1948 WAF file deals with training and statistics for women in the Air Force.

319.18. The Plans and Operations records include **formerly security classified** (313 ft.) and **formerly top secret** (114 ft.) **correspondence, 1946–50**, used with the aid of **cross-reference sheets** (34 ft.). Each series is arranged in two chronological segments, 1946–48 and 1848–50, and thereunder according to the War Department decimal classification scheme. The formerly security classified correspondence is further arranged by case number. Under 320, Reports of the General Board, United States Forces, European Theater (ETO Board Reports), ETO Board Study No. 11, "Study of Women's Army Corps in the European Theater of Operations," 1945 (3 vols., processed), is filed with Case No. 20. Appendixes provide statistics and copies of documents. Case 18 under file 320 contains information about the utilization of WAC personnel in the postwar Army. Study No. 114 is titled "Special Service Companies" and includes a section on the WAC Special Service Company formed in May 1945 to provide entertainers, librarians, projectionists, and musicians for the occupation forces in Europe. Study No. 117 (Case 20/2) "Live Entertainment" provides information on the use of civilian actresses and technicians, USO personnel, and Wacs. Under file 324.5 there are records about mobilization planning for women in the Army, the establishment of a Plans and Policy Committee in the WAC, and the appointment of Lt. Col. Mary A. Hallaran as Deputy Director of the WAC.

319.19. The G-3 **security classified correspondence, 1950–55** (1,034 ft.), is arranged in five chronological segments—1950–51 and one segment for each of the other four years, and thereunder according to the War Department decimal classification scheme. The **subject indexes to the security classified and top secret correspondence, 1950–55** (82 ft.), consist of lists of documents filed under each decimal and cross-reference sheets for individual documents filed under a different decimal arranged the same way as the correspondence. The procurement and selection of WAC personnel and subsequent training for them appear as subjects under files 211 and 324.5 "WAC" and under 201 by name of individual trained.

Records of the Special Staff

319.20. Statistical records relating to the Army in World War II, 1940–52 (19 ft.), consist of ASF data collected for use in writing a statistical history of the Army in World War II, drafts of which are in the file. **Military and civilian monthly strength reports of the Army Service Forces, 1943–46** (5 ft.), include statistical analyses of civilian employment in the Army by wage and occupational class for men and for women, strength reports for nurses and Wacs with data concerning race and military status, and additional statistical information at the end of the war for civilian employees, Wacs, nurses, dietitians, physical therapists, and wives and widows of veterans.

319.21. Historical notes relating to the organization and operation of overseas Army units of World War II, 1947–48 (2 ft.), contains records created by the War Department Special Staff, which eventually became the Office of the Chief of Military History. Arranged by arm of service and thereunder by unit, the notes include manuscripts, historical reports, monthly reports, and related records arranged by theater, army, service, program, or some other subdivision. A monograph produced by the Office of the Chief of Transportation about the Army's overseas passenger traffic during World War II contains information about the movement of dependents in 1941 and of war brides in 1945–46. There are reports from hospitals in the Africa-Middle East Theater of Operations which include descriptions of professional, social, and health activities of Army nurses; women with the American Red Cross; the WAC Detachment, Middle East command; and the WAC Detachment with the Cairo Military District. A "Supplementary History of Training: Special Service Units and Companies, June 1945–January 1946," prepared by the Special Services Division of the ASF includes a history of the 1st WAC Special Services Company in the European Theater.

Records of the Office of the Secretary of Defense

Record Group 330

330.1. The Office of the Secretary of Defense (OSD) was created in 1947 to head the National Military Establishment, which was renamed the Department of Defense (DOD) in 1949. The DOD is responsible for providing for the security of the United States by integrating policies and procedures for Government departments, agencies, and functions relating to national security. The Department of the Army (formerly the War Department), the Department of the Navy, and the Department of the Air Force were established as military departments under Assistant Secretaries of Defense within the DOD. Records relating to all of the women's military services, families of military personnel, and civilian women employed by bureaus and agencies within the DOD are in this record group.

Records of the Office of the
Assistant Secretary of Defense (Comptroller)

330.2. The **correspondence relating to organizational functions of the Office and to military assistance programs, 1947–55** (13 ft.), of the Assistant Secretary of Defense (ASD) (Comptroller) is filed in two subseries, one arranged according to a numerical scheme and the other arranged alphabetically by subject. A file on housing (5 in.) includes reports and correspondence with members of Congress and others concerning DOD housing policy and legislation. There are specific references to family units.

Records of the Office of the
Assistant Secretary of Defense (Manpower and Personnel)

330.3. The Office of the Assistant Secretary of Defense (Manpower and Personnel), usually referred to as OASD (M&P), was established in 1950 to develop policies and coordinate programs relating to men and women in all of the military services, civilian employees, and families of military personnel. When the Office later assumed responsibility for the same policies and programs for reserves, the acronym became OASD (MP&R).

Records of the Executive Office

330.4. In 1951 Secretary of Defense George C. Marshall appointed the Defense Advisory Committee on Women in the Services (DACOWITS), consisting of 49 prominent women educators, civic leaders, and business and professional women, to assist the defense establishment in recruiting women for the armed services. Lt. Col. Geneva F. McQuatters (WAC) was appointed executive secretary to the committee. Dr. Esther Strong was made a representative of women's interests in the OASD (M&P) and a staff member for women's affairs in the Military Personnel Policy Division, OASD, in 1952. There is correspondence of both women in **correspondence relating to the formulation of plans, policies, and procedures of the Office of the Assistant Secretary (Manpower, Personnel, and Reserve) ("Staff Signature Files"), 1952** (4 ft.), arranged alphabetically by surname of writer. Strong corresponded with women's organizations and military officials concerning community and government relations with women on assembly lines, in service occupations, in the professions, and in family life.

330.5. In January 1954 DACOWITS was given a new charter increasing its responsibilities. Committee members thereafter actively participated in recruiting women through personal appearances, lectures, and media programs. **Public information radio programs and spot announcements, 1952** (2 sound recordings), among the records of DACOWITS include 30-second announcements in the "Women in the Services Recruiting Campaign," and a public service radio special entitled "A Letter to Joan" performed by Helen Hayes, also a vehicle to recruit women.

330.6. Anna Rosenberg was Assistant Secretary of Defense (Manpower and Personnel), 1950–54. **Records of Anna Rosenberg, Assistant Secretary of Defense (Manpower and Personnel) relating to manpower and personnel matters of the Department of Defense, November 1950–December 1951** (1 ft.), arranged chronologically, consist largely of replies to congratulatory letters, requests for assistance, personal invitations, and similar matters.

330.7. Rosenberg made inspection trips to American military bases. **Formerly security classified records relating to manpower requirements for the Armed Forces and manpower and personnel matters in member countries of the North Atlantic Treaty Organization and in the Far East, 1951–52** (8 in.), include records of the preparation for these trips, briefing papers presented to her by field units, and her reports to the Secretary of Defense. The records are arranged in geographical segments (Europe, North Africa, Far East), followed by a segment of files on manpower requirements. Rosenberg observed a need for Wacs and Wafs in Korea in addition to the women already in Japan and Okinawa. One set of statistics includes the number of wives of military personnel at military bases in England.

330.8. Weekly activity reports ("Thursday reports"), September 1951–December 1953 (2 ft.), arranged chronologically, were filed by unit heads of OASD (M&P) and by committees, commissions, and boards. The reports relate to industrial relations; manpower supply and utilization, including women; military personnel policy, including civilians; reserve forces; information and education; domestic security programs; DACOWITS; Negro affairs; and chaplains.

330.9. The OASD (M&P) **formerly classified decimal classification correspondence file, 1949–54** (108 ft.), and its **indexes** (16 ft.), are both arranged in chronological segments and thereunder by the War Department decimal classification scheme. The chronological segments cover calendar years 1949–50, 1951, 1952, 1953, and 1954, but some overlapping of dates occurs within each segment. Many records about women can be found in file 291.3 in the 1949–50 segment, which includes records of 1950–51. Among these records are: a February 1951 report (27 pp.) submitted to Anna Rosenberg by the Personnel Policy Board (PPB) on actual and prospective utilization and recruitment of military and civilian women by the military services; records of the June 1950 Conference of Civilian Women Leaders convened by the PPB, including a processed report (195 pp.) of the conference proceedings that includes photographs and biographical information on attendees, press releases, and follow-up correspondence; records relating to policies about foreign service, regulations relating to homosexuals of both sexes in the armed services, and the discharge, detention, marriage, pregnancy, sex hygiene, and maternity of servicewomen; a processed report (M-7-51) of an October 1950 study, "Maximum Utilization of Military Womanpower," submitted in April 1951; correspondence, January–March 1951, about Project C-3-50, "Employment and Utilization of Civilian Women"; and pamphlets and memorandums about orientation for wives and families of military personnel going to Germany and Japan. Entries referring to records about women in the index covering the 1949–50 segment of the correspondence include "Legislation," "Reserve Officer Training Corps (ROTC)," "Sex hygiene," and "Statutes."

330.10. File 291.3 in the 1952 segment of the correspondence includes two reports on enlisted women in the military services prepared by the Attitude Research Branch of OSD's Office of Armed Forces Information and Education. One report (98 pp.) concerns the attitudes of enlisted servicewomen toward reenlistment, and the other (42 pp.) is entitled "The Servicewoman as a Public Relations Agent for Her Service." There is a two-volume copy of responses of the services to questions from the chief counsel of a congressional committee relating to the utilization of women in the military. The report of the Attitude Research Branch, "Women in the WAC: A Study of Recent Enlistees," May 1952 (33 pp.), is accompanied by Rosenberg correspondence about the utilization of women in the reserves and security classification of reports on the utilization of women. There are similar records in file 291.3 in the 1954 segment of the correspondence involving Rosenberg's successor, John A. Hannah. The records include guides for the utilization of Navy enlisted women (30 pp.) and officers (33 pp.) during mobilization, prepared by the Billet and Qualifications Research Branch of the Analysis Division of the Bureau of Naval Personnel.

330.11. File 292 for 1951 includes reports and correspondence concerning the implications of and policies about aid to families of reservists recalled to active duty, family units overseas, and evacuation of families from occupation zones. File 292 for 1952 also contains records relating to family members overseas. Records in file 324.5 "WASP" for 1951 show that recall of women pilots from civilian status was considered.

330.12. In file 334 for 1952 there is a "Special File: Housing for Women in the Military Services" and a DACOWITS file (334W) that includes agenda and minutes of the committee's meetings, Rosenberg's comments, her correspondence with committee members, and her reports to the Secretary on committee recommendations.

330.13. A copy of the PPB February 1951 report (see **330.9**), with additional attachments, is in file CD 324.5 of a subject correspondence file of the Office of the Secretary of Defense. This **confidential-top secret**

subject correspondence file, 1947–53 (101 ft.), is organized in three segments: a numerical file, 1947–50; a decimal file, 1950–53, arranged by year and thereunder by the War Department decimal classification scheme; and a subject file, 1943–45, arranged alphabetically by subject. Among the attachments is another document, "USAF Military Personnel Requirements for Women," June 1950 (67 pp.).

330.14. The **records of the Citizens Advisory Commission on Medical Care of Dependents of Military Personnel ("Moulton Commission"), April–June 1953** (6 ft.), arranged alphabetically by subject, include reports of previous studies of medical care; testimony of witnesses from the military services, the American Medical Association, the American Hospital Association, and servicemen's organizations; correspondence; minutes; the final report of the commission; and several publications including *Maternity and Infant Care Provisions for Servicemen's Dependents*, Publication No. 13, Research Department, Welfare Council of Metropolitan Los Angeles, 1952 (108 pp.).

Records of the Office of Administrative Services

330.15. Projected statistics on dependent care in the continental United States for fiscal year 1950, drafts of an attitude survey, and correspondence relating to problems in medical care for dependents are in a section labeled "Armed Forces Medical Policy Council," in the **formerly security classified reading file of J.R. Loftis, Director of Administrative Services, 1948–50** (3 ft.), arranged alphabetically by subject. Records relating to the attitude survey of married officers and enlisted men at Army, Navy, and Air Force installations concerning medical care for their families are filed under "Hospital and Medical Care Program."

Records of the Office of Armed Forces Information and Education

330.16. In 1942, the War Department began to conduct a series of surveys of the attitudes of military personnel. Collectively referred to as the "American Soldier in World War II," these surveys were designed to provide factual information on which to base policy-making decisions. Many of the surveys and associated analyses addressed women's issues. Examples include three surveys conducted in 1945: two surveys of Army nurses (surveys S-192 A and B) and one survey of Wacs (survey S-194). The questions in these surveys dealt with attitudes toward the overall treatment, condition, and use of women in the Army. Included were questions about job assignments; regulations affecting women; the importance of women's role in the war effort; equality of treatment for men and women; social life in the Army; leisure time facilities for women; opportunities for advancement; and postwar education, occupation, and marital plans. Some of the other surveys, of enlisted men and officers, included questions about USO clubs (surveys S-72, S-170, and S-174), dating "English girls" (survey S-122), venereal diseases (surveys S-146 and S-233), and attitudes about women in the military (surveys S-193 and S-215).

330.17. The **decimal correspondence file, 1943–52** (126 ft.), of the Office of Armed Forces Information and Education, arranged according to the War Department decimal classification scheme, and **records relating to the organization, development, and functions of the Research Division and of its predecessor, the Army Research Branch, 1941–55** (2 ft.), arranged alphabetically by subject, provide useful background material on the survey program.

330.18. The National Archives has an **electronic copy of raw data from the American Soldier surveys** (i.e., a computer tape version of punch cards representing responses to 138 of the surveys conducted by the Army Research Branch between 1942 and 1945). These data were written to tape in the late 1970's by the Roper Center, with funding from the Army Research Institute. Among the 138 data sets on tape are responses to the surveys of Army nurses and Wacs described in paragraph **330.16**.

330.19. Reports and analyses of attitude research surveys, 1942–55 (23 ft.), arranged by study number with a few unnumbered studies interspersed, begin with a list, arranged by survey number, showing for each study its number, title, and date; the samples drawn; and the total number of responses. Questionnaires, sampling and coding instructions, work sheets, statistical data, brief outlines, and related material for developing and analyzing the data are also in the records. The resulting administrative reports relating to women are too numerous to list here. For example, Wac responses in the United States to survey number S-194 resulted in the following reports:

C-102   How Enlisted WACs in the United States View Their WAC Officers

C-103   Fatigue as a Problem Among WAC Enlisted Personnel in the United States

C-120   WAC Attitudes Toward Overseas Occupation Service

C-130   Satisfaction With Assignment in the Women's Army Corps

C-132   Attitude Toward Recreation in the Women's Army Corps

B-158   Postwar Education Plans of Enlisted WACs

B-166   Postwar Job Plans of Enlisted WACs

WST15   How WACs View Their Officers

330.20. Some of the reports were distributed in a series of processed papers under the title "What the Soldier Thinks," which are filed with some reports of interviews with Wacs and other preliminary reports in **reports of studies of attitudes, prejudices, and desires of American troops, ("What the Soldier Thinks"), 1942–June 1955** (9 ft.), arranged numerically in six segments by report or memorandum number. The following relate to women:

48   Report on Leisure Time Activities

49   Preliminary Report on Motivations in Joining the WAC, January 1943

B-4   Preliminary Memorandum on Attitudes of White Enlisted Men Toward the WAAC

Report 13-6347
Enlisted Women in the Service: Some Satisfactions and Dissatisfactions of Service Life, 1952

Report 17-309 O,B
Housing Problems of Army Personnel in the Zone of the Interior, March 1947

Report 62-314 Xb,c
What the Soldier Thinks About Housing, March 1948

Report 83-322SN
Opinions of Army Nurse Corps Officers, November 1948

Reports 110 and 110A
Medical Care for Dependents, An Attitude Survey, May and June 1950

Report 129-349
Attitude of Girls' Nation Toward Military Service for Women and Toward Current Recruiting Appeals, 1952

Special Memorandum 55-347
Some Attitudes of Enlisted WAF, May 1953

330.21. In addition to reports of surveys taken in the United States, there are **reports of overseas research units showing the results of studies of opinions and attitudes of military personnel stationed overseas, 1942–53** (9 ft.), arranged by report number, each including a geographical designator. For the European Theater of Operations (ETO) there are reports on magazine preferences of enlisted black and white Wacs and their attitudes toward their Army assignments. Other reports deal with opinions of Army nurses and enlisted Wacs about the magazine *Overseas Woman*, and soldiers' evaluation of care received at Army and Red Cross hospitals. In the central Pacific, Army nurses were questioned about the quality of recreation facilities and other matters. There are reports of opinions of married Wacs in the Mediterranean area about discharge and Wacs' interest in courses that might be offered in an Army postwar education program. For the China-Burma-India (CBI) Theater of Operations there are reports on what enlisted men thought of Red Cross women as dates and as staff, the opinion of Army nurses of the CBI prohibition of their marrying, and other matters. There is a **subject index** (5 in.).

330.22. Other records remaining from the American Soldier studies include blank copies of the **questionnaires used in surveys . . . , 1942–55** (7 ft.), arranged by study number, and a **microfilm copy of a card index file of survey questions and marginals, Dec. 7, 1941, to Dec. 31, 1945,** (4 rolls).

Records of the Office of Manpower Utilization

330.23. The Office of Manpower Utilization **correspondence and reports relating to the review and evaluation of civilian and military manpower requirements, 1951–54** (6 in.), arranged alphabetically by subject, include records about housing and living conditions for military families in Alaska and Berlin and long hours for nurses with the 8th Army in Korea. A report entitled "Personal Data for the Assistant Secretary of Defense as Presented at Headquarters, European Command" includes complaints about overseas tours for nurses. Separate data on men and women civilian employees appear in "Manpower Requirements—Strengths." Military policies concerning shipment of household goods and proposed legislation to provide survivors' benefits are included in 1953 records.

Records of the Office of Personnel Policy

330.24. Records of the Military Personnel Policy Division include some files that pertain both to women in the military and to wives of military personnel. **Records relating to morale and welfare in the Armed Forces, 1949–52** (5 ft.), arranged by subject or project number, include scattered documents relating to survivor's benefits. There is one study of severance pay for servicewomen who were separated because of pregnancy or maternity. Records of Project M-7-50 pertain to a basic allowance for quarters for married personnel and the proposal that the allowance be improved "from the women's standpoint." For Project M-8E-50 correspondence and reports relate to policies dealing with uniform implementation of the basic allowance for quarters authorized for dependents of deceased servicemen. Other records relate to medical care for dependents of military personnel.

Records of the Personnel Policy Board

330.25. The Board's **studies concerning personnel matters referred to designated subcommittees, 1948–51** (9 ft.), arranged numerically, followed by a small group arranged by subject, include several studies relating to women. In addition to projects relating to survivors' benefit legislation, the following projects relate to women:

M-40	Recruitment of Civilian Physicians for the Care of Dependents of Military Personnel, 1949
M-46	Study to Revise Regulations for the Handling of Homosexuals in the Armed Forces, 1949
M-50	[Completion of a] Joint Publication Concerning Sex Hygiene Among Women in the Services
M-54	Policy Concerning Marriage, Pregnancy, and Maternity of Women in the Armed Forces

M-75   Medical Care for Dependents of Military Personnel

M-79   Review of Provisions Affecting Women Personnel in the Revision of the Officer Personnel Act of 1947

M-80   Foreign Service Policies of Women's Military Services

M-1-50 Review of Records of the National Research Council Concerning Venereal Disease Program of the Armed Forces

M-7-51 Transfer of Study Concerning Maximum Utilization of Military Womanpower (see **330.9**)

M-18   Rental and Subsistence Allowances, Payment of, Where Women Are Involved, 28 April 1949

Records of the Office of the Assistant Secretary of Defense (Legislative and Public Affairs)

Records of the Office of Public Information

330.26.   Records relating to the production of motion pictures for the Armed Forces, 1943–52 (15 ft.), arranged in rough alphabetical order by name of motion picture, were created by the Pictorial Branch of this office. They include scripts sent to the office or its predecessors for review, photographs, and correspondence with independent film companies under contract to the branch. Some films deal with women in the military, "girlfriends" of military personnel, and venereal disease. Titles of some scripts relating to women are "Because You're Mine," "Miracle of Living," "Never Wave at a Wac," "Skirts Ahoy," "The Real Miss America," and "This Lady Says No." Not all of the scripts were produced as films.

330.27.   Feature films about military events or incidents produced by commercial studios were often reviewed in the Pictorial Branch. In **records relating to the filming and releasing of motion pictures based on military operations or activities, 1951–53** (5 ft.), arranged alphabetically by subject, among the films relating to women are "Flight Nurse," which depicts WAF nurses evacuating the wounded from Korea to hospitals in Japan; "The Girls Have Landed," envisioned as a tribute to a USO troupe in Korea; "The Lady Laughs Last," an abandoned film idea about a woman doctor on a troop transport ship; and "Three Sailors and a Girl," which starred Jane Powell.

330.28.   Audiovisual records of the American Forces Information Service include **sound recordings of the "Command Performance" radio program, 1942–49** (68 items), arranged by program number. Produced by the War Department and the Armed Forces Radio (AFRS), they feature interviews, entertainment, and information broadcast to American military personnel stationed overseas. During the 1942–45 period the women entertainers recorded include Lauren Bacall, Talullah Bankhead, Joan Davis, Ella Fitzgerald, Betty Lou, Myrna Loy, the Peters sisters, Dinah Shore, Kate Smith, Barbara Stanwyck, Rise Stevens, and Margaret Whiting. Those making recordings between 1946 and 1949 include June Allyson, the Andrews Sisters, Lucille Ball, Janet Blair, Gloria de Haven, Ava Gardner, Betty Grable, Gloria Graham, June Havor, Rita Hayworth, Kitty Kaller, the King Sisters, Angela Lansbury, Peggy Lee, Marilyn Maxwell, Mary Pickford, Ginger Rogers, Shirley Ross, Dinah Shore, Kay Starr, Margaret Whiting, and Esther Williams.

330.29. Sound recordings, 1949–73 (1,772 items), cover press conferences, briefings, speeches, radio and television programs, and statements of the Secretary of Defense, other Federal officials, and political and military leaders relating to defense policy, foreign affairs, military aid, Korea, and other matters. Among women's events recorded are a 1949 presentation to war correspondent Helen Kirkpatrick; Anna Rosenberg at a November 1950 Women's National Press Club meeting; Col. Alice Gray, Director of Women in the Air Force (WAF), speaking on the seventh anniversary of the WAF; a 1951 discussion among several women of the Defense Advisory Committee Roundtable (3 tapes); and President Dwight D. Eisenhower's April 30, 1954, address to DACOWITS. In September 1952, Anna Rosenberg appeared on a broadcast in the "Time for Defense" television-radio series.

330.30. The Analysis Branch of the Office of Public Information collected news clippings, editorials, magazine articles, and other published material reflecting public opinion and news of interest to the military services. In the 1940–47 segment of the Branch's **general subject file, 1940–52** (8 ft.), arranged alphabetically by subject in two chronological segments (1940–47 and 1950–52), there are war bibliographies compiled by Dorothy C. Tompkins, research assistant in the Bureau of Public Administration at the University of California in Berkeley. One bibliography concerns the day care of children of working mothers (9 pp.).

330.31. Television network news broadcasts relating to Department of Defense activities, 1965–76 (574 reels), arranged numerically, consist of excerpts from the news reports of the three major TV networks relating to the Vietnam war, videotaped as they were broadcast by the DOD Directorate for Defense for internal DOD use. The film is accompanied by **news summary sheets, 1965–76** (7 vols., 1 ft.), which are printed summaries of the segments recorded. There are scattered references to women in the services, celebrities, war protesters, and Vietnamese women and children entering the United States as refugees. There was a June 21, 1966, report of a married couple working together as nurses in Vietnam, and a June 27, 1966, interview with a navy recruiter seeking nurses. President and Mrs. Nixon's trip to Vietnam in July 1969 was reported as was Betty (Mrs. Gerald R.) Ford's visit to a Vietnamese refugee camp at Camp Pendleton, CA, in May 1967, and her talk with former Vietnamese Premier Ki. Summaries for February 15, 1967, include

June 28, 1967: Capt. Elizabeth Finn, during her tour in Vietnam with the 93d Evacuation Hospital, watches two orphan girls perform a native dance. 111-C-41472.

NBC's "film story concerning women picketing to stop the war in Vietnam," and ABC's "film story concerning the Women's Strike for Peace." Families of draft evaders, servicemen, casualties, prisoners of war, and persons missing in action were frequently interviewed. All three networks reported aspects of and changes to military policy toward women in the services. Examples include: "Wacs and GIs living in the same barracks" (NBC, September 1, 1974), "Two Wacs facing discharge for homosexuality" (NBC, June 12, 1975), "Report on opportunities for Wacs . . . [in] weapons training" (CBS, summer 1975), "Report on status change for pregnant women in the military" (ABC, summer 1975), and brief reports about women cadets at the U.S. Coast Guard Academy (CBS, November 21, 1975), and the first women cadets at West Point (CBS and NBC, early 1975).

Records of the Office of the Administrative Secretary

330.32. The **unclassified subject correspondence file, 1947– 53** (216 ft.), of the Office is arranged by year and thereunder by the *Navy*

Filing Manual (for the period 1947–49) or the War Department decimal classification scheme (for the period 1950–53) with annual **name and subject indexes** (58 ft.). Under "VIP Correspondence" in the index for the September 1950–December 1952 period, there are references to a significant number of Anna Rosenberg's letters, many of which are routine replies to worried mothers of servicemen and women and to service personnel who wanted to return to school. A small subseries of correspondence filed alphabetically by name and subject, 1947–49, includes letters from women's organizations protesting or advocating specific defense policies. Filed under 334 in 1951 are records relating to DACOWITS. File 334 in 1953 includes records relating to the Moulton Commission and to the Family Housing Advisory Committee. In 1954 file 701 contains records relating to medical care for military families. The records include a reminiscence of a former American official in Germany about nurses' complaints that hospital beds were occupied by officers' wives and family members and "frauleins who are favorites of senior officers," in numbers that occasionally precluded treatment of military personnel.

Records of the Armed Forces Medical Policy Council

330.33. A **subject correspondence file, January–July, 1951** (8 ft.), arranged numerically according to the Council's file plan, includes records about commissioning women physicians and male nurses and matters relating to the military nurse corps and women medical specialists and to sex hygiene for women in the military services.

330.34. One area in which practice in the military varied from service to service was medical care, particularly the care available for families of military personnel. One of the earliest of several studies of the matter is documented in **records relating to a study of the medical services of the Armed Forces, 1948–49** (13 ft.), arranged by subject. The records include those of the "Hawley Committee or Board," chaired by Dr. Paul R. Hawley, relating to the care for dependents.

330.35. The Office of Medical Services **subject correspondence file, May 1949–January 1951** (12 ft.), arranged in rough alphabetical order by subject, includes records about the military nurse corps and women medical specialists.

Records of the Defense Management Council

330.36. Formerly top secret management improvement records, 1949–53 (ca. 150 ft.), arranged by subject include scattered records relating to women. For example, a file labeled "Housing" contains USAF statistics on the number of black women and WAC, Army Nurse Corps, and Women's Specialist Corps personnel in the Air Force. "Human Behavior Working Group Pamphlets" include one on marriage of service personnel prepared June 3, 1951, by a Navy chaplain. A file about the creation of the position of ASD (M&P) includes copies of memorandums transferring responsibilities from other offices, reassigning personnel, and establishing internal organization. Anna Rosenberg's testimony before the Preparedness Subcommittee of the Senate Armed Services Committee is in the file.

Records of Washington Headquarters Services

330.37. The **Combat Area Casualties Current File**, a machine-readable data set with technical documentation, includes final records for 58,152 casualties of the conflict in Southeast Asia, 1957–91. Among these casualty records are those for the eight women who died as a result of that conflict. Data available from the file includes name, date of death, branch of service, rank, serial or Social Security number, country of casualty, military and pay grades, home of record, military occupation code, birth date, cause of casualty, aircraft involvement, race, religion, length of service, and marital status.

Records of
Allied Operational and Occupation Headquarters, World War II

Record Group 331

331.1. In this record group are records of the Supreme Headquarters, Allied Expeditionary Forces (SHAEF), established in February 1944 to direct the Allied military operations in Western Europe; the Allied Force Headquarters (AFHQ), established in September 1942 as an Allied command to plan and direct ground, air, and naval operations and military government activities in the North African Theater of Operations (renamed the Mediterranean Theater of Operations in November 1944); the Allied Commission and Allied Military Government of Italy; the Allied Military Government, British-United States Zone, Free Territory of Trieste; and the General Headquarters, Supreme Commander for the Allied Powers (SCAP), organized in October 1945 to carry out the occupation of Japan. Series, including indexes, are arranged by the War Department decimal classification scheme unless otherwise noted.

SHAEF Records

331.2. In the **decimal correspondence file, 1944–45** (17 ft.), of SHAEF Headquarters G-1 (Personnel), file 291.1 "Marriage Policies" includes correspondence about mixed racial marriages. File 324.5 "Women's Services" consists of correspondence relating to women personnel in Germany during the occupation, including conditions under which women were to be employed, their duties and promotion requirements, their location and living conditions, and Gen. Dwight D. Eisenhower's instructions relating to women.

331.3. File 211.3 "Nurses" in the **unclassified through formerly secret decimal correspondence file, 1944–45** (68 ft.), contains copies of messages related to requests for and assignment of Army Nurse Corps liaison personnel and women war correspondents to evacuation hospitals to prepare news stories about Army nurses in the field. These records document Eisenhower's concern about an imbalance in publicity between the Army nurses and the Wacs.

331.4. The **decimal file, 1944–45** (14 ft.), of the Office of the Headquarters Commandant includes in file 291.1 (8 in.) records relating to marriages of American soldiers to foreign women and, in a few instances, to Wacs. There are declarations of intention to marry, investigative reports, oaths, and certified copies of cables of parental approval. In file 324.5 there are reports, correspondence, and cross-references relating to WAC morale, living conditions, assignments, and discipline.

331.5. SHAEF sent missions to liberated countries to deal with reestablished governments. In the records of the mission to France the general records of the Adjutant General's Division include **personnel name files of British and U.S. officers, enlisted men, and civilians assigned to duty with the mission, 1944–45** (3 ft.), arranged alphabetically, including the names of many Wacs and a few Red Cross women who were working with the Displaced Persons Branch. For each person listed there are personal information forms and requests for furloughs.

331.6. The 12th Army Group was under the operational control of SHAEF. In the records of the Morale and Personnel Branch of the G-1 (Personnel) Section of the 12th, **correspondence, memorandums, reports, and other papers relating to awards and decorations, promotions, assignments, redeployment, and other matters affecting personnel, 1944–45** (1 ft.), arranged alphabetically by subject, contain material on nurses, Wacs, and Red Cross workers. To a great extent these are requests for furloughs to England, passes to Paris, and leave. Registers at the front of the **recommendations for awards and decorations, 1944–45** (4 ft.), in this branch show that two American Red Cross nurses were recommended for the Bronze Star by their theater commander. **Policy books, 1944–45** (6 in.), maintained by the Morale and Personnel Branch consist of European Theater and other issuances for military and civilian personnel, including civilian women on the clerical staff and American Red Cross personnel. There are sections on leave, uniforms, and furlough policies as well as a 291.1 "Marriage Policies" file.

331.7. The **formerly classified and unclassified general correspondence, 1943–45** (92 ft.), of the 12th Army Group Adjutant   229

General's Section includes in 322 "Wac units" reports and correspondence on subjects such as manpower shortages, official visits to detachments, homes, and administrative matters.

331.8. Photographs of Supreme Headquarters Allied Expeditionary Forces (SHAEF) taken during invasion and occupation of Europe, 1944–45 (3,000 items), are accompanied by a subject index. Two-thirds of the fully captioned black-and-white prints are arranged geographically and thereunder by subject; the rest are arranged by subject only. Approximately 100 of the photographs include women. Most show activities of American Red Cross workers after the invasion of Europe providing aid to refugees and other civilians, teaching kindergarten, and conducting interviews with displaced persons. A small part of the portrait section is devoted to individual WAC staff officers, group portraits including Wacs, and photographs of WAC training activities. A few photographs include wives of officers in social settings and at least one woman war correspondent. Most of the women photographed served with the G-5 (Civil Affairs) Section of the 12th Army Group.

SCAP Records

331.9. In the **decimal correspondence file, 1945–April 1952** (429 ft.), of the Adjutant General Section of the Office of the Chief of Staff, arranged in classified and unclassified segments, there are records in file 291.1 that concern marriages between American soldiers and Japanese citizens and between American nurses and U.S. Army officers. A small amount of material in file 292 pertains to housing for military families. The records in file 230 and its subparts are voluminous, and most pertain to employment of Japanese civilians, but in file 230.42 there is a copy of a January 14, 1952, SCAP message to Washington listing the names of visiting experts, some of whom were women.

331.10. Reports, correspondence, and other documents relating to the activities of women leaders in Japan, 1945–51 (7 ft.), is a subject file of the Policy and Programs Branch of the Civil Information and Education (CI and E) Section. It includes records of Ethel Weed, a former WAC lieutenant who became the civilian chief of CI and E.

331.11. Florence Powdermaker, M.D., a Navy lieutenant during the war, a professor of psychiatry, and an official of the Veterans Administration, was one of the experts in the CI and E Section. Her trip reports are in **records relating to the organization, personnel, and activities of the Public Opinion and Sociological Research Division, 1946–51** (7 ft.), arranged by type of record. She reported on education, women, and public health and welfare in several Japanese cities. The records include names and titles of the U.S. Military Government personnel with whom she met, some of whom were American women. There are also minutes of meetings and conferences that were attended by Powdermaker, other CI and E women, and women from the Public Heath and Welfare Section of SCAP.

331.12. Among the records of the Administrative Branch (formerly the "Manila Branch") of SCAP's Legal Section are **reports on investigations of illegal acts committed by the Japanese in the Philippines (the "Manila Case Files"), 1945–46** (15 ft.), accompanied by **name files of Allied prisoners of war, witnesses of illegal acts, and victims, 1945–47** (18 ft.), and indexes to the reports and the name files. The reports include accounts of the experiences of American nurses and civilian women who were imprisoned in the Philippines and in Japan. There are similar records in **questionnaires completed by former prisoners of war, 1945** (5 ft.), in the Investigative Division of the Legal Section.

331.13. Records of the Administration Division of the Public Health and Welfare Section include a **miscellaneous subject file, 1945–53** (85 ft.), arranged by type of record or by subject. It includes records of the Nursing Division and the Division of Nursing Affairs. There are reports and correspondence of Army Nurse Corps personnel, American civilian nurses, and nursing education consultants who met with Japanese nurses and nursing associations to plan for the Tokyo Demonstration School of Nursing at the Red Cross Central Hospital. In the same series are memorandums from women in the Social Work Training Branch and birth control advocate Margaret Sanger's application for an entrance permit to lecture on planned parenthood. The records of the Welfare Division include files on "Social Work Education" (1 ft.), which document the career of Florence Brugger, a social work consultant and chief of the Welfare Administration and Organization Branch.

Records of U.S. Theaters of War, World War II

Record Group 332

332.1. After strategic direction of the war was made a joint Army-Navy and Allied responsibility through the establishment of the Joint and Combined Chiefs of Staff, the term "theater of operations" came to embrace a specific geographical area and all commands in it. The Army often used the term to designate its own headquarters in an area. Most records in this record group are those of units at the theater level. There are many more records about women in the records of the European Theater of Operations (ETO) than in any of the other theaters; all of the examples below are from the ETO. Records are arranged according to the War Department decimal classification scheme unless otherwise noted.

332.2. The **general correspondence, 1943–46** (12 ft.), of the Administrative Branch of the G-1 (Personnel) Section includes in file

320.4 proposed staffing tables for WAAC companies. The tables show the number and ranks of personnel assigned and the work to be performed. There is also correspondence concerning the utilization of black Wacs.

332.3. The records of the Women's Army Corps Branch of the G-1 Section include **subject correspondence, 1942–43** (9 in.), which includes lists of personnel, activities reports, and correspondence about policy and administrative matters. A series of WAC **histories, historical reports, and related records, 1942–46** (5 in.), includes reports and memorabilia concerning Air WAC, Special Services, and WAC rest homes and leave areas. There are also copies of the speeches of Col. Oveta Culp Hobby, first director of the WAC. **Correspondence and reports, 1944–46** (10 in.), include correspondence of the WAC staff director for the ETO, inspection reports, speeches, menus, and statistical WAC health reports.

332.4. In file 211 of the **general correspondence, 1943–44** (17 ft.), of the Surgeon General's Section there are reports, correspondence, copies of periodicals, and cross-reference sheets concerning Army nurses. Subjects include marriage policy, combat clothing, dietetic training, black nurses, the care of burn victims, convalescent homes, and the new periodical *The Army Nurse*. Records relating to the general health of nurses as well as Wacs are in file 322.099 "WAC Corps."

332.5. Reports of troop movements in the **general correspondence, 1942–46** (32 ft.), of the Transportation Section include the names of military personnel shipped overseas and also the names of civilians visiting the troops at the front, such as entertainers and other celebrities, many of whom were women.

332.6. Activities of American women in postwar Europe are documented in the **subject correspondence, 1945–47** (5 in.), of the Civilian Personnel Branch of the Seine Section of the Western Base Section, arranged alphabetically by subject. Under the heading "W.D. Civilians" there are records dated 1946 about policies relating to married couples and the hiring of dependents of military personnel. The series also contains records relating to women military personnel.

332.7. The series **administrative histories, 1942–January 1946** (90 ft.), consists of many reports arranged numerically, accompanied by an index and a list of reports. Included in folder 204 are Army Nurse Corps annual reports and the daily diary of the corps director, 1942–43, a North African trip diary, and information on Army Nurse Corps training programs in the ETO. G-2 (Intelligence) and base censors' semiannual reports on the morale of the troops in folder 212 include comments from nurses identified only by a number, duty station, and date. Comments in nurses' outgoing letters were extracted and tabulated by type. Also in folder 212 is a special report on WAC morale dated February 15, 1944, and comments about servicewomen excerpted from outgoing letters in the base censors' semimonthly reports on the morale of the troops. There are photographs, reports of WAC officers, press releases, and correspondence in folder 365. Folder 596D contains an undated draft history of the WAC Detachment, Normandy Base Section, prepared by Capt. Elizabeth Egan, the detachment commander.

Records of Interservice Agencies

Record Group 334

334.1. During World War II about 75 major interservice agencies representing two or more military services were created to deal with particular aspects or phases of the war. Some of these agencies helped determine top-level policy; others engaged in fact-finding activities, coordinated Army and Navy activities, or engaged in procurement operations. Most were discontinued after the war, but some concerned with peacetime military activity were placed under the Office of the Secretary of Defense.

334.2. The Joint Army-Navy Disciplinary Control Board was established in August 1944 primarily to deal with venereal disease and prostitution. **Correspondence, reports, and other records pertaining to the reduction and repression of conditions inimical to the morals and welfare of service personnel, 1944–49** (1 ft.), arranged alphabetically by name of restaurant, bar, club, dance hall, or other establishment, relate largely to conditions in the Army's Military District of Washington and in the Potomac River Naval Command. The minutes of monthly board meetings noted that certain establishments would be off limits to both male and female military personnel. Two files in the series are labeled "Commercialized Prostitution Conditions in Washington, D.C., 1948," and "Places of Encounter and Exposure, 1947, 1948."

334.3. The Industrial College of the Armed Forces developed in 1946 out of the Army Industrial College that had been established in 1924. Its courses dealt primarily with procurement and contracts, but the **case files of security classified research projects, 1944–48** (6 ft.), arranged numerically with a list of project titles at the beginning of the series, include a study of employment trends before 1944 with predictions for the future that speculate on the continuation of women in the labor force. Several lectures in its **conference branch lectures, 1950–58** (8 ft.), arranged alphabetically by subject, analyze the World War II experience in utilization of manpower including women. The **publications file, 1927–60** (9 ft.), arranged alphabetically by subject, includes under "Economic Mobilization Studies" Report No. 155 entitled " Manpower, 1952," which contains similar material. "Biographies of students, 1947– 233

60," include those of a few women officers. Other reports, filed under "Student Papers," were prepared by officers at the college for training. Among them are M55-94 "A Study of Military Family Housing, 1955" (29 pp.), and M56-53 "Military Survivors' Benefits, 1956" (40 pp.). Catalogs of the processed reports include several by women and show that a seminar was conducted in 1946 by three women on "Women in War and Industry."

334.4. The Medical Education for National Defense (MEND) Program was established in 1952 as an experiment in cooperation with five U.S. medical schools to improve the training and motivation of medical students in the practice of military and civil disaster medicine. Eventually all of the nation's undergraduate medical schools participated. Women took part in conferences, symposia, and other educational activities as students and as instructors. The security classified **general correspondence, 1951–69** (14 ft.), of the National Coordinator is arranged by fiscal year and thereunder by subject. One file title is "Work Conference on Disaster Nursing, American Nurses' Association, Washington, D.C., 1956."

Records of the
Office of the Secretary of the Army

Record Group 335

335.1. The Office of the Secretary of the Army was established when the National Security Act of 1947 transformed the Department of War into the Department of the Army and made the Secretary of the Army responsible to the Secretary of Defense. The Secretary of the Army is responsible for administration, training, operations, logistics, welfare, preparedness, and effectiveness of the Army. The Women's Army Corps (WAC), the Women's Medical Specialist Corps (WMSC), the Army Nurse Corps, and civilian women employees of the Department come under his administration. Many of the records in this record group are security classified.

335.2. The general correspondence of the Office of the Secretary and the cross-reference sheets that serve as finding aids to it are all arranged in chronological segments and thereunder by the War Department decimal classification scheme. The correspondence is divided into two series: **security classified general correspondence, 1947–64** (366 ft.), and unclassified **general correspondence, 1947–64** (569 ft.). There are three sets of cross-reference sheets: the **top secret cross-reference sheets to security classified general correspondence, 1953–62** (8 ft.); **security classified cross-reference sheets to the security classified general correspondence, 1947–64** (112 ft.); and **unclassified**

cross-reference sheets to general correspondence, 1947–64 (504 ft.), filmed as M1101 (485 rolls). There are subject or project files at the end of each of the five series. The following citations to records relating to women in these series are examples of the kinds of records these series may contain.

335.3. Among the unclassified records there is a subject file for the WAC, 1947–50, which consists of correspondence with Members of Congress and officials of the Department of Defense about establishing permanent corps of women in the National Military Establishment. File 020 "Surgeon General," 1951–53, contains a processed copy of an inspection report of the Far East Command for February 1953 that includes the report of Col. Ruby Bryant, Chief of the SGO Nursing Division, on the activities, clothing, and staffing of nurses in Korea and Japan. There are many entries for records of and about Anna Rosenberg, Assistant Secretary of Defense (Manpower and Personnel), 1950–54, in M1101, including those under file 201. Filed under 211 "Nurses" is a memorandum from the Assistant Secretary about a bill to permit the appointment of male nurses. Policy in regard to resignation of women from the Army because of marriage is treated in file 291.2 "Marriage," 1951–53. File 291.3 was used for correspondence relating to women in the Army in general, including their detention, the military status of women who served overseas with the Army in World War I, the Defense Advisory Committee on Women in the Services (DACOWITS), and further records relating to marriage of women in the Army. File 292 was often used for reports, memorandums, directives, and studies pertaining to wives of military personnel. For example, 1951–53 cross-reference sheets mention day care of children at military installations and legislation to provide maternity and infant care for families of enlisted men. SSO (Standards and Systems Office) Report No. 57-63E, "Career Attitudes of Wives of Junior Officers, U.S. Army, 1963" (67 pp.), prepared by the Office of Personnel Operations, is also filed under 292. File 321 "Army Nurse Corps and Women's Medical Specialist Corps" contains material relating to union activities, alleged discrimination in Japan, and amendments to the Army-Navy Nurses Act of 1947 drafted by the Secretary of the Army.. There is also a separate file 321 "WMSC," 1951–53. File 322 "WAC" includes information relating to black enlistments in the WAC and the promotion of the WAC officer training program on college campuses.

335.4. Among the security classified records, the following citations are examples of available records relating to women. Most are taken from security classified cross-reference sheets. Sheets for a WAC project file, 1949–50, refer to correspondence with the White House about promotion lists. There are sheets filed under both 020 "G-1" and 292 for 1951–53 relating to movement or evacuation of families of servicemen in critical areas of the world. Sheets under 292 for 1959–60 mention memorandums and meetings about reducing the number of family members overseas to help the balance of payments, the gold outflow, and general savings. Strengthening the Army Nurse Corps and the Army Reserve nurses during the Korean war is a subject on cross-reference sheets for 321 "Army Nurse Corps," 1951–53. Cross-reference sheets for 321 "WMSC," 1951–53, refer to the appointment of a new WMSC chief. File 321.02 "Medical Officers," 1953–56, includes statistics on the nursing population, including the number of nurses who were professionally active, married, and with children. File 324.5 for 1953–54 also contains records relating to the selection of a director for the WMSC. Cross-reference sheets under 324.5 for 1959–60 refer to an investigation of alleged homosexual activity among certain Wacs. Cross-reference sheets under file 700 in August 1953 refer to records relating to the numerical adequacy of the Army Nurse Corps officers, other medical personnel, and the enlisted WAC.

335.5. Records about Anna Rosenberg also appear in **security classified general correspondence, 1947–54** (366 ft.), of the Undersecretary of the Army, which includes Secretary of Defense George C. Marshall's January 4, 1951, letter announcing her appointment. In the **security classified cross–reference sheets, 1949–54** (278 ft.), to this correspondence there is reference under file 324.5 "Independent volunteer organizations" to file 700 "Medicine, hygiene, and sanitation," which contains memorandums, procedural directions, and policy statements, January–May 1950, regarding the health and medical care of women in the armed services. A reference in cross-reference file 291.3 "Sex" leads to file 620 "Barracks and quarters," which contains memorandums and reports about housing for women in the services.

335.6. The **security classified general correspondence, 1949–50** (36 ft.), of the Assistant Secretary of the Army (Manpower and Reserve Forces) is accompanied by **security classified cross-reference sheets to security classified general correspondence, 1949–50** (42 ft.), both arranged according to the War Department decimal classification scheme with project or subject files at the end of the series. In file 320 "Strength" there is a 1950 Personnel Policy Board (PPB) report on manpower utilization, the Assistant Secretary's comments on it, and another 1950 report on women on the staff of Murphy General Hospital in Massachusetts, where a staffing test was conducted by the Surgeon General's Office. An October 1950 PPB report recommended a study of personnel policy, the formulation of principles, and research regarding the utilization of women in the military in wartime and the problems of their service in certain occupational fields. A reference in file 321 in the cross-reference sheets leads to file 326.02 in the correspondence where there are figures approved by Secretary of Defense Marshall in September 1950 to support calling Reserve Army nurses and WMSC personnel to active duty.

335.7. Reports and other records relating to personnel, 1940–48 (2 ft.), in the Office of Civilian Personnel (OCP) is arranged by type of report and gives statistics of grade, pay, distribution, numerical strength, and turnover of civilian employees, including some separate reports about women. Most of the reports were prepared for congressional hearings. Reports consisting mainly of statistics and lists of names and positions of civilian women in key positions ("CAF-9 and above") were prepared in response to a request from Representative Mary T. Norton in April 1948. It is in report 18 of OCP **numbered reports, 1946–52** (3 ft.), arranged numerically. A similar report, number 101, was prepared in March 1952 about women in grades GS-13 and above. The date of birth, marital status, and number of years of Government service are given for each woman.

335.8. Beginning in 1955 the Office of the Chief of Legislative Liaison was responsible for formulating the Department of the Army legislative program for submission to the Secretary of Defense. **Records relating to proposed legislation, 1955–64** (20 ft.), **records relating to congressional bills and resolutions, 1955–65** (181 ft.), and **records relating to legislative affairs, 1955–64** (10 ft.), are all arranged by Congress and thereunder variously. All three series are served by **cross-reference sheets, 1955–64** (25 ft.), arranged by session of Congress and thereunder by War Department decimal classification scheme. Subjects encountered most frequently are pay allowances, veterans' benefits, and medical care for families of servicemen. The admission of men to the previously all-woman Army Nurse Corps and Women's Medical Specialist Corps occurred during this period and is documented in these series.

335.9. Sound recordings of the "Army Hour" radio program, 1942–74 (611 items), are arranged by program number with some gaps. The "Army Hour" was a series of public service programs produced by the Command Information Unit of the Office of the Chief of Public Affairs for broadcast to U.S. military personnel overseas and at posts in the United States. The series began broadcasting in April 1942 and continued through the end of World War II. It was revived in September 1953 and ceased production in 1974. The format featured interviews with service personnel, reports on current events, and entertainment. The recordings are accompanied by **program resumes, 1953–74** (3 ft.). Additional finding aids are available at the National Archives. Servicewomen are among the interviewees. A 30-minute program on the WAC (335AH#4) aired on November 13, 1953, and part of another 30-minute program (335AH#11) that was broadcast on February 5, 1954, is entitled "The Story of How Army Nurses Helped Restore the Health of the Wounded." Four months later "the many jobs efficiently handled by the Women's Medical Specialist Corps" shared part of a program. Features on other programs included a husband-and-wife team of Army nurses, and an Army wife and an Army nurse, each of whom was chosen "U.S. Lady of the Year." Among well-known entertainers who appeared on the program were the Andrews Sisters, Fannie Brice, Claudette Colbert, Marlene

Dietrich, Lena Horne, Jayne Mansfield, and Barbara Stanwyck. The WAC and the Army Nurse Corps were featured during the 1960's.

Records of Headquarters Army Ground Forces

Record Group 337

337.1. In 1942 Army combat arms were placed under the Army Ground Forces (AGF), which was responsible for organizing, training, and equipping ground force units for combat operations. Redesignated the Office of the Chief of Army Field Forces (AFF) in 1948, its authority was extended in 1953 to include the general direction, supervision, and coordination of the development of tactics, techniques, and materiel for field force use. In February 1955 the Continental Command was established as successor to the AFF.

337.2. Inspection reports relating to the training of units of the Regular Army, the National Guard, Organized Reserve Corps, and Reserve Officers' Training Corps, 1948–54 (34 ft.), in the records of the Combat Arms Advisory Group, are arranged geographically by location of training facility through 1950 and thereafter by year and thereunder numerically. Copies of the semiannual inspection reports and related correspondence for the WAC Training Center at Fort Lee, VA, for 1950 are filed under Fort Lee; in 1951 similar reports are numbered 190 and 192. Inspection reports of the training of Wacs in the Organized Reserve Corps in 1951 are numbered 30 and 343.

337.3. File 320.2 "WAC" is the principal source of correspondence about the WAC in the **formerly classified general correspondence, 1942–48** (6 ft.), arranged according to the War Department decimal classification scheme, of the G-1 Section (Personnel), of which the Women's Army Corps Division was a part.

337.4. Correspondence, reports, pamphlets, and related records of the Women's Army Corps Division are in the Division's **formerly security classified subject correspondence file, 1943–48** (3 ft.), arranged alphabetically by subject, under the following headings for the pre-1946 period: "Health," "Index to WAC Policy FIle," "Policy File," "Readjustment and Regulation," "Telephone Conversations," "WAC Detachment, Headquarters, AGF," "WAC File—Demobilization," and "WAC Separation Criteria." Plans for making the WAC part of the Regular Army are covered under the postwar subject headings: "Assignments of WAC Staff Directors"; "Health"; "Inspections"; "Letters to all WAC Staff Directors"; "Office of the Director, WAC"; "Plans for WAC Organized Reserve Corps"; "Policies and Index to WAC Policy File"; "Reenlistment, AGF WAC Requirements in Peacetime"; "Re-entry Program"; "Reserve WAC"; "Surgeon

General's Office—Correspondence"; "Transportation Corps—Correspondence"; "Telephone Conversations"; "WAC Officers in the AGF"; and "WAC Regular Army Training Center."

337.5. A few records of the Office of the Chief of Army Field Forces pertain to training women in medical and nursing subjects. Programs of instruction at the Medical Field Service School, Brooke Army Medical Center, Fort Sam Houston, TX, for example, are in the **correspondence, lists of Army extension courses, and other records pertaining to training (project files), 1945–50** (85 ft.), arranged in three segments: according to the War Department decimal filing scheme (8 ft.), alphabetically by school and thereunder by course number (74 ft.), and alphabetically by school (3 ft.). For 1948 there are summaries of subject matter and hours for each course and a description of the scope, references, and type of instruction for each subject in neuropsychiatric nursing and intermediate psychological social work. In the "project file" section of the series under the heading "medical school," there are records about extension courses established for nurses in 1949 in ward management, administration, and in-service education.

337.6. The **formerly confidential and secret general correspondence, 1942–55** (202 ft.), of the Communications and Records Division of the Adjutant General's Section is arranged according to the War Department decimal classification scheme in chronological subseries. In file 211 "Nurses" there is information about nurses in evacuation service and maneuvers and their field equipment. In project files at the end of chronological subseries and under file 321 "WAC, 1943–45" there are monthly activity reports to Col. Oveta Culp Hobby for transmission to the NCAC and other reports relating to WAC detachments, the Anti-aircraft Command, the Infantry Replacement Center, the Tank Destroyer School, and the Parachute School. There is also the report of Col. Emily C. Davis, AGF WAC Staff Director, December 1944–March 1945.

337.7. The Communications and Records Division's **unclassified general correspondence, 1940–54** (686 ft.), arranged according to the War Department decimal classification scheme, contains correspondence and cross-references relating to courses for nurses and women medical officers and enlisted personnel in file 352 "Medical School." Training for Wacs is documented in files 321 "WAC" and File 322 "WAC Training Center," at Fort McClellan, AL, which was dedicated on September 27, 1954. There is a 1953 file 352 "WAC School."

337.8. Among the records of the same division **studies conducted by the military occupational specialty panel concerning the enlisted military occupational specialty structure of the Army, 1952** (4 ft.), arranged numerically, include under the heading "Mobilization" a series of questions about the ability of Wacs to handle particular assignments.

Records of United States Army Commands

Record Group 338

338.1. A War Department reorganization of February 28, 1942, restructured the Department for wartime operation. All Army activities were grouped under Commanding Generals of the Army Air Forces, the Army Ground Forces, and the Army Service Forces. The fighting units created by these separate commands entered combat under commanders of the various theaters of operations (TO), defense commands, or task forces. By the end of World War II, there were WAC contingents in nearly all commands and Army nurses in most TO's.

338.2. The records in this record group are voluminous, and at this writing they are still being processed by the National Archives staff. The description that follows can serve only to note the types of records available about women.

Records of Headquarters U.S. Army, Europe

338.3. The top administrative headquarters of the U.S. Army's combat and service forces in Europe was known as Headquarters U.S. Army European Theater of Operations (ETOUSA) from June 1942 to July 1945. After two name changes, it became the U.S. Army Europe (USAREUR).

338.4. The **general correspondence, 1949–52** (118 ft.), of the Operations and Records Branch, Adjutant General's Division, USAREUR, is arranged chronologically by year and thereunder according to the War Department decimal classification system and is accompanied by **personal name card indexes** (10 ft.) and a smaller series of **subject card indexes**. The correspondence relates to women among civilian and military personnel and to servicemen's fiancees and wives and to such subjects as family transportation and adoption of children as well as routine administrative personnel matters. The **classified general correspondence, 1952** (17 ft.), of the Administrative Branch under the Secretary of the General Staff, USAREUR, also arranged according to the War Department classification scheme, contains similar material, including in file 501 (1 in.) correspondence about permission to have family members with military personnel in Berlin.

338.5. Several women held positions of responsibility in the Intelligence Division, USAREUR, and at War Criminal Prison No. 1 (Landsberg Prison). The records that document women's activities consist of personal name dossiers for prisoners interrogated and prosecuted, 1948–54.

338.6. Mildred Gillars, also known as Mildred Elizabeth Sisk, was an American citizen who broadcast enemy propaganda designed to undermine American troop morale in Europe. She called herself "Midge," but was dubbed "Axis Sally" by American servicemen. Records relating to her extradition to the United States to be tried for treason in the U.S. District Court for the District of Columbia can be located by using the **index to war crimes case files, 1945–55** (36 ft.), in records of the International Affairs Branch, Judge Advocate's Division.

Records of the Western Defense Command

338.7. The Western Defense Command (WDC) was established in March 1941 to provide for the defense of the U.S. west coast. The western halves of Washington, Oregon, and California and the southern part of Arizona were designated as Military Area No. 1, and all men, women, and children of Japanese descent living in that area were first advised and then ordered to evacuate the area. The WDC created a civilian agency, the Wartime Civil Control Administration, to establish assembly centers from which the Japanese were sent to relocation centers administered by the War Relocation Authority, a civilian agency. The records of the Army's activities in the evacuation are in the **records of the Western Defense Command, 1941–46** (70 ft. and 620 rolls of microfilm), arranged by type of record.

338.8. The **records of the assembly centers** are on microfilm and are accompanied by an **index** (1 vol., 4 in.), which consists of a master table of contents and tables giving the roll numbers for each assembly center. Records for each family group in the Sacramento Assembly Center are filed under 2.1. For most other assembly centers, these "family folders" are found under 3.1 or 3A, evacuee personnel records. Records identify each individual and his or her family connections, including in-laws, cousins, and friends. Files contain copies of records concerning property, instructions about movement to a relocation center, orders to report for work, and other similar material. Filed under 2.5 for Sacramento and 3.3–3.5 for other centers are rosters and other records of departures, which include records of births and deaths of related persons inside and outside the center and names of persons released or repatriated.

338.9. Personnel records—Caucasian, file 2A for Sacramento and 2.1–2.4 for other centers, relate to men and women employed by the Army in the evacuation program. Other personnel records are in files of the Finance Division, Payroll Section, of the Central Office in San Francisco. Hospital reports, recreation records (including "girls' singing and dancing"), and records documenting transfers of evacuees into private employment are also available.

Records of the Eastern Defense Command

338.10. **Records of headquarters, Eastern Defense Command (EDC), 1941–46** (13 ft.), arranged by sector or type of record, include records about evacuating persons of other than Japanese lineage who were considered too dangerous to leave in strategic defense areas.

338.11. Among the records of Army posts, camps, and stations the records of the Fort Lee, VA, WAC Training Center include the **training program outline, 1948–49** (1 in.), **historical reports, 1949–50** (5 in.), **training memoranda, 1951–52,** and **unnumbered memoranda, 1951.** There is a **"History of the Third Women's Army Corps Training Center,"** 1943–45 (1 in.), filed with records for Fort Oglethorpe, GA, and a description of the First WAC Training Center in a **"History of Fort Des Moines," 1946** (½ in.).

Records of U.S. Army Forces in the Pacific

338.12. The records of the WAC Staff Director, Special Troops, Headquarters, Army Forces in the Pacific (AFPAC), include records concerning Wacs with the Army Air Forces in detachments throughout the Southwest Pacific Area (SWPA) and at SWPA's Allied headquarters in Melbourne, Australia. The **"History of WAC's [sic] in SWPA," May 12, 1944–October 15, 1945** (2 in.), is an account prepared by Capt. Velma P. Griffith, Chief, Women's Interest Section, Public Relations Office, General Headquarters, AFPAC. It includes lists of WAC units showing, for each, duty assignments accompanied by Army Post Office (APO) numbers and names of commanding officers; a section on WAC casualties; biographies of SWPA's three WAC Legion of Honor recipients; detachment histories; and narrative accounts of activities in five different headquarters: U.S. Army Services of Supply (Southwest Pacific), U.S. Army Forces in the Far East, Far East Air Forces, Far East Air Service Command, and General Headquarters.

338.13. In addition, the WAC staff director's **monthly reports, 1944–45** (2 in.), include more historical reports, troop movement directives, and a checklist for WAC inspections. **Shipping rosters, 1944–45** (3 in.), provide, by contingent, the name and rank of every Wac sent to the SWPA.

338.14. The records also include those of the 8th Army's Sugamo Prison Supervisory Detachment. Among the prisoners there was Iva Ikuko Toguri, an American citizen of Japanese descent who, as "Little Orphan Annie" or "Tokyo Rose," broadcast Japanese propaganda to U.S. troops in the Pacific area. There are records about her in the 8th Army's **released prisoner 201 ["Personal records"] files, 1945–52** (22 ft.), arranged alphabetically by prisoner's surname.

Other Records

338.15. Records of Army medical units, 1942–54 (ca. 230 ft.), arranged alphabetically by type of unit and thereunder numerically, include copies of annual reports, historical reports, general orders, activities reports, photographs, venereal disease reports, and unit histories. They include many records about or created by nurses in various theaters of operations. For example, in the records of the 4th Field Hospital attached to the Army Air Force Service Command, Mediterranean Theater of Operations, is a nurse's report (9 pp.), dated January 1, 1944. Photograph albums (1 ft.) from the 67th Evacuation Hospital in the Philippines include scattered pictures of nurses and their quarters. A lengthy report of the American Red Cross unit at the 135th U.S. General Hospital in England tells of Red Cross work in solving patients' marital problems and of baby picture and "Big Baby" picture contests. Among the records of the Office of the Surgeon, Headquarters, USAF Middle Pacific, there is information on Army Nurse Corps morale, medals, and public health programs. Records relating to nurses and other medical personnel in the U.S. Army, Mediterranean Theater of Operations, include correspondence in file 200 about unit personnel requisitions, 1944; in file 200.3, personnel assignment and allotment, 1945; and in file 333, inspections.

Records of the
Office of the Secretary of the Air Force

Record Group 340

340.1. The Office of the Secretary of the Air Force had its origin in the National Security Act of 1947, which established the Department of the Air Force as part of the National Military Establishment and provided that certain functions and responsibilities be transferred to it from the Department of the Army. The Secretary is responsible to the Secretary of Defense for the administration of all aspects of the Air Force, including the Women in the Air Force (WAF), civilian employees, and families of Air Force service personnel.

340.2. The Secretary's **unclassified and security classified general correspondence, 1947–54** (670 ft.), is arranged largely in chronological segments separated into unclassified and security classified records and thereunder according to the War Department classification scheme. Unclassified and security classified records for 1948 and 1949 are mixed and include file 080 "Air Force Aid Society," which contains correspondence with the society about its efforts and suggestions to help servicemen's families solve housing and hospitalization problems. The marriages of Air Force personnel are the subject of file 291 for 1948–49. The unclassified part of the series for 1951 contains a 292 file relating to a proposed policy about allowing military families to remain in Germany after assessing the morale value of their presence. File 322 contains most of the records relating to the Wafs. In the file for 1948–49 there is correspondence about former Women Airforce Service Pilots (Wasps) who became Wafs, and the determination of some correspondents to prevent their being utilized as pilots in peacetime. Also filed under 322 are legislative records including the implementation of and proposed amendments to the Women's Armed Services Integration Act of 1948. Filed in later chronological segments are a copy of the Defense Department's Personnel Policy Board "Study on the Maximum Utilization of Military Womanpower" and correspondence generated by it. In the 1951 segment the 322 file includes the historical report of the first 3 years of the WAF by Director Col. Geraldine P. May and records about her resignation in June 1951. There are also recruiting materials from the Defense Advisory Committee on Women in the Services (DACOWITS) program for a Volunteer Air Reserve and correspondence and draft regulations relating to women with children. Filed under 334 in various unclassified chronological segments are a 1951 DACOWITS file containing correspondence and schedules for meetings and conferences of the committee, notes for presentations at meetings, and memorandums from Anna Rosenberg. Also filed under 334 is a processed copy of a final report and recommendations (2 in.) to the Secretary of Defense dated January 15, 1951, concerning family housing for military personnel along with earlier reports and correspondence. Among its chapters is one entitled "Justifications for Government-financed Construction of Family Housing for Military Personnel" and another dealing with women in the military services. A list of files within the 1951 classified part of file 334 identifies several other documents that may relate to women. Cited are reports, correspondence with Members of Congress, and excerpts from letters from constituents regarding housing in various parts of the country near Air Force installations. A folder numbered 5045 for the Interagency Committee for Critical Defense Areas contains similar records. File 600.12 "Housing for Dependents" covers housing requirements and availability at particular locations, authorization bills, and construction.

340.3. Title III of the Women's Armed Services Integration Act provided for the enlistment and appointment of women in WAF. In the records of the Office of the Administrative Assistant, **records relating to programs of the Air Force ("special interest files"), 1947–50** (24 ft.), are arranged in chronological segments and thereunder by a subject-numeric system. File 12 of the 1948 segment is a legislative file, January–August 1948 (2 in.), on the WAF part of the bill (S.1641). The file documents the changing status of the bill, the question of integrating the former Wasps into the WAF, and the types of work considered suitable for women. Among correspondents are Mrs. Oswald Lord and Jacqueline Cochran. Other records in the series relating to women are:

1948—file 1 (housing on USAF bases, especially in Alaska), file 30 (housing at Perrin Field, Sherman, TX), and file 34 (housing initiatives for the 81st Congress)

1948–49—file 6 (recommendations of the Hook Board regarding pay and analysis of the effect of military pay scales on families)

1949—file 1 (housing at various bases including photographs of AAF housing in Alaska)

1950—file 1 (housing, especially in Alaska), file 2 (USAF medical program, 1949–50, including family care and an October 1949 proposal by the Bureau of the Budget to discontinue medical, dental, and hospitalization benefits to military dependents), and file 4C (a preliminary study of public laws and pending legislation including housing for families)

340.4. The **security classified correspondence of Under Secretary Roswell L. Gilpatric, November–December 1951** (4 in.), arranged chronologically, contains correspondence about commissaries, dispensaries, and charity work, all of which affected military families.

340.5. The **security classified records of Frank T. McCoy, Deputy for Civilian Components, 1947–51** (3 ft.), arranged alphabetically by subject, contains records documenting the debate about women in the Reserves program and policies in regard to USAF construction, particularly that under the Wherry Housing Act. This law encouraged private sector construction of rental housing units near military bases for dependents of military personnel.

340.6. Among the subjects of the **security classified records of the Deputy for Personnel Management Clarence Osthagen, 1948–50** (10 in.), are studies relating to emergency utilization of personnel, including women; joint Army-Navy-Air Force recruiting for overseas service; and attempts to get full civil service status for persons who had been temporarily employed during World War II.

340.7. Housing in Alaska and the implementation of the Wherry Housing Act are among the subjects of the **security classified records of Scott W. Donaldson, Deputy for Air Installations and Family Housing, 1948–51** (2 ft.), arranged alphabetically by subject.

340.8. The **security classified records of the Assistant Secretary (Materiel), 1951** (10 in.), arranged chronologically, include the proceedings of the Family Housing Policy Committee.

340.9. In the records of the Public Information Division of the Office of Information Services, some **manuscripts of speeches prepared for Air Force officials, June 1942–November 1947** (5 ft.), arranged alphabetically by name of official, relate to training for women pilots. An address to be given November 29, 1943, at the induction of the first Air WAC company into the Army Air Forces is filed under the name of Brig. Gen. William G. Hall. Under "Articles" in the file of Gen. Henry H. Arnold is correspondence about the publication of his articles in national magazines, including women's magazines. One draft article, addressed to mothers, is entitled "Is Your Son an Army Flier?" In the same division, **records relating to motion pictures, 1947–53** (1 ft.), arranged alphabetically by subject, contain a file labeled "Flight Nurse," 1951–53, which deals with the review of the story treatment of a commercially produced film.

Records relating to special film projects, March 1946–April 1954 (3 ft.), are arranged by project number. Project SFP 258 "Women in the Air Force," 1950–52 (2 in.), deals with a screenplay about the recruitment of women for military service written for the Department of Defense in the early 1950's.

340.10. Records of the Office of the Director of Legislation and Liaison include **congressional correspondence, 1948–56** (612 ft.), arranged, beginning in 1952, by year and thereunder alphabetically by subject or name of congressman or constituent. Records in the series include material relating to medical care for USAF dependents in the 1953 segment; references to pilot and technical training for Wafs under "Pilots, women" and "Training" and a file labeled "Marriage" in the 1955 segment; and, in the 1956 segment, records about housing at USAF facilities and a file labeled "Civilian," which contains references to women employees. **Case files relating to congressional investigations, 1950–55** (51 ft.), arranged by year and thereunder numerically, include cases relating to benefits for USAF dependents.

Records of Headquarters, U.S. Air Force (Air Staff)

Record Group 341

341.1. Headquarters U.S. Air Force, also known as the Air Staff, was established under the terms of the National Security Act of 1947 to succeed to the functions of the Army Air Forces Headquarters. The Air Force Chief of Staff is responsible to the Secretary of the Air Force and is a member of the Joint Chiefs of Staff. Many series consist of both Army Air Force (AAF) as well as U.S. Air Force (USAF) records.

Records of the Vice Chief of Staff

341.2. References to the transition from "Air Wacs" to Women in the Air Force (WAF) as well as records relating to military families are in the general correspondence of the Executive Services Division. The correspondence is in three parts: **unclassified numerical correspondence, 1942–52** (52 ft.), arranged according to a numerical scheme; **confidential and secret correspondence, 1942–52** (8 ft.), arranged the same way; and **general and congressional correspondence, 1946–52** (6 ft.), arranged by year and thereunder alphabetically by initial letter of Congressman's name. All three are served by a **subject index to parts of the unclassified and classified numerical and decimal correspondence, 1946–51** (20 ft.). There are records about regulations and issuances regarding the travel of widows of servicemen after World War II, new problems of military families due to the Korean war, and educational and hospitalization needs of families of Air Force personnel in general. There are a few references to the utilization of nurses during the Korean war. The index contains many entries under "WAC" and "WAF."

Records of the Office of the Air Adjutant General

341.3. The Publications Review Branch maintained **formerly security classified microfilm copies of rescinded Air Force administrative publications, 1941–56** (401 rolls), arranged by type of publication and thereunder numerically. The series contains background material about the publications, including memorandums, notes, and comments on drafts. The records document the approval, revision, and rescission of AAF and USAF publications. On roll 35 are the following records relating to women: AAF Regulation 35-44 "Allotment, Assignment, and Administration of WAC Personnel" of November 10, 1943; AFR 35-44 "Military Personnel Assignments and Administration of the WAF Personnel," of October 25, 1949; and AFR 5-2A, which rescinded AFR 35-44 on January 4, 1954. Records relating to AAF Manual 120-2, *Women's Army Corps Inspection Manual* appear on roll 166. (See RG 287, Publications of the U.S. Government, for a copy of the manual.) Correspondence and a draft of letter 36-4, effective April 27, 1951, concerning appointment of officers in the WAF Reserve are on roll 270. The letter was superseded by AFM 36-5C in June 1, 1952; it is on roll 141. AAF Regulations 40-8 and 40-9 (roll 56) relate to the organization and function of the Women Airforce Service Pilots (WASP) as uniformed civilian employees of the AAF.

Records of the Office of the Surgeon General

341.4. The Air Force Nurse Corps and the Air Force Women's Medical Specialist Corps were both established in 1949. Administrative correspondence of both Corps are filed in the **general correspondence, 1950–51** (39 ft.), of the Office of the Executive Officer, arranged according to the War Department decimal classification scheme. Filed under 210.1 and 210.3 are applications for appointment in the regular and reserve forces, for overseas transfers, for training, and for discharge or extensions of duty. Frequently, records for both organizations are found in files labeled with either organizational title. File 327.052 in this correspondence series is used for records relating to Air Force women in general, including the WAF.

341.5. Among the records of the Historical Branch **historical branch background information, 1940–54** (147 ft.), contains correspondence, activities reports, studies, and publications relating to the functions of the Office of the Surgeon General, arranged by subject. Included are annual reports, quarterly activity reports, trip reports, 247 speeches and related records of the Air Force Nurse Corps and the Air Force Women's Medical Specialist Corps, some of them filed under "Medical Support Group." The series includes records about both organizations in reports of the Directorate of Medical Staffing and Education, and there are statistics and other information on medical education, aeromedical evacuation, Air Force nursing in the Far East, and the Defense Advisory Committee on Women in the Services (DACOWITS).

341.6. In the records of the Aviation Medicine Division's Technical Information Branch there is a series of indexed **monthly publication issues ("medical service digests") with background materials, June 1950–December 1953** (1 ft.), arranged chronologically, that contains many articles about the Air Force Nurse Corps and Women's Medical Specialist Corps. There is also an article about the first woman doctor sworn into the Air Force Medical Service.

Records of the
Office of the Deputy Chief of Staff, Comptroller

341.7. Among the records of the Personnel Statistical Division of the Office of the Director of Statistical Services **security classified microfilm copies of statistical reports relating to civilian and military personnel, March 1944–February 1956** (455 rolls), arranged by an alpha-numeric filing scheme, include reports relating to women in all parts of the Air Force and dependent families of Air Force personnel. The following titles are examples of reports containing information about women: SC-ZR-169, 24 August 1950, "Air Force Personnel Survey by Year of Birth, Race, Sex, and Place of Pre-service Residence"; SC-PS-25 (Officers) and SC-PS-26 (Enlisted), issued monthly, "Worldwide Strength Reports Showing Military Occupational Specialty, Race, Sex, Grade, and Department Status"; SC-PS-398, October 1952, "Dependents Overseas"; SC-PSD-720S, May 1951, "Enlisted Personnel by Grade and Marital Status" (provides statistics concerning dependents, educational levels, overseas service credits, requests for release, and college enrollment); SC-PSD-1118, January 1951, "Survey of Air Force Personnel by Grade and Number of Dependents Residing at or near Duty Station"; SC-PSD-808, April 1951 (no title but similar to report above); ZR-195, including data as late as 1954, "USAF Military Personnel Reflecting Component Within Sex and Departmental Status Group, June–December 1952"; SC-PS-431, April–October 1952, "Assigned Strength of the WAF by Unit"; SC-PS-425 "Female Personnel by SSN/AFSC and Command, July–December 1952" and "WAF Personnel by AFSC with Career Field Command, March–December 1952"; SC-PSD-733S, no date, includes data pertaining to WAF personnel, May 1951, in such categories as quarters, allowance, marital status, dependency status, residence of dependents, and grade.

Records of the Deputy Chief of Staff, Personnel

341.8. The director of the WAF was placed in this office, and many WAF records are filed under 210.10 "WAF" of its Executive Office **administrative and policy correspondence, 1947–54** (6 ft.), arranged according to the War Department classification scheme. Included are records relating to the naming of the WAF; WAF procurement, training, and housing; meetings of the Defense Advisory Committee on Women in the Services (DACOWITS); and the call of reservists to active duty. WAF activities are the subjects of reports, correspondence, press releases, newspaper clippings, and issuances and directives in the series. The files contain originals and copies of reports and correspondence of WAF Directors Col. Geraldine P. May and Col. Mary J. Shelly and Deputy Director Kathleen McClure; a summary examination of the WAF program by the Office of the Inspector General conducted April 1–June 30, 1951; a report to the Secretary of the Air Force by the Committee on Personnel Utilization and Training submitted June 1951; and statistical summaries.

341.9. Microfilmed records of the Office of the Chief of Chaplains provide vital statistics concerning Air Force families. **Records of baptisms, marriages, and funerals conducted by Air Force chaplains ("Chapel Records"), July 1, 1949–December 31, 1955**, filmed as P2002 (44 rolls), are arranged in chronological segments and thereunder alphabetically by surname.

341.10. In the records of the Executive Office of the Office of the Director of Personnel Planning, the **decimal correspondence file pertaining to plans, policies, and programs for the procurement, promotion, separation, and utilization of Air Force military personnel, 1948–53** (24 ft.), is arranged according to the War Department decimal classification scheme. File 324.5 "WAF" (4 in.) consists of unclassified through secret folders. One of the secret folders contains "USAF Mobilization: Military Personnel Requirements for Women," June 1, 1950 (67 pp.), and related correspondence. There are also memorandums and statistics about USAF Reserve requirements for women as of October 27, 1950. There are proposed regulations and correspondence about policies and procedures for separating commissioned WAF officers because of marriage or pregnancy. Other correspondence deals with the status of Wasps and recommendations from Jacqueline Cochran and DACOWITS. Also included are correspondence on the recommendations made in the Personnel Policy Board's "Study on Maximum Utilization of Military Womanpower" and records relating to nurses, women doctors, and medical specialists, as well as Colonel May's May 15, 1952, report on the WAF program during her first year as director.

341.11. The **correspondence and studies relating to organization, staffing, budgeting, and work measurement, 1952–54** (8 ft.), of the Management Planning Branch of the Standards Division of the

Office of Civilian Personnel are arranged by subject. One subject is "Reports—Women Civilian Employees in Grades GS-13 or Over."

Records of the
Office of the Deputy Chief of Staff, Operations

341.12. The **decimal correspondence file, 1948–49** (2 ft.), of the Air Force Manpower Group in the Office of the Director of Manpower and Organization, is arranged according to the War Department decimal classification scheme. In file 524 "Movement of Household Goods" there are studies of the comparative costs of transporting personal possessions and providing furnished quarters for Air Force personnel in the United States and overseas.

341.13. Among the records of the Executive Office of the Policy Division of the Office of the Director of Plans, the **correspondence and publications relating to policy, administration, and Air Force planning, 1947–49** (3 ft.), are arranged numerically. There are several sections relating to women; for example: 1-0 "Personnel, general" (including marriage); 1-1 "Personnel" (with a list of issuances and regulations in the file so that WAC- and WAF-related material can be located easily, and including a few issuances relating to Air Force family members); 1-4 "Transfers, procedures for movement of family groups"; 1-6 "Training" (including eligibility for the aviation cadet program); 1-13 "Pay and allowances, married men;" 1-17 "Health'; and 1-20 "Housing." The "A-1 Policy" file contains resumes of principal policies of the Assistant Chief of the Air Staff (AC/AS), and in a binder labeled "AC/AS Policy File" a WAC section (13 pp.) covers assignment, discipline, enlistment, grades, leave, maternity care, pay and allowances, promotion, recreation, separation, training, uniforms, and volunteers for extended service. Attached to each policy statement is a regulation, circular, Air Force letter, or some other documentation. A February 11, 1949, Air Force letter (53-18) pertains to flight nurse training.

Records of the
Office of the Deputy Chief of Staff (Materiel)

341.14. The Passenger and Household Goods Branch was in the Movement Control Division of the Office of the Director of Transportation. In the branch **decimal correspondence file relating to policies and regulations governing the transportation of civilian and military personnel and their dependents, 1951–54** (4 ft.), arranged according to the War Department decimal classification scheme, correspondence (2 in.) filed under 512 relates to the travel problems of particular families. Filed under 512.2 are a few form letters, instructions, and an organizational chart. There is similar material in a congressional correspondence section of the branch **correspondence and reports re-**

lating to the movement of passengers to and from overseas ports and estimated passenger requirements, 1945–53 (5 ft.), arranged alphabetically by subject.

Records of U.S. Air Force Commands, Activities, and Organizations

Record Group 342

342.1. The U.S. Air Force (USAF) was established in 1947 as the successor of the Army Air Forces (AAF), which had developed from a series of military air services dating back to 1907. This record group consists of the records of the field organizations of the USAF and its predecessors.

342.2. A few women flyers and wives of famous aviators appear in **motion pictures, 1900–64** (4,095 reels), made or collected by the USAF on the history of the development of flight. Included is footage about Amelia Earhart, Ruth Elder, Elinor Smith, Mary L. Schofield, Ruth Cheney Streeter, and Anne Morrow (Mrs. Charles A.) Lindbergh. Women ferry pilots (USAF No. 13074, 9 min.) and women in defense industry jobs (USAF No. 16979, 18 min.) are also featured. "Air Force News Reviews" (USAF No. 13736, 10 min.) includes footage of USAF nurses receiving medals, discussing their experiences on Guadalcanal, and marching in review. Women pilots, USAF dependents, and Air Force Officer Training Corps enrollees are represented in "Air Force Digest," "News Releases," and "Special Film Projects," all of which are USAF motion picture series. Script sheets are available.

342.3. Prints and negatives: U.S. Air Force Occupation of Germany 1945–59 (342-G, 43 vols.; 3072 items), are arranged by subject. In the albums relating to ceremonies and decorations (342-G, albums 4–8) there are numerous photographs of USAF families and nurses, awards ceremonies honoring USAF women, and American civilians assisting in civil affairs and relief and welfare programs, mostly in the 1950's. In album 6 there are photographs of Margaret Divvers, Chairman of the Defense Advisory Committee on Women in the Services, and of Senator Margaret Chase Smith (Lt. Col., USAF Reserve) in Wiesbaden, Germany.

342.4. Photographs in album 38, "Medical—Nurses" in **prints and negatives: U.S. Air Force occupation of Japan, 1945–59** (342-J, 69 vols., 4,608 items), arranged by subject, show USAF nurses at survival training in the field, in hospitals and touring Japan. In album 13 are photographs of three USAF women who received the Bronze Star. Part of album 69 includes a section on "Women in the Air Force" and contains 43 prints of the 1st WAF Squadron, 1951–55.

Sgt. Doris E. Brown controls air traffic at a U.S. Air Force Base near Tokyo in 1952. 342-J-68-81382.

Records of Joint Commands

Record Group 349

349.1. In December 1946 the President approved a comprehensive system of joint commands recommended by the Joint Chiefs of Staff. When a unified command is deemed to be in the interest of national security, the system places responsibility for conduct of military operations of all U.S. forces under a single commander in a strategic area, such as the U.S. European Command (US EUCOM). The commander of a joint command has full operational control over these forces, including women who are in the armed services or connected with them.

349.2. Unclassified through secret decimal correspondence files for each command are arranged chronologically by year and thereunder usually according to the War Department decimal classification scheme. Records in classifications 291 and 292 usually relate to marriage and families of service personnel. In Headquarters, US EUCOM, **decimal files, unclassified, confidential through secret, 1952–54** (37 ft.), decimal

291.1 for 1952 was used for a few requests for marriage approval and 292 for some arrangements for dependents traveling as tourists. For most commands, file 322 "WAC" is the location for most WAC-related records, and file 045 "Navy Department" contains most records relating to Waves. There are references to wives and daughters and to women among military and civilian personnel and relief organization workers in file 510 "Transportation of persons" in the records of most commands.

349.3. The **correspondence, 1953–54** (73 ft.), of the Far East Command, includes in file 080 "Societies and Associations" some records (2 in.) of the American Girl Scout Association of Japan. A "Report on American Red Cross Services to Ill and Wounded Repatriated Personnel," dated May 21, 1953, mentions women staff workers at Army hospitals in Korea and Japan and Gray Ladies and other volunteers at the Tokyo Army Hospital.

349.4. General, special, and letter orders relating to the assignment, promotion, travel, and temporary duty of military and civilian personnel ("administrative publications"), 1952–54 (5 ft.), of the US EUCOM are arranged by type of record and thereunder chronologically. The orders identify women who traveled to and from and within the US EUCOM by name, rank or status, and branch of service with which they were connected. A similar series for the Far East Command, **general, special, and letter orders; staff memorandums; and daily bulletins, 1953–54** (15 ft.), arranged by type of record and thereunder chronologically, deals with dependents located in Tokyo and contains letter orders authorizing travel to Korea for certain wives, journalists, American Legion Auxiliary officials, American Red Cross representatives, and other women. The "daily bulletins" consist of skeletal narratives of events, mainly at headquarters, including notices about families within the command.

349.5. The records of the G-1 Division (Personnel), Headquarters, Far East Command, contain considerable information about military families overseas and separated by duty assignments. Some security classified **reports relating to the activities of the division and its sections ("command reports and unit histories"), 1953–54** (3 ft.), arranged chronologically, deal with family housing, the entry of alien dependents into the United States, and such detailed matters as air travel for infants from 6 weeks to 6 months old. The Personnel Division **minutes of meetings, correspondence, reports, and other papers relating to the administration of the Joint Welfare Fund, 1945–55** (8 ft.), include chronologically arranged minutes and other records arranged by subject. Recreation, education, and relief activities and facilities for military and civilian personnel and their families are among the subjects of the records.

Records of the Defense Intelligence Agency

Record Group 373

373.1. The Defense Intelligence Agency was established by a Department of Defense (DOD) directive in 1961. Its director is responsible for producing and disseminating military intelligence to satisfy the requirements of the Secretary of Defense, the Joint Chiefs of Staff, and major components of the DOD. DIA also provides military intelligence for "national foreign intelligence and counterintelligence products."

373.2. The U.S. Army and Marine Corps units that landed on Grenada in October 1983 seized a large quantity of the island's documents. These documents, most of which date from 1979 to October 1983, were microfiched, and document summaries were prepared in machine-readable form. Approximately 14,000 microfiche and finding aids constitute the Grenada documents collection among the DIA records in the National Archives. The documents include administrative records of the former Grenadian government, files of the New Jewel Movement and its leaders, and documents of Soviet, Cuban, and other East Bloc countries, as well as papers of private persons. Approximately 30 percent are in languages other than English. A few items concern American women. An incomplete **name index** to the collection includes that of Gail Reed Rizo, the U.S.-born wife of the Cuban Ambassador to Grenada. Other women about whom there are records are Barbara-Lee Chisom and Carlottia Scott, aides to U.S. Congressman Ron Dellums (fiche 2016, 3353, and 4744); Angela Davis, who appeared as a guest at an International Women's Day rally and on other occasions (fiche 4781, 4852, 7267, and 7276); Esmeralda Brown, resource coordinator in the Latin America and the Caribbean area for the United Methodist Office for the United Nations (fiche 4226 and 6708); and the Honorable Sally A. Shelton, U.S. Ambassador to Grenada, Barbados, and Dominica, and Minister to St. Lucia (fiche 4779). There is also a list of members of the faculty of the St. George's Medical School (fiche 7034), which includes several women.

Records of the
Office of the Provost Marshal General

Record Group 389

389.1. A permanent Office of the Provost Marshal General was established in 1941 to be responsible for protective services, preservation of law and order, Army-wide crime prevention, criminal investigations and law enforcement, traffic control, military police, and prisoner-of-war activities. The principal records relating to women are about those who were POW's.

389.2. Among the records maintained by the Mail and Records Section of the Executive Office is an alphabetically arranged **subject correspondence file relating to the maintenance of internal security, 1942–45** (2 ft.). Filed there under the heading "subversives" are records about a black woman Communist Party member employed at an Army field office in the United States whose loyalty was questioned.

389.3. Several types of records were maintained by the Prisoner of War (POW) Division. Its **correspondence, camp reports, diaries, rosters, and other records relating to Americans interned by Germany and Japan during World War II, 1942–46** (64 ft.), arranged alphabetically by subject, include bound rosters (3 ft.) for such groups of POW's as American missionary religious sisters, military personnel, and civilian internees (which include U.S. Navy nurses who were not on lists of U.S. military personnel). Varying amounts of information are supplied with entries on these lists, which may include the place and date of internment and the date of death with citations to other records in the series such as cables, repatriation lists, and casualty reports from which the information on the rosters was derived.

389.4. In the same series is a report numbered CFN-208, a computer printout produced by the Strength and Accounting Branch of the Adjutant General's Office, consisting of a 1950 alphabetical list of Army and Air Force personnel who were captured by the enemy. For each internee the full name, rank, service number, and date span of internment is given. Report CFN-127 is a similar list of American civilian POW's of the Germans, 1941–45, and a report on Japanese detainees. In a section of diaries and interview reports there is a report of an interview with a woman who was interned at Shanghai. There are camp reports about POW camps in Los Banos, Baguio, Santo Tomas, and Mindinao in the Philippines, as well as camps in China. Lists of internees and narrative reports include information provided by internees and observers about prison experiences. Passenger lists on ships returning former POW's to U.S. jurisdictions include the names and "status" of "officials" including clerks, wives, maids, daughters, and Navy nurses.

389.5 Toward the end of the series are summary reports of the International Committee of the Red Cross International concerning prisoners of the Japanese. Following these is a file labeled "War Crimes Information Series No. 1, November 13, 1945" (200 pp.), which contains a processed report from the Military Intelligence Division that includes the names of the sisters interned at Shanghai and Tokyo compiled from lists prepared by former POW's in those cities. There are also lists of Americans repatriated on the *Gripsholm*, June 9, 1942–February 20, 1946. At the end of the series in a file for Mrs. Jennifer White, who was returning on the exchange ship SS *Gripsholm* in June 1942. There are unofficial lists of Americans, many of them women, who were formerly interned at Santo Tomas, January 4–June 5, 1942, with remarks on internee experience.

389.6. Summary information as of June 1943 derived from loyalty investigations of women is in a file labeled "WAAC" (4 in.) in a **formerly security classified correspondence file relating to the internal security program, 1941–46** (58 ft.), arranged by broad subject matter areas and thereunder alphabetically by specific subject, in the records of the Provost Division. Included are statistics regarding suspect activities among the women of the Women's Auxiliary Army Corps (WAAC), arranged by subject and by Army command; statistics of the racial descent of the more than 1,000 women whose cases were reviewed; and memorandums, reports, and pamphlets on the promotional work of the Adjutant General's Office for the WAAC, changes in the procedure for conducting loyalty and character investigations of recruits for the Women's Army Corps (WAC), and related plans and activities. In addition, there is a file (1 in.) of correspondence, investigative reports, and memorandums concerning possible espionage among hostesses in the Stage Door Canteen, a unit of the American Theater Wing War Services, Inc., that originated as "Stage Women War Relief."

Records of U.S. Regular Army Mobile Units, 1821–1942

Record Group 391

391.1. U.S. Regular Army mobile units in 1821 consisted of seven infantry regiments and four artillery regiments. The number increased during each war but usually decreased in peacetime. After the Civil War only the infantry was decreased, and there was a great increase in the numbers and kinds of mobile units during World War I. The records of a typical unit include orders, returns, and some correspondence.

391.2. Women did not play a prominent role in the history of mobile units. Records about laundresses and other women are few and brief. For example, among 6th Infantry regimental records **orders issued and received, 1817–24** (17 vols., 18 in.), arranged in rough chronological order, Col. Henry Leavenworth's Order 94 relates to rations for laundresses and "unauthorized women" at Fort Atkinson, a frontier post on the Missouri River in present-day Nebraska, and his Order 94 relates to courts-martial, including that of a laundress named Hannah.

Records of U.S. Army Continental Commands, 1821–1920

Record Group 393

393.1. A War Department general order of May 17, 1821, divided the United States into two geographical Army commands, the Eastern and Western Departments. The names and jurisdictions of the commands were frequently changed after 1821, and new commands were created as the area of the United States grew. During the Civil War, departments that functioned virtually as armies and military divisions had jurisdiction over armies, army corps, and such units as railroad defenses, U.S. forces, detachments, and parts of armies and army corps. The former Confederacy was divided into five military (reconstruction) districts comparable to geographical departments between May 1867 and January 1870. Army organization into divisions and departments was replaced in 1920 by the creation of nine corps areas for the continental United States. The interaction of various military units with women is documented in some of the small series that make up this record group, although few of the series pertain obviously or entirely to women. The items described below are *examples only*, and researchers interested in records of a particular period and place must use the five-volume preliminary inventory.

393.2. Documentation relating to women can be found among records of geographical divisions, departments, and military reconstruction districts. A four-page letter from Clara Barton to Brig. Gen. Quincy A. Gilmore is in file B-310-1863 of **letters received, 1862–67** (13 ft.), by the Department of the South, arranged by year and thereunder by initial letter of the name of correspondent. It discusses her personal background in addition to her volunteer relief work among Union soldiers.

393.3. Among the records of the provost marshal of the Department of Washington there are a few documents pertaining to women in the records for 1862 in **papers relating to refugees, prisoners, and miscellaneous cases, 1861–65** (1 ft.), arranged by year. They refer to activities such as peddling liquor, buying medicine to take to the South, and securing a guard or escort for women traveling between Washington and northern Virginia.

393.4. An office of civil affairs was established in each of the five military districts in the South after the Civil War. The office served as liaison between the occupation forces and the civilians they controlled. Documents scattered throughout the records of those offices and of others in the field structure of the U.S. Army commands during the Reconstruction period provide glimpses of the experiences of many Southern women, white and black. A few letters from women to the military government describe their plight as widows, heads of households deserted by husbands, or victims of lawless persons of the district. Series of letters received by the various military destricts or posts for the period 1867–70, most accompanied by name indexes and registers, and companion series of letters sent are available. Some series have been microfilmed. Typical of these records is the *Correspondence of the Office of Civil Affairs of the District of Texas, the Fifth Military District, and the Department of Texas, 1867–1870* (M1188, 40 rolls).

393.5. General correspondence, 1905–13 (223 ft.), arranged numerically, of the Department of the East is accompanied by a **name**

and subject index (56 ft.) which includes references to women under "Nurse," "Matron," "WCTU," and "Ladies" and under subjects such as "Assault" and "Rape." One case referred to under "Rape" is documented in correspondence file 30361 containing letters, reports, testimony, and newspaper accounts (3 in.) relating to an incident in Sackett's Harbor, NY. A black soldier of the 25th Infantry regiment was accused of an assault on a white woman. An investigation by the Office of the Inspector General cleared the soldier and in the process examined the attitudes of local women toward the troops. A **name and subject index** (8 ft.) to the Judge Advocate's **record cards and general correspondence, 1908–11** (47 ft.), of the Department of the East also includes a few cards under "Rape." Other entries in the index refer to letters from women on behalf of friends and relatives in the service.

393.6. In the **general correspondence of the Eastern Department, 1915–20** (30 ft.), arranged according to the War Department decimal classification scheme, are a number of memorandums, reports, and circulars about the employment of women after World War I as instructors and service club hostesses at Army camps, as supervisors of women's relations in the Army's geographical departments (in files 230 and 231), and as volunteer hostess assistants (in file 353.8). File 291.1 (8 in.) consists of questionnaires designed by the Provost Marshal General and completed by servicemen applying for marriage licenses. The information required includes names and addresses of the soldier and his fiancée, their places and dates of birth, where they met, when the soldier arrived in New York City, the couple's parents' names and addresses, and when they wished to be married.

393.7. Lower echelon command records also contain information about women. Among **lists of rations furnished, issued and requested; and lists of employees, prisoners, and deserters, 1865** (1 vol. [no. 165 DMY], 1 in.), of polyonomous command No. 186, is evidence that most of the employees were women while this command was headquartered in Edgefield, TN, in late 1865. The occupation and employer of each woman is given.

393.8. A letter sent from the Headquarters, District of Southwest Missouri to the Commanding General of the Department of Missouri reported "the return of a brace of female spies" presumably reporting on affairs in areas of the South where they had been traveling. It is in the fourth volume (no. 258/5591, pp. 50–51) of the Department's **letters sent, May 1862–July 1865** (4 vols., 6 in.).

393.9. Among the records of the Provost Marshal field organizations of the Civil War for Onancock, VA, are several small series that relate to women. **Letters sent by the Assistant Provost Marshal, March 1864–May 1865** (1 vol. [no. 249/633 VaNc], 1 in.) include a reference to the protective role that Union soldiers sometimes played toward women in the occupied areas of the South. The next four series noted are all smaller than one-half inch. The Assistant Provost Marshal's **orders, special orders issued, February 1864–May 1865** (in vol. no. 249/635 VaNc), include several that applied to women. A **list of charges and specifications, August–October 1864** (in vol. no. 249/634 VaNc), includes charges against local women. Following the charges and specifications is a brief register of prisoners confined to Onancock, which contains women's names. There is also a **list of females enrolled as U.S. citizens, February–April 1864** (in vol. no. 249/636).

393.10. Records of Union prisons during the Civil War frequently include records about women. For example, the records of the Julia Street Prison in New Orleans include a **list of female prisoners, 1865** (in vol. no. 375/916DG). **Records relating to prisoners held at Old Capitol Prison in Washington, DC, 1862–65** (10 in.), include Rose Greenhow's name on one of its rolls, as well as names of a few other women confined there. Among **visitor passes, 1862–65** (2 in.), are those for many women visitors to that prison, and the record of a visit to Belle Boyd by her father.

393.11. Women's activities and lives are also documented among widely scattered records of U.S. Army posts. The evacuation of troops, wives, and laundresses during a yellow fever epidemic in Key West is mentioned in a May 1880 letter in **letters sent, March 1880–December 1882** (2 vols., 1 in.), among post records for Fort Brooke, FL.

393.12. Among miscellaneous records of Fort Monroe, VA, **reports of women occupying public quarters, May 1879** (½ in.), list wives of military personnel, laundresses, a hospital matron, and others living on post. They also include copies of 1869 and 1879 general orders relating to laundresses and to local citizens and squatters, many of whom were women.

393.13. Records of Fort Richardson, TX, include a few relating to courts-martial at the post. Among **charges and specifications for garrison courts-martial, April 1869–December 1877** (3 vols., 3 in.), there are records relating to a garrison court-martial of a corporal who pleaded guilty to assualting a black woman. In another case, a contract physician was charged with neglect of duty for failure to comply with requests to attend families of enlisted men and laundresses. Special orders issuing the determinations of the court and the sentences are in the post's **general orders and circulars issued, October 1868–May 1878** (4 vols., 5 in.).

393.14. The **private letters received, November 1856–December 1865, December 1892, and April 1899** (1 in.), among the records of the engineers at Fort Taylor, FL, are mostly those of an engineer storekeeper at Key West. They include letters from women friends.

393.15. Unusual types of "records" sometimes appeared anomg reports from the field. In **miscellaneous records, 1857–58** (1 vol., ½ in.), for Fort Kissimmee, FL, for example, there are a few poems and

259

love letters entered by a surgeon at the post during the Third Seminole War.

Records of U.S. Army Continental Commands, 1920–42

Record Group 394

394.1. In August 1920 the continental United States was divided among nine U.S. Army Corps, whose functions included performing administrative and training services for the Army and tactical command functions for all major ground units and defense forces in the United States. In March 1942 all headquarters of corps areas were placed under the Services of Supply (later Army Service Forces), and all corps areas were designated service areas. Records about women relate to those who were employed as civilian clerks, wives and other dependents of soldiers, and hostesses in recreational facilities. All series are arranged according to the War Department decimal filing scheme unless otherwise noted.

394.2. The **general correspondence, 1917–38** (141 ft.), of First Corps Area Headquarters includes a few references to women as civilian employees under file 211, specifically mentioning "female army field clerks." The First Corps Inspector's **reports of investigation, 1918–39** (18 ft.), arranged alphabetically by name of individual or post, deal with divorce as well as such matters as fire, theft, and complaints.

394.3. The **general correspondence, 1916–21** (114 ft.), of the Sixth Corps Area headquarters in Chicago, includes in files 230 and 231 "Civilian employees" scattered memorandums, circulars, and reports relating to women employed as Army field clerks and stenographers. File 230.14 deals with policy in regard to hiring women during World War I. Other pertinent files are 231.3 "Army field clerks," 231.8 for references to hostesses, and 319.1 for reports that mention women librarians and drama assistants. In the continuing series, **general correspondence, 1921–26** (142 ft.), there is a large file 211.1 "Army field clerks" (3 ft.), arranged alphabetically by name of clerk, that includes personal history forms and records of leave and discharge.

394.4. There is similar material among the records of field installations. For example, in the **general correspondence, 1920–21** (2 ft.), of Camp Marfa (later Fort D.A. Russell), TX, file 319.1 "Moral [sic] Reports" contains references to hostess work and dances for enlisted men in reports on education and recreation.

394.5. Other records relating to the families of military personnel are series of birth and death certificates, such as **birth certificates, March 1921–September 1922** (1 in.), and **death certificates, May**

1935–October 1938 (8 in.), in the records for Fort Douglas, UT, 1919–39. Both series are arranged alphabetically by first letter of surname.

Records of
U.S. Army Overseas Operations and Commands

Record Group 395

395.1. To this record group have been allocated the records of Army overseas geographical divisions, departments, districts, and subordinate posts; Army corps and armies; and expeditions and troops sent to Mexico, Cuba, the Philippines, Hawaii, China, and Siberia. The records of the American Expeditionary Force, World War I, are in Record Group 120. Wives and children of military personnel often accompanied the troops sent overseas during this period. Members of the Army Nurse Corps were also assigned to overseas posts. The records described below are *examples only* of the kinds of materials available in this large record group. Records are filed according to the War Department decimal classification scheme unless otherwise noted.

395.2. The 5th Army Corps was one of seven Army corps organized to go to Cuba at the beginning of the Spanish-American War in 1898. Although battlefield casualties were few during the brief period of combat, many U.S. servicemen were infected with yellow fever. **Letters received, May–October 1898** (2 ft.), arranged chronologically, include a few inquiries from mothers and wives of Corps personnel.

395.3. When internal strife in Mexico threatened U.S. interests, including the safety of U.S. civilians and members of religious orders, U.S. naval forces occupied Veracruz in April 1914 and were soon replaced by the U.S. Expeditionary Forces. **Orders, special orders, and memorandums issued by Headquarters U.S. Expeditionary Forces and office of the depot quartermaster, Veracruz, Mexico, July–November 1914** (¼ in.), deal with some of the problems of American women and children caught in the troubled area.

395.4. Women were among the civilian employees of the Division of the Philippines and its successor, the Philippine Department of the U.S. Army between 1900 and 1942, but few of the divisional or departmental records have survived. There are, however, many records of subordinate commands. In the quartermaster records for the Department of Mindanao and Jolo, for example, a few of the **record cards and correspondence relating to personnel, 1904–5** (1 ft.), arranged alphabetically by name of employee, document the presence of women employees.

395.5. Wives and families and welfare workers accompanied U.S. Army and Army Nurse Corps personnel to China after the Chinese revolution of 1911. The **general correspondence, 1925–38** (53 ft.), of the 261

U.S. Army Troops in China, 1912–38, includes records about women under the following file numbers: 080 "Army Relief Society"; 211.31 "Nurses—Assignment"; 211.32 "Nurses—Change of status"; 211.48 "Nurses—Detached service"; 211.481 "Nurses—Foreign service"; and 292 "Wives."

395.6. General correspondence of the station hospital, 1928–37 (2 ft.), at Tientsin includes birth records in file 053.1, pay vouchers for Army nurses in file 112.4, correspondence and regulations relating to ANC conduct, uniforms, and quarters in file 211, a list of injuries sustained by two nurses in file 313.5, and instruction in nursing in file 352. **Records of the station hospital, 1916–38** (2 ft.), include the names and ranks of nurses, January 1927–February 1934; monthly reports of sick and wounded, 1913–33, including a census of nurses and attached civilians; and reports of births, marriages, and deaths among the American military community in China.

395.7. American nurses and welfare workers also joined the American Expeditionary Forces, Siberia, 1918–20. Among the records of the general headquarters in Siberia, **general correspondence, 1918–20** (20 ft.), includes letters about housing for YWCA workers in file 080 and about nurses' quarters in files 211.31, 622, and 632. There are also letters from mothers and wives of military personnel inquiring about particular soldiers or nurses and a list of officers and men who had families, some of them destitute, living in the Philippine Islands.

395.8. Historical files of the American Expeditionary Forces in Siberia, 1918–20 (6 ft.), filmed as M917 (11 rolls), include records relating to both Army Nurse Corps and American Red Cross nurses. Arranged according to a War Department historical decimal classification devised by the Army War College, records relating to the nurses are reproduced on roll 11 in files 21-43.3 "Chief Surgeon's report on sanitary personnel, August 1918–May 1919"; 21-43 "Chief Surgeon's report of operations during 1919"; and 21-43, "Medical History of the Siberian Expedition, August 1918–June 1919."

395.9. The **general correspondence of the Chief Surgeon, 1918–20** (2 ft.), includes, in file 080, several letters and reports of the work of American Red Cross nurses in field hospitals during the influenza and pneumonia epidemics in Siberia. In files 230, 211, 500, and 632 "EH 17" there are memorandums that relate to Army nurses' duties, working conditions, and administrative decisions about their tours of duty. There is a description of the building occupied by nurses' quarters in file 600 and requests for rocking chairs, rugs, wardrobes, linens, and china for Army nurses at Evacuation Hospital No. 17 in file 620. Alphabetically arranged correspondence relating to individuals at the end of the series includes some letters relating to women.

395.10. Bulletins, 1919 (2 items), of the Chief Surgeon outline medical procedures, including the duties and responsibilities of nurses.

Aviation heroine Amelia Earhart stops for a pre-flight photograph. 306-NT-172.254.

Strength reports, 1918–19 (2 in.), and **reports of the Chief Surgeon, 1918–20** (3 in.), show for Army nurses the number on duty, sick, and absent in the American Expeditionary Forces, Siberia.

395.11. Correspondence about problems with allotments owed to dependents between December 1918 and February 1920 are in file 243.4 of the **general correspondence, 1913–23** (2 ft.), of the Army's Hawaiian Department.

395.12. The Hawaiian Department was also involved with Amelia Earhart's ill-fated attempts at circumnavigating the globe. On her first attempt in March 1937, she crashed on takeoff from Luke Field. Over 50 pages of documentation, including proceedings of a board of Army officers convened on March 22, 1937, to investigate the accident and a July 27, 1937, report from the observation officer at Howland Field, where Earhart was to have refueled during her second attempt, are filed under decimal 334 in the **general correspondence, 1931–42** (3 ft.), of the Air Officer.

395.13. Also in the records of the Hawaiian Department, the **annual reports of the Department Surgeon, 1914–39** (2 in.), consist of narrative reports and statistics that include information about Regular

Army nurses and Reserve nurses on duty at the Honolulu Department Hospital.

Records of the U.S. Naval Academy

Record Group 405

405.1. The U.S. Naval Academy was established in 1845 to provide midshipmen appointed by the President with an effectively organized system of education and training in preparation for service as officers of the U.S. Navy. The records that have been accessioned into the National Archives predate the admission of women in 1976. They are in the physical custody of the Naval Academy in Annapolis, MD.

405.2. There is correspondence with women in the records of the Office of the Superintendent in **letters received, 1845–87** (12 ft.), arranged by time period and thereunder alphabetically by subject and filmed as M949 (11 rolls), and in **letters sent, August 1845–November 1865** (2 ft.), arranged chronologically and filmed as M945 (3 rolls). The women's letters were usually written on behalf of sons who wished to enter the Academy or who, once there, had disciplinary or academic problems.

Records of the Adjutant General's Office, 1917–

Record Group 407

407.1. The Adjutant General's Office (AGO) was reestablished in the War Department in 1907. The pre-1917 records of this office and of an earlier AGO have been assigned to RG 94, Records of the Adjutant General's Office, 1780's–1917. The AGO provided administrative services, including personnel administration, staff and administrative communications, and current and noncurrent records administration, to the War Department and, after 1947, to the Department of the Army. The AGO was abolished in November 1986. Because of its involvement with personnel matters, the AGO produced some records relating to military families, civilian employees, and women in the Army. Records are arranged according to the War Department decimal classification scheme unless otherwise noted. They are often accompanied by related bulky files under the same decimal number. Project files frequently appear at the end of a series subdivided according to the War Department classification scheme.

General Correspondence

407.2. There are references to a woman lawyer's complaints about immorality in training camps in New York and near the Mexican border in **correspondence with the office of the Secretary of War, 1917–19** (3 ft.), which is accompanied by an **index** (1 ft.).

407.3. The AGO's **unclassified general correspondence, 1917–39** (ca. 2,790 ft.), is arranged in two chronological segments, 1917–25 (790 ft.) and 1926–39 (2,000 ft.), and is served by **cross-reference sheets to the formerly classified and unclassified file of the Adjutant General's Office, 1917–39,** filmed as T822 (1,956 rolls).

407.4. Among decimal classifications in the 1917–25 segment containing records about women are the following:

055.9   "World War," including records about nurses, yeomen (F), and telephone operators

061.3   "Maps and Charts," including a chart purportedly linking various women's organizations to communism and letters written by Anita Phipps, director of Women's Relations of the War Department, and Maud Wood Parks, chair of a special committee of the Women's Joint Congressional Committee

080   "Societies and Associations," including records about the American Defense Society, American War Mothers' League of America, General Federation of Women's Clubs, National American Woman Suffrage Association, National League for Women's Service, National Women's Army, Winthrop Women's Civic League, Women's Army and Navy League, Women's Motor Corps of America, Women's Overseas Service League, Women's Reserve Camouflage Corps, and the YWCA

080   "American Red Cross," including petitions to grant military status to nurses and correspondence about a Red Cross nurse wounded in France

095   records about nonmilitary individuals such as wives of military personnel

150   "Claims and Accounts"

210.3   "Nurses," including assignments and transfers

211.31   "Nurses and reconstruction aides," including records about Spanish-American War nurses and nuns who served as nurses before 1900

220.5   "Rewards," which is subdivided according to type of award with women's names appearing most frequently under 220.54 "Certificate of Merit"

231   "Civilian employees," which is subdivided according to type of work, such as 231.35 "Hostesses," including, in both main and bulky files, records about Mrs. John B. Casserley and her successor, Anita Phipps, who were Directors of Women's Relations and of the Hostess Service of the War Department, and photographs and reports (1920–24)

231   "Nurses, emergency," including the names of civilian nurses and of the employing military installation under Civilian Conservation Corps contract

250.1   "Morals and Conduct," including documents relating to a scandal involving an incident of April 30, 1918, with four young girls on a truck convoy. Other documents contain further complaints from the woman lawyer in the case about immoral conditions cited in paragraph **407.2**.

291.9   "Women," including responses to a War Department questionnaire about the utilization of women during the war as welfare workers, hostesses, librarians, telephone operators, nurses, and clericals

292   "Quasi-military persons" including wives, widows, and mothers of military personnel—292.1 for families of officers; 292.2 for families of enlisted men, including a few memorandums encouraging enlisted men to make family allotments; and 292.12 concerning recruiting married enlisted men

516   "Transportation, civilians," including proposals for a pilgrimage to European cemeteries for Gold Star Mothers, and 516.2, which deals with the travel of families of military personnel and of war brides of American soldiers

407.5. The following project files are among those in the 1917–25 segment that relate to women:

"American Forces in China," including a 291.12 file on married enlisted men

"Organizations," including, under 322.9 "Telephone Operators' Unit," documents concerning an investigation of accommodations for women at the Hoboken, NJ, port of embarkation

"Organizations—Army Schools—School of Nursing" concerning the use of student nurses instead of nurses' aides in Army hospitals, with letters of opinion on the matter filed under 352.4

"Countries—France," including 1924–25 records filed under 293.2 about the burial of wives, mothers, and daughters of military personnel in national cemeteries in the United States and Europe

"European Expedition," including records about organizing a telephone unit and, under 231.32 "Female typists in the AEF," a proposal by Miss E.L. Gunther, head of the Female Labor Bureau of the Service of Supply, that a Women's Overseas Corps be established

407.6. In the 1926–39 segment are the following examples of records relating to women:

000.5   "Crimes, criminals, offenses, and domestic subversion," including a 1929 incident involving the death of a young corporal in a "love triangle"

080   "Societies and Associations," including Gold Star Mothers, National Society of Women Builders of America, Wisconsin Federation of Women's Clubs, Woman's National Defense Association, Inc., Woman's Pioneer Aircraft Association of Chicago, Woman's Relief Corps, Women of Army and Navy Legion of Valor, Women's Auxiliary of the American Medical Association, Women's International League for Peace and Freedom, Women's Patriotic Con-

ference on National Defense, and YWCA as well as a detailed plan prepared in 1938 by Mary Charles of Los Angeles for a Women's National Air Corps

095   "Custer, Elizabeth B.," relating to her bequest of certain items to the U.S. Government

095   "Davies, Ethel Alice," relating to her award of the British War Medal for her service as a member of a Chicago medical unit in World War I

210.3   "Nurses," dealing principally with assignments overseas and to transport vessels

231.37   "Telephone operators," including legislation proposed in 1935–39 to recognize operators' service as bona fide military service

250.1   "Morals and conduct," including in file 250.11 a 1930 letter from President Herbert C. Hoover to Secretary of War Patrick Hurley in response to the complaint from an Army officer's wife about drinking in the Army

291.12   Records relating to the enlistment of married men

516   "Transportation of civilians," including the arrangements for the Gold Star Mothers' Pilgrimage

407.7. The AGO's **unclassified general correspondence, 1940–54** (ca. 3,900 ft.), is arranged in five chronological segments: 1940–45 (1,900 ft.), 1946–48 (740 ft.), 1949–50 (462 ft.), 1951–52 (438 ft.), and 1953–54 (355 ft.). The 1940–45 segment is accompanied by a **microfilm copy of cross-reference sheets to part of the unclassified general correspondence, 1940–45** (1,522 rolls), which provides a synopsis of each document indexed and includes cross-references to related records under other headings.

407.8. Among the files relating to women are the following:

095   Records arranged alphabetically by individuals' surnames including those of women of military families or business women dealing with the Army

210.3   "Nurses," relating to assignments and changes of station

211   "Nurses," including correspondence with Congressmen; a bill to grant temporary commissions to male nurses; and records relating to morale problems of nurses overseas, utilization of black nurses, clothing allowances for dependents, nurses for air evacuation service, and demobilization after World War II

230.14   "Civilian employees," including a draft of a "Guide to the Immediate Maximum Utilization of Civilian Womanpower," October 1943, prepared by the Industrial Personnel Division of the Army Service Forces

245.7 and 246.7   Records relating to family allowances for officers and enlisted men respectively

291.1　Records relating to marriage, pregnancy, and minorities among civilian employees, the WAC, and the Army Nurse Corps

291.3　Records relating to women pilot trainees, clothing, the length of the working day for women, and women's volunteer committees

291.9　"Status of Women" (1940–45), including letters from women and girls offering service, documents about replacing women factory workers with Wacs; correspondence with Congressmen about organizing women for war service; and correspondence with the Women's Overseas Service League, Women's Legion of Defense, American Women's Volunteer Services, Inc., and the Women's Ambulance and Defense Corps of Los Angeles

292　"Military families," 292.1 for officers' families, and 292.2 for enlisted men's families, including the evacuation of military families from Pacific installations in February 1941, the Servicemen's Dependents Allowance Act of 1942, and records relating to housing and hospital benefits

321　"Nurse Corps," including records about the organization of the Army Nurse Corps, recruiting for it, and efforts to change laws relating to nurses, dietitians, and physical therapists

322.23　"Women's Auxiliary Ferrying Squadron"

324.5　"WASP" (Women Airforce Service Pilots)

510　"Transportation of persons," including that of World War II European war brides of American servicemen

407.9. Among the project files the following are examples of records relating to women:

"Military Schools—Army Schools—WAAC," including in file 451.2, an entry on the cross-reference sheets suggesting that Waacs were being taught about trucks

"WAC, 1940–45" (21 ft.), including records relating to recruiting (4 ft.), training, uniforms, minorities, medical examinations, morals and conduct, desertion, detention, separation, and discharge; muster rolls and returns; orders, circulars, regulations, rosters, strength reports, and narrative reports; correspondence with civilians, Congressmen, WAC headquarters, and military officials such as Gen. Brehon B. Somervell and Gen. George C. Marshall; and small separate project files on WAC schools including the first WAAC training center at Ft. Des Moines, IA.

407.10. Cross-reference sheets, 1946–48 (166 ft.), provide access to the 1946–48 segment of the unclassified general correspondence. Sheets filed under 020 relate to the new WAC, and those filed under 032.1 document proposed legislation to integrate the WAC and women medical personnel into the Army. Filed alphabetically by name of organization under 080 and by name of person under 095 are references to many letters from women.

407.11. In the 1946–48 correspondence there are small files of correspondence and other records relating to women such as 210.1

"Nurses," 210.2 "Women's Medical Specialist Corps," 210.31 "Nurses," 260 "Pensions," 321 "Nurse Corps," 321 "WAC," and 321 "Women's Medical Specialist Corps." In file 334 "WAC National Civilian Advisory Committee" (NCAC) is the September 19, 1946, report of Mary Pillsbury (Mrs. Oswald) Lord, chair of the NCAC, to Col. Westray Battle Boyce, Director of the WAC, July 1945–May 1947, with NCAC recommendations for the future. In the same file is a copy of Gen. Dwight D. Eisenhower's reply. A WAC project file (8 in.) includes records about the WAC Training Center at Camp Lee, VA, and reports for the services regarding plans for a Women's Army Corps in the Regular Army. "Race" is one element in the plans.

407.12. Access points for records relating to women are provided in the **cross-reference sheets** (125 ft.) for the 1949–50 segment of the unclassified general correspondence. Among the relevant decimal designations are file 020 "Women's Army Corps"; 080 "Associations and Societies," including National Council of Negro Women, Women's Overseas Service League, and American War Mothers; 291.1 "Marriages," including those of servicewomen; and 291.3 "Women," which includes references to Wacs and proposed legislation to authorize the appointment of women doctors in the Army. The WAC project file (5 in.) in the 1949–50 correspondence segment contains a prospectus for a course for officer candidates in the WAC ar d records relating to appointments in the WAC section of the Organized Reserve Corps, a new procurement program, the use of Wacs in static antiaircraft units, military occupational specialties, and WAC uniforms.

407.13. The 1951–52 segment of the unclassified general correspondence includes under file 095 "Freda K. Giffen," correspondence about a military dependent and former nurse who received a Medal of Freedom for her service in evacuating families from Korea at the outbreak of hostilities there. A WAC project file (5 in.) contains records about the Organized Reserve Corps, physical standards for enlisted personnel applying for commissions in the WAC, routine personnel policies and actions, special regulations relating to the fit of women's clothing, and proposed legislation relating to the WAC. In the same file there is a copy of an Attitude Research Report (126-345W) entitled "Women in the WAC, A Study of Recent Enlistees," May 1952 (33 pp.), prepared by the Department of Defense Office of Armed Forces Information and Education Attitude Research Branch.

407.14. The 1953–54 segment of the unclassified general correspondence contains a large WAC project file.

407.15. The **secret and confidential general correspondence, 1940–54** (ca. 1,700 ft.), is arranged in six chronological segments: 1940–42 (443 ft.), 1943–45 (964 ft.), 1946–47 (81 ft.), 1948–50 (80 ft.), 1951–52 (69 ft.), and 1953–54 (59 ft.). At this writing, these records have been declassified only through 1950.

407.16. An important finding aid to the AGO correspondence is the **security classified microfilm copy of cross-reference sheets to part of the secret and top secret general correspondence, 1940–47** (1,485 rolls). Recognition of the service of Philippine Army nurses is referenced under file 091. Under file 095 are references to records under the names of female relatives of servicemen and of other civilians, including women entertainers. A large alphabetical 201 file at the end of the cross-reference sheets includes references to civilian women employees and to women in the Army. Under decimal 292 are references to records relating to living conditions for military families overseas in 1940–45 and later. All of roll 895 of the cross-reference sheets microfilm in the projects section is devoted to the WAC.

407.17. Three subseries of the **cross-reference sheets to 1948–54 segments of the formerly secret and confidential general correspondence files** (150 ft.) have not been microfilmed. In each subseries there are several references to WAC project files, including references to mobilization planning, sex offenses, and discharges. Other references to women are filed under 201, which is arranged alphabetically by surname of service person, and 322 "WAC detachments." In the 1948–50 segment of the cross-reference sheets many references to file 220.8 "Discharge of enlisted personnel" deal with the investigation and separation of Wacs for alleged homosexual activities.

407.18. The 1940–42 segment of the correspondence contains records of the early history of the WAC, beginning with the planning of the WAAC. Plans for the types of units required and quarters for women are among the subjects in file 291.9. Among other decimal classifications containing records about women are 231.35, which contains records about two hostesses who were discharged, and 250.18, which contains statements of the Provost Marshal for the 1st Army about the suppression of prostitution in North and South Carolina.

407.19. In the 1943–45 segment, the final report and papers relating to the Japanese evacuation from the West Coast, December 1941–May 1943 (3½ ft.), submitted by Gen. J.L. DeWitt of the Western Defense Command is filed under 014.311. It includes descriptions of cases coming before the Federal Reserve Bank of San Francisco relating to evacuee property, some of which was owned by women. File 080 "American Red Cross" (1 in.) contains scattered correspondence about women workers. Records about promotions for WAC officers and inspection of the WAC training center at Ft. Oglethorpe, GA, are filed under 210.2 "WAC," and records about the eligibility of husbands, children, and dependent parents of deceased Wacs for benefits are filed under 322 "WAC," which includes a G-3 (Organization and Training) study, entitled "Employment of WAAC Personnel in Antiaircraft Artillery." Several files relate to nurses: 210.1 "Nurses," 211 "Nurses," 211.31 "Army Nurses," and 321 "Nurse Corps."

File 291.1 "Marriage" in the 1943–45 segment contains records relating to policy about the return of unmarried enlisted men to the United States to marry women pregnant with their children. Reports and correspondence in file 095 of the declassified 1943–45 correspondence under the name of Virginia Hall support her nomination for a Distinguished Service Cross for her work behind enemy lines with the Office of Strategic Services.

407.20. In the 1948–50 segment, records relating to preparation for the trial of Iva Ikuko Toguri (Tokyo Rose) are filed under 000.5. Under 095 there are alphabetical files of applicants, including some women, for Officer Candidate School and of military wives registering complaints or seeking transportation to join husbands overseas and correspondence with Elsie Wallace Moore, an American woman who had been a civilian prisoner of the Japanese at Santo Tomas. File 220.8 "Discharge of Enlisted Personnel" relates to investigations and separations of Wacs for alleged homosexual activities. The correspondence includes complaints, investigative reports, testimony, polygraphic and psychiatric studies, recommendations of the Army Personnel Board, and sworn statements of the women accepting discharge. Most of the records concern events at the WAC Training Center, Ft. Lee, at Petersberg, VA, and the WAC Detachment, Ft. Bliss, TX, but a few relate to Wacs stationed overseas. In file 334 a report of the President's Committee on Religion and Welfare in the Armed Forces includes information about problems at the WAC Training Center at Ft. Lee.

407.21. The **top secret general correspondence, 1940–54** (58 ft.), has also been declassified through 1950. Filed under 334 "Boards, committees, commissions, councils, and missions" in the 1946–47 segment is a report prepared by the War Department Policies and Program Review Board. Appendix 39 in records relating to this report consists of a May 11, 1947, memorandum written by Col. Mary A. Hallaren who became the third director of the WAC on May 5, 1947. It sets forth her plans for mobilizing, paying, housing, and clothing the WAC in the Regular Army.

407.22. The **classified and unclassified general correspondence and cross-reference sheets, 1955–58** (780 ft.), include references to women under the usual file numbers, including 291.3 "Women," and 321 "Army Medical Service for Army nurses and Wacs."

Records Relating to Personnel

407.23. The **personnel correspondence ("201") file, Old Records Section, 1923–53** (579 ft.), arranged alphabetically by name of service person, includes requests for verification of service of contract nurses in order to qualify them for such benefits as grave markers.

Records of the Enlisted Division

407.24. In a **policy and precedent file,** ca. 1921–40 (10 ft.), there are copies of a few precedent-setting decisions of the War Department about wives of soldiers in the post-World War I period. Filed under 291.12 is correspondence relating to women whom enlisted men married and left destitute. An alphabetical index to the file (7 ft.) contains entries for "Marriage," "Widows," "Wife (Rations)," and "Wives of Soldiers."

Records of the Military Personnel Procurement Division

407.25. The **monthly publication *Recruiting Journal* with related source material, 1950–54** (3 ft.), arranged chronologically, includes copies of the journal and drafts of articles submitted for it. The records include features on WAC, Air WAC, and Army Nurse Corps programs and about individual recruits.

407.26. There are a few application forms from Army nurses in the alphabetical file of **approved and disapproved applications for decorations and awards, 1905–51** (36 ft.), arranged alphabetically by name of applicant, among the records of the Personnel Actions Branch.

407.27. Following legislation in 1947 and 1948 to integrate the women's military organizations into the Army, the names of servicewomen with their ranks and serial numbers are included on **lists of individuals nominated for appointment in the Regular Army, 1947–52** (1 ft.), arranged chronologically, in the records of the Officer Placement Branch. Personnel actions resulting from this legislation are recorded in a **card file of commissions and assignments, 1898–1947** (58 ft.), arranged alphabetically by name of service individual.

Records of the Administrative Services Division

407.28. Personnel correspondence, 1916–40 (10 ft.), arranged alphabetically by name, includes many records about civilian women—those in the families of military personnel and those employed by the welfare agencies that provided services to the Army and by the War Department. A worker's permit, usually bearing a photograph of the worker, occasionally appears in a personnel correspondence file. These were issued to representatives of the American Red Cross, the YMCA, and other organizations authorized to serve with American troops during and shortly after World War I.

407.29. An **administrative medical file, 1933–41** (53 ft.), includes general correspondence in which the names of civilian nurses employed by the Civilian Conservation Corps can be found in file 231 "Surgeons, contract."

407.30. Among the records of the Civilian Personnel Branch, the **monograph history of the Machine Training School, A.G.O., November 1942–September 1945** (2 in.), includes records about the training of men and women in the use of machines from key punchers to "Advanced Wiring." The records include directives and a narrative report. An alphabetical register of students, many of whom were civilian women, and a WAC register give the names, race, education, ratings, and starting and ending dates of training.

407.31. Among the records of the Statistics and Accounting Branch the **statistical tabulations relating to casualties, prisoners of war, civilian internees, general prisoners, civilian and military strength, and other personnel matters, 1940–53** (462 ft.), arranged according to an alpha-numeric scheme, reduce to numbers and lists almost every aspect of Army personnel information. In addition, there are numerous reports, either in processed or computer printout form. A few examples of reports containing information about women are listed below.

CFM-10	Statistics of U.S. Army battle casualties including those among the WAC and the Army Nurse Corps by theater [of operations], 1944–45
CFN-95	List of Army nurses who died in the line of duty, 1941–46, including date, grade, and theater for each nurse
CFN-117	Lists of surviving officers, warrant officers, and nurses who were prisoners of war or missing in action before May 31, 1942, with a follow-up list by serial number of those later reported dead or returned
OTN-199	List of WAC officers worldwide by military occupational specialty (MOS), June 1945
OTN-248	Listing of Regular Army officers, warrant officers, and nurses, October 3, 1945
OTN-319	WAC officers willing to remain in service after World War II
OTN-490	Regular Army promotion lists by grade and seniority, December 31, 1947. Parts C and D are for the Army Nurse Corps and the Women's Medical Service Corps, respectively.
OTN-529	Alphabetical lists of male Regular Army officers (Part I) and members of the Army Nurse Corps (Part II) and the Women's Medical Specialist Corps (Part III), May 31, 1948
OTN-535	List of Regular Army Nurse Corps
OTN-537	Regular Army women commissioned officers by constructive service, September 29, 1948
OTN-770	Army Nurse Corps Reserve officers not on extended active duty, August 10, 1950
OTN-774	Reserve officers by branch of the Army including the WAC and the Women's Medical Specialist Corps by MOS and grade with separate lists for blacks and "other than" blacks

SFM-351   Monthly strength reports of nurses, dietitians, and physical therapy aides in each grade stationed outside the continental United States, 1943–45

STM-30   *Strength of the Army, 1943–47,* a publication that gave monthly worldwide strength returns by command and department, showing, among other things, the number of Wacs, Army nurses, dietitians, and physical therapy aides in each grade

The EDN series of reports, including a few reports that relate entirely to the WAC, concerns enlisted personnel. Two reports concern the separation of officers and enlisted personnel respectively, noting date and cause of each discharge or resignation.

Records of the Personnel Research Division

407.32. The Personnel Research Division produced a number of Army personnel **training and evaluation studies, 1944–72** (4 ft.), arranged by study. Several papers focused entirely on women in the Armed Forces, and women are included in other studies of the general military population. The following files from the series are examples of records of studies that included women:

"WAC Selection," 1962–68, including memorandums about WAC enlistment standards and procedures, and Report No. 32-66-E "Supplemental Findings Concerning the Personal History Characteristics in Relation to Retention and Separation of WAC Trainees Under Normal Standards, 1 May 1963–30 June 1964" (7 pp.) of the Office of Personnel Operations (OPOSS).

"Psychological Testing Programs in the U.S. Army," July 1959 (50 pp.), including discussion of enlistment screening, selection of women for Officer Candidate School; and appointment of women to commissions in the Regular Army and the Army Reserve

"An Attempt to Develop a Personality Test for Enlisted Women," Research Memorandum 62-4, August 1962 (8 pp.)

"Opinion Survey: Effect on WAC Recruitment of Offering Electronics Training Options," Research Study 59-4, June 1959 (12 pp.)

Records of the Career Management Division

407.33. File 210.31 "WAC" (5 in.) in the Division's **unclassified general correspondence, 1949–52** (24 ft.), arranged in two chronological segments, 1949–50 and 1951–52, consists of routine correspondence about assignments and training. In file 334 "Personnel Policy Board" (PPB) there is a copy of the recommendations of the PPB Committee on Detention of Women Personnel of the Armed Services. The committee included representatives of all five armed services. **Cross-reference sheets** (8 ft.) for this series include a large alphabetical 201 file relating to individuals, including women. There is an additional series of **cross-reference sheets**

(3 ft.) to the Division's identically arranged **security classified general correspondence, 1949–52** (10 ft.), which may include references to women.

Records of the Office of the Comptroller

Records of the Technical Information Branch

407.34. Publicity records relating to the War Department civilian recruiting program, 1944–46 (8 in.), consist of forms filled in by recruiters indicating civilians available for employment, newspaper clippings, photographs, and scripts for media campaigns. The latter half of the series documents the recruiting of women for overseas jobs and includes interview reports and photographs of candidates. **Photographs used in the War Department civilian recruiting program, 1943–45** (9 vols., 1½ ft.), depict the life of civilians in wartime Washington, including women at the Army Staff Forces Civilian Reception Booth, in class at the AGO Training School, at work at the Pentagon, and enjoying the sights of Washington.

Records of the Legislative and Precedent Branch

407.35. One of the AGO's functions as the central office of record was to research and answer inquiries from the War Department and the general public on matters of precedent. The **legislative policy and precedent files, 1943–75** (49 ft.), arranged according to a subject-numeric scheme, include press releases, newspaper articles, historical surveys, and copies of correspondence and reports. File 135 "Entertainment" documents performances for the troops of Martha Raye and Mary Martin. Filed under 163 "Women" is a list of women casualties in World War I, giving for each residence and the date, place, and cause of her death; a list of women awarded American decorations; passports for wives and mothers of officers; a statement of the duties of the position of Director of Women's Relations of the War Department; records of the Defense Advisory Committee on Women in the Services (DACOWITS); records about Assistant Secretary of Defense Anna Rosenberg; and a pamphlet, *You're Going to Employ Women.* File 212 "Women's Army Corps" includes additional records about the WAC. File 340 "Manpower" includes some records about women, and file 858 "Female personnel" contains subfiles about the WAC, the Women's Medical Specialist Corps, the Women's Auxiliary Ferrying Squadron, and Women Airforce Service Pilots. File 1378 "Casualties" includes cumulative statistics for Army Nurse Corps and WAC personnel by theater of operation, December 7, 1941–June 30, 1946. File 1382C "Joint Agreements Originated by the Joint Army-Navy Personnel Board, the Armed Services Personnel Board, and the Military Personnel

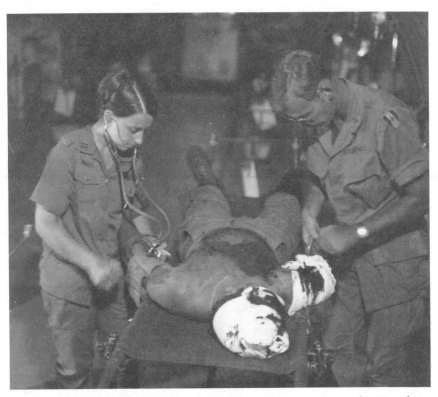

September 1969: Capt. Bernice Scott checks a patient's blood pressure, and Lt. David Van Voorhis removes his bandages at a field hospital in Vietnam. 111-CC-61548.

Policy Committees, June 1942–April 1949" contains a report (165 pp.) by that title, compiled and edited by Maj. Ruth E. Paul, that includes several parts that pertain to the recruitment of women for military service. File 2285 "Wives" relates to protocol for the social activities and conduct of military wives and to the Dependent's Medical Care Program. There are two indexes to the series. A subject index summarizes each document in a subject category such as "Nurses" or "Dependents, military personnel" and identifies records on subjects ranging from the first woman doctors and dentists in the Regular Army in 1951 to the participation of servicewomen in Vietnam. There is also an index to military boards and committees, 1943–63 (7 in.).

407.36. The **biography file, 1943–76** (7 ft.), arranged alphabetically by surname, includes records about several women. The file of Anna Rosenberg contains the texts of several of her public statements. A file for Elizabeth P. Hoisington contains a press release announcing the ceremony in which she became the seventh director of the WAC on August 1, 1966. In a file for Clara Louise Maas is correspondence about whether or not she should be officially recognized as a "yellow fever hero" in recognition of her efforts earlier in the century.

Records of U.S. Armed Forces in the Far East

407.37. The U.S. Armed Forces in the Far East (USAFFE) was established before Pearl Harbor with headquarters in the Philippine Islands. After the surrender of Corregidor and Bataan in 1942, the USAFFE disappeared but was later revived as the name for Gen. Douglas McArthur's command headquartered in Australia.

407.38. The records known as the "Philippine Archives" are those that were created, compiled, or collected by the Recovered Personnel Division (RPD). USAFFE records created before the fall of Corregidor are in the RPD **general correspondence, 1938–60** (1 ft.); **special orders, 1941** (1 in.); **pre-surrender general correspondence files, 1937–42** (1 roll of microfilm), arranged by organization; and **rosters and lists, 1938–42** (1½ ft.), arranged by organization and thereunder alphabetically or by serial number. Records relating to women are largely about nurses and civilian employees. Other RPD records document the experiences of prisoners of war (POW's) and civilian internees of the Japanese, many of whom were women. There are **civilian internee rosters, 1942–46** (16 ft.), and **rosters and lists of POW's, 1942–47** (26½ ft. and 15 rolls of microfilm). The textual and microfilmed records duplicate each other to a certain extent, and both are arranged by name of camp and thereunder alphabetically, sometimes within groups by nationality. On some lists the physical condition of the former POW or internee at the time of recovery by U.S. forces was recorded. **Medical records of POW's and civilian internees, 1942–45** (10½ ft.), are arranged the same way. **General correspondence files pertaining to civilian internees, 1943–45** (2 ft.), arranged by internment camp, give vivid accounts of the experiences of a group of civilians assembled in Los Banos and Santo Tomas prisons "for temporary protective custody" by the Japanese in December 1941 and liberated by the Allies in 1945. Also available are **civilian internee death report files, 1941–43** (3 in.).

407.39. Diaries and historical narratives of POW's and civilian internees, 1940–46 (9 ft.), arranged alphabetically by surname of author, contain firsthand personal accounts of the prewar situation in the Philippines, the Japanese attack, American surrender, Bataan death march, and prisoner-of-war life. Included in the series are diaries or accounts for Lt. Mary Bernice Menzie (file 999-2-14) and civilian nurses or hospital workers Clara L. Mueller (file 999-2-84) and Mrs. M.R. Williams (file 999-2-85). Some of the diaries are available in a collection of Army microfilm (rolls 1–110), which follows at the end of the textual records in the "Philippine Archives" collection. Roll 88, for example, contains

Menzie's diary, and roll 3 includes a file 610-7, identified as "Corregidor Nurses Interned at Santo Tomas Internment Camp."

Reports

407.40. Narrative reports and supporting documents relating to operations and activities of the Army during World War II and the postwar period ("operations report file"), 1940–48 (8,035 ft.), are arranged by command level, so it is necessary to know the name and number of particular military units in order to make full use of this large quantity of material. The series includes references to a few reports concerning nurses, including one relating to operations during the invasion of Normandy, an intelligence report from the Southwest Pacific, and an observer's report from the European Theater, and to Wacs in reports on Okinawa and on military intelligence. Other possibly useful index terms are "Recreation," "Red Cross," and "Entertainment." Additional references to potential subjects are not indexed under these obvious headings but can be picked up from the table of contents that precedes most reports at the theater, Army group, Army, and corps levels. For many reports there are appended staff section reports. At the theater level there is a pictorial and textual history of Wacs in the Western Pacific and a pamphlet (34 pp.) entitled *Story of the WAC in the ETO*, which contains photographs and description of the work of Army women on the Continent (SuDoc W109.202:W84 in RG 287). Among records of nonorganic units (independent units not a part of a hierarchy such as infantry or cavalry) filed at the end of the series are reports of hospital units and WAC units. Files for each are subdivided by type of unit. The reports of general, field, surgical, and evacuation hospitals, like the headquarters reports mentioned above, give details concerning conditions and activities at the site, and a few include reports on nursing service or references to particular nurses, dietitians, or physical therapists. Occasionally there is more information concerning female Red Cross welfare and recreation workers in medical reports than there is pertaining to Army Nurse Corps personnel and activities. Among records in the nonorganic subseries for WAC units (1 ft.) are a unit history for the 6714th WAC Communications Platoon organized in Naples and processed copies of "WACKERY Bulletin," a newsletter of the 6716th WAC Headquarters Company in Italy, monthly historical summaries from the 5220th WAC Service Unit in New Guinea, and an organizational history of the antiaircraft artillery unit WAC Detachment, AAAC, Military District of Washington, which began as the 62d WAAC Operations Company, Aircraft Warning Service. A history of the 400th Band (WAC) (file BAND-400-0.1) is in the band section of the subseries for nonorganic units. There is also material for the 7692d WAC Detachment, U.S. Forces in Austria.

407.41. Histories of peacetime WAC units, mainly during 1946 but including Headquarters Co., U.S. Army WAC, South Post, Ft. Myer, VA, from July 1948 to June 3, 1949, and other WAC units stationed at Ft. Myer during that time, are filed in a subseries for nonorganic units.

407.42. Some records in the **unclassified through formerly secret narrative reports and supporting documents relating to operations of the Army ("command report file"), 1949–54** (2,107 ft.), which are arranged by level of command, mention activities involving or administrative matters relating to female military and associated personnel and to wives and military dependents mainly overseas. Additional records in the still classified **top secret "command reports file," 1949–54** (20 ft.), mainly for the General Headquarters, Far East Command/United Nations Command, deal with some of the same classes of persons. Reports at command, force, and army levels include a useful table of contents to the main report. Appended are staff section reports such as those for medical/surgical, G-1 (Personnel), and morale and personal services. Knowing where a unit was situated organizationally and geographically speeds research. Much more accessible are the reports filed at the end of the series, of nonorganic units, those for which designations stand outside of the command hierarchy. Several feet of nonorganic reports, from evacuation hospitals, field hospitals, and Mobile Army Surgical Hospitals (MASH), filed under MDDP, MDFA, and MDSU respectively, contain statistics or rosters of female medical personnel with the unit. Activities in the continental United States prior to U.S. participation in the Korean war, as well as combat operations and effects of the war are described. In the numerous reports from station hospitals in 1950, under file designation MDSH, there are sections on the Nursing Service, scattered information regarding obstetrical and gynecological matters in Vienna and Yokohama, and reference to the work of Gray Ladies and female recreation and social service workers. Reports of medical activities at Port of Embarkation, Bremerhaven, 1952–53 (TCPT-7802), also encompass several women-related areas. Files for nonorganic units include those (1 in.) for separate units of only WAC personnel. Among them are the 8225th WAC Company in Tokyo with the Headquarters and Service Command, General Headquarters, Far East Command, and the 7692nd WAC Detachment, U.S. Forces in Austria. For the latter there is a considerable amount of material concerning mission, function, organization, policy, morale and discipline, and recreation, 1949–53.

Miscellaneous Records

407.43. In the **microfilm copy of the Army serial number file, 1938–46**, filmed March 26–May 7, 1947 (1,586 rolls), arranged in serial number order, rolls 1–21 are labeled "WAC." In addition to serial number, information for each person includes name, grade, date of enlistment, source, birthplace, birthdate, State and county of residence, civilian occupation, and marital status.

407.44. Records of Camp Shows, Inc., 1941–57 (8 vols., 3 ft.), arranged by time periods (1941–47 and 1947–57) and thereunder by type of record, consist of processed copies of activities reports, minutes of meetings, informational literature that was sent to entertainers who were considering overseas tours, lists of persons who served in various touring units, the locations of their performances, and assessments of their work. Camp Shows, Inc., was funded by the United Service Organizations (USO) and furnished live entertainment to troops from World War II through the Korean war. There were women performers and managers in the organization.

407.45. Records of the Army Music School, 1941–44 (4 in.), include a small file showing that Waacs (and later, Wacs) were allowed to attend the Army Music School at Ft. Myer, VA.

Reference Aids

407.46. Some records series such as the one described below were microfilmed by the War Department or the Department of the Army, and the microfilm is the only record in the National Archives.

407.47. Among the records of the Organization and Directory Branch of the Miscellaneous Division is a **microfilm copy of historical data cards of Army units, 1776–1970**, filmed in 1971 (116 rolls), which is arranged by type of unit and thereunder numerically and includes active and inactive units. The cards provide information about the location, movement, and composition of specific Army units, including dates of activation and disbandment, references to the War Department or AGO issuances establishing each unit, and changes of unit names. On rolls 13 and 14 are cards for disbanded Regular Army Medical units including numbered WAC hospital companies. Rolls 84 and 85 contain cards for WAAC training centers and other assignments for women. Cards for hospital units include references to unit histories filed with AGO correspondence.

407.48. Directories and station lists of the United States Army, 1942–53 (46 ft.), are arranged alphabetically or numerically by command worldwide and thereunder by month and year. These records are useful in locating a particular unit in records arranged by unit. The monthly station lists for the Far East Command, for example, name the WAC detachments assigned to it and show where they were stationed at any given time. In an index with the station list for the 7th Service

Command, as another example, are entries for training centers for cadet nurses, for Wacs, and for members of the Army Nurse Corps.

General Records of the Department of the Navy, 1947–

Record Group 428

428.1. From its creation by an act of Congress on April 30, 1798, until 1947, the Department of the Navy functioned as an independent unit directly responsible to the President of the United States. By the National Security Act of 1947 the Department became a part of the National Military Establishment, which became the Department of Defense in 1949. Records are arranged according to the *Navy Filing Manual* (NFM) within various chronological and organizational schemes. Records about women are largely statistical.

428.2. The **formerly security classified general correspondence of the Chief of Naval Operations and Secretary of the Navy, 1948–51** (236 ft.), are arranged by year, thereunder by security classification, and thereunder according to the NFM. In file P16-1 of the formerly secret correspondence there are annual statistics on the number of "Navy military personnel (female)," excluding the Navy Nurse Corps, employed in segments of the Naval Establishment during the first 3 years of mobilization and the percentage of billets filled by women in various activities. In file L20-4 for 1949 there are memorandums relating to transporting dependents of marine and naval personnel located overseas. The series is served by annual **indexes** (110 ft.).

428.3. In file A18 of the **formerly classified correspondence of Secretary of the Navy John L. Sullivan, 1947–49** (3 ft.), there is a list of the 10 most important bills in the Navy's legislative program for 1948. Item number 3 on the list is S. 1641 "To authorize the enlistment and commissioning of women in the regular and reserve establishments of the Army, Navy, and Air Force." In a file labeled "Miscellaneous" is a July 29, 1948, "Report of the Board to Examine, Study, and Report Upon the Functions and Personnel Requirements of the Medical Department, United States Navy" (5 in.). It includes postwar plans for nurses and statistics of services provided to dependents and industrial employees of the Navy.

428.4. Formerly classified correspondence of Secretary of the Navy Francis P. Matthews, 1949–50 (2½ ft.), contains in file P a memorandum from Acting Secretary Dan A. Kimball to the Personnel Policy Board, Office of the Secretary of Defense, containing Kimball's comments on a "Study of Maximum Utilization of Military Womanpower."

428.5. The **formerly security classified general correspondence of the Deputy Chief of Naval Operations (OP02–OP05 and OP20), 1948–51** (ca. 200 ft.), is arranged by office, thereunder by year, thereunder by former level of security classification, and thereunder by the *NFM*. In the 1949 formerly secret correspondence under OP04 (Chief of Logistics) the only document filed under QR8 is a reference to Bureau of Naval Personnel studies relating to women. Among the formerly secret correspondence filed under OPO4 for 1950 are management survey reports including "Survey Report on the Bureau of Naval Personnel," prepared by Sub-board 2 of the Management Survey Board submitted June 14, 1950, recommending a reduction in staff for the Chief of Naval Personnel's special assistant for women. A "Comparative Study, Officer Personnel Act of 1947," November 18, 1949 (2 in.), prepared by a subcommittee of the Military Personnel Policy Committee, includes comparisons between permanent and temporary promotion laws affecting women in the Army, Navy, Air Force, and Marine Corps. Separate sections of the report deal with nurses and other women medical specialists, women commissioned officers, male commissioned officers, and male and female warrant and chief warrant officers. It is filed under OP20 (Chief of Naval Communications), 1948–49, among designated files that follow file P11. Also under OP20 there are references to the WAVES in files P16-1 "Personnel strength and distribution" and P16-3 "Duty and detail."

Part II

RELATED MATERIALS IN PRESIDENTIAL LIBRARIES

PL 1. The Presidential Libraries, one for every President beginning with the Herbert C. Hoover, are repositories for the personal papers of the President and of persons associated with him or his administration as well as the records of the White House and certain Presidential committees, commissions, and boards. Accordingly, there are a few records and manuscript collections in various Presidential Libraries relating to American women who have had some connection with the Armed Forces or with national defense. Examples of such documentation are noted below for each Presidential Library in chronological order.

Herbert Hoover Library

PL 2. The **Presidential subject file, 1929–33** (155 ft.), includes "correspondence, 1930–32" (82 pp.), on Gold Star Mothers of World War I.

PL 3. The **papers of Lou Henry Hoover, 1874–1973** (141 ft.), document the activities of Mrs. Hoover as a Red Cross volunteer during the Spanish-American War and during the siege of Tientsin in the Boxer Rebellion of 1900 and her participation in relief activities in both world wars. During World War I she was an officer in the American Citizen's Relief Committee, an organization that the Hoovers launched to repatriate stranded American tourists at the outbreak of World War I, and in the American Women's War Relief Fund, 1914–19. She assisted her husband when he was director of the Commission for Relief in Belgium and the U.S. Food Administration by organizing the sale of Belgian lace and speaking at popular rallies. She organized the Food Administration Women's Club as a dining club and youth hostel for young women who came to Washington to hold clerical positions. She was also associate director of the Red Cross Canteen Escort Service to accompany troop trains bearing wounded war veterans. In World War II she worked extensively with the Salvation Army.

PL 3. The **papers of Rose Wilder Lane, 1865–1969** (27 ft.), a writer and journalist, include accounts of the work of the American Red Cross in Europe during World War I, which she produced as a publicist for the Red Cross in 1918.

PL 4. The **papers of Frank E. Mason, 1892–1979** (19 ft.), contain the diaries of his wife, Ellen Speltan-Thomsen Mason, January 1941–June 1942 (2 in.), while she, an NBC executive, was on loan to the Secretary of the Navy as a public relations adviser.

PL 5. The **papers of Rosalie Slaughter Morton, 1898–1955** (14 ft.), consist of fragments of her correspondence documenting her work as a physician and surgeon who volunteered in 1916 at a French Army hospital as a special commissioner of the American Red Cross. She organized and directed the American Women's Hospitals, 1917–18.

PL 6. The **papers of Truman Smith, 1916–46** (3 ft.), a career Army officer who served as American military attaché in Berlin, 1935–39, include a two-part unpublished autobiography of his wife, Katherine A.H. Smith, in which she recounts her efforts to assist her husband in his intelligence-gathering activities, 1935–39, and their life in Washington, 1939–46.

Franklin D. Roosevelt Library

PL 7. The **President's official file, 1933–45** (1,174 ft.), is arranged according to a subject-numeric system. Material related to women in the military is filed under the following headings:

OF 18E   Marine Corps and Women's Reserve

OF 25JJ   Women's Army Auxiliary Corps

OF 357E   Women's Army Corps Service Medals

OF 379B   Women's Auxiliary Naval Reserve

OF 461   Gold Star Mothers of the World War, Inc.

PL 8. The **President's personal file, 1933–45** (608 ft.), arranged by a subject-numeric system, contains at least one relevant file: PPF 1534 Gold Star Mothers of the World War, Inc.

PL 9. An alphabetical card index to the **papers of Anna Eleanor Roosevelt, 1933–45**, includes entries for Oveta Culp Hobby, Women's Air Corps, Women in Defense, Women's Volunteer Reserve Corps, Women's Army Auxiliary Corps, and Women's Defense Cadets of America.

PL 10. An **oral history interview with Anna Rosenberg Hoffman** deals more with her association with the Roosevelts in New York State than with her experiences under her maiden name, Anna Rosenberg, while she was an Assistant Secretary of Defense. Documents relating to Rosenberg as regional director of the War Manpower Commission in Region 2, New York, and as a member of the advisory board of the Office of War Mobilization and Reconversion are located in various files including OF 4025 and PPF 8101.

PL 11. The **papers of Caroline Ware, 1925–80** (32 ft.), a consumer advocate, include materials on her membership on the National Defense Advisory Committee during World War II.

Harry S. Truman Library

PL 12. The records in the **official files of the White House central files, 1945–53** (2,784 ft.), are arranged by a subject-numeric classification scheme. Those relating to women in the military are filed under the following headings: 18N "Navy Nurse Corps," 18CC "WAVES," 1285B "Army Nurse Corps,"1285B Women's Army Corps," 1285B

"Women's Medical Specialist Corps (Army)," 1285C "Women Marines," and 1285D "Women in the Air Force."

PL 13. The **President's secretary's files, 1945–53** (136 ft.), are made up of personal and confidential materials that President Truman wished to keep under his personal control. In this file and in President Truman's **Post-Presidential name file, 1953–72** (364 ft.), there is correspondence with and about Anna Rosenberg under her married name, "Hoffman."

PL 14. Records about the WAC appear in the **records of the President's Committee on Religion and Welfare in the Armed Forces, 1948–51** (17 ft.).

PL 15. **Eleanor Bontecou** was a legal adviser in the War Crimes Branch of the Civil Affairs Division of the Department of Justice during 1946–47. Her **papers, 1938–65** (6 ft.), include information about this period.

PL 16. The Civil Affairs Division in the War Department Special Staff formulated and coordinated U.S. policy concerning liberated and occupied countries after World War II. In the process, the Division worked with United Nations agencies. The **papers of Ann Laughlin, 1936–57** (2 ft.), cover her work as director of the United Nations Relief and Rehabilitation Administration in the Netherlands in 1946 and as chief of mission for the United Nations International Children's Emergency Fund (UNICEF) in Bulgaria, 1946–50.

PL 17. Westray Battle Boyce was director of the Women's Army Corps, 1945–47. Her **papers, 1933–62** (2 ft.), under her married name, **Westray Battle Boyce Long**, deal largely with that service.

Dwight D. Eisenhower Library

PL 18. The **papers of Margaret Chase, 1942–60** (ca. 175 items), include letters written by Chase to her parents describing her experiences as a Red Cross volunteer in London, France, Italy, and North Africa (1942–45) and diaries covering the same period.

PL 19. The **Jacqueline Cochran papers, 1932–75** (150 ft.), contain extensive documentation on most aspects of her aeronautical and political activities. Most of the collection is arranged by subject. There are files covering her work for the British Air Transport Auxiliary, 1941–42; as director of the Women's Airforce Service Pilots, 1942–45; and as a reserve officer in the U.S. Air Force, 1948–70. The collection also contains material on the early history of the Ninety-Nines, an international women pilots association, and its role in national defense during the 1930's and 1940's.

PL 20. The **papers of Eleanor Lansing Dulles, 1880–1973** (20 ft.), contain diaries, correspondence, and scrapbooks documenting her

PL 21. The **papers of Oveta Culp Hobby, 1952–55** (73 ft.), are largely the documentation of Hobby's tenure as Secretary of Health, Education, and Welfare in the Eisenhower Cabinet, but also included are a scrapbook and a few other papers about her experience as first director of the WAC.

PL 22. The **papers of Katherine Howard, 1917–75** (12 ft.), contain correspondence, memorandums, newspaper clippings, speeches, and publications documenting her work in civil defense, Republican politics, and the 1958 Brussels Worlds Fair. During the Eisenhower administration she served in the Federal Civil Defense Administration and represented the United States on the NATO Civil Defense Committee.

PL 23. The **papers of Mary Pillsbury (Mrs. Oswald) Lord, 1941–72** (1 ft.), and the **transcript of an oral history interview** (428 pp.) contain little about her work as chair of the National Civilian Advisory Committee for the WAC and deal largely with her experience as a member of the United Nations Human Rights Commission.

PL 24. The **papers of Pearlie and Michael McKeough, 1941–69** (400 pp.), contain copies of newspaper clippings that describe their military service and copies of their social correspondence with Dwight D. Eisenhower. Mrs. McKeough served in the Women's Army Corps during World War II and was assigned to General Dwight D. Eisenhower's staff.

PL 25. The **papers of Elizabeth Margaret Phillips, 1918–55** (5 ft.), document her service as a nurse in France during World War I and as a Red Cross volunteer who organized aid to Allied prisoners of war during World War II.

PL 26. An **oral history interview with Inez G. Scott** (34 pp.), describes her experience as driver for General Eisenhower during World War II.

John F. Kennedy Library

PL 27. The **President's office files, 1961–63** (73 ft.), are President Kennedy's working papers maintained by his secretary. They include a file under "Speech files" labeled "Women Pilots, 99 Club 7/26/63 speech."

PL 28. The **subject file, 1961–63** (440 ft.), in the White House Central Files is arranged by an alpha-numeric scheme. In it there are the following files for the women's military services: ND 009 "Selection Board Lists: Women Marines"; FG 120 "Women's Army Corps"; FG 125 "WAVES, Navy"; and ME 003 "WAVES, Navy." Among the **White House staff files, 1961–63** (559 ft.), arranged alphabetically by name, the file for Gordon McHugh (17 ft.) contains material about women under the heading "Promotions and Descriptions, 13 and 14." McHugh was Air Force Aide to the President.

heading "Promotions and Descriptions, 13 and 14." McHugh was Air Force Aide to the President.

PL 29. The **papers of John Harllee, 1945–69** (3 rolls of microfilm), include an essay entitled "Can Women Help Us Fight?" Harllee was a naval officer and Chair of the Federal Maritime Commission.

PL 30. The **papers of Elvis Jacob Stahr, Jr., 1938–67** (35 ft.), include an essay entitled "Army Lady Today." Stahr was Secretary of the Army, 1961–62.

PL 31. Adam Yarmolinsky was a special assistant to the Secretary of Defense. His **papers, 1961–63** (159 ft.), contain material about women filed under "Organizations and Agencies: Armed Forces and Society Papers."

PL 32. The Kennedy Library holds microfilm copies of the records of some Federal agencies dealing with issues important in the Kennedy administration. Among them are records of the Veterans' Administration (17 rolls), which include the following headings: "Records of the Office of the Administrator: Civil Rights—Personnel, Women" (roll 6); "Records of the Assistant Administrator for Personnel: Recognition of Women" (roll 8); and "Records of the Office of the Director of Information Services: Women in Government" (roll 9).

Lyndon Baines Johnson Library

PL 33. In the **White House central files, 1963–69**, arranged according to an alpha-numeric classification scheme, material about women in the military is filed under the following headings: FG 110-4 "Coast Guard" (3 in.), FG 120-7 "Women's Army Corps," FG 125-5 "Marine Corps" (3 in.), FG 125-6 "Waves," FG 130-7 "Women in the Air Force." There is material of a more general nature about the status of women, including women in the military, under HU 3 "Equality for women" (5 in.), and FG 737 "President's Commission on the Status of Women." LE/ND 9 "Legislation—Military Personnel" contains a small amount of material about the enactment of Public Law 90-130, an act to improve the career opportunities of women in the armed services. A small amount of additional material on PL 90-130 is in **reports on enrolled legislation,** "PL 90-130 (HR5894)."

PL 34. Office files of the White House aides consist of working files of Presidential assistants. Under the heading "Advertising Council," the file "Military Nurses Recruitment" contains three items about a 1966 drive to increase recruitment. Filed under "William R. Sparks," the file labeled "Women in the Armed Services" contains a copy of the draft of the final statement of President Johnson made upon signing PL 90-130.

PL 35. The **papers of Clark McAdams Clifford, Secretary of Defense, 1968–69** (10 ft.), include one file labeled "DACOWITS—Defense Advisory Committee on Women in the Armed Services."

Mary Anne Gasser, a Wave stationed in Jacksonville, FL, rebuilds a generator that had been cleaned, September 1943. 80-G-471714.

PL 36. The **House of Representatives papers of Lyndon Baines Johnson, 1937–49** (140 ft.), include in the case files, some constituent mail concerning wartime appointments to the WAAC, WAVES, and WAFS.

PL 37. The Library's Oral History Collection includes interviews with Virginia Milke English, a Red Cross volunteer in Europe in World War II, and Anna Rosenberg Hoffman (31 pp.). Interviews with Jacqueline Cochran and Oveta Culp Hobby are closed.

Gerald R. Ford Library

PL 38. The **subject file, 1974–77** (1,350 ft.), of the White House central files is arranged according to an alpha-numeric scheme. Under ND 8 "Military personnel," FG 13-4 "Defense Advisory Committee on Women in the Service," and FG 14-10 "Women's Army Corps," there are correspondence, memorandums, reports, and speeches about the WAC, veteran's preference in civil service hiring, admission of women to the military academies, abortion on military bases, the President's remarks to groups such as the Women's Forum on National Security, and especially relations with families of service personnel listed as missing in action (MIA's) in Southeast Asia. Scattered items on equality for women in

Government positions can be found under HU 2-5 "Women." The **name file, 1974–77** (1,420 ft.), is arranged alphabetically. The part of this correspondence, invitations, proclamations, etc., that relates to women consists primarily of Presidential greetings and messages to various support organizations related to women in the military and women who were relatives of service personnel, such as the Gold Star Mothers.

PL 39. Among the papers of the Public Liaison Office, the **files of Special Assistant for Women's Affairs Jeanne M. Holm, 1974–77** (21 ft.), are divided into 10 series and arranged thereunder alphabetically by subject or chronologically. Among the subjects are "Military and Women," "American Legion Auxiliary," and "11/16/76—DACOWITS meeting." The **files of Special Assistant for Human Resources, Theodore C. Marrs, 1974–77** (48 ft.), are divided into eight series and arranged thereunder alphabetically by subject or chronologically. They include records about MIA's and their families, refugees, and clemency for draft dodgers. The **files of Deputy Special Assistant for Human Resources, Milton E. Mitler, 1973–77** (17 ft.) in four series, relate largely to the MIA question.

Appendix A

Frequently Used Acronyms

(Note: U.S. Postal Service two-letter abbreviations for State names are used throughout the text of this guide.)

AAF	Army Air Force
ABCMR	Army Board for the Correction of Military Records
ACP	Appointment, Commission, and Personal Branch (Adjutant General's Office)
AEF	American Expeditionary Force (World War I)
AFB	Air Force Base
AFF	Army Field Forces
AFG	American Forces in Germany
AFHQ	Allied Force Headquarters (World War II)
AFRS	Armed Forces Radio Service
AGF	Army Ground Forces
AGO	Adjutant General's Office
ASD	Assistant Secretary of Defense
BUPERS	Bureau of Naval Personnel
BPR	Bureau of Public Relations
CAD	Civil Affairs Division
CBITO	China-Burma-India Theater of Operations
CIA	Central Intelligence Agency
CI and E	Civil Information and Education Section (of SCAP)
CNO	Chief Naval Officer
COMINCH	Commander-in-Chief (U.S. Fleet)
CTCA	Commission on Training Camp Activities (World War I)
DACOWITS	Defense Advisory Committee on Women in the Services
DOD	Department of Defense
EDC	Eastern Defense Command
ETO	European Theater of Operations (World War II)
ETOUSA	U.S. Army European Theater of Operations
EUCOM	European Command
G-1	Personnel Division (Army)
G-2	Intelligence Division (Army)
G-3	Organization and Training Division (Army)
G-4	Supply Division (Army)
GPO	Government Printing Office
IG	Inspector General

IGO	Office of the Inspector General
IMT	International Military Tribunal
IMTFE	International Military Tribunal for the Far East
JAG	Judge Advocate General
NCAC	National Civilian Advisory Committee (to the WAC)
NFM	*Navy Filing Manual*
OASD	Office of the Assistant Secretary of Defense
OASD(M&P)	Office of the Assistant Secretary of Defense for Manpower and Personnel
OASD(MP&R)	Office of the Assistant Secretary of Defense for Manpower, Personnel and Reserves
OCE	Office of the Chief of Engineers
OCMH	Office of the Chief of Military History
OCP	Office of Civilian Personnel
OMG	Office of Military Government
OMGUS	Office of Military Government for Germany, U.S.
ONI	Office of Naval Intelligence
OSD	Office of the Secretary of Defense
OSS	Office of Strategic Services
POE	Port of Embarkation
POW	Prisoner of War
ROTC	Reserve Officer Training Corps
SCAP	Supreme Commander for the Allied Powers
SGO	Surgeon General's Office
SHAEF	Supreme Headquarters, Allied Expeditionary Forces
SOS	Services of Supply
UMT	Universal Military Training
USAEUR	U.S. Army, Europe
USAF	U.S. Air Force
USCAR	U.S. Civil Administration of the Ryukyu Islands
USCC	U.S. Christian Commission
USN	U.S. Navy
USO	United Services Organization
WAAC	Women's Auxiliary Army Corps
WAC	Women's Army Corps
WAF	Women in the Air Force
WAFS	Women's Auxiliary Ferrying Squadron
WASP	Women Airforce Service Pilots
WAVES	Women Accepted for Voluntary Emergency Service
WCTU	Woman's Christian Temperance Union
WDC	Western Defense Command
WFTD	Women's Flying Training Detachment

WMSC	Women's Medical Specialist Corps
YMCA	Young Men's Christian Association
YWCA	Young Women's Christian Association
ZI	Zone of the Interior

Appendix B

The War Department Decimal Classification Scheme

Many records of the War Department and its component agencies are arranged according to the War Department decimal classification scheme. First issued in 1914, it was revised in 1918 and in 1943. It was abandoned in the early 1960's with the introduction of the Army Functional Files System (TAFFS), which was implemented at different times by different Army components. Many components went over to TAFFS by 1963.

The War Department decimal classification scheme is a subject classification scheme. Under ten general classifications to which even multiples of 100 (000–900) were assigned, more specific classifications were inserted bearing whole numbers under each multiple of 100, and even more specific subjects thereunder were given decimal numbers. Below are some of the decimal classifications most frequently assigned to records relating to women.

000	General	
	000.51	Rape
	080	Societies and Associations
	095	Individual persons
200	Personnel	
	201	Personal records
	210	Officers
	210.2	Promotions
	210.3	Assignments, change station, transfer
	211	Titles and grades ("Nurses")
	220	Enlisted
	230	Civilian employees
	231	Titles and grades among civilians
	231.22	Inspectors
	231.23	Medical
	231.28	Teachers, social workers, flying instructors
	231.3	Clerical personnel, horsebuyers, interpreters, translators
	231.35	Women's relations and hostess service
	231.37	Telephone operators
	231.4	Maids, cooks, laundresses, and other laborers
	240	Pay and allowances
	241.3	Family support (officers)
	241.4	Family support (enlisted)
	245.7	Family allowances
	250	Discipline
	250.1	Rape

251.1   Prostitution
260   Pensions
290   Miscellaneous
291.1   Genealogy (Marriage)
291.2   Race "(Negroes . .; Filipinos . .: American Indians)"
291.3   Sex
292   Quasi-military persons. (Families of officers and enlisted personnel, servants, sutlers, post traders, camp followers)
293   Funerals and burials

300 Administration
320   Organization of the Army
321   Arms of service and departments
324.5   Independent volunteer organizations, including "WAC" and "WASP"

500 Transportation
510   Transportation of persons
512   Officers, nurses, etc., including families
513   Enlisted men, recruits, and their families

600 Buildings and Grounds
620   Barracks and quarters

700 Medicine, hygiene, and sanitation
710   Diseases, including venereal disease

Appendix C

List of Microfilm Publications Cited

M22   Registers of Letters Received by the Office of the Secretary of War, Main Series, 1800–1870. 134 rolls.

M89   Letters Received by the Secretary of the Navy from Commanding Officers of Squadrons, 1841–1886. 300 rolls.

M123   Schedules Enumerating Union Veterans and Widows of Union Veterans of the Civil War, 1890. 118 rolls.

M124   Letters Received by the Secretary of the Navy: Miscellaneous Letters, 1801–1884. 647 rolls.

M148   Letters Received by the Secretary of the Navy from Officers below the Rank of Commander, 1802–1884. 518 rolls.

M186   Progress Reports of the Advisory Commission to the Council of National Defense, July 24, 1940–May 28, 1941. 1 roll.

M209   Miscellaneous Letters Sent by the Secretary of the Navy, 1798–1886. 43 rolls.

M221   Letters Received by the Secretary of War, Registered Series, 1801–1870. 317 rolls.

M222   Letters Received by the Secretary of War, Unregistered Series, 1789–1861. 34 rolls.

M246   Revolutionary War Rolls, 1775–1783. 138 rolls.

M253   Consolidated Index to Compiled Service Records of Confederate Soldiers. 535 rolls.

M273   Records of General Courts-Martial and Courts of Inquiry of the Navy Department, 1799–1867. 198 rolls.

M313   Index to War of 1812 Pension Application Files. 102 rolls.

M345   Union Provost Marshal's File of Papers Relating to Individual Civilians. 300 rolls.

M346   Confederate Papers Relating to Citizens or Business Firms. 1,158 rolls.

M347   Unfiled Papers and Slips Belonging in Confederate Compiled Service Records. 442 rolls.

M409   Index to Letters Received by the Confederate Secretary of War, 1861–1865. 34 rolls.

M410   Index to the Letters Received by the Confederate Adjutant and Inspector General and by the Confederate Quartermaster General, 1861–1865. 41 rolls.

M416   Union Provost Marshal's File of Papers Relating to Two or More Civilians. 94 rolls.

M437   Letters Received by the Confederate Secretary of War, 1861–1865. 151 rolls.

M492   Letters Received by the Secretary of War, Irregular Series, 1861–1866. 36 rolls.

M495   Indexes to Letters Received by the Secretary of War, 1861–1870. 14 rolls.

M522   Letters Sent by the Confederate Secretary of War, 1861–1865. 10 rolls.

M565   Letters Sent by the Office of the Adjutant General (Main Series), 1800–1890. 63 rolls.

M566   Letters Received by the Office of the Adjutant General, 1805–1821. 144 rolls.

M567   Letters Received by the Office of the Adjutant General (Main Series), 1822–1860. 636 rolls.

M598   Selected Records of the War Department Relating to Prisoners of War, 1861–65. 145 rolls.

M599   Investigation and Trial Papers Relating to the Assassination of President Lincoln. 16 rolls.

M619   Letters Received by the Office of the Adjutant General (Main Series), 1861–1870. 828 rolls.

M625   Area File of the Naval Records Collection, 1775–1910. 414 rolls.

M666   Letters Received by the Office of the Adjutant General (Main Series), 1871–1880. 593 rolls.

M686   Index to the General Correspondence of the Record and Pension Office, 1889–1920. 385 rolls.

M698   Index to the General Correspondence of the Office of the Adjutant General, 1890–1917. 1,269 rolls.

M711   Registers of Letters Received, Office of the Adjutant General, 1812–1889. 85 rolls.

M725   Indexes to Letters Received by the Office of the Adjutant General (Main Series), 1846, 1861–1889. 9 rolls.

M740   Records Relating to Investigations of the Fort Philip Kearney (or Fetterman) Massacre, 1866–1867. 1 roll.

M742   Selected Series of Records Issued by the Commissioner of the Bureau of Refugees, Freedmen, and Abandoned Lands, 1865–1872. 7 rolls.

M745   Letters Sent by the Office of the Quartermaster General, Main Series, 1818–1870. 61 rolls.

M752   Registers and Letters Received by the Commissioner of the Bureau of Refugees, Freedmen, and Abandoned Lands, 1865–1872. 74 rolls.

M797   Case Files of Investigations by Levi C. Turner and Lafayette C. Baker, 1861–1866. 137 rolls.

M803   Records of the Education Division of the Bureau of Refugees, Freedmen, and Abandoned Lands, 1865–1871. 35 rolls.

M804   Revolutionary War Pension and Bounty-Land Warrant Application Files. 2,670 rolls.

M847   Special Index to Numbered Records in the War Department Collection of Revolutionary War Records, 1775–1783. 39 rolls.

M853   Numbered Record Books Concerning Military Operations and Service, Pay and Settlement of Accounts, and Supplies in the War Department Collection of Revolutionary War Records. 41 rolls.

M859   Miscellaneous Numbered Records (The Manuscript File) in the War Department Collection of Revolutionary War Records, 1775–1790's. 125 rolls.

M860   General Index to Compiled Military Service Records of Revolutionary War Soldiers. 58 rolls.

M880   Compiled Service Records of American Naval Personnel and Members of the Departments of the Quartermaster General and the Commissary General of Military Stores Who Served During the Revolutionary War. 4 rolls.

M881   Compiled Service Records of Soldiers Who Served in the American Army During the Revolutionary War. 1,096 rolls.

M889   Records of the U.S. Nuernberg War Crimes Trials: *United States of America* v. *Josef Altstoetter et al.* (Case III), February 17–December 4, 1947. 53 rolls.

M892   Records of the U.S. Nuernberg War Crimes Trials: *United States of America* v. *Carl Krauch et al.* (Case VI), Aug. 14, 1947–July 30, 1948. 113 rolls.

M900   Letters and Telegrams Sent by the Confederate Quartermaster General, 1861–1865. 8 rolls.

M901   General Orders and Circulars of the Confederate War Department, 1861–1865. 1 roll.

M903   Descriptive Commentaries from the Medical Histories of Posts. 5 rolls.

M904   War Department Collection of Post-Revolutionary War Manuscripts. 4 rolls.

M905   Compiled Service Records of Volunteer Soldiers who Served from 1784 to 1811. 32 rolls.

M910   Virginia Half Pay and Other Related Revolutionary War Pension Application Files. 18 rolls.

M912   Indexes to the Records of the War College Division and Related General Staff Offices, 1903–1919. 49 rolls.

M917   Historical Files of the American Expeditionary Forces in Siberia, 1918–1920. 11 rolls.

M930   Cablegrams Exchanged Between General Headquarters, American Expeditionary Forces, and the War Department, 1917–1919. 19 rolls.

M935   Inspection Reports and Related Records Received by the Inspection Branch in the Confederate Adjutant and Inspector General's Office. 18 rolls.

M945   Letters Sent by the Superintendent of the U.S. Naval Academy, 1845–1865. 3 rolls.

M949   Letters Received by the Superintendent of the U.S. Naval Academy, 1845–1887. 11 rolls.

M983   Reports and Correspondence Relating to the Army Investigations of the Battle of Wounded Knee and to the Sioux Campaign of 1890–1891. 2 rolls.

M984   Navy Department General Orders, 1863–1948. 3 rolls.

M997   Annual Reports of the War Department, 1822–1907. 164 rolls.

M999   Records of the Assistant Commissioner for the State of Tennessee, Bureau of Refugees, Freedmen, and Abandoned Lands, 1865–1869. 34 rolls.

M1000   Records of the Superintendent of Education for the State of Tennessee, Bureau of Refugees, Freedmen, and Abandoned Lands, 1865–1870. 9 rolls.

M1003   Pardon Petitions and Related Papers Submitted in Response to President Andrew Johnson's Amnesty Proclamation of May 29, 1865 ("Amnesty Papers"). 73 rolls.

M1023   Record Cards to the Correspondence of the War College Division, Related General Staff, and Adjutant General Offices, 1902–1919. 37 rolls.

M1052   General and Special Indexes to the General Correspondence of the Office of the Secretary of the Navy, July 1897–August 1926. 119 rolls.

M1055   Records of the Assistant Commissioner for the District of Columbia, Bureau of Refugees, Freedmen, and Abandoned Lands, 1865–1872. 21 rolls.

M1064   Letters Received by the Commission Branch of the Adjutant General's Office, 1863–1870. 527 rolls.

M1067   Name and Subject Index to the General Correspondence of the Office of the Secretary of the Navy, 1930–1942. 187 rolls.

M1080   Name and Subject Index to the General Correspondence of the War Plans Division, 1921–1942. 18 rolls.

M1091   Subject File of the Confederate States Navy, 1861–1865. 61 rolls.

M1094   General Orders and Circulars of the War Department and Headquarters of the Army, 1809–1864. 8 rolls.

M1101   Unclassified Cross-Reference Sheets to General Correspondence of the Office of the Secretary of the Army, 1947–1964. 485 rolls.

M1105   Registers of the Records of the Proceedings of the U.S. Army General Courts-Martial, 1809–1890. 8 rolls.

M1125   Name and Subject Index to the Letters Received by the Appointment, Commission, and Personal Branch of the Adjutant General's Office, 1871–1894. 4 rolls.

M1140   Secret and Confidential Correspondence of the Office of the Chief of Naval Operations and the Office of the Secretary of the Navy, 1919–1927. 117 rolls.

M1141   Indexes and Register to the Correspondence of the Office of the Chief of Naval Operations and the Office of the Secretary of the Navy, 1919–1927. 9 rolls.

M1188   Correspondence of the Office of Civil Affairs of the District of Texas, the 5th Military District, and the Department of Texas, 1867–1870. 40 rolls.

M1194   Name Index to Correspondence of the Military Intelligence Division of the War Department Staff, 1917–1941. 262 rolls.

M1239   War Production Board Press Releases and Indexes, 1940–1947. 53 rolls.

M1278   Nuernberg Trials Records: Register Cards to the NG Document Series, 1946–1949. 3 rolls.

T251   List of Photographs and Photographic Negatives Relating to the War for the Union (War Department Subject Catalogue No. 5, 1897). 1 roll.

T252   The Mathew B. Brady Collection of Civil War Photographs. 4 rolls.

T288   General Index to Pension Files, 1861–1934. 544 rolls.

T289   Organization Index to Pension Files of Veterans who Served Between 1861 and 1900. 765 rolls.

T316   Old War Index to Pension Files, 1815–1926. 7 rolls.

T317   Index to Mexican War Pension Files, 1887–1926. 14 rolls.

T318   Index to Indian Wars Pension Files, 1892–1926. 12 rolls.

T822   Cross Index to the Central Files of the Adjutant General's Office, 1917–1939. 1,956 rolls.

T900   Index to Correspondence of the Office of the Commander in Chief, American Expeditionary Forces, 1917–1919. 132 rolls.

T1013   Department of the Army: Records of the General and Special Staff (Indexes and Tally Sheets), 1921–February 1942. 17 rolls.

T1139   Records of the U.S. Nuernberg War Crimes Trials: NG Series, 1933–1948. 70 rolls.

Appendix D

National Archives Regional Archives

National Archives–New England Region
380 Trapelo Road, Waltham, MA 02154
[Connecticut, Maine, Massachusetts,
New Hampshire, Rhode Island, Vermont]

National Archives–Northeast Region
201 Varick Street, New York, NY 10014-4811
[New Jersey, New York, Puerto Rico, the Virgin Islands]

National Archives–Mid Atlantic Region
9th and Market Streets, Room 1350, Philadelphia, PA 19107
[Delaware, Pennsylvania, Maryland, Virginia, West Virginia]

National Archives–Southeast Region
1557 St. Joseph Avenue, East Point, GA 30344
[Alabama, Georgia, Florida, Kentucky, Mississippi,
North Carolina, South Carolina, Tennessee]

National Archives–Great Lakes Region
7358 South Pulaski Road, Chicago, IL 60629
[Illinois, Indiana, Michigan, Minnesota, Ohio, Wisconsin]

National Archives–Central Plains Region
2312 East Bannister Road, Kansas City, MO 64131
[Iowa, Kansas, Missouri, Nebraska]

National Archives–Southwest Region
501 West Felix Street, P.O. Box 6216, Ft. Worth, TX 76115
[Arkansas, Louisiana, New Mexico, Oklahoma, Texas]

National Archives–Rocky Mountain Region
Building 48—Denver Federal Center, Denver, CO 80225-0307
[Colorado, Montana, North Dakota, South Dakota, Utah, Wyoming]

National Archives–Pacific Sierra Region
1000 Commodore Drive, San Bruno, CA 94066
[Northern California, Hawaii, Nevada (except Clark County),
American Samoa, the Trust Territory of the Pacific Islands]

National Archives–Pacific Southwest Region
24000 Avila Road, P.O. Box 6719, Laguna Niguel, CA 92607-6719
[Southern California, Arizona, and Clark County, Nevada]

National Archives–Pacific Northwest Region
6125 Sand Point Way NE, Seattle, WA 98115
[Idaho, Oregon, Washington]

National Archives–Alaska Region
654 West Third Avenue, Anchorage, AK 99501
[Alaska]

Index

Entries in this index refer to the relevant paragraph number. Record group titles appear in **boldface** type. *Italic numbers* refer to paragraphs in which photographs are described.